CW01375810

The Four Seasons of Venice

12 Historical Walking Tours

by
John Costella

authorHOUSE

AuthorHouse™ UK Ltd.
500 Avebury Boulevard
Central Milton Keynes, MK9 2BE
www.authorhouse.co.uk
Phone: 08001974150

© 2008 John Costella. All rights reserved.

No part of this book may be reproduced, stored in a retrieval system, or transmitted by any means without the written permission of the author.

First published by AuthorHouse   4/25/2008

ISBN: 978-1-4343-7959-7 (sc)
ISBN: 978-1-4343-7958-0 (hc)

Printed in the United States of America
Bloomington, Indiana

This book is printed on acid-free paper.

For Caitlin

Contents

ACKNOWLEDGMENTS ix

INTRODUCTION xiii

CHAPTER 1 SEPTEMBER: Let the Journal Begin 1
                        'Crossing the Sestieri by Land and Water'

CHAPTER 2 OCTOBER: Treasures of the Grand Canal 29
                        'This Passage of Water Frozen in Time'

CHAPTER 3 NOVEMBER: Cannaregio 75
                        'The Unspoilt Sestiere'

CHAPTER 4 DECEMBER: Santa Croce and San Polo 109
                        'Neighbours of Change and Tragedy'

CHAPTER 5 JANUARY: Piazza San Marco 153
                        'From the Malamocco rises the Citadel'

CHAPTER 6 FEBRUARY: The Eastern District 193
                        'From the Age of Decadence to the Age of War'

CHAPTER 7 MARCH: Murano, Burano and Torcello 225
                        'In Search of the Northern Archipelago'

CHAPTER 8 APRIL: The Southern Islands 261
                        'Time and Tide in Competition with the Lagoon'

CHAPTER 9 MAY: Dorsoduro 321
                        'Piety, Enmity, Dexterity and the Plague'

CHAPTER 10 JUNE: San Marco 357
     'Merchants, Music and Revolution'

CHAPTER 11 JULY: Castello 385
     'Home to the Pantheon of Venice'

CHAPTER 12 AUGUST: Further East 421
     'Seclusion and Solitude Energized by Art'

INDEX 443

EPILOGUE 451

ACKNOWLEDGMENTS

First and foremost to my patient, understanding and supportive wife, Avril, who not only has spent many hours checking and proofreading this journal but also is continually supportive of my regular visits to the 'Serenissima', and without whose help this book would not have been possible. In addition to my wife, I must say a fond thank-you to my immediate family, Louise, Anthony, Michelle and Julie, who have listened constantly to my aggravating enthusiasm and provided constructive advice and encouragement with this book

I am also extremely grateful to Julian Batson (Oakhill Publishing), who is not only my friend but has been a helpful adviser when I required publishing information.

As a constant reader of books, journals and publications related to Venice (too numerous to name), may I thank each author for providing me with endless hours of enjoyable reading material about the Veneto in general, as well as expressing my appreciation to Mini Gallery ™ for providing the opportunity to display my artwork online. My thanks also to the staff from the scores of churches, museums, palazzos and galleries that I have visited over a period of years, who have provided me with a host of valuable information which on occasions has proved extremely helpful.

I would also like to thank Tate Britain for allowing me to visit their Prints and Drawings Rooms to view original works of Venice by JMW Turner, which encouraged and inspired my own work.

Finally, it would be remiss of me not to thank the following: easyJet for providing affordable flights, which have enabled me to travel so often to Venice, the staff at the Hotel Santa Chiara for continually providing such comfortable accommodation on the occasions when I have extended my visit, and last, but not least, my friend Enrico at Bar S. Lucia for the hospitality he has shown whenever I visit Venice.

Mille grazie

ILLUSTRATIONS

Fig.1   Santa Maria Gloriosa dei Frari 140

Fig.2   Grand Canal 141

Fig 3   Piazza San Marco 142

Fig.4   Bar S. Lucia 143

Fig.5   Santa Chiara Hotel 143

Fig.6   Santa Maria Formosa 144

Fig.7   Rio Bacino Orseolo 145

Fig.8   Palazzo Salviati 146

Fig.9   Santa Maria e Donato 146

Fig.10   Santa Maria Assunta & Santa Fosca 147

Fig.11   Fondamenta San Mauro 147

Fig.12   Rio dei Frari 148

Fig.13   Santa Maria della Salute 149

Fig.14   Squaro San Travaso 150

Fig.15   Campo Manin 151

Fig.16   The Rialto Bridge 152

Fig.17   Pescheria 304

Fig.18   Ponte dei Pugni 305

Fig.19   Santa Maria Miracoli 306

Fig.20   Scuola Grande di San Marco 307

Fig.21   Santi Giovanni E Paolo 308

Fig.22   Santa Pietro di Castello 309

Fig.23   Fondamenta Barbarigo 310

Fig.24   Campo San Angelo 311

Fig.25   Rio del Vatral (Murano) 312

Fig.26   Rio Ognissanti 313

Fig.27   Rio del Gafaro 314

Fig.28   Cloister of Santissima Trinita (Frari) 315

Fig.29   Piazetta 'Basilica San Marco & Palazzo Ducale' 316

Fig.30   San Giorgio Maggiore 317

Fig.31   Ca' Pesaro 318

Fig.32   Ca' da Mosto 319

INTRODUCTION

The Four Seasons of Venice – 12 Historical Walking Tours provides the reader with a wealth of useful information for planning a visit to Venice for just one single day or several at a time as well as providing a fairly comprehensive but easy-to-follow schedule of my personal travels to the 'Serenissima' during the course of one year. This journal is not an attempt to rewrite previous travel books, nor is it a tuition guide on the practicalities and protocol for artists to paint outside; it will, I hope, invigorate the reader who has an adventurous mind by identifying interesting, descriptive and sometimes amusing events which will generate enough interest for others to follow in my footsteps. As a tourist, I have recorded and detailed 12 historical walking routes while on my travels, starting from my flight out from Gatwick, the journey from Marco Polo airport to Piazzale Roma, the wonderful trips on the *vaporetti* (waterbuses) and the sheer pleasure in walking and exploring so many interesting places in Venice, and of course locations to eat and drink. The walking tours were recorded between 2006-2007 but remain the same today as they will tomorrow, simply because the plethora of interesting and magnificent buildings and streets which I take you down are timeless and will never change. As an artist, I explore all six districts of Venice and the surrounding islands with a view to discovering the abundant opportunities available to paint both in the tourist gateways as well as in isolated pockets hidden by time.

In planning this journal, I have mapped out what I consider to be helpful, descriptive and, more importantly, enjoyable routes to explore, as well as providing many interesting, historical and architectural facts at each location I visit, having spent a considerable amount of time researching each itinerary before travelling. Although I am not in any way an accomplished historian or an expert in Venetian architecture and certainly no authority on classical art, I have made every attempt to research my work thoroughly even though I occasionally use some 'creative' words for my own benefit. My journal was written over a period of 12 months, as I wanted to capture each month and season as it evolved, but this proved difficult at times due to the uncertainty of climatic change. Therefore I have merged the inconsistent seasonal weather pattern into monthly reviews; having done this I have still retained the calendar year in Venice to portray seasonal events such as Carnevale, which take into account the occasion, the emotional warmth and unsurpassed beauty of this city. The journal includes several of my sketches to supplement the dialogue, which I hope will flavour the occasion for tourists, journeymen and artists alike, but more importantly bring to life a beautiful island that has much history and many treasures to enjoy.

I should also add at this point that the vast majority of trips I make to Venice are usually undertaken in a 'single day', out early each morning and back home each evening. To most readers this may seem far too exhausting and repetitious, but this pattern of travel serves me well as I can visit Venice on a monthly basis and enjoy the rich experience that each season has to offer. I make every effort to keep my travelling costs affordable; this information

I share with readers whenever charges are incurred. In compiling this journal, I was armed with a good travel guide and map to plot my itinerary around the mainland and the many surrounding islands, and although I no longer depend on these guides, as I know Venice reasonably well, I still refer to them on occasions. Having said that, although Venice itself is a surprisingly small island, which can be walked from the extreme north to the south in just over an hour, new as well as seasoned travellers, can still lose themselves in the maze of enchanting streets. Knowing this, I feel sure that the descriptive routes I have mapped out will maximise the reader's time to enjoy all that Venice has to offer, either as a day trip or for those who are considering staying for a longer period.

Having read numerous biographies from past artists and writers of the 19th and early 20th centuries, I realise just how difficult travel abroad must have been for them compared to today, and I constantly remind myself just how easy it is today to experience part of a 21st-century 'Grand Tour', or simply enjoy centuries of Venetian history in just a few short hours. My passion for Venice really only began as recently as 1997 when I visited the island as part of a short excursion prior to watching a European Cup football match in Vincenza. As with most European football matches involving British clubs, each participating country seems to adopt delaying tactics for visiting supporters by finding drop-off zones where the police and officials can regulate and control fans prior to kick-off time. On this occasion, they decided that a long coach trip from the airport to Laguna Veneta (Tronchetto to be exact) and a short boat trip to Bacino di San Marco would account for most of the day before the evening kick-off. This decision would have a major impact on my artwork in future years, and started my love affair with Venice. Since that day, I have become completely besotted by the wealth of history and culture that Venice and its surrounding group of islands have to offer.

In writing this journal, my intention is to portray sufficient information for the reader to discover and get a taste for the culture, customs, history and architecture of Venice, as well as the Venetians themselves, who have battled through centuries of evolution, toil and achievement.

Occasionally, I remind myself of the wonderful treasures, so carefully described by John Ruskin, which are there to be discovered, and often I use some of my favourite quotations by noted people which seem to summarise the moment so well.

Each route that I have mapped and recorded would normally include at least 12 memorable locations and will interest both new and experienced travellers, at the same time providing excellent material for both the photographer and artist. Having said that, almost everywhere in Venice provides cherished reminders of a splendid and glorious history.

As an artist, I have attempted to paint a journalistic picture of just how much pleasure there is in painting 'real time' in a city of a thousand opportunities, but realising that not everyone paints I have only featured one 'typical creative day', which the reader will discover in Chapter 1, but having said that, I like to sketch at predetermined locations. However, the weather and permitted time on location dictate my daily itinerary, so photographs are generally the order of the day. As a rule, I usually only photograph, sketch and dictate notes between November and March, and occasionally paint selected subjects back in my studio at a later date. If the weather is inclement and could affect my plans, I never despair, as I always pack a digital camera and sketch book as there is as much to record and illustrate 'inside' each church and museum as there are bridges, campi, piazzas and palazzos around every street, passageway and alley.

As a traveller, I hope that each passage throughout this adventure will also bring to the reader both a descriptive and often humorous insight into the joy and the occasional painful experience, which seem to be part and parcel of our modern age. In capturing the spirit and culture of this wonderful island, I ensure that each of the six districts, or *'sestieri'*, are visited on their own merit as individual chapters, as well as the occasional mention when 'passing through each one' to arrive at pre-determined locations. This becomes obvious in the September, October, March and August chapters where the locations I've chosen to explore traverse several districts before arriving at the end of the walking tour.

Wishing to capture some of the surrounding islands of Venice (to visit them all would fill another journal), chapters March, April and August concentrate on interesting locations around Murano, Burano, Torchello, Giudecca, San Giorgio Maggiore, Lido and San Lazzaro.

One important factor that I should mention again is that I do take a very good map with me, 'my bible', on almost every journey I undertake, and I thoroughly recommend that anyone following my travels will also follow my example, as I use the place names as they are illustrated. I have found the *Touring Club Italiano Map* (ISBN 8836537405) to be the best. The scale is 1:5000 and includes a good index of street names, palazzos and monuments, with instructions on how to find them easily on the map. Together with my trusty map, I also take my amazingly helpful travel guide *DK EyeWitness*, which illustrates each piazza on the Grand Canal in graphic form. This proves extremely useful in Chapter 2 when I describe various buildings for photographing and painting on the wonderful journey from Piazzale Roma to Basin di San Marco (the full length of the Grand Canal).

As each daily itinerary could be considered 'fairly active', especially when taken as a day trip, I recommend that new travellers simply photograph what they see in order to get the most out of their day trip. More experienced travellers who have a reasonable understanding of the geographical layout of the island will discover that sketching 'moments' are achievable whilst still keeping a check on the time allocated for each route. As a guide, I regularly provide 'real time' updates on each walking tour, as it is very easy to become totally engrossed whilst exploring this enchanting island and lose all sense of time. These should prove useful to 'day visitors' who have a return flight the same day. I can, however, confirm that the airport lounge at Marco Polo airport has some comfortable chairs whilst waiting for the next flight home! For travellers staying in Venice for a few days, the majority of historical walks I have mapped are easily achievable, and would certainly provide the reader with ample time to explore each Scuola, gallery and museum.

Although I make numerous day trips each year to paint, photograph and explore, I should confess that I do occasionally stay over for a couple of days, accompanied by my wife, Avril, simply to shop and enjoy the ambience and atmosphere, which radiates from every corner and street of the 'Serenissima' (a name I use often which is lovingly associated with Venice).

Occasionally, when recording my journal, I sometimes reminisce about my previous visits to Venice and sometimes speculate about my future plans, and every so often I will fantasise about the romance and history that this city has experienced. I will occasionally criticise the apparent apathy in preserving such a wonderful legacy of the past, but never will I tire from travelling the length of the Grand Canal or exploring the alleyways of Venetian history, history that in the 5th century brought the first travellers and settlers to the marshy Venetian Lagoon as a place of refuge. Once here, they then made their mark on the empty, barren and hostile terrain and went on to establish the most powerful city in Europe for almost a millennium. Today most of the Lagoon remains the same as it has for thousands of years, no longer is it hostile or empty; it now serves to proudly display Byzantine, Gothic, Renaissance and Baroque architecture, coupled with a an indigenous population who have developed in custom and tradition.

The Four Seasons of Venice – 12 Historical Walking Tours will, I hope, provide each reader with both an armchair journal of Venice throughout each season and also encourage both new and previous visitors to follow in my footsteps and experience the 'Venetian fever' to which all visitors eventually succumb.

CHAPTER 1
SEPTEMBER: Let the Journal Begin
'Crossing the Sestieri by Land and Water'

This is the start of a new adventure for me, simply because whenever I travelled to Venice in the past I inevitably used my busy day excursions to explore this wonderful island at random and occasionally sketched or photographed wherever my curiosity took me. Today, and for the following twelve months, although my visits will still give me the same level of enjoyment experienced over a decade, there will be one fundamental difference: I will now be planning interesting routes for the reader to follow and, more importantly, recording almost every detail of my travels.

Having solely used my artistic skills in the past to capture the beauty of Venice on canvas or paper, I now have to concentrate on my writing, rather than my brushes, to capture the essence of Venice. This presents quite a challenge, and therefore only Chapter 1 will have an artistic theme, whereas the following chapters will concentrate on recording detail, which I hope will translate into the grandeur, beauty and history of this wonderful group of islands.

From today, my backpack will include new tools such as a digital recorder and an electronic notepad, which will enable me to recapture in each chapter, precisely where I go, what I see,

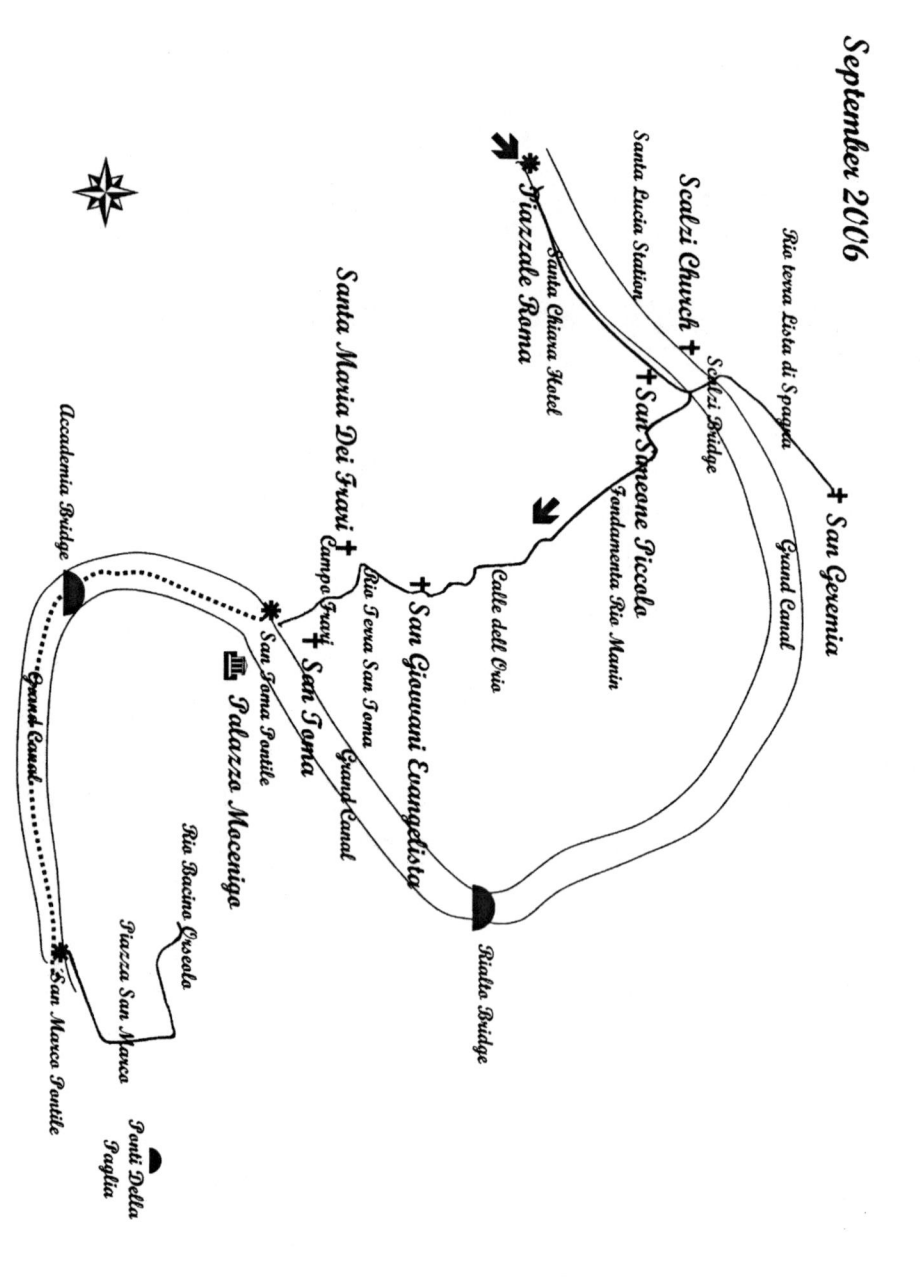

September 2006

Map of Venice

Locations and labels:

- Rio terra Lista di Spagna
- San Geremia
- Grand Canal
- Santa Lucia Station
- Santa Chiara Hotel
- Scalzi Church
- Scalzi Bridge
- Piazzale Roma
- San Simeone Piccolo
- Fondamenta Rio Marin
- Calle dell Ora
- Santa Maria Dei Frari
- Campo Frari
- Rio Terra San Toma
- San Giovanni Evangelista
- San Toma Pentile
- San Toma
- Grand Canal
- Rialto Bridge
- Palazzo Moceniga
- Rio Bacino Oseola
- Piazza San Marco
- San Marco Pentile
- Accademia Bridge
- Grand Canal
- Ponti Della Paglia

and more importantly how much I enjoy visiting this group of enchanting islands within the Venetian Lagoon. My objective by the end of Chapter 12 is to ensure that the reader will have a good knowledge of Venice, its surrounding islands, people and history and realise that a simple day trip for that special occasion is achievable, or better still a short holiday.

By way of an introduction to exploring Venice, the first two chapters of this journal will concentrate firstly on a walk which crosses three districts of the island, namely Santa Croce, San Polo and San Marco, and secondly follows the passage of the incredible Grand Canal. These early itineraries will, I hope, give the reader a good understanding and grounding for future chapters, where I plan to focus my travels on individual districts and the surrounding islands of this archipelago within a lagoon.

***September 5th 2006**

The alarm on my telephone tells me that it is 4.00am and time to rise on this wonderful autumnal morning. On this occasion, I have to drive to Gatwick and check in two hours before my 6.50am flight to San Marco Airport, Venice. Getting up at this ungodly hour is never a problem for me when I know that I may be on the Grand Canal by 10.00am GMT. So I shower, shave, dress quietly and sidle down the stairs with my backpack already prepared, into the car and I'm on my way.

The contents of my backpack today consist of the electronic aids I mentioned earlier, my folding seat/case, which holds my small easel and paint materials, together with my plastic portfolio case with some finished watercolours and a watercolour block. I generally take the plastic portfolio just in case I find a tourist who likes my work; we artists have to make the most of every opportunity available, even if it means labouring with the kit on my shoulder throughout the day.

After a slight delay in taking off due to fog at Marco Polo airport, the flight was excellent. I always marvel when I fly over the Alps, but never seem to have my camera available. The mountain range is quite a sight at 11,600m and a subject I shall paint at some time.

I arrive at Marco Polo airport around 10.45am Italian time; collect my luggage, and proceed to the public transport ticket office, situated directly to the left when entering the arrival lounge. Here a 48, 36, 24 or 12-hour ticket may be purchased that gives unlimited travel on both ATVO buses and ACTV *vaporetti* (waterbuses). Believe me, this is great value for money at only 12 euros for a 12-hour ticket, compared with a single water taxi journey just from the airport to Venice, which is in the region of 80 euros on a good day! Incidentally, I must compliment the airport staff at Marco Polo, as each member of staff at the administration counter for bus tickets and general travel needs seem to be bi-lingual, which is a great help when your Italian is poor.

Having purchased my ticket from the appropriate office, I walk straight through the airport exit doors, across the service road pedestrian crossing, and arrive at the bus terminal areas. Immediately to the left is the sign for the No. 5 bus, which arrives every half hour, usually displaying Piazzale Roma on the front. More often than not, there is a seat available when boarding and usually ample space for luggage, but on this occasion the bus was full. However, this is not a major problem as the journey usually only takes 20 minutes. Next, I must remember to validate my ticket once on board the bus in the machine provided. Once this is done, I can simply hop on and off all selected transport throughout the day. The bus will make a few drop-off stops en route before reaching the terminus at Piazzale Roma. Once the bus is out of the airport, one immediately appreciates how important the Veneto region is for transport links to northern Italy, a labyrinth of roads merging and disappearing to closely located cities and towns such as Padua, Vincenza and Verona. Each one of these locations is worth a visit for they also provide a plethora of locations to paint and photograph. I digress – back to Venice!

The first sighting of Venice appears when the bus enters the Ponte della Liberta (Bridge of Freedom), the road bridge that links the mainland to the island. As a traveller and tourist, I consider this structure to be extremely important as this highway is the main link to Venice, and it forms part of the 'futuristic' dream held by Mussolini in the 1930s, which was to create a new and modern metropolis. Running parallel with Ponte della Liberta is the railway bridge which, when built in 1846, was considered by Venetians to be 'the end of their independence and security' as a unique and isolated community. Even though Venetians lost their independence long before the bridge was built, following Napoleon Bonaparte's invasion in 1797, which, incidentally, destroyed the Republic, there was still a great deal of resistance by Venetians to the construction of this rail bridge, so much so that when it was finally built during the clamour of the industrial revolution, allowance was made for 48 voids in its structure to accommodate dynamite should they feel the need to sever their links with the mainland!

Now the magic begins when I first catch sight of Venice as a silhouette in the distance: campaniles and palazzos all there to discover and paint, which is just what I am about to do. Can't wait. I try to avoid looking to my right at the industrial mayhem called Marghera, which I consider to be a blot on a wonderful landscape, with its hideous collection of 20th-century mechanical architecture deemed so important for commercial needs. Behind me, on such a clear day as today, I can see the range of Dolomites in the distance, which serve as a perfect backdrop to the lagoon … excluding Marghera!

Once over the Ponte della Liberta, I finally arrive at the Piazzale Roma bus terminal. This is an extremely busy area as it is the last staging post for land motor transport together with its neighbour, the Santa Lucia Railway Station, which is close by. Between them they provide the main arterial links for Venetians and journeyers to the mainland. This particular location becomes busy between 5.00pm and midnight, when the working population of weary Italians make their way home across the Lagoon.

Piazzale Roma is where my journey really begins, and is featured in all the forthcoming chapters because it is the staging post for each district I visit, and therefore plays an important part in my journal. Situated at the very top of the Grand Canal in the district known as Santa Croce, Piazzale Roma is positioned in the mid-west of this district. Santa Croce is one of six districts (*sestieri*, singular *sestiere*) which form the island of Venice, the others being San Polo, Cannaregio, Castello, San Marco and, finally, Dorsoduro. Interestingly enough, the first sighting of the Grand Canal occurs almost immediately after getting off of the No. 5 bus, as almost everyone leaving the bus terminal make their way to the narrow passageway leading to Fondamenta Croce and eventually the new canal bridge, which is the main thoroughfare to the city. For several years now, I have watched with interest as work progresses on this new bridge, which will eventually cross the northern part of the Grand Canal, and as there are only three bridges that cross the canal at present, this is a major undertaking for the city planners. Unfortunately, because of planning and financing problems, the completion of the new bridge has been delayed for what seems like an eternity, and all that can be seen today are the concrete base foundations on either side of this historic waterway. Having discussed the ongoing political saga relating to construction of the bridge with several Venetians, who incidentally feel passionate about getting the bridge completed, I sensed a tone of conservative distrust in their voices, which was directed at the city planners, and I guess this problem is still a long way from being resolved.

It is now 11.30am and my Venetian journey is well underway, but first I must give you a brief resume of where I will visit and what I will see today. My walk will start at St Simeon Piccolo, which is close to Piazzale Roma, following which I travel on to St Geremia, having crossed the Grand Canal, then return over this historic waterway and amble through wonderful back streets until I get to Santa Maria Gloriosa dei Frari, and finally from there I make my way to Rio e Bacino Orseolo, which is close to Piazza San Marco.

The first three locations have wonderful churches, which have featured in many former works of art, and the path I take to reach them will give you the opportunity to instantly experience the joy of being in Venice. The Rio e Bacino Orseolo is a delightful minor canal staging post for gondoliers, which is at the back of the Piazza San Marco and a perfect spot to sketch or photograph gondolas and people in general. Finally, my homeward journey back to Piazzale Roma takes in a trip on the *vaporetto* (waterbus, singular of *'vaporetti'*) along the entire route of the Grand Canal, to savour this Venetian dream.

Several important pieces of information are needed before we start, as throughout the journal I will continually refer to places by the titles below, especially when navigating through the city. The majority of street signs are printed in a Venetian dialect, which has a variation to the Italian spelling. However, all major signs are labelled in Italian. A *fondamenta* is a street which runs alongside a canal, *calle* is a street, *rio* is a canal, *rio terra* is a filled-in canal which often forms a square, *sotoportego* is a covered passageway, *salizada* is a main street, *riva* is a wide *fondamenta*, often facing a lagoon, *rugagiuffa* is a street lined with shops, and *corte* is a courtyard – confusing to say the least, but exciting to navigate. I often use the word *pontile* when describing a vaporetto landing stage, and *ponte* is simply a bridge. The Venetian *campo* (square) varies considerably in shape and size and is generally considered to be the hub of a community. It may have as many as four abandoned drinking water wells within its square, which once served as the fresh water supply for the local population.

Equally important are the orientations of the wonderful churches and basilicas I will visit throughout the journal, so for those who are unfamiliar with church layouts I will explain. The *nave* is the main body of the church where the assembled congregation either sit, stand or kneel. The *chancel* lies beyond the nave, separated by a step and usually has choir stalls on either side. The *sanctuary* sits just beyond the chancel and accommodates the altarpiece, while the *apse* is the area directly behind the altar at the far end of the church. If a church or basilica has a *rood screen*, it is generally used as a divisional screen, which spans the width of the nave, separating it from the chancel. The *transept* is the recessed area, usually north and south at the two ends of the nave, while the *aisles* act as open corridors either side of the nave.

Obviously, in order to achieve this fairly active itinerary, today there will be a limited amount of time for sketching but, like all my routes, I know that I personally will return and spend more time at individual locations at a later date, and my camera will capture the moment equally as well.

Leaving the bus depot at Piazzle Roma, I head towards the Santa Chiara Hotel, which sits directly opposite where I alighted from the No. 5 airport bus. This bus stop, incidentally, is where I return to for my journey back to the airport, so a check is made on the timetable. At the time of writing, buses leave every 10 and 40 minutes on the hour.

The Santa Chiara Hotel sits on the site of an ancient monastery and was once a *tintoria*, or dye works, in the 18th century, it is also featured in paintings as well as numerous sketches of the Grand Canal by Canaletto and is the only hotel in Venice to offer car parking. Having stayed there on several occasions, I can thoroughly recommend its Venetian-style accommodation and, more importantly, its position, as it is perfectly situated for the journeyer arriving in Venice, and it sits right at the beginning of the Grand Canal, which is perfect for future transportation to each district and the surrounding islands.

I pass the front of the hotel, continue along the Fondamenta San Simeon Piccolo for 200m and arrive at the church of St Simeon Piccolo. Unfortunately the church is closed to the public, but is nevertheless a wonderful subject to sketch or photograph. In order to get a better view, I have to cross the Grand Canal via the Scalzi Bridge, which, as I mentioned earlier, is one of three bridges that cross the Grand Canal. As I pass the church, I continue walking for another 20m and finally reach the Scalzi Bridge, which faces me on the left. This bridge was built as recently as 1934, replacing an earlier, 19th-century wrought iron bridge, which like the earlier Accademia crossing, was dismantled and sold as scrap. This would have pleased John Ruskin, as he was an advocate of preserving Venice in its former glory, more of that later. Once over the bridge, I turn left and arrive at Santa Lucia Railway Station, which faces St Simeon Piccolo.

The view across the Canal provides a good opportunity to get the easel out or simply sketch or photograph it, but I have to be mindful of time as I should move on by 12.30pm to get the best out of the day, and, of course, stop for some lunch. The church of San Simeon Piccolo was founded in the 9th century, but the present building dates between 1718 and 1738. It was built by Giovanni Scalfarotto to mimic the Pantheum in Rome and has a wonderful copper roof, which is now a distinctive green colour through age. The attractive external staircase leads to the Istrian stone columned entrance, which has a magnificent pediment, with relief work designed and sculptured by Francesco Renso. Unfortunately, as I previously mentioned, visitors are not permitted to enter the church at this present time as it is closed for essential restoration work, but still it is a joy to paint. Moving on, I am now ready for lunch and there are several good bars and restaurants nearby. One, in particular, which is on my route is situated at the start of the Rio Terra Lista Di Spagna, and I have decided to eat there before setting off for Campo San Germia. This small but busy restaurant, which is positioned facing the Scalzi Bridge, has a reasonably priced set menu and is a perfect place to sit and watch people come and go along this busy concourse. After having had a delightful lunch of fried squid with a salad, washed down with a glass of beer, I am now fully refreshed, as that will keep me going till I arrive back here in the late afternoon once my travels are over.

The time now is 1.30pm and, as I leave the restaurant, I travel along the Rio Terra Lista Di Spagna for 300m until I arrive at Campo San Germia. This campo is one of the few piazzas (squares completely surrounded by buildings) that have four separate wells – wonderful subject matter for painting and sketching. I am now confronted with the magnificent church of San Geremia, which was founded in the 11th century and later rebuilt in the 13th century, following which, the current design of this truly remarkable building was later transformed by the architect Carlo Corbellini. The modern façade, which is seen today was introduced in 1871, after the original one was destroyed by fire, following the Austrian bombardment of Cannaregio, a feature that I intend to detail in a later chapter when I talk about the 'Siege of Venice'. The campanile (belltower), which is constructed of red brick and has two narrow Romanesque windows, is worth photographing as it is one of the oldest in the city and is thought to have been built in the 12th century. Internally, the floor plan is similar to that of the 'Salute', a masterpiece of a church, which features in Chapter 9. There are several notable pieces of artwork on display inside, one being *The Virgin Attending the Crowning of Venice* by Jacopo Palma the Younger. Incidentally, San Geremia also holds the relics of St Lucia, who was martyred in Sicily, and whose remains are entombed in a glass coffin at the rear of the church.

Adjoining the church is the Palazzo Labia, built between the 17th and 18th centuries by the wealthy Labia family. When, in a later chapter, I travel to the island of Murano, I will have the opportunity to photograph San Geremia whilst aboard a vaperetto, when it turns off of the Grand Canal and weaves it way along the Canale di Cannaregio and out to the open lagoon north of Venice. I now have time for a quick pencil sketch of San Geremia and will most probably do a watercolour at a later date as the sky offers a beautiful hazy background for the dome. The light at this time of the day would be perfect to paint, but on this occasion time doesn't permit.

It's 2.00pm, so I must now press on to Santa Maria Gloriosa del Frari, and therefore I have to backtrack on my route and re-cross the Scalzi Bridge, where I am back again in the Santa Croce district. Once across the bridge, I head south down Calle Lunga Chioverette, which is directly in front of me.

Whilst walking down this *calle*, I cross a canal and then cross back over again. Seems crazy, but this is the only direct route and I will often be following similar paths throughout my journal. That's what makes Venice so special: you just don't know for sure if your route is direct, even following the maps that are available.

I continue walking until I reach the end of Calle Lunga Chioverette and then turn left and cross over a small canal bridge, which spans Rio Marin. Once over the bridge, I turn right into Fondamenta Rio Marin Garzotte, which runs parallel with the canal, continue past a small bridge on my right, walk another 100m and then turn right over the next bridge, which brings me onto the Fondamenta Rio Marin. During this delightful walk, I have passed scores of small houses, which appear in need of some careful love and attention. Any sensitive improvements certainly wouldn't spoil the atmosphere and intimacy, which abounds everywhere along this specific route. I consider myself to be a conservationist first and a reformer second, and would like to see more effort made in preserving these historic buildings in their original state. I can't believe that some simple and sensitive maintenance programme could not be adopted for the majority of façades I have just passed. I know for a fact that there are preservation orders in place almost everywhere on the island and certain listing criteria are administered.

Enough of my views ... for now at least. Let's get back on track. Once over the bridge, I turn immediately left and walk a few metres, and then turn right into Calle Dell 'Olio. I continue walking until I reach Calle Magazen and arrive at Rio Terra San Toma. I'm close to my first location now; I just have to turn immediately left at the end of Rio Terra San Toma, walk 50m and onto the Fondamenta Dei Frari. I then turn right and walk a further 10 metres, cross the small bridge on my right and I am now at Campo Frari in the district of San Polo.

By this time, I need a drink, and luckily there is a small shop near the bridge which sells a variety of drinks; cold water is the order of the day. The time now is 2.40pm and a perfect time to visit the majestic and beautiful church of Santa Maria Gloriosa dei Frari (better known as 'Frari' to the locals), as the main body of tourists will have been and gone and there is some good shade outside for me to work in.

The 'Frari', which was built by Franciscan monks in the mid-15th century, stands on the same spot as the original church built in the 11th century. I have to say that this location has provided me with endless hours of enjoyment in the past, as its graceful demeanour provides artists and tourists alike with several nice views to sketch or photograph. Incidentally, this was the first spot in Venice where someone asked if they could purchase some of my work. Occasions like that are always memorable as they are few and far between. The two pieces I sold went to a Canadian lady called Marian who said she was taking them back to Ottawa.

I've decided to spend nearly an hour here today, 45 minutes to finish a watercolour, which I started on my last trip but didn't finish, and a few minutes (you need an hour to really do it justice) exploring the interior of this magnificent church once again. The view I am painting in the Campo is one that looks from the 'Frari' along the small canal I crossed earlier, which leads to another minor bridge about 30m away. Unfortunately, there were no gondoliers by the bridge when I started the painting but there was a group of artists sitting opposite, facing me, probably on an organised tour, who were painting a scene of the front of the church. You never know, I might be in their paintings, as they are in mine. I've also decided to take several more photographs of this idylllic location to add to those I have already, as there are some nice shadows forming. Incidentally, where I am painting is completely in shadow, which is very comfortable as the afternoon is very warm, sunny and humid. It might be worth noting now that I take a great deal of photographs during my travels in Venice as I use them constantly for reference when I'm back in my studio. Some artists wouldn't dream of using photographs as an aid to their work; I frequently do, as I think it's the only way possible to capture, and freeze in time, the magic of the moment, providing you get the right perspective.

My picture is complete. Not bad, but alas no purchasers. Still, there's the inside of the 'Frari' to explore, which is compensation enough. Treasures abound inside this church, so I make my way to the entrance where there is an admission fee of 2.5 euros. Worth every penny. As I enter the church, immediately to my left is the important and formidable Canova's Tomb, a symbolic and notable marble pyramid, which he designed as a tribute to Titian but never built. In fact his students built it from his original drawings in 1822 as a tribute to him, following his death. Other treasures to savour are Titian's *'Madonna di Ca'Pesaro',* the tomb of Monteverdi, the tomb of Doge Nicolo Tron, the tomb of Doge Francesco Foscari, Titian's *'Assumption of the Virgin'*, Bellini's *'Madonna enthroned with Saint'* and the Choir Stalls, to name but a few.

The Choir Stalls consist of 124 wooden stalls, sculptured by Marco Cozzi in 1468, which form a spectacular centrepiece. It is said that these stalls have no equal, and I thought I would mention these as my great great uncle was said to have carved stalls in the village church of Bratto in northern Tuscany albeit on a much smaller scale, Bratto being the village that my mother's family descend from.

I never tire from visiting 'Frari' to gaze at its Gothic-style beauty, with its three-part façade in red brick, the ornate rose windows and the beautifully sculptured cornices, not forgetting its campanile, which is only second in scale to the one we shall see later in Piazza San Marco. The time now is 3.35pm and reluctantly I have to move on, and I remind myself that I still haven't had my ride on the vaporetto today. I have to confess that a relaxing boat trip in the heat and sun of the afternoon sounds good. I leave Campo Frari with a good heart, knowing that I will return again sometime, and walk around the south wing of the church to Salizzada San Rocco, which adjoins Camp San Rocco. At Salizzada San Roco I walk down Larga Prima eastward in the direction of the Grand Canal for about 100m until I get to Campo San Toma, where there has been a square since the 10th century. Having visited this area many times before, I know that there are some really interesting buildings to sketch or photograph here, but for today I have an appointment with a vaporetto. I cross the Campo and head for the Calle Campaniel, which I turn into and walk another few metres before turning left in the direction of the

ACTV San Toma vaporetto landing stage (known, as I mentioned earlier, as a *pontile*).

Now is perhaps a good time to explain the vaporetto waterbus system. Basically this service is run by ACTV (Azienda Consorzio Trasporti Veneziano) and the ticket which I purchased earlier at the airport allows me to jump on and off this transport system all day long in addition to using the airport bus that I used this morning and will return on later. The landing stages for the vaporetto cannot be missed, as each one is painted a bright yellow and there are clear signage instructions for everyone to see on the *pontile* platforms.

My vaporetto will be coming from my left if I'm facing the Canal. It's always a good thing to watch which direction they arrive from as that's the direction they will go when they leave. As a general guide, even numbered watercraft travel clockwise, odd numbers anti-clockwise. If you are not sure, then ask the boatman who controls passenger traffic getting on and off. As I had my ticket punched earlier at the airport, when I first got on the bus, it is not necessary to show it again unless an inspector asks to see it, which is extremely unlikely. It never ceases to amaze me how casual the ticket system appears to be and I feel sure it is abused as it seems so easy to dodge paying fares; I am told, however, if someone is caught without a valid ticket, the punishment is heavy and the Bridge of Sighs comes into mind (a pun that will have more meaning in a later chapter).

There are 16 landing stages (*pontiles*) along the length of the Grand Canal alone and each stage is clearly marked with its name, in this case San Toma. The boat I am waiting for is the No. 1, which sails the entire length of the Canal, stopping off at each landing stage (usually takes 40–45 minutes to travel from Piazzale

Roma to San Marco). This is particularly useful if you want to see everything that is going on in slow motion as it gives you ample time to view, even though it may be crowded at times. In later chapters, when I travel to the surrounding islands, I will use the same system but different boat numbers to get me to all my destinations, and I can't emphasise enough just how much of a bargain the day ticket is at 12 euros when you compare it to our rail and bus fares in the UK.

While I am waiting at San Toma landing stage for the vaporetto, I gaze directly across the Canal to the Palazzo Mocenigo, where Lord Byron stayed in 1818 when he wrote *Don Juan*. This palazzo is formed of four palaces, which are linked together with a wonderful facade made of Istrian stone, its typical Venetian design being functional as well as being equipped for seasonal change: having a central *portego* so common with 17th-century Venetian design, the trading floors being on the ground floor accessed from the Canal, with offices on the first floor and residential quarters on the top (third) floor. There are garrets (attic space) in the roof space and these were allocated to the servants and must have been pretty warm in the height of a Venetian summer. Today the Palazzo serves as a remarkably well-preserved museum both internally and externally, and is the Centre for the History of Costume.

The vaporetto arrives (usually every 10 minutes during the day, and 20 minutes in the evening), I board and within a minute we are off heading towards the last of the three bridges that cross the Grand Canal and is known as the Accademia. In next month's chapter I will focus on the Rialto area and of course, the famous Rialto Bridge, which is without doubt the most splendid of the three Grand Canal bridges. Incidentally, I propose to write in far more detail about the Grand Canal next month when I can bring to life some of the wonderful palazzos which grace this historic and beautiful watercourse, at the same time focusing on the two prime Canal bridges and their surrounding areas.

The vaporetto is now nearing the Accademia Bridge, which I have crossed a hundred times in the past and will no doubt cross several times again throughout the journal, but my immediate thoughts are currently on the view looking west towards the Santa Maria della Salute, a view which I and thousands of other artists have painted time and again over the years and which provides an amazing atmospheric view that changes throughout the day, season upon season; absolute magic.

After a few more stops along the Grand Canal I now arrive close to the most popular location in Venice, the majestic and imposing Piazza San Marco, and alight from the vaporetto. The time now is 4.25pm and I feel I have accomplished so much already in a few hours. Before moving on, I must just mention the passengers I shared the vaporetto with, as they were a complete mixture. People watching has become an important part of my Venetian trips as I really do want to understand the Venetians themselves and their culture.

The majority of passengers were in fact tourists, as one would expect in September; then there is a split between Italians living and working in Venice and the true Venetians. The tourists, from all over the world, like myself were jockeying to take photographs and record their travels and seemed slightly impatient as I guess some had a limited amount of time to spend on this wonderful island. By limited time, I mean that a large number would have arrived mid-morning from the two tiered *motonave* or smaller *motocafo* boats which ferry tourists from the mainland (probably Tronchetto) and back into San Marco, probably on guided tours from mainland locations such as Lake Garda or from European coach tours, making these passengers predictable; the remaining ones are slightly less calculable.

The split between Italians and true Venetians is slightly more difficult. Unfortunately, my limited Italian cannot pick up the Venetian dialect, which is somewhat different from the basic Italian. However, I can sometimes feel a sense of bitterness from the true Venetians whereas the Italians feel more united and accept change. One has to appreciate that the true Venetians have experienced far more difficult times in the last three hundred years than most. As well as relinquishing their independence, a passage of change has been forced on them by the economy and climatic evolution, which must seem unstoppable for such a proud and historic race. Statistics tell me that only 10% of the population of Venice are true Venetians, a population that has reduced by half since the end of World War II, a population that has an average age of 45! The average age is high because the majority of young people have been driven out by the high rents imposed as prices on mainland Veneto can be as much as 40–50% cheaper.

Enough of social history, for now at least. I have now turned right, after alighting from the vaporetto at San Marco, and continue to walk along the Giardinetti Reali which, as a building, provides the perfect frontispiece for the Zecca, which we will see more clearly from Piazza San Marco. I should add, at this point, that I am one of thousands of tourists who arrive at this spot by the boatload, so I am fully prepared for the melee that awaits me. This may sound a little unfair, but the practicalities are that unless you arrive out of season, you have to share San Marco with the world. Having said that, I have been known to sit comfortably in the Piazza San Marco and paint, but that has been at seven in the morning.

Despite the crowds, the magnificent buildings I am about to see again have provided me with endless material for my art over the years. I now turn left, once reaching the columns of San Marco and San Teodoro, walk past the Palazzo Ducale (Doge's Palace), which is on my right, and directly facing me is the majestic Campanile. From this point, I can see the Piazza San Marco quite clearly even though it is covered with pigeons (mustn't knock them as they feature in quite a few of my paintings, without asking for sitters' fees) and I make my way diagonally across the Piazza to where the arches of the Procuratie Vecchie end. Once I have reached this corner point between the Procuratie Vecchie and the Ala Napoleonica, there is a small passageway, which takes me to the Rio e Bacino Orseolo, our final destination for today. You will have gathered that I have deliberately crossed the Piazza with little or no reference to the wealth of architecture, history and beauty which abounds, the reason being that I propose to dedicate a major part of the January chapter to this spectacular and historical part of Venice. As I previously mentioned, the Piazza and its surrounding buildings provide endless material for future works, and artists for hundreds of years have portrayed this scene in many different ways for the world to admire.

The time is now 4.45pm and when I arrive at Rio e Bacino Orseolo it is so tranquil and peaceful even though the gondoliers are still plying their trade in this small basin, the queues of passengers who normally await them when they arrive back at this spot having now disappeared. This particular place holds fond memories for me, as it was literally the first location that I pencil-sketched on my second visit to the island, and it has also proved to be a valuable place to promote my artwork. Views from either end of this small basin are perfect material for painting, one being from the passageway leading from Piazza San Marco looking north towards the small bridge that spans this tiny canal, the other from the opposite direction facing the narrow thoroughfare which leads from the bridge to the backdrop of the hotel wall where the gondolas are moored. I should perhaps mention that I have experienced some problems from the people who organise the gondola tours. It may be that they see me as being a slight threat when I am sketching and possibly worry that their customers might buy my sketches rather than their photographs. On occasions, I have been asked to move along by these people who, after all, are simply artisans like myself and really have no authority to move me on.

As I intend to use this location for future work I generally resist arguing with them, and have even humoured them in the past, which they seem to take in good heart, so I simply finish my sketching quickly today and move on. Again, I have taken several photographs which I can use as reference at a later date. When I am journeying around Venice I usually carry a small rigid transparent plastic case, measuring 33cm x 43cm, which enables me to transport finished watercolour work without the fear of it getting damaged. It being transparent, I can advertise my work simply by resting the case against my easel or folding seat when I am working, and it is surprising just how many people stop and comment on the work, and occasionally, and I stress occasionally, they purchase some. The fact that I rotate what's on view in the case to match the location I am working at probably helps! Sales don't happen often, but when they do it does help with my air fares and expenses and frees up my collection for new work to be added.

For the non-artist, I should add that, over the course of a year, I seem to amass a large volume of finished work, and therefore it is important to sell. Once the joy of painting is over, it's time for someone else to enjoy your work!

Commercial over, the Rio e Bacino Orseolo provides a wonderful vista to paint, as it nearly always produces movement from the gondoliers, and seems to capture what Venice is about in one picture.

Although I have no time to paint today, I must find some time to photograph certain areas of the Ponte della Paglia, which is the main pedestrian thoroughfare at the Lagoon end of San Marco and where I board the vaporetto for my final boat trip for the day.

I say farewell to Rio e Bacino Orseolo and the tranquillity and benevolence of this small oasis for now, as I head back across Piazza San Marco, where I am surprised to see that the heaving crowds have reduced considerably in such a short period of time. Heading past the Campanile on my right and the Doge's Palace (Palazzo Ducale) on my left, I arrive back on this wonderful promenade and turn directly left for the Ponte della Paglia. It is very opportune that I have chosen this spot to photograph as it gives me the opportunity to seek out a fellow artist whom I have met several times in the past and who is generally found working under the portico alongside the Palazzo Ducale. He is Danish by birth and has lived in Venice since 1966, and we often pass the time of day discussing art in general. I particularly like the work he produces, which is best described as abstract/contemporary, in oil, depicting the Basilica San Marco as a complex design of horizontal, vertical and curved lines which look stunning on his wonderful blue canvas background. Alas, today it is fairly late in the afternoon and he has obviously moved on, but I am sure to see him at a later date and talk about his work and Venice in general.

Having photographed the Ponte della Paglia, I realise that I do actually need more tourist traffic to fashion a future piece of work, and late afternoon is not the best time, so I decide to get more detailed photographs on another day. There is still time, however, to photograph the famous Bridge of Sighs, which spans this small canal that flows into the Lagoon. The Bridge of Sighs, in fact, links the Palazzo Ducale to the infamous New Prisons (no longer in use), which were originally built in the 14th century.

This particular location today reminds me of a quotation by Samuel Johnson which reads 'Worth seeing, yes; but not worth going to see', simply because the tourist traffic in this area during the peak season is stifling. I thoroughly recommend leaving locations like this for visits during the 'off-peak season'. I intend to return here in a later chapter, as not only are there fewer people to circumnavigate, but areas like this come alive when they are less crowded and it is easier to experience and fully enjoy this incredible scene.

It is now 5.15pm and I must catch the vaporetto back to Piazzale Roma (remember, our starting point this morning? Seems a long time ago now). That is the wonder of Venice for me; a day can sometimes seems like a week. I am back at the vaporetto landing stage for the No. 1 boat, and have boarded and got a seat, which pleases my tired legs, I can now sit back and marvel at travelling the entire length of the Grand Canal. What could be better, a drink perhaps? Well, I hope to have enough time to visit a small bar which is located directly at the rear of the bus terminal at Piazzale Roma.

Sitting on the vaporetto, I have time to reflect on my day, at the same time looking at the world around me, and I know the boat will take about 50 minutes to get to Piazzale Roma so it's time to sit back and enjoy the rich experience that the day has given me. Having read a copious amount of books about Venice and particularly the periods of its history between the 15th and 19th centuries, my imagination starts to wander and I visualise the millions of merchants and seamen who have traded along this waterway, the artists who have painted every building, bend and skyline, the mystique of Carnivale, the feuding of families, Marco Polo setting out for China, the hundreds of regattas, the pestilence and plague that crippled the population, the courtesans and other women of the world looking for trade, the legend of Casanova, the freezing over of the Canal, the architectural grandeur of each palazzo ... it goes on and on forever and the 50-minute slot becomes an epic film, all of which I intend to explain to the reader in future chapters.

As the Grand Canal forms a major part of this wonderful city, I propose to give a detailed description of the wonderful façades along the length of its seven sections in my October chapter, at the same time concentrating on the Rialto Bridge and its markets, and the Galleria dell Accademia. But that is all for next month, now back to today.

I arrive at Piazzale Roma at 6.10pm, which leaves me 30 minutes before my bus departs; time for a quick drink. I make my way over to a local bar for a cold beer. The bar in question sits in a small area of Piazzale Roma directly at the back of the bus terminal and is a perfect place to catch your breath before the journey home. I remember the very first time I used this bar; it was on a pleasant summer's evening, similar to today, when I noticed how peaceful and shaded this spot was, and how interesting the customers looked sitting outside. On this particular occasion, I had at least an hour to spare as, in those early days, I was concerned about getting back to the airport well before time, so this was a perfect spot before catching the bus. Anyway, a waiter appeared for my order and I was pretty thirsty so I ordered a '*birra grande*'; immediately, the waiter positioned his hands to signify the difference between large and small, so, being extremely thirsty, I simply nodded. A couple of minutes later, he arrived back with my drink, a full litre of lager in the largest glass I have ever seen, the size of a large flower vase! Now this may not have seemed at all odd to a Bavarian drinker but to the group of Italian customers spread around the other tables, with their small glasses of Campari and miniscule espresso coffees, it created quite a discussion point for the remainder of my time at the bar. Being British, I said nothing and just sat there nonchalantly sipping from this vessel for the next 30 minutes before leaving feeling and looking like the Michelin Man.

Today, I have a small glass of larger and I sit shaded from the afternoon sun and feel at ease with the world. I recognise some English tourists by their accents and casually pass the time of day with a young couple; they have noticed my paintings and want a peek. It is always nice to get some comment on your work. After all, artists are performers and need an audience to appreciate what they do. A small working barge pulls up alongside the quay close to where I am sitting and two tired boatmen moor their vessel to the adjoining fleet of similar small craft. They, being on the other side of the small canal which separates the bar from them, immediately cross over the small bridge nearby and head directly to the bar where two glasses of what appear to be Campari await them; obviously regulars. They are soon joined by others fellow boatmen and within a couple of minutes all are drinking and discussing their day's work. Boats like theirs play an important part in the commercial life of Venice. I suspect their particular boat is used for deliveries, as there are lots of small wooden boxes on board, and one can't help but notice throughout the day, from early morning to late at night, these craft are constantly travelling the canals. As an artist, I just feel that even on a misty wet day one can create a good sketch from these highly decorative vessels as well as the local architecture.

I am reluctant to leave as I look around and see a typical Mediterranean scene at early evening, with people of all ages just appearing with their partners, some taking their pets for a walk others casually sitting at a bar table with their newspaper, having a drink and watching the world go by. How civilised they are. Next month I intend to visit a new bar, which I passed today, called Bar S. Lucia. I noticed that it sells cold draught Guinness and looks very comfortable and is also close to Piazzale Roma: perfect for a tipple before heading home.

My bus departs from the terminal at 6.40pm, so I reluctantly leave my little oasis and, after a couple of minutes, walk back past the Santa Chiara Hotel, which conveniently backs onto the bus terminal. Although my bus arrives five minutes late, there is still plenty of time to get to the airport, as the route back follows a reasonably quite arterial road once it has circumnavigated the autoroute junction around Mestre. I board, sit down and immediately think about the conversation I had with a delightful couple I met on the bus on the way out this morning, who were on their way to the International Jewellery Fair in Milan later in the week. I remember sharing with them the magic that Venice unfolds and how they, like me, smiled with joy when we first saw the silhouette of the island as we crossed the motor bridge. Now I am returning home again and journeying back to the airport as I gaze hesitantly at Marghera and quickly realise that I am now leaving Venice and entering the 21st century again. Fortunately, even though my mood changes slightly on the homeward journey, I can look forward to recreating Venice at home in my studio whilst listening to Vivaldi. Not a bad compromise.

Checking in at Marco Polo airport presented no problems and, feeling peckish, I decided to have a delicious pizza and espresso coffee in the departure lounge prior to my flight home, which departed on time and was very comfortable. A fairly empty Gatwick awaited me on my arrival home at 10.00pm GMT, and 25 minutes later I was back home, slightly weary, but full of inspiration. I look forward to pleasant dreams of Venice with its green canals, those red, pink and russet-coloured palazzos, and the joy of future visits exploring and investigating its prolific history. I simply can't wait till next month when I really start to get to terms with the historical data that will supplement my travels in the 'Serenissima', but in the meantime there is a great deal of research to complete before my next trip.

Buonasera, Venezia.

CHAPTER 2
OCTOBER: Treasures of the Grand Canal
'This Passage of Water Frozen in Time'

October, and autumn is with us, bringing another chapter and introducing another season for me to investigate and enjoy on my travels in Venice. Last month's chapter took me on a journey through three districts (*sestieri*) of this wonderful island and provided several really interesting areas to explore and paint. Whilst I bridged three districts to complete my travels in September, I really only glimpsed at the splendour and history that was around me, but that was more than enough to whet my appetite and inspire me to plan and design the layout of my journal for future chapters. Having had a month at home to reflect, paint and write, I am now fully charged up to return to the 'Serenissima', my city of dreams, and begin the second chapter of this journal.

On this trip, I intend to focus my travels on three specific areas of Venice and actually circumnavigate all six districts in one day. Impossible, one might think. Not really, as this time I will make full use of my favourite means of travel, the vaporetto. My route today will take me along the complete length of the Grand Canal and back again, at the same time enabling me to explore the Rialto area and the Accademia Gallery. I consider

October 2006

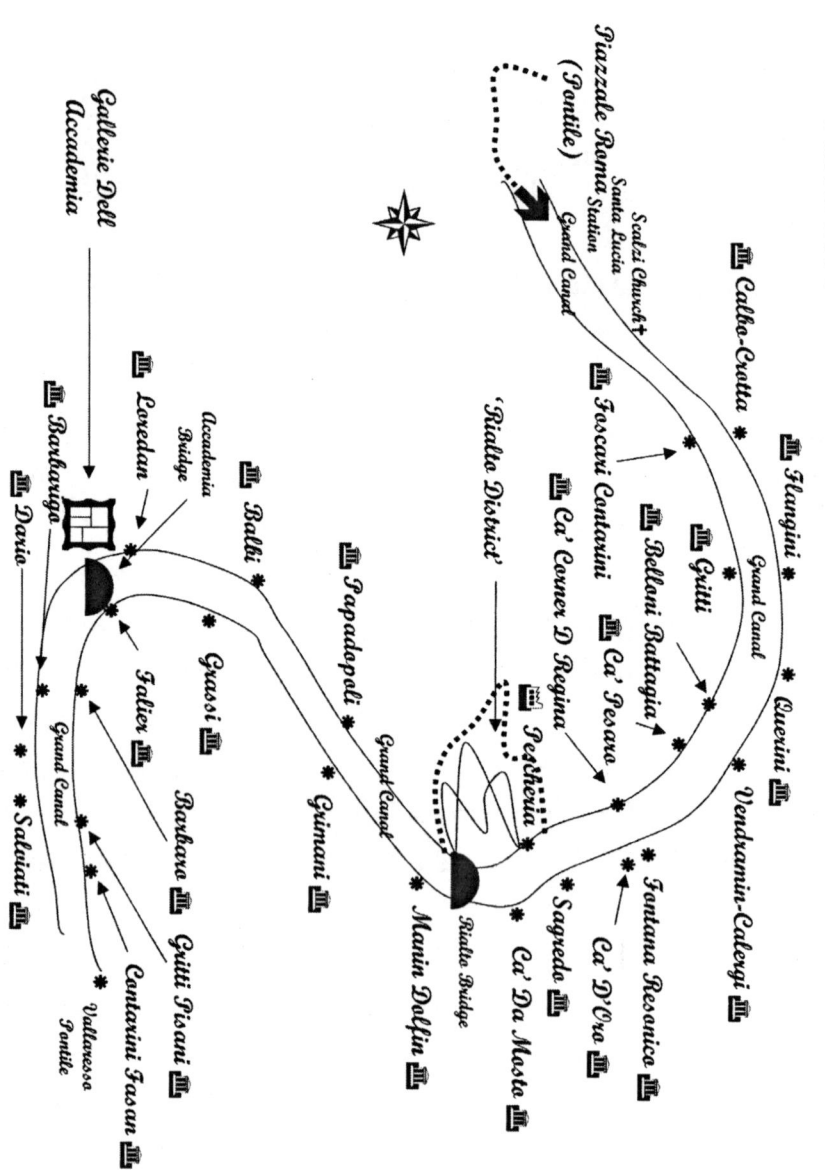

Piazzale Roma Station (Pontile)
Scalzi Church
Santa Lucia
Grand Canal

- Calbo-Crotta 🏛
- Flangini ✶
- Querini 🏛
- Vendramin-Calergi 🏛
- Foscari Contarini 🏛
- Belloni Battagia 🏛
- Gritti 🏛
- Ca' Pesaro 🏛
- Ca' Corner D Regina 🏛
- 'Rialto District'
- Pescheria
- Fontana Resonico ✶
- Ca' D'Oro 🏛
- Sagredo ✶
- Ca' Da Mosto 🏛
- Rialto Bridge
- Marin Dolfin 🏛
- Papadopoli ✶
- Grimani 🏛
- Balbi 🏛
- Grand Canal
- Accademia Bridge
- Loredan
- Barbarigo 🏛
- Doria 🏛
- Gallerie Dell Accademia
- Grassi ✶
- Falier 🏛
- Barbaro 🏛
- Gritti Pisani 🏛
- Contarini Fasan 🏛
- Vallaresso Pontile
- Salviati 🏛

that the Grand Canal and its palazzos should be prime topics in my Venetian journal and therefore I should spend a reasonable amount of time writing about them. The Canal journey alone will give me the opportunity to highlight many palazzos of interest and some that are artistically special, which will also provide me with a wealth of material for future paintings. My aim today is also to capture on camera the splendid and glorious architecture that abounds along the Grand Canal, and marvel at the dignified and austere Byzantine, Gothic, Renaissance and Baroque structures, which stand in collective grandeur. To fully explain these palazzo designs would take several chapters. *The Stones of Venice* by John Ruskin is such a publication, which provides all the detail you will ever need. However, I think my brief synopsis will provide a wealth of interesting facts.

By way of a simple guide to the architectural designs that I constantly refer to, a classification of the four periods can be summarised as the *Byzantine* period, being the 12th and 13th centuries, with round arches on the ground floor and open galleries running on the first floor of the buildings; the *Gothic* period, from the 13th to the mid-15th century, whose buildings have pointed arches and beautifully carved window heads, far more ornate than earlier buildings, which account for the largest selection of buildings in Venice; the *Renaissance* period, spanning the 15th to 16th centuries, with buildings usually of local sandstone, rather than brick, which look more symmetric in design, fashioning themselves on the Roman and Greek style with sculptured columns and semi circular arches; and the *Baroque* period, focused on the 17th century, in which the building façades are completely covered with ornamental work and usually have heavy stone fronting on the ground floor.

I should also explain again that the majority of routes I plan to travel, within this journal, are completed usually in one day, so I am limited to the amount of time I have to sketch. However, a two-day trip would provide ample time to experience the joy of painting 'live', as so many artists have done in the past.

My travel bag today will therefore be restricted to a camera, notebook and sketchbook. These few items will allow me to work on several pieces once I am back home in my studio. As usual, I will take my trusted travel guide (an important reference for today in identifying each palazzo graphically) and my well worn but useful street map, simply to plot and record my route.

* October 12th 2006

The alarm on my mobile phone tells me that it is 4.30am and time to get up and get to Gatwick for the 6.50am flight to Marco Polo airport, Venice. Doesn't seem like five weeks ago since I was last there. Can't wait to return and savour beautiful Venice again. Some of my friends still cannot understand why I travel on day trips and think that I would be far better staying in Venice for a couple of weeks once a year. They still haven't got the plot yet. Apart from being more economical to do it the way I do, I am simply besotted by Venice and can't wait to start planning my next trip. How else would I get to see and feel the changing seasons? Not by staying there for a two-week period.

My flight was uneventful other than for the remarkable views of the Dolomites as the aircraft circled this range of mountains when making its final descent before landing at Marco Polo airport. We landed at Marco Polo at 10.15am Italian time, and when I emerged from the plane the air temperature was perfect for me and I thought to myself that today is going to be a great day, and so it was, other than one slight mishap in the evening, which I will explain later.

Having purchased my ACTV day ticket, my journey on the bus from the airport to Piazzale Roma allows me the opportunity to photograph the 3-kilometre stretch of the Ponte della Liberata (Bridge of Liberty), which crosses the Lagoon and terminates in the 'Serenissima'. Today, weather conditions are brilliant, which gives me the perfect opportunity to witness fishermen working from their small dingees (*bragozzo)*, resetting their nets and other associated traps for the next tide and their next catch. There are several ways in which these fishermen make their catch, as the season dictates what is available; for instance, this part of the Lagoon generally provides only eels and mullet in the summer. Each species of fish is caught in a different manner within the Lagoon, one common method being the square dipping technique that comprises of large net supported by four posts, which move in accordance with each tide. Hoop nets are for the bass and bream whereas the wicker *vieri* are normally employed for crabs and other shellfish. There are many species of fish available for the fishermen to catch in the Lagoon, and even more in the seaward parts beyond the protection of its natural harbour defences, which arrive via the Adriatic, and all of this produce will be transported to the wonderful fish market (*pescheria*) in the early hours of the morning, for Venetians to savour.

My bus arrives at Piazzale Roma terminal and already I feel that the past twenty or so minutes journey from the airport have been extremely enjoyable, especially when sighting the silhouette of the campaniles and churches of the city which invite me in like the pull of a magnet. I'm off the bus and have checked the timetable by the bus stop just in case there have been some seasonal changes made. All is well, so I walk the short distance to the vaporetti waterbus terminal, which is directly to my left and about a 5-minute walk away from the bus terminal. The No. 1 vaporetto pontile is at the far end of the group, and when I arrive I am just in time for departure, so I quickly jump on board and I am away on the Grand Canal. The vaporetti are extremely punctual and arrive or depart from their pontiles every 10 minutes, so there is no precious time lost anywhere along the Canal. Now is a good time to explain briefly how wonderful this service is. For my 12-euro ticket, I can travel on any ACTV craft within and around the main island and also travel to the surrounding islands within the Lagoon (when time permits). Exploring these islands is a must and I will feature some in later chapters such as Murano, Lido, Torcello and Burano, not to mention the closer islands of the Giudecca and San Giorgio Maggiore. The main vaporetti routes cover all these extremely picturesque places and I will be using numbers 1, 42, 61 and 82 among others for most of my travels throughout the journal. I also use their website regularly to ensure that I have the correct timetable. The vaporetto will serve me well today, as I will use it as a platform for my main article, being the Grand Canal and its palazzos.

Careful to have my camera and guidebook at the ready, I take my position on the vaporetto, which fortunately is not crowded, and grab a prime seat at the rear of the craft in order to have a good vantage point to photograph the collection of palazzos I have chosen to write about today. Normally, the seven seats which are situated to the rear of the main seating area are difficult to obtain, as every passenger wants one on a nice summer's day. However, today is my lucky day and I have a seat which I share with two locals and several American tourists. From my vantage point, I get the opportunity to view both left and right banks of the Canal as well as being able to stand up, sit down and turn around whilst photographing. Sometimes this does prove to be more difficult when the vaporetto is full, and one has to appreciate the fact that there are other passengers, but invariably they are keen to capture the moment on film, so a little give and take is the order of the day. Again, looking around me, it is fairly easy to spot the indigenous Venetians as they offer a slight look of resentment and shy contempt of the situation, primarily because we as tourists are seen as an imposition at times even though we do generate substantial income for the Island. There are those, however, who are extremely hospitable and offer a distant smile, especially if I look completely overawed by the occasion, which I generally am even though I have been here many times before. My fellow group of Americans are equally enthusiastic to record their trip, so I am in the majority for the time being.

The plan for today, as I previously mentioned, is to capture several palazzos on camera to sketch later in the studio, and also to highlight a collection of special buildings which I am very fond of. Even though I probably could identify my favourites without any help from my guidebook, I have still marked each one with a marker pen in the travel guide so that I don't miss them when they come into view. My travel guide is particularly good for this purpose as it follows the contour of the Canal perfectly and the graphical reproduction of each building is remarkably well illustrated.

The cruise begins as we pull out on the vaporetto from Piazzale Roma pontile and navigate this rich and historic waterway. Before we arrive at our destination, where the Grand Canal ends and the Canal di San Marco begins, I will have sailed under three wonderful bridges, passed over 200 palazzos (former palaces), seen 46 side canals which enter the Canal, and also noticed 48 alleys that terminate by the Canal. and gazed at the splendour of the 10 magnificent churches that stand on its edge. I will have travelled just 3.2km over a waterway that is approximately 2.75m deep, and my thoughts once again would be trained to the rich history and occasion that has made this the most attractive canal in the world.

In order to keep a level plain on the Canal and not become completely disorientated, I have decided to highlight the palazzos of my choice on the left bank (which happens to be on my left in the direction I am travelling) until I reach Canal di San Marco. This will become more clear when I disembark from the vaporetto to first visit the Rialto area, and then on the return trip when I explore the Accademia.

I am now passing Santa Lucia railway station on my left and notice that even at 11.00am there is a melee of tourists and locals either sitting on the station steps photographing, eating their snacks or simply enjoying the view, whilst others are casually entering this busy terminal. Given more time, I would have enjoyed walking around this fashionable station again, as it is an interesting place to explore and it also provides plenty of material for future sketches. I remember the first time I visited the station and was impressed just how clean and tidy it was, having no raised platforms like those back home, which made the locomotives seem enormous, as they stood stationary in their prescribed terminal position. The Eurostar looked splendid amongst the other relatively commonplace engines that would eventually transport passengers to many distant Italian cities. Although my thoughts are to return to the station at a later date to fully appreciate once again just how efficient the modern

Italian railways are, I should point out that the original church of Santa Lucia once stood on this very site and was demolished for the purpose of progress. Knowing how much Venetians feel about their island, I can only assume that they were mortified when this transformation finally took place. Not only were they losing a piece of living history but the station was ultimately responsible for bringing the world to Venice. There is, however, a wonderful painting by Canaletto titled *'The Upper Reaches of the Grand Canal with San Simeone Piccolo'* showing the Santa Lucia church as it once stood, which was painted in 1738.

Having just passed under the Scalzi Bridge, I immediately catch sight of Palazzo Calbo Crotta, which is my first selected building en route. Calbo Crotta stands proud and adjacent to Ferrovia pontile, with its sunblinds decorating the pavement in front of the now 4 star hotel, built originally in the 14th century and later altered in the 17th century. Considerably restored but still retaining its Byzantine appearance, this wonderful building was once filled with beautiful Venetian furniture now displayed in the Ca' Rezzonico (18th century museum) further down the Canal. I particularly like the sympathetic way in which the traditional windows form a symmetrical pattern across the façade, a feature I consider to be important for my work, and one which I will regularly endorse as we travel further on our route. Today, like many palazzos on the Canal, Calbo Crotta caters for the tourist and is known as the Hotel Principe, and by way of its location provides a double aspect view of the Canal, Calbo formerly being a wealthy resident of Venice who also owned several other houses near the Rialto area and married Lucrezia Crotta, hence the double-barrelled name. As the pontile is alongside this Palazzo, I get some good shots of the apartments within the footprint of the hotel, which I am told by a local trattoria owner is tastefully appointed but very expensive.

As I leave Ferrovia pontile, I notice that the vaporetto has become far more crowded, probably due to railway commuters coming on board, so I have to position myself more strategically in order to photograph my next palazzo, which is the Flangini.

Palazzo Flangini is almost connected to the church of San Geremia, which is located just before we reach the Cannaregio Canal on my left, and is a slightly oblong-looking building with a Baroque façade. I like this palazzo as it offers some wonderful window studies for future sketching, again with an asymmetrical façade. It was built by Giuseppi Sardi, who incidentally made every effort to purchase original buildings on either side, but failed, resulting in Palazzo Flangini remaining unfinished. The 18th century decoration remains to this day, as the palazzo currently houses the Hellenic Institute, which specialises in Byzantine studies, and is rich with archives and social history. The Institute is proud to also own several rare documents of Crete and Cyprus, which were once colonies of the Venetian Empire. Cardinal Lodovico was the last member of the Flangini family. After his death in 1804 the Panciere family bought the palazzo and kept it in extremely good condition, preserving its heritage for all to enjoy today.

As the vaporetto slowly passes Flangini, the church of San Geremia immediately imposes itself on the Canal and, although not completely visible to the eye (it can be enjoyed better from terra firma), I am aware of its eloquent and expressive splendour, having visited it several times in the past. Passing Canal Cannaregio on the left, I quickly get positioned to photograph Palazzo Querini, which is directly in front of me as the contour of its façade is gracefully angled on the bend, as the Canal veers slightly to the right. Querini is a Renaissance palazzo built in the 16th century and has the family coat of arms clearly displayed on its façade. Although I haven't been inside this palazzo, I could imagine that the view from the interior facing back towards Piazzale Roma is breathtaking. In the 18th century, Palazzo Querini went to the Guistinan family and had several owners up until the 20th century. Today it is owned by the Italian Mail and is used for exhibitions and conferences. The interior is decorated with 19th-century frescoes and stuccowork, all created by lesser-known artists (by lesser known I simply mean those that have not been artistically prominent in historical works, but who are none the less masters of their trade). The research I have compiled on this palazzo tells me that on the second floor there remains the original terrazzo flooring, which is still perfect today. History states that several of the Querini family went into refuge on a Greek island when they were accused of being part of the Bajamonte Tiepolo plot of 1316. To explain this plot I go back to 1297 when a move was put forward to abolish popular elections. Venice, then being a true democracy, diffused the situation by luring most of the conspirators to the Doge's Palace (*Palazzo Ducale*) and then drowning them all in the Lagoon! Ten years later, Bajamonte Tiepolo, armed with a force to overthrow the Doge, set forth for the Palazzo Ducale when, as legend would have it, the perpetrators were stopped in their tracks when an old woman accidentally knocked a mortar from her balcony, killing Tiepolo's standard-bearer, which signalled an unhappy ending for Tiepolo and his followers. Venetian history is littered with thousands of remarkable stories, which I never tire from reading or hearing.

The vaporetto sluggishly moves on, with its engine straining at the gears, passing palazzo after palazzo as it does every day, oblivious to the history facing it on each bank, and then finally arrives at the pontile San Marinola. Fortuitously, the pontile is only yards away from my next selected palazzo, which is Vendramin Calergi.

Palazzo Vendramin Calergi is an early Renaissance building constructed in 1502–1509 and was designed and part-built by Mauro Codussi for Andrea Loredan (Codussi also built the Palazzo Corner Spinelli a decade earlier); Tullio Lombardo eventually completed the building. The palazzo embraces a garden area, which is linked to the main building, but unfortunately the 'terra firma' side entrance is on the northern bank of the Maddalena district of Venice, which is looking very shabby, compared to other areas. Having said that, the palazzo has had a great deal of restoration in the past and the majority of the interior remains intact. After Loredan's death the palazzo passed to the Duke of Brunswick, then to the Duke of Mantora, and was later purchased by the Vendarim Calergi family who, after a few years, passed it on to the Grimani family, at which time it was redesigned by Vincenzo Scamozzi in 1660. The current 'White Wing' is a reconstruction of Scamozzi's design since the original was pulled down as a punishment for a capital crime committed by the Grimanis. Apparently the two sons of the house conspired to murder a member of the Querini-Stanpolia family and were eventually exiled. Richard Wagner was said to have rented 15 rooms in the palazzo, but only used the mezzanine floor and later died in the 'White Wing'; reports state that his body was taken by gondola to the station and returned to Bayreuth for burial. Today the once grand palazzo serves as a winter casino.

Pulling away from the pontile, I casually glance at the church of San Marcuola and feel slightly sad that this wonderful church façade was never completed and, even today, set back from its neighbouring buildings looks forgotten; the interior however is well worth a visit.

I am now heading towards the Palazzo Fontana Rezzonico, and by now the American tourists are totally besotted by the incredible amount of building history that is available to view from our small vessel, and all are envious of the travel guide I have which really does help to identify the majority of buildings we pass.

Traffic on the Canal is extremely busy and I always marvel at the way in which each floating vessel seems to avoid a collision and how each navigator demonstrates a genuine courtesy for fellow mariners, especially the armada of gondolas which circumnavigate the island.

Considering it is October, the weather is perfect. In fact, the forecast was cloudy but I see only blue sky and turquoise water. Perfect.

Again, the reflections of each building in the Canal are countless and indescribable, a sight I always record in my mind, as this combination always seems to enhance whatever sketch or final painting I'm currently working on. The continuity of colour and sparkle in the Canal never ceases to amaze me, as this iridescent phenomenon never seems to alter in colour, only tone. Even when the sun is missing, the colour of the water seems to blend in with the buildings and creates a passage to follow and a picture to record.

Palazzo Fontana Rezzonico is now ahead, its pink façade and attractive windows making such a good subject to paint at a later date. Ideally, the view from the right bank would be a perfect location to set up an easel, but today it is a photograph only. This fine palazzo sits protected by foliage on either side, a rare characteristic for buildings on the Canal. The palazzo was the birthplace of Count Rezzonico (1693), the fifth Venetian Pope (Pope Clemens XIII). Although the palazzo is extremely well preserved, it has been divided to a large extent internally over the centuries. Most of the interior decoration was removed and utilised elsewhere in the 19th century, so very little original craftsmanship remains. The external façade is finished with small horizontal limestone pieces, which are so common for buildings of its time. When I first noticed the beauty of this building, I was surprised to find that it did not feature on general maps, but it is clearly defined in my travel guide and I often wonder if there is some mysterious reason for this or simply that it was overlooked. How can you overlook a palace? I normally look to the right bank when travelling in the direction of San Marco as I know this wonderful palazzo is opposite Ca' Corner della Regina, which I will feature on the return journey later in the day.

Before I have time to fully savour the Fontana Rezzonico I am adjacent to my next selected palazzo, which is the Ca'd'Oro. This wonderful palazzo is better known as the 'House of Gold' and was built for the Procurator Mario Contarini in 1421–1440, to a Gothic design. The name was taken from the original 13th century palazzo building constructed on the same spot, and incorporates part of that original building today. The original façade was finished in gold leaf, with ultramarine and vermilion materials, to signify the wealth of its owner. Unfortunately, the current façade, compared to its original design, has totally changed. However, the internal gallery does hold a wealth of art treasures by Mantegna, Lombardo,

Bellini and Pisanello. Baron Giorgio Franchetti once restored the palazzo to its former glory but there have been substantial alterations over the centuries. The canal façade has recently been restored, highlighting the finely carved windows with traces of exotic marble. There are six arches on the *piano nobile* (main living area), which now accommodate apartments. Today I sometimes use gold leaf on my abstract paintings and would have loved to have produced a painting of the original Ca'D'Oro in its natural colours. Perhaps one day, when I can find detailed drawings of this palazzo, I'll make some vain attempt to reproduce it in all its former glory.

The vaporetto is now stopping at the Ca'D'Oro pontile, which is ideally situated for my next palazzo, the Sagredo, being situated to the right of the docking stage. This palazzo was built between the 14th and 15th centuries and was originally owned by the Morosini family, who sold it on to the Sagredo family in the 18th century. It provides me, as an artist, with a perfect Venetian/Byzantine façade to sketch. The interior staircase and frescoes are by Pietro Longhi and the tracery of the piano nobile remains 14th century and therefore later than the floors below. The right wing dates from the 14th century and is currently being converted into a hotel, which hopefully will mean it will be sympathetically restored and maintained for many years to come.

Fortunately I have sufficient time to photograph this wonderful palazzo before the vaporetto leaves the pontile, as there appears to be some congestion on the Canal, which is preventing our vessel from moving off. My commentary on the palazzos appears to have labelled me an authority on Venice, according to my American friends, who seem to be drilling me with questions. I assure them that I am not an authority on Venetian architecture, just someone who reads a great deal and has spent a considerable amount of time researching Venetian buildings. Having spent many hours in libraries and on the web, I am amazed just how much information there is if you search hard enough. My only regret is that, with my limited Italian, I cannot take advantage of the research documentation in Venice itself. That apart, my commentary must be reasonably interesting, as my American fellow passengers seem to be enjoying what information I can share with them.

Moving off again after the short delay – it appeared that the landing-stage platform rail was not operating properly, which caused the hold up – I am eager to photograph my next palazzo albeit one that appears to be in total disrepair when viewed from the Canal side. It is, of course, the Ca'da Mosto, which recently featured in a superb Venetian television documentary written and narrated by Francesco Da Mosto, a Venetian directly related to the original family owners.

Ca'da Mosto is one of the oldest palazzos in Venice and perfectly illustrates and exemplifies 13th-century design even though it has since been extended and now has a mezzanine floor, which was added to the building in the 16th century. I find the Canal façade to be somewhat in need of restoration but nevertheless a perfect subject to sketch as its Venetian/Byzantine style is perfectly fashioned to capture early building craftsmanship at its best. This building gets my sympathy vote because of its memorable and glorious history and it is one that should be restored to its former glory because it holds so much that Venice is about. Alvise da Mosto, was born 1432, and was an early owner of this historic building. He was apparently famous for his navigational skills and is credited with discovering the Cape Verde islands. Between the 16th and 19th centuries the palazzo was one of Venice's most popular hotels with patrons that included J M W. Turner amongst others, and less notable guests such as the two German officers who fought a duel within the palazzo in the 18th century.

With so many wonderful buildings to see on each side of the Canal, my American friends are constantly reminding me that there are equally wonderful palazzos on the right bank as we cruise along, and I remind them that I intend to keep to my original plan and concentrate only on the left bank until I reach San Marco.

As I pass Ca'da Mosto, the vaporetto turns slightly to the right down the Canal and I see the Rialto Bridge for the first time today and prepare to leave the vaporetto for the time being. Sailing underneath this amazing bridge prepares me for my next assignment, which is to explore some of the Rialto district, and as I approach the Rialto pontile I bid farewell to my American friends, who have patiently watched me cavorting from side to side on the back of the vaporetto in order to photograph the treasures we have all enjoyed. As I leave the vaporetto I turn left and make my way along the *fondamenta* and arrive at the Bridge, and what a bridge it is.

The Rialto Bridge was at one time the only bridge to span the Canal and remained so until 1854. There have been several former structures on this site, which were mostly wooden, but in 1591 Antonio da Ponte built the bridge we see today in all its glory. Prior to the bridge being built, several notable designers competed with one another for the contract, designers such as Michelangelo, Vignola, Sansorino and Scamozzi, each producing wonderful designs, which varied in style. I feel sure that each one would have looked magnificent and met the design criteria, but would they have stood the test of time as well as the one I am now standing on? The decision to build a stone bridge was taken following several disasters that occurred, the most notable being in 1450 when, during a festival, the then wooden structured bridge collapsed, with a considerable loss of life. From my research, I have discovered that the current bridge is 46m long and 15.5m wide, has a span of 27.5m, and at its highest point is 9m above water. The arch rests upon 12,000 elm piles each 12.2m in length. The wide thoroughfare is divided into three passageways with 12 shops on either side. All the land to the right when travelling from San Marco belongs to the island of St Mark, and on the left to the island of the Rialto, and close to the left-hand entrance (Rialto Island) is the site of the first church in Venice, which was erected in AD 420. On show between the facings of the bridge on the San Marco side is a late-16th century relief work of the Annunciation, by Agostini Rubini, with figures of St Mark and Theodore by Tiziano Aspetti on the opposite side. All in all, the Rialto Bridge is a marvel of design architecture and demonstrates just how good Venetian craftsmen were in that period, and one must appreciate just how well it has served the Venetian population over centuries of wear, not to mention 200 years of tourism. Whenever I cross the bridge I am amazed just how well it has survived and how attractive it still looks considering the constant traffic it is subjected to.

The Rialto Quarter lies within the San Polo *sestiere* (district) and research tells me that there were settlers on this site as early as the 9th century. These early settlers called this small area 'Rivoaltus', referring to the left bank of the Canal. In 1097 the first market was established and access was provided to this area by wooden boats, which spanned the Canal. Within a few years there was a semi-permanent structure formed as trade increased. As trading escalated, the Rialto became the financial district of the city, dealing in both retail and wholesale goods. It also housed the city's abattoir.

When I walk across the bridge, on either passageway, I immediately feel a sense of tradition, even today with its shops selling 21st century-goods. I think this is because I pick up the 'scent' of the food markets even though they are situated several hundred metres away. Once across the bridge, I am immediately made aware of the thoroughfare known as Ruga d. Orefici; which forms an aisle and draws pedestrians through. Today, the goods they sell in this thoroughfare are not so dissimilar to those of times gone by, the difference being that the materials of our modern age are on show in their non-biodegradable form. I now make my way through a small passageway to the right, dodging the busy antique and food stalls to arrive in a small square, which leads to the church of San Giacomo di Rialto. This church with its beautiful small bell tower and attractive dome makes a terrific study piece for future work. In fact, I have noticed that it can be photographed more easily from the steps of the bridge whilst standing on the intermediate stairwell that leads down into the market. Once into the small square where the church is situated, I look to my left and see an array of arches leading to a group of small colonnades, which will eventually take me to the food markets.

Looking directly at the entrance door to the church, which is wide open, I can see clearly down the aisle to the main altar, which is beautifully finished in gold. Unfortunately, I don't have time to explore today but will certainly return again in the future. I now walk diagonally to my left and notice the street sign Sotoportego Del Banco Giro, which translated means 'a covered passageway leading to a bank'. Around this area there are four marble steps, which lead down to the water and were once part of the Palazzo

Manin (1560), the residence of the last Doge of Venice before the Republic fell. This building was also once the Bank of Venice. History tells me that there was bank trading in this area for almost 1,000 years and amazingly it never fell into bankruptcy. Quite a feat! The word 'giro', which is used in modern banking terms today, originated from this area also. Another interesting fact I discovered was that, many centuries ago, close to the bank, merchants created what was to be the very first insurance company in the world. Behind the square stands the Palazzo dei Camerlenghi (Palace of Treasures), built in 1525 to a Renaissance design, which was built by the Republican Senate for their treasures.

Once called the Bazaar of Europe, Rialto was the centrepiece for trading Italian fabrics, precious stones, silver plate, gold jewellery, spices and dyes. In the winter of 1514 a fire destroyed almost everything in the Rialto area following 400 years of trading. This tragedy might have been avoided had the Canal not been frozen over at the time, thereby making water more readily available to douse the flames.

I now enter the open area known as the *Erberia* (greengrocery market), which boasts an enormous variety of vegetables and fruit. Each stall is meticulously clean and the goods on sale look so fresh and artistically presented that it seems a shame to purchase these goods and disturb the presentation. Incidentally, when buying produce, remember not to touch any item by hand; these Venetian traders become upset if you do. Although it is only 11.50am, the volume of customers has reduced considerably and most stall owners are carefully packing their goods ready for transportation by boat elsewhere. I wonder what happens to this produce once it leaves the Erberia.

Moving on and having crossed the Erberia, I am now close to the *pescheria* (fish market), which even at this time of the day has some produce on show. The Venetians buy their food really early in the morning. I guess, like most other markets around the world, the Pescheria is at its best at around 7.00am, when trading is really busy. Today I am late but still enjoy the atmosphere this market generates and I take some great photographs for future work in my studio. The Pescheria is a remarkably interesting and architecturally attractive structure to paint and is immediately recognizable by its bright-red canvas hoardings, which enclose the wonderful archways of this historic building and the colour of which for me brings a watercolour to life.

Market time is over for today so I decide to make my way along Ruga d. Orefici in order to photograph the magnificent ceiling paintings that adorn this passageway, which runs parallel with the street market. This scruffy thoroughfare has a few carefully preserved shops but the ceiling panels above this passageway are the real treasure, quite magnificent and generally overlooked by tourists. On each archway between each vault are beautifully painted works of art that would adorn any galley. Well worth seeking out. I sincerely hope that the restoration societies within Venice have these lovely works pencilled in for future attention.

Each time I visit the Rialto area, I leave thinking that there is so much more to see, such as the fruit sellers around Campo San Gracomo, and all the vegetable and butchers' shops as you walk through Campo Battisti, and today is no exception, but I have a vaporetto to catch which will take me down to San Marco.

Having returned to the Rialto Bridge, I take one last opportunity to view its beauty from the right bank. This symbolic and notable edifice must have been inspirational in its day, and looking over to the pontile I remember that several remarkable artists have lived close to this area, one being Vincenzo Catena, who lodged in a low building on the side of the Tedeschi, which is situated back across the bridge to the right. What sketches he must have made during his time there. German merchants also occupied part of this area (Tedeschi means Germans); the exact location is indicated by the buff coloured building on view with a pointed cornice, which can clearly be seen again across the Canal to the right of the bridge.

The time is now 12.30pm and I have crossed back over the Rialto Bridge and boarded the vaporetto again for the remainder of my journey to San Marco. I can now see my next selected palazzo, which is the Manin-Dolfin. As this palazzo is situated immediately adjoining the pontile at the Rialto, I have to be quick in photographing it before the vaporetto moves off. This is not as easy as before, as I am now standing at the front of the vessel jockeying for a vantage point. Fortunately, I am fully prepared for photographing this building and a kind tourist moves to one side so I can see this wonderful palazzo close up. Jacopo Sansovino built this Palazzo (his second palazzo in Venice) between 1538 and 1540; unfortunately only the classical façade remains, which is probably one reason why I am attracted to it. The original interior was completely changed for Ludovico Manin (the last Doge, who died in 1797). Drawings were commissioned to extend the palazzo, but never realised. However, it is one of a few palazzos that still have a passageway, which runs under the façade (a fairly common feature of Venetian buildings of that time). I particularly like the general design of the façade, which is finished in Istrian stone, and the graceful semi-circular arches that are perfectly symmetrical and balance well with the decorative balconies. As an artist, I love to paint this type of building as the heavily shadowed ground floor arches provide perfect subject matter for my watercolours. The palazzo was built on the site of two medieval houses, which probably dated back to the 13th century. The Manin family were said to have rented the palazzo for many years, before eventually purchasing it in 1787. Today the current owners are the Banco Nazionale de Rigno (Bank of Italy).

Moving on a few yards, I arrive at the Palazzo Grimani, situated almost opposite the San Silvestro pontile. This palazzo provides me again with a perfect study for sketching, as it has lots of detail to choose from. Originally built by Sanmicheli for the Procurator Givolamo Grimani, between 1559 and 1575, it was only completed after his death. John Ruskin, the art critic, features Palazzo Grimani in several of his literary works, as it was one of the few buildings he liked. Legend has it that the Palazzo Grimani was built by an admirer of the daughter of the owner of the opposite-facing palazzo in revenge for being turned away for not being suitable. The windows of this palazzo were deliberately designed to be much larger than its facing building the Coccina Tiepolo, which infuriated its owner. In 1807 it was purchased by the State and is now the city's Court of Appeal.

I particularly like this stretch of the Canal, known as La Volta, as it provides the ideal finishing strait for the famed Venetian Regatta and is featured in many famous works of art.

Having now settled for a reasonable viewing position on the vaporetto, I glance to the right bank and photograph the Palazzo Papadopoli as it is easier to get some good shots from the left side of the Canal (more about Papadopoli later on the return trip). The vaporetto now stops at Sant' Angelo pontile, before making a turn to the left on the final part of the journey to San Marco.

Ahead, just before the bend in the Canal, is Palazzo Balbi, which is in fact on the right bank, which I will photograph now and discuss later together with the Papadopoli Palazzo. The vaporetto makes its turn around the bend of the Canal and I can see San Samuele pontile ahead, and just before we dock Palazzo Grassi is in sight. Grassi, designed by Giorgio Massari and constructed during the 1730s, was the last of the great palazzos to be built on the Canal. In the 19th century it was known as the 'bathhouse'. In 1984 the Fiat Foundation purchased it as an exhibition centre, later being redesigned by Gae Anlenti. It now stages extravagant exhibitions and is owned by the French billionaire impresario Franco Pinault. The exterior façade is Venetian/Baroque, which is based on a Renaissance-Classical style, and incorporates a limited but serviceable access from the Canal entrance.

I am now catching site of the Accademia Bridge from my vantage point on the vaporetto and must not forget to photograph the next of the palazzos on my list, which is Falier. Palazzo Falier sits snugly on the southern stretch of the Canal and provides me with a slightly different building design to sketch. Its façade is finished with two covered balconies, which are made of wood and aligned with the piano nobile on either side of the building, thereby creating a recess and attractive courtyard. The second oldest home in Venice, parts of which date back to the 13th century, it is modelled on the Venetian/Byzantine style. Historians remind me that this is the house of the ill-fated Doge Marin Falier who conspired to overthrow the Republic with the help of the Governor of the Arsenale. Falier was beheaded on the spot where he was crowned Doge and his name is marked with a black flag in the honours list of Doges that is displayed in the Palazzo Ducale (more information in a later chapter).

Moving on from the Falier, the vaporetto is now crossing the Canal to the right bank and stopping eventually at the Accademia, which I will visit on my return trip. For now though, I make sure that I am ready to photograph Palazzo Barbaro, which comes into view on my left directly after passing underneath the Accademia Bridge. Pallazo Barbaro was built in 1425 in the Gothic style, having four floors with two loggias containing four wonderfully painted arches in the piano nobile. The right wing was extended in 1700 and has a Baroque façade; at that time it was regarded as being a popular ballroom. Now privately owned, it has retained some of its original artwork and furniture. However, the Baroque ceiling artwork was removed after the fall of the Republic in 1797. Bought by an American family from Boston family in the 19th century, it was substantially renovated and more recently has undergone additional restoration work especially on the exterior, which was originally designed by Antonio Gaspari. History tells me that both Monet and Whistler painted here. I seem to remember reading once that, when Monet spent some time in Venice, he continually praised the quality and comfort of his stay, and I would like to think that he was referring to Palazzo Barbaro when he made that statement.

I can now see the end of the Canal where it opens up into the Bacino di San Marco and I have just two more buildings to capture before I reach the San Marco pontile.

Palazzo Gritti-Pisani is a 16th- century building, which was commissioned in 1525 as the residence for the Doge Andrea Gritti, a really attractive façade from all directions with its arched windows carefully spaced apart to allow a greater amount of its fascia to be exposed and enjoyed. Gritti-Pisani has wonderful views over to the Salute and beyond and is now a fashionable 5 star hotel. In its time, it has been the official residence of the Vatican's Ambassadors to Venice and more recently boasted such guests as John Ruskin, who stayed there in 1851, and Ernest Hemmingway, who remarked that this was his favourite hotel, as did Somerset Maughan.

Before I disembark from the vaporetto at the Vallaresso pontile, I must mention one last Palazzo on the left, which is the Contarini Fasan, built in the 15th century. It is quite small in size but nevertheless a very attractive palazzo, with a rich decorative façade surpassing the usual Gothic architecture of the day. The romantic aspect of this building lies in the fact that legend has it that Shakespeare portrayed this palazzo when writing *Othello* and it is known as the Casa di Desdemona, where Othello performed his dastardly deed. Well, that's what the gondoliers believe, and who is to say they are wrong!

Time for lunch, as it is now 1.10pm, and, having left the vaporetto, I make my way past the Giardinetti Reali (Royal Gardens) and head towards Piazza San Marco. As in chapter one, I am deliberately avoiding the splendour of San Marco for a later chapter (January 2007), when it hopefully will be less crowded and I can concentrate on this subject for a whole day; there really is so much to see and record. Incidentally, my eldest daughter, Louise, has asked if she could join me on one trip, so I thought she would enjoy the January one even though it may be cold, this being her first visit to beautiful Venice.

Today, although the weather is perfect and everything I do seems to be working well, my diet is suffering as I have this urge again for fast food, so I am making my way to the next culinary delight, which is another high street fast-food outlet, but one with a difference. As I walk diagonally across the piazza, through the passageway at the corner of the Procuratie Vecchie, past Basino Oreolo (sketched last month), and continue to follow the small canal, I arrive at Campo S. Luca, and lunch is waiting. By now I'm hungry, over six hours since Gatwick and at last I am standing in the best burger bar in Venice. Here I can order a great pizza meal (yes, a real pizza) with a dressed salad with olives and chicken for 10 euros and sit comfortably on the first floor restaurant enjoying my meal with a view of the small *campo* below. I should also add that the washing and toilet facilities are very good too.

My enjoyable lunch over, and feeling fully refreshed, I now check my digital camera before moving off. I still marvel at the technology that is available today. After leaving the pizza bar, I now make my way back to San Marco, retracing the same route that got me here, and within a few minutes I am crossing Piazza San Marco.

At the Vallaresso pontile I wait a few minutes for my vaporetto to arrive, board it when it eventually docks and secure a reasonably good position at the back of the craft for the next short journey, which will be to photograph palazzos on the right bank before leaving the vaporetto once again to explore the magnificent Accademia Gallery.

It is now 2.40pm and I am on my way again for the very short vaporetto ride to the Accademia. Even though the first part of my return journey along the Grand Canal will only take a few minutes, I still have some palazzos to photograph and record. I have a good view of the Canal from the rear of the vaporetto and almost immediately photograph the Salute on my left as we pass the palazzos on the right bank (left side of the vaporetto). The first building to appear is the Palazzo Salviati, which is one of two selected buildings, not on the map, but featured in the travel guidebook, which I will explain shortly. Palazzo Salviati is a relatively new building, which was constructed in 1924 by the glassmakers of Murano, and viewed by many to be garish and unsightly. I think quite the opposite. As an artist, I feel that both Salviati and Palazzo Barbarigo provide me with an array of colourful studies, and, although considered to be 'technicolour' (a term adopted by locals) by Venetian standards, are in my opinion in keeping with the earlier palazzos.

Salviati has a wonderful façade with undeniable charm and is adorned with mosaics designed by craftsmen, and today currently houses exhibition rooms for the Salviati family who are famous glass blowers from Murano. The fact that this Palazzo is kept in good order although built in the 20th century does not, in my opinion, degrade other more historical buildings, but should in fact pressurise other owners to maintain their Palazzos in a similar condition. Moving along from Salviati we come to Palazzo Dario, which I will explain shortly, and although not mentioned before does actually sit between Palazzo Salviati and Barbarigo. Palazzo Barbarigo like Salviati is again considered to be out of character with other buildings, but I think that this is a foolish statement to make as this building was originally built in the 16th century and has a graceful Renaissance style, which accommodates three floors. In 1886 the glassmakers of Murano sought to advertise their wares by decorating the façade of Barbarigo, which also has colourful mosaics (Carlini), and was again criticised by the locals and is still a bone of contention today. The original interior decoration was by Fontebasso and Tiepolo and another interesting design feature is that the open loggia gives access to the Canal.

Personally, I think that both of these Palazzo's provide a great deal of material for artists, are ascetically pleasing to the eye and do not in any way spoil the Venetian dream, after all it was the glass makers of Murano (who incidentally were physically removed from Venice to Murano) that brought considerable trade to Venice for many decades and still do today.

Enough of my political statements for today, my next choice of Palazzo is actually squeezed between the previous two and can easily be missed; it is of course the very attractive Palazzo Dario, built by Pietro Lombardo for a Ventian diplomat named Giovanni Dario. The building features 2 piano nobile's with a splendid marble finish, which was also remarked upon favourably by John Ruskin. Its ornate chimneys are regarded as being very special as they are original and still functional. Chimneys were an important feature of Venetian architecture in particular the 'inverted bell' design, which is remarkably well preserved on the roof of Dario, and similar designs can be seen in many wonderful paintings by 17th and 18th century painters. Dario is small in comparison to other Palazzos and was once described by Henry James as being as fragile as a 'House of Cards'. History tells me that this Palazzo is infamous for many strange reasons, notably that several of its former owners have allegedly died under strange circumstances: an English Scholar who commited suicide, an English pop group manager who was murdered, an Italian Count who was murdered, an Italian industrialist who committed suicide and an Italian businessman who went bust and his sister was murdered. We move on!

I am now going underneath the Accademia Bridge, ready to disembark and explore this marvellous gallery. Incidentally, this bridge is the second of two temporary structures on this site that were built to span the Canal in the last 70 years, and I can't help thinking that this 'modern structure' is no worse than the glassmakers palazzos. So what is all the fuss about? The Accademia is virtually opposite the pontile, which is moored alongside the bridge, so I only have to walk a few metres and I will be at the entrance to this magnificent gallery.

It is now 2.50pm and I am entering the Accademia by the front door where, as one would expect, there is a security check, but it is a more intense check than any I have experienced in other galleries I have visited. The usual hand luggage restrictions apply at the admission counter (a subject that I will mention when I visit the Doge's Palace in a later chapter), but getting a taped guide seemed to be unusually laboured, all of which was quickly forgotten once my tour started. Incidentally, the Galleria does have an admission charge of 6.50 euros, but that's not bad considering what's on offer.

The Accademia Galleries were created in the mid 18th century by the Venetian Authorities, and in the early 1800s contained arguably the most important collection of 14th–18th century Venetian paintings in Venice, its prime objective being to provide examples of fine art for students and, secondly, to house all manner of art from public buildings, churches, monasteries and convents which had suffered due to the fall of the Republic. A decree issued by Napoleon Bonaparte enforced all public pallazi and religious buildings to be closed, and some even destroyed, a command that was enforced to an unspeakable degree. The Venetians were then faced with many organisational problems in accommodating hundreds of abandoned and retrieved masterpieces, and eventually produced a plan, which would accommodate these works. Their recovery plan meant that three religious buildings, namely the Convent of the Lateran Canons, the Chiesa della Carita and the Scuola della Carita, would have to be grouped into one building and utilised for this sole purpose, and after many building projects this grouping eventually became the Galleria we know today.

Upon entering the first of the 24 rooms in the Accademia, I realise just how important this collection of art is to Venetians, as it records both social and religious history held so dear by these former Republicans. *Room 1* demonstrates just how powerful were the secular guilds of the 15th century and how much effort they put into assisting the poor and infirm. The pieces on show are known as the 'Primitives' collection, and the numerous panels on display reminded me of just how talented these early artists were and how each piece represented the variety of artistic guilds there were working in Venice at that period. The recorded commentary for my tour, which I hired at the reception, was certainly money well spent because the Galleria really is a labyrinth of intercommunicating rooms, which do not, at least to my mind, run in any systematic order. Walking through each room, I soon realised that the 'churn' of artworks has been substantial and almost continuous since the late 19th century, when certain pieces were eventually returned to their former churches, as well as new treasures introduced. In accommodating this transformation, ceilings have been replaced, new stairways created and windows redesigned all by notable designers of their time, such as Carlo Scarpa and Francesco Lazzari.

To describe each room and their amazing collections would fill an entire journal on its own, so I have decided to concentrate on a just few which I particularly like. I should also mention that there are extensive renovation works currently taking place both internally and externally, which provide additional entertainment purely because of the noise factor and the embarrassed Galleria staff who make every effort to contain the enthusiasm shown by the restorers/builders, at the same time being very apologetic to each visitor. My trusted *DK* travel guide tells me to visit the Galleria on a bright morning as the paintings are dependent on natural light, a tip worth remembering, I am fortunate today as the early afternoon light is very good.

Room 2 was constructed between 1886 and 1895 to house Titian's *'Assumption'*, which, incidentally, was returned to the Frari in 1919. It currently contains some super works by Giovanni Bellini, *'Virgin Enthroned with Child'*, and Carpaccio's *'Presentation of Christ in the Temple'*. To restore the balance and harmony of this room, Carlo Scarpa actually replaced the entire ceiling with a dark green plaster as well as introducing the terrazzo and creating a new stairway.

Room 6 is the 'Nuorissima' room, which connects rooms 9 and 11 and was built between 1840 and 1857. In 1988 the room was extensively restored for the Paolo Veronese exhibition. Within this room are pieces by Titian, *'St John the Baptist'*, Jacopo Tintoretto, *'The Creation of Animals'* and Paolo Veronese, *'Venice Receiving Gifts from Hercules and Ceres'*. The Veronese was originally on the ceiling of the Corn Magistrates room in the Doge's Palace. After being sold in 1792, it was moved to the ceiling of the Napoleonic Wing, and then later to the Accademia.

The commentary on my personal recorder has so far given me a very comprehensive overview of the art I am viewing albeit I still have to look carefully at room numbers in order to keep aligned with the commentary. I generally pack my digital recorder together with my camera and have decided today to record the salient commentary points for my journal. In doing so, I appear to be proving an interesting attraction, as well as the surrounding artwork, due to the fact that I have my recorder held between the commentary phone and my right ear!

Room 11 is situated at the far end of the Galleria and was reopened in 1946 by Carlo Scarpa. The entire area was covered with a thick grey canvas as a temporary arrangement, which lasted until 1980! Renovated in 1980, the room remained untouched till 1996. There are a number of frescoes by Tiepolo, which have had specially designed supports made to enable these works of art to be positioned in this room. These detached frescoes, which are spectacular in every sense of the word, must have looked incredible in their original home. One set depicts worshippers facing a loggia, whilst others depict biblical scenes and religious cycles, all demonstrating the remarkable craftsmanship of this period.

Other masters in this room include Leandro Bassano's *'Resurrection of Lazarus'*, Bernardo Strozzi's *'Feast in the House of Simon'*, Luca Giordano's *'Crucifixion of St Peter'*, Bonifacio Veronese's *'Lazarus the Beggar'*, Pordenone's *'The Blessed Lorenzo Giustiniani and Saints'*, and Tintoretto's *'Madonna dei Camerlenghi'*.

The Camerlenghi family were financial magistrates of the Venetian Republic, and an inscription on the lower left states that this piece was destined for the Camerlenghi Palazzo at the Rialto and is dated 1566.

Room 16 has retained the same original dimensions of the convent cell it was once, and was remodelled by Carlo Scarpa in 1947. There are some particularly nice portraits in this room, and one I especially like is *'The Fortune Teller'* by Giambattista Piazzetta. Piazzetta really does capture the grace of the occasion: the assured smile of the woman in the centre and the expression of the youth to her left. Other masters who feature in this room are Alessandro Longhi's *'The Family of Procurator Luigi Pisani'* and Fra' Galgario's *'Portrait of Count Giovanni Battista Vailetti'*.

Room 17 is my favourite room, as it displays works of art by my favourite Italian artist, Canaletto. I was somewhat surprised to discover that there are very few works by Canaletto in Venice, considering that he painted this fair city hundreds of times, but I now realise that the vast majority of his work was commissioned for buyers all over the world. My favourite painting in this room is *'Capriccio of a Colonnade'* (1765), which was a trial piece of work completed after Canaletto was awarded the title Professor of Perspective Architecture. This particular piece was copied by Canaletto several times as well as by many other major artists. Other artists in this room include Francesco Guardi, *'Basin of Saint Mark's Square, with San Giorgio and the Giudecca'*. Gaurdi's works are also very special to me as I see a similarity to Canaletto's work even though his canvases hold a certain graininess, which compliments each scene he paints. Another featured artist I really admire in this room is Rosalba Carriera. She has several portraits on display, one of which *'Portrait of a Girl with a Bussola'* is a piece that features in her personal diary, where she recorded that she received a snuff box with 10 zecchinis from the French Ambassador as payment for the work.

Room 21 provides the viewer with an amazing group of works by Vittore Carpaccio. Carlo Scarpa remodelled this room between 1959 and 1960, lowering the paintings and fitting a strip of light oak with a gilt border as a special feature to complement the overall design. Carpaccio's paintings used to grace the Scuola di Sant'Orsola, a religious group founded in the 14th century. Many aristocrats including the Loredan family were members of this group as were the 'Company of the Stocking' a sort of club set up by young men, most of them from nobility, who chose to combine their forces and who wore stockings quartered in different colours as an emblem.

Carpaccio's work *'The Arrival of the English Ambassadors'* forms part of a group of paintings depicting the occasion perfectly and I was pleased to have the Galleria commentary to guide me through each piece. In doing so, I really did understand this masterpiece and the tale it had to tell.

I spent almost two hours in the Accademia, but could have spent all day there. Like everything else in Venice, there is hopefully 'always the next time', and I will certainly make every effort to return again. Before leaving the Galleria, I had a short conversation with a member of the Galleria staff who spoke perfect English and I asked why there were so few Canalettos on show. I was told that there are more in the Ca'Rezzonico, which is close by. Having said that, there were still only two additional pieces of his works on display there. Just five Canalettos in Venice, it's hard to believe. It's a good job there are more in our own National Gallery to enjoy.

Leaving the Accademia Galleria, I walk straight ahead to the vaporetto pontile to embark on my final trip along the Canal for today, and wait a couple of minutes for transport to arrive. The time now is 4.50pm. While waiting, my thoughts return to the wonderful collection of art that I have just witnessed and I think how lucky Venetians are today in having this wealth of treasures around them, not just in the galleries and palazzos, but everywhere. History tells me that, in 1848, just prior to the Siege of Venice, works of art throughout the city were considered for mortgaging purposes by the interim government in order to raise

1,000,000 lire to aid their financial problems. Luckily, this was semi-resolved by the rich Venetian merchants and patriarchs who managed to raise sufficient funds as an interim solution, thereby retaining priceless works of art.

My vaporetto arrives and, again, like other journeys, I make every effort to get either a front or back seat, but now realise that it is the Venetian rush hour and people are making their way either home, or to Santa Lucia station, so I have to settle for a position mid-craft where passengers get on and off. Not the best place to be, but at least I can get some camera shots of my remaining palazzos, so, camera and guidebook at the ready, the vaporetto sluggishly moves off from the Accademia pontile.

Within a minute or so, I have spotted Palazzo Loredan to my left (right bank) and straight away marvel at the decorative central piano nobile, which has a small balcony running in front of its four sculptured windows. The symmetry of its façade really does work for this attractive building. Palazzo Loredan was built in the 15th century and now houses the British Vice Consulate. The original features of this Veneto/Byzantine building have been well preserved, as it was when once the house of Doge Francesco Loredan. The Loredan family, being extremely wealthy, owned several palazzos on the Canal. This building was once the home of Elena Corner Pisopia, who it is said became the very first woman to gain a university degree, in 1678, when she graduated from Padua University, after which it became the Austrian ambassador's residence in 1572, gaining the nickname 'The Ambassador's House'. The Austrian government of the time was originally asked to pay 29 years' rent in advance. Obviously, even 200 years before Austrian rule, Venetians were not enamoured with their European neighbours.

Sailing past the Loredan, I take note of the Ca 'Rezzonico, which I mentioned earlier, and notice from my guidebook that it was once the home of Robert Browning, in 1888, and is now the museum of 18th century Venice, and therefore and an important building to visit. Although I have not included the Ca 'Rezzonico in my itinerary for today, it is a building which cannot be overlooked in my journal, and therefore I intend to visit this palazzo in a later chapter.

Just as the Canal turns to the right, I see my next palazzo literally on the bend and hastily get a photograph of Balbi, perhaps one of the most important functional palazzos on the Canal, built in the 1580s by Alessandro Vittoria (also a sculptor) for Nicolo Balbi. Tragically, Nicolo Balbi was so keen to see his palazzo being built that he moored a boat alongside the building works and died of a chill from sleeping in the boat during the construction of the building. Palazzo Balbi is now the seat of the Veneto Regional Council. More famously perhaps, Napoleon viewed a regatta from the balcony of this building in 1807, during his very short and only visit to Venice, more of which I will disclose in a later chapter. I can easily see why Balbi was chosen as a good vantage point for this particular event, as it does command a strategic viewing position on the Canal and is perfectly positioned to capture the splendour of the annual regatta. Viewing the spectacle of the regatta from this magnificent Renaissance façade, on both of the balconied floors, must have made a powerful political statement to all of Europe regarding Venetian wealth in earlier days, and this was surely one palazzo that earned a great deal of respect from visitors and dignitaries from abroad.

The vaporetto is now chugging painlessly back towards the Rialto Bridge and just passing the San Toma pontile. At this point, I notice that I could disembark and cross the Canal via the Traghetto di San Toma, for here are gondolas which cross the Canal daily for a nominal fee. I have used them in the past but was not very happy with the fact that they like you to stand up rather than sit down while being transported. Having planned to remain on the Canal, as there are still many more marvellous palazzos to see before reaching my next chosen building, I will give the traghetto a miss today and simply enjoy the cruise and watch the wealth of activities going on around me.

Before reaching Palazzo Papadopoli, my next building, I pass two small inlets entering the Canal which would provide some excellent photographs for future reference, and record geographically where they are in relation to my map for when I get home. That's the joy of Venice: there is always another view or spot where you haven't noticed before, and new ground where you can return to another day.

I am now almost parallel with Palazzo Papadopoli, having sighted the garden area to its left, again another Renaissance-style building, built in the 1560s to a relatively conservative design for its period. By that I mean that there are blank wall spaces broken up with small areas of decoration on its façade, but none the less attractive for sketching purposes. The palazzo was originally built for the Coccina's family, who were jewellers of some note in the 16th century. It was later purchased by the Papadopoli family in the 19th century, who brought with them a fine collection of coins, art and glass. The interior is extremely well preserved, especially the famous 'Hall of Mirrors'. Today Papadopoli is used by the University of Venice.

I am now on the homeward stretch of the Canal and will shortly pass under the Rialto Bridge. Again my mind wanders to early Venetian history as I try to imagine just what it must have been like 400 years ago. Everything that I have read in the past about this area suddenly comes to life. I don't have time to dream for long, however, because my next palazzo will be coming into view shortly. As the vaporetto veers left, I pass the Tribunale Fabbriche Nuove, which is the Assize Courts and originally formed part of Sansovino's market buildings, which were constructed in 1555. This interesting structure features in many works of art, but because of its size I find it difficult to photograph in its entirety, and therefore I shall concentrate on the smaller details along its façade. My disappointment in not capturing the Tribunale is soon forgotten, as the adjoining building is the Pescheria, which I walked around earlier in the morning; and the Canal view provides me with the perfect vista to photograph this colourful scene.

Passing Ca' d'Oro on my right I now get ready to snap the next palazzo, which is approaching on my left and is the Ca'Corner della Regina, which was constructed in 1724 by Domenico Rossi and follows the Baroque style of its day. This palazzo was originally named after Caterina Cornaro, the Queen of Cyprus, who was born on this site in 1454. History reminds me that Caterina was married to James II of Lusignan, who after his death was forced to surrender the island to the Venetian Seignory. Caterina was, however, received and welcomed in Venice, with every honour bestowed upon her, and lived comfortably in an area near Treviso for 20 years. The current palazzo houses historic archives of contemporary art and is currently being restored. I personally like its present form for the same reasons that I mentioned earlier, the recessed windows and balconies, which provide excellent sketching material, and the small columns on the first and second floors, which provide recessed, shaded areas, making it perfect for watercolour paintings.

Cruising past several interesting buildings, each one deserving some recognition, the vaporetto takes me to the large Palazzo Ca' Pesaro, which today houses the Gallery of Modern Art and the Oriental Museum. Ca' Pesaro is a huge and stately Baroque palazzo, designed by Baldassare Longhena, which was originally built for Leonardo Pesaro, a procurator of San Marco. The façade is in a classic style of its time, with two doorways on the ground floor and loggias on the first and second floors, having a light-brown stone finish, . Today, alas, it has a large fabricated hoarding with its name boldly printed on it. Great pity. Construction of this monolith was interrupted in 1682 following the death of Longhena, and the architect Antonio Gaspan completed the third floor. The palazzo has a wonderful wellhead in the courtyard designed by Sansovino. Ca'Pesaro became the property of the City Council of Venice in 1899, following the death of the Duchess Felicita Berilacqua La Mastra, who bequeathed the building to Venice to become a permanent exhibition centre. Again I enjoy the size and shape of this palazzo in a similar fashion to the previous one, as they follow very similar lines.

The time is now 5.15pm and I am looking forward to some refreshment again as the early evening is still warm and my travels today seem to have incorporated a great deal in just a few hours. The Grand Canal has over 200 palazzos and I will have mentioned just a few today, but I feel that the time I have given to their beauty is fully justified. However, one has to see this splendour first hand to really appreciate how wonderful it is. Frederick Barnard's quotation sums it up very nicely: 'One picture is worth ten thousand words.'

Leaving Ca'Pesaro, the heavily laden vaporetto grinds its gearbox once again and, seemingly without much effort, makes for the final bend in the Canal for my journey today, before arriving at Piazzale Roma. As it cruises by the San Stae pontile, I see the next palazzo, which is Belloni Battagia, with its distinctive obelisks standing proudly on either side of its roof. Palazzo Belloni Battagia was built in the mid-17th century for the Belloni family, who, amazingly, bought their way into Venetian aristocracy and found later that the cost of the palazzo was too much for them so they had to rent it out rather than live in it. The Baroque façade has segmented arches, and the great coat of arms, which is clearly on show, forms a rich decoration, heralding a powerful statement about its owner. All of the 18th-century frescoes inside have been restored and conserved, either by an early owner and merchant named A. Caporilla or later, in 1804, when they underwent more restoration when passed on to the Brazzi di Savorgnan family. I have just passed Belloni Battagia and see the Cannaregio Canal and San Geremia to my right, which means that I will arrive at my next palazzo in a couple of minutes. Palazzo Gritti is fast approaching and, despite being much smaller than the previous palazzos, is equally attractive. Gritti is a 16th-century building constructed in a Renaissance style, and was the home of the wealthy Gritti family, who were responsible for producing one of the most dynamic, forceful and intellectual Doges of Venice, Andrea Gritti, who ruled from 1523 to 1538. Andrea was, in his day, a well-respected general and diplomat who served his country well. During the Italian Wars, he drove the Imperial army from Padua and defeated the French in 1512. The Carnival season was brought to another dimension during his reign and he was responsible for building the Marciana Library, Procuratie Nouve, several government offices and the Mint and, most importantly, he developed Piazza San Marco in the style we see it today. Unfortunately, this wonderfully clever man finally succumbed to a surfeit of eels in 1538! Although Palazzo Gritti is relatively modest in its appearance, it does provide interesting sketching material. Even though it is not symmetrically formed, it does have a rather nice little balcony on the second floor, which I have painted several times in the past.

With the Scalzi Bridge in front of me, the vaporetto takes me past the final palazzo on my itinerary today, which is the Foscani Contarini. Palazzo Foscani Contarini consists of a pair of delightful but small buildings, constructed in the 16th century, which form two *palazzettis* adjacent to one another and which, remarkably, are featured on a canvas by Canaletto, which he painted looking southwest from the Chiesa dagli' Scalzi to the Fondamenta della Croce. The palazzo was originally decorated with frescoes by Lattanzio Gambara, and was initially the home of Doge Francesco Foscari, who ruled from 1423 to 1457. It was also once a bank, but now the Palazzo is in private ownership after recently being renovated and offered on the property market for 5 million euros.

My journey on the Grand Canal is now over for today as I pass under the Scalzi Bridge and the vaporetto heads for the Ferrovia pontile where my journey started nearly seven hours earlier. During those seven hours I have visited so many historic places that the day seems like a week. That's one of the reasons why I love Venice so much.

Having disembarked from the vaporetto, it is time for some welcome refreshment again, as I still have over an hour before my bus leaves the terminal to take me back to the airport. Although I do enjoy finishing my day in Venice sitting at the little bar behind the bus terminal, today I have a slightly longer period of time to rest, so I have decided to visit a small bar a few minutes' walk down the Rio Tera Lista di Spagna; this is the street that runs from the Scalzi Bridge to Campo San Geremia. This attractive little bar has caught my attention several times in the past, but I have always been too busy to stop and have a drink. Today I will. Another attraction of this bar, as I mentioned earlier, is the fact that it sells my favourite British (though, actually, it's Irish) beer, which is Guinness, and what's more it's on draught, and on an evening like this a cold drop of the 'Liffey Water' is the order of the day. Bar S. Lucia is a small but very comfortable place to stop off for a late-afternoon tipple and today is no exception. Unfortunately, the tables outside are taken, so I move inside and take a relaxing seat near the doorway. The guy behind the bar has a perfect Irish accent but speaks fluent Italian and I place my order of a pint of Guinness and a small spinach pastry dish which is on display in the bar cabinet. The beer arrives within a couple of minutes with my spinach snack, and how delicious that snack was, so much so that I ordered another! Looking around the bar, I noticed several tourists enjoying their Guinness like me, and discovered that they were from the Czech Republic; the reason I knew this was that, apart from speaking very good English, they were all searching for a currency note from their motherland, as the bar has an extremely large Perspex-covered wall with almost every nationality in the world represented in monetary form. Seeing that their own country was not represented, they immediately offered a Czech note to the barman, who then added it to the collection. I didn't notice an English note while quickly looking at the wall and, knowing that it would cost me a fiver to put things right if there wasn't one, I quickly ordered another drink and sat down!

In conversation with my Czech friends, I gathered that they were in fact living and working in Lincolnshire and were over in Venice on holiday. I'm sure there must be a story line there somewhere. The guy behind the bar finds time to have a chat and tells me that the bar is open throughout the winter months, so I have yet another watering hole to visit at the end of my daily excursions throughout the coming months. Having satisfied my taste buds, I now bid farewell to the occupants of the bar and make my way back to the Scalzi Bridge for my return trip home. When crossing the bridge, I take a couple of photographs of the Canal still busy with gondolas and other water traffic, the sun gradually setting creating wonderful reflections on the water. Today has been a perfect day: good weather, good food, good photography and lots of new discoveries.

Next month, when I return to Venice, I will in fact be concentrating on the Cannaregio District and I have a super itinerary and route to follow, which I scheduled earlier in the year. The route will take me to several places of historic interest including the Ghetto quarter, and I hope to map a route that will be interesting to either photograph or sketch. Before then, however, I have to record today's trip and the many places and palazzos that I have visited and photographed. Once that is done, I will have to select some suitable work for sketching and painting in my studio as possible material for the journal. Apart from my journal artwork, I must also find time to work on my new collection of fairly large abstract pieces for my website, which, interestingly, will focus on Venetian colours and tones, mainly earth colours, and represent each of the six ancient districts, or *sestieri*. In fact, I might even feature one or two of these abstract pieces in later chapters. Whatever, I have to complete my new collection by the end of November as my website is quite demanding and there is some pressure to update the 75 current pieces on display. I am continually asked where and how I find inspiration to paint. The simple answer is, that each time I visit the 'Serenissima' my imagination goes into paint mode and I seem to have new ideas developing in my mind everywhere I travel, which luckily provides me with ideas that cater for a fairly comprehensive portfolio.

From the Scalzi Bridge I have a 5-minute walk to the bus terminal at Piazzale Roma and I reach there minutes before the No. 5 bus arrives. At Marco Polo airport I am second in the queue at the easyJet check-in and within 15 minutes have checked in and I am looking for a coffee. The flight home took 1hour 45 minutes and when I arrived at Gatwick I didn't need to wear my jacket, as it was a nice Indian Summer evening, much the same as the weather had been all day in Venice.

I seem to remember, at the start of this chapter I said everything went wonderfully well throughout the day except one slight mishap in the evening, and that was still to happen. As I left the plane and passed through immigration and customs, I headed towards the short-term car park and as usual I was in conversation with a fellow passenger. When I arrived at the ticket machine, and whilst still talking, I placed my ticket in it when suddenly the machine stopped working with my ticket lodged inside its mechanism. After trying in vain for several minutes to retrieve the ticket, I pushed the button to summon help. Within 10 minutes a car park attendant was on the scene and the machine was opened. By now, I am feeling a bit tired, but I patiently wait for him to retrieve my ticket and, after several minutes, I am told that my ticket has completely screwed up the machine and the attendant will have to remove the mechanism that holds the ticket. This has to be done in his office, where he can then dismantle the damaged part and free the ticket. I then make my way with him to his secure office and wait behind a counter while he works on the mechanism with the patience of a surgeon. After some minutes, the attendant had successfully removed the offending ticket and was scrutinising it like a forensic investigator. Then he said, with some authority, 'This is not a car park ticket, sir. I'm not sure what it is but I seem to be able to make out the word 'vaporetto'. I immediately looked in my wallet and there, sure enough, hidden away in one of the sleeves was my car park ticket.

Buonasera, Venezia

CHAPTER 3
NOVEMBER: Cannaregio
'The Unspoilt Sestiere'

November has suddenly descended upon us and it is noticeable that winter has heralded its arrival, as the first frosts have appeared and left their crystallised calling cards. I seem to take more interest in our weather during the winter and spring periods as there are often restrictions placed upon my activities due to inclement conditions, albeit that our planet seems to be warming and seasonal change can arguably be said to be less predictable nowadays. More importantly for me, at this present time, are the weather conditions in Venice, as I need to visit the 'Serenissima' each month, good weather or bad, to complete my journal. Venice experiences all weather conditions, much the same as other European cities, though generally the winters are considered to be mild, in fact mild enough to allow certain fruits to grow. However, I have experienced snow and high winds in Venice at this time of the year, which is to be expected in this age of unpredictability, but I would be grateful for some stable conditions over the next three to four months in order that I can record my travels and photograph what I need in relative comfort.

It has only been three and a half weeks since I was last in

November 2006

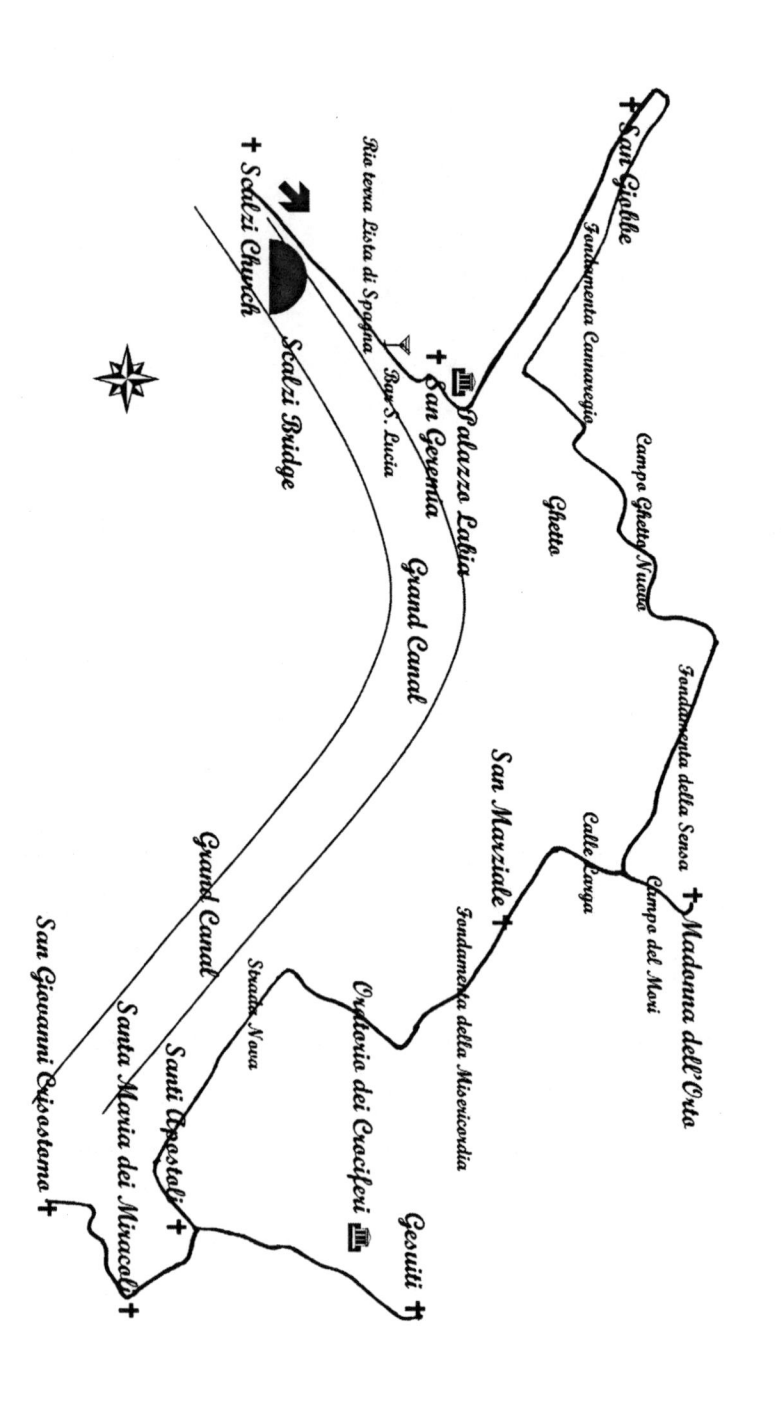

Venice, cruising down the magnificent Grand Canal, visiting its markets and, most memorable of all, visiting the Accademia, not forgetting the joy of recording just a few of its palazzos with their rich history, history incidentally that does at times rely on folklore and tradition. Thinking about it, what historical event does not have stories to tell that fire the imagination beyond certainty at some time? My research is simply based on historical facts which I believe to be accurate, facts that appear to have been researched many times in the past by historians as well as authors and which, I hope are authentic. But then who can deny those 'other' stories told by Venetians both past and present, stories that have been handed down from generation to generation, facts that are perfectly plausible though not always recorded?

My travels at least are recorded and factual but I find I need that element of historic mystery to build a picture of the areas I visit and wish that I could converse more freely with the indigenous residents of each of the *sestieri* I feature, for I feel sure there must be innumerable tales to tell that would be very interesting to hear. Having said that, I have been able to build a small network of friends in Venice who, alas, cannot always help me with historical facts but are extremely helpful in providing me with a better understanding of the 21st-century Venice.

Last month's journal entry was fairly long, as I simply did not want to discredit the marvel of the Grand Canal and I have only just finished the first draft with help from my wife, Avril, who meticulously checks my grammatical errors and who not only critiques my art but also supplies constructive views which I sometimes take on board. In addition to that, she unselfishly puts up with me spending a great deal of time in my studio, as well as travelling the 'Serenissma', and all without the slightest whinge or complaint. *'Mille grazi, Avril.'*

Today I propose to journey solely around the Cannaregio *sestiere* (district), which lies to the northeast of Venice and north of the Grand Canal, which is sometimes referred to as the 'unspoilt district' because it appears to be less visited by tourists and therefore slightly better preserved than most. On my travels today, I hope to see the fairly active Cannaregio Canal, which serves as an important waterway into the northern Venetian Lagoon, and whilst trekking the streets of Cannaregio I will get the chance to visit the Ghetto area, which features in many history books and will prove to be a memorable experience. I will visit several churches of note, two of which will be the *Gesuiti* (Santa Maria Assunta) and the Madonna dell' Orto, a church used by Tintoretto. Surprisingly enough, there are also other palazzos situated away from the Grand Canal and I will pass Palazzo Labia among several others and get some sketching material for a later date. The walk will include the Palazzo Ca'D'Oro, which I passed on the Canal last month, and with a bit of luck I should have enough time to see its treasures. As a humble emerging artist, I will stand in reverence when I pass the house of Tintoretto and, of course, will visit his church, as I mentioned earlier. The route for today will end at the church of San Giovanni Crisostomo, which is just to the north of the Rialto Bridge, and I will probably take the vaporetto back to Ferrovia pontile for my customary refreshment break, time permitting. I am not quite sure at this point in time where I will have lunch but I know that there will be a small eating emporium to rest and recharge the batteries somewhere along my route.

In order to see all of the sights I have planned for today, there will be several 'cul-de-sacs' which I take throughout my route: in other words, thoroughfares which I will return down as there are no other means of getting to the next destination in a reasonable amount of time. For those who want to venture off of my scheduled route, there is plenty more to see and many other interesting rambles to take, which I intend hopefully to return to in another travel journal.

My travel bag will be much the same as last month, perhaps one extra pocket map, which will have the route highlighted for easy reference, giving me more time to enjoy the scenery and take notes.

* **November 7th 2006**

Again, like October, upon arrival at Gatwick I was pleasantly surprised to see how small the crowds were at the security check area and just how efficiently the staff got passengers through with the least amount of fuss. Hopefully the new controls are now fully operational and everyone travelling by air does appreciate just how important the current restrictions are in ensuring that their journeys are made safe.

The Alps today were a wonderful sight again, even though our flight path seemed to be over mountainous regions which had little snow. I guess that will change soon, once winter is fully upon us. The weather today in Venice is supposed to be dry but cloudy and between 4C and 15C.

Upon arrival in Venice, the temperature is just about right, and the sky clear and blue, perfect for my travels today. It is important to have dry weather when one is sketching and photographing and it makes the journey far more relaxing as everybody else around seems to be generally more sociable and friendly as they too go about their daily routines. Up to now, I have been very lucky with the weather on most of my trips, though I am always mindful of the *'Acqua Alta'* during the winter months and hope that I manage to miss this event. Acqua Alta has been a weather phenomenon which Venetians have had to endure for centuries, and simply means 'flooding'. For the time being, I have opted not to discuss this element of seasonal events, but I do however intend to discuss the implications of this phenomena in a later chapter, probably February, that is, if I don't experience an event of this nature before then.

The flight to Marco Polo airport was fast and comfortable and I arrived at the terminal building around 10.00am Italian time and made my way to the ACTV ticket office. The journey to Piazzale Roma took about 20 minutes and again I was able to view the fishermen quite clearly setting their nets and pots on the Lagoon as we travelled over the Ponte della Liberta to the bus terminal and the start of today's adventure.

Arriving at Piazzale Roma, I quickly step off the bus and make my way to the Santa Chiara Hotel (which is close by), as I want to confirm an overnight booking for my March visit, which I reserved on the web a few days earlier. The reason for the overnight stay is simply because in March I intend to travel to several surrounding islands, some close, some far away, which will need extra time as I want to include them all in one chapter. As I mentioned before, Santa Chiara Hotel is a very comfortable hotel and is situated right at the end of the Grand Canal and almost opposite Santa Lucia railway station, perfect in every way for transportation, and it does provide good accommodation.

Having completed my short business in the hotel, I now have my map ready to start my travels and proceed to make my way to the Scalzi Bridge. Once there, I cross over the bridge and then head down Rio terra Lista di Spagna towards the Palazzo Labia. On my route, I casually look out on the left for the Bar S. Lucia, which I intend to visit on my way back to enjoy a couple of beers and some conversation with the locals. When I reach Campo S. Geremia, I notice how busy it is and just how many people are crowding around the street traders. This time of the year must be very quiet for these vendors, not to mention the chilly winter months ahead. I have noticed that the traders do use the bars around this area when things are quiet; they simply pop in for a drink while keeping an eye out for customers from the bar doorways. Although the prime tourist season has passed, there is always a high volume of pedestrian traffic along this passage, as it is a main link to Santa Lucia station, so I suppose local traders probably maintain a reasonable trade during the winter months.

Ahead of me stands the Palazzo Labia, which was built between the late 17th and early 18th century by the wealthy Labia family, who were Catalan merchants and supported Venice during the war with Candia. The Labias were said to be one of the richest families in Venice at that time, and it was their generosity that enabled them to buy their way into society. Tiepolo was commissioned to cover the magnificent ballroom with frescoes depicting Anthony and Cleopatra, in the mid-18th century, and this is said by some to be his finest work in Venice. The external appearance of this palazzo remains in tact, as have parts of the interior, which is a surprise as my research tells me that it has been used as a school, a base for a religious culture and a doss-house! Although Labia has lost some of its original splendour, it was more recently owned by the Italian Broadcasting Network, RAI, between 1964 and 1992, when a considerable amount of restoration took place. Today, paintings by Mengozzi Colonna can be viewed, but by appointment only.

When I view this incredible palazzo, I am saddened to see what time has done to erode this once beautiful structure, even though there has been some major works commissioned to preserve it, and I can only wonder just how magnificent it must have been in its heyday when the original Labia family were in residence.

Weather conditions remain perfect for November as I now journey on to the Ponte D. Guglie (the small bridge that crosses the Cannaregio Canal), which is situated just a few metres to the left of Labia. When I reach the bridge, I pause and savour the view I have of the Cannaregio Canal as it enters the Northern Lagoon, and watch the vaporetti and other boat craft manoeuvring themselves along this very busy waterway. I continually remind myself that this canal was once the main access point to the island before the arrival of the railway, and provides vital transportation routes to other smaller canals that support this *sestiere*.

Cannaregio acquired its name from the word *canne* (canes) and is by far the most unspoilt *sesteiri* of the six in Venice, as well as being the most populated, probably because of its close proximity to the railway and bus terminals, as well as it being less explored by tourists. I particularly like Cannaregio, as it appears to have this healthy vitality even though it is not overwhelmed by tourists, a fact which I find incredible, as it has many interesting facets to enjoy, such as: magnificent buildings to visit, mysterious alleyways to explore, opportunities to watch a variety of craftsmen at their work, small shops to peruse and a host of 'local' bars and restaurants to sample. I have been reliably informed that the majority of Venetians eat and socialise in this district, which offers authentic Venetian cuisine and, I suspect, local gossip to match.

As I stand on the steps of the Ponte d. Guglie, I have noted a small hotel to my left with seating outside which looks interesting, and one that I will visit on another day, perhaps for some lunch next summer.

I am now walking down the Fondamenta Veneir, which runs parallel with the Cannaregio Canal. I take note that it is only 10.55am and I marvel at how much I have seen and enjoyed already today. Across the canal to my right, sits the Palazzo Surian with its Baroque façade and wonderful balconies, which highlight each of the ornate windows on view. Moving along, I now see the Ponte Te D. Tre Archi (a small brick bridge) ahead, which will take me across the Cannaregio Canal on my return along this waterway. It is a great temptation for me at this point to jump on an awaiting vaporetto No. 42 on its way to Murano, but I must keep to the journal schedule and leave Murano until my visit in March. I notice several boats carrying what appears to be furniture and I guess that they may be Venice's equivalent to our removal vans and I think how awkward it must be to load these vessels with heavy furniture, apart from the access problems getting the furniture to their respective buildings, again a unique display of the adaptability of these islanders and the matter of fact spirit they show to everyday life.

Before I cross back over the Cannaregio Canal, I turn left into Campo S. Giobbe, where there stands the church of San Giobbe, which sits on the same site as an early oratory built in the 14th century and dedicated to a saint of the same name. Construction of San Giobbe commenced in the middle of the 15th century following designs produced by Antonio Gabello, and was originally financed by Doge Christofano Moro, whose tomb lies inside. Having said that, various silk traders provided the funding for the chapels. In 1470 Pietro Lombardo completed certain modifications by adding some Renaissance touches such as statuettes, and the church remains virtually as we see it today. Research tells me that these masterpieces by Lombardo were probably his first works in Venice. Originally there were several works by Bellini and Carpaccio above the altars, but today they have been removed and are housed in the Accademia. Works that have remained in situ include pieces by Gerolamo Savoldo, Vivarini, Lombardo and other great masters.

Although I couldn't gain access into San Giobbe, I did record the number of 'cats' in the Campo who, judging by their condition, were obviously well fed. I also observed that there were several Venetians either sitting or standing around the campo who seemed to view my presence as an imposition on their privacy. Their calculating looks seemed to be suspiciously aimed at me whilst I was photographing their church and I did detect a look of satisfaction from them when I tried to enter the front door of the church to discover that it was locked. Not wishing to be judgmental on Venetians, as I can appreciate that they probably feel very exposed to the multitude of visitors they receive each year, they do however at times need to appreciate the fact that tourists do bring income into this beautiful city, and this income is paramount to its survival. Having said that, Cannaregio, as I mentioned earlier, probably receives fewer tourists than the other five *sestieri* and appears to be left to run its own affairs much as it has for many centuries. Despite my comments regarding certain Venetians, I do understand that, to preserve the heritage and charm of Venice, it must be difficult to accommodate millions of tourists each year, and I am of the opinion that perhaps there could be certain limitations enforced to restrict large numbers of tourists at any one time entering the city. One solution that has been suggested, if not actually enforced, was to levy certain charges on tourists, which would be distributed to the various organisations working hard to preserve the 'Serenissima'. Enough sermons for the time being!

Having now reached the 17th- century three-arched bridge, which incidentally is the only one in Venice, modelled on a design by Palladio for the Rialto, I cross over and stop to look at the view facing east from where I have just walked. How quiet and serene the view is looking back to the Ponte D. Guglie, which is the direction I am now heading. The next palazzo that I photograph is the Savorgnan, which is on the opposite side of the canal and again Baroque in design, with wonderful balconies and heavy relief work on two panels on either side of the piani nobile. Turning left now, into Calle del Forno, I am now close to the world's oldest Ghetto district, which I am looking forward to photographing and recording, as there is so much historical fact built around this particular area of Venice. Walking along the Ghetto Vecchio, I notice a small shop sign advertising the work of musician and artist Tony Green. The poster on the shop doorway states 'entrance free' and, having read the external poster, I decide to go inside and have a look at what appears to be an artist's gallery, a gallery with a difference as there is great jazz guitar music playing in the background. I am immediately welcomed by the artist himself, Tony Green, who then goes on to provide me with some really interesting background information about his work and his travels. Tony has been more or less a permanent resident in Venice since 1982, moving between New Orleans and the 'Serenissima' as well as travelling to other European venues touring with his jazz group and producing a really interesting art portfolio

I have to confess to being a traditional jazz enthusiast and have myself travelled to New Orleans, in addition to being the owner of a collection of 'plastic LPs' from masters like Kid Ory, Louis Armstrong and George Lewis to name but a few, so to hear a CD of Django Reinhardt playing in the background was a double result for me on the day. Tony's style of playing is very similar to Django's, and he also play's live music in Venice on occasions. All this he told me whilst preparing posters for a session he was performing the following evening, which, sadly, I could not attend as I would be back in the U.K. Unfortunately, I didn't purchase one of his CDs on display, which I regret now, but will hopefully get the opportunity to do so at a later date. Having mentioned Tony's music, I should also mention his artwork, which is full of vibrant colours, especially those works I saw depicting New Orleans, which record the energy, colour and tradition of an era which, thankfully, was responsible for creating jazz itself and producing some of the finest jazz musicians and composers of the 20th century. Most of the artwork on display depicted interesting scenes of Venice, beautifully portrayed in a range of sensitive colours so typical of the city, together with contrastingly dynamic portraits of New Orleans street musicians performing, which captured both the festive atmosphere and movement of the occasion in the equally interesting French Quarter of the birthplace of jazz.

As I now enter Campo Ghetto Nuovo, my mind immediately focuses on the past research I undertook in order to fully understand just how meaningful this district was to Venetian history. A Jewish community established itself here illegally during the second half of the 14th century, when as merchants they arrived to both buy and sell their wares in the lucrative Venetian ports. They were officially authorised to reside and trade in Venice following a *condotta* (contract) being drawn up which outlined conditions of finance and status, thereby controlling their activities. The Jews, however, were constantly checked by the voice of authority and threatened with expulsion in 1397 because Venetians were afraid that they would overtake and run both commerce and finance in the city. Because of these fears, certain stipulations were imposed, namely that each Jew wore bespoke clothing, initially yellow and later red hats, and that they did not reside in the city for periods of more than 15 consecutive days at any one time. This *condotta* remained law for almost 100 years, but was inevitably abused although reasonably well marshalled during this period. In the Cambrai Wars of the early 16th century, Jews sought refuge in Venice and, in doing so, donated substantial funds to the Republic, which, in turn, justifiably offered a more reasonable settlement for cohabitation. In 1516 the Jewish population were moved en masse (exodus) to the Ghetto Nuovo, where I am currently standing, but they had several restraints imposed on them. As Nuovo was then an island cut off from the rest of Cannaregio by canals, two gates were built to enclose its occupants, which were manned by Venetian Christian guards, ironically financed by the Jews themselves. These gates were only opened at dawn, and closed at midnight, for access. Interestingly enough, the original fixing points for these gates can still be seen today at the entrance to the Sottoportio. This then, in effect, became the first 'ghetto' that we know in modern terms and served as an effective curfew area that partitioned Jews from the indigenous population of Christians in the city. By controlling these two access points leading into the Ghetto, Venetians felt that they were protecting their own interests even though they allowed money-lending and pawn-brokering enterprises to function, which incidentally provided considerable revenue in the form of taxes for the Venetian government. The original Ghetto site, before the Jews occupied it, had been an ironworks that produced ammunition and weapons for the Venetians, and the word 'ghetto' originates from the Venetian medieval name for a foundry.

There were several versions of the *condotta* issued in the late 16th century which allowed higher tax rates to be imposed. However, a more sensible approach was eventually made whereby Jews were given the opportunity to trade within their own quarter and also share commodities and leisure pursuits with their Christian neighbours. The infamous Ghetto Gates were eventually demolished in 1797 during the French occupation, but containment within this area was still enforced until the Unification of Italy in the 19th century. Today there are still three sections of the Ghetto area remaining, which are justifiably cherished by both Jews and Christians alike: Vecchio (old), Nuovo (new) and Nicoro (newest). Unfortunately, I don't have time today to visit the wonderful synagogues and museums within this quarter which I described earlier, but would recommend travellers to do so whenever in this area. A good number of the Jewish population today have relocated to each of the other *sestieri*'s on the island, but they still retain a strong presence in this historic quarter.

Architecturally, the terraced group of buildings within the Ghetto Nuovo are colourful and well preserved and one day I will attempt to recreate this area on canvas. Again, research tells me that it was forbidden to use any marble on either the interiors or exteriors of their buildings, so what you see today are grim reminders of the pointless sanctions imposed on the Jewish population, which restricted architects in achieving similar styles in common with Venetian architecture. Most of the buildings are several storeys high, built deliberately to accommodate large numbers of people in as closely confined an area as possible. In doing so, the ceiling height for each floor was reduced considerably. Before I leave the Ghetto area, I will always remember this particular *campo* for the inscriptions, which were carved in stone centuries ago by Venetians, the first of which offers the threat of medieval punishment to any Jew who is found guilty of blasphemy. To supplement this statement, it also added that the governing body of Venice would offer payment to informers, payment taken from the offenders no less, for arguably the questionable information that was submitted, which must have been a temptation for many ruthless individuals. The second inscription, which I thought was very moving, serves as a testimonial for all those years of oppression: it simply informs everyone that of the 8,000 Italian Jews who were killed in World War II, 200 were Venetians. What was missing, or at least I couldn't find, was any testimonial to the courageous Venetian Jews who volunteered to serve with the Bandiera e Moro artillery regiment, as a defence unit prior to the Siege of Venice in 1848, a remarkable sacrifice when you consider how their forefathers were previously confined to the Venetian Ghetto. I think William Shakespeare summarised my thoughts quite succinctly in his quotation, 'I am a man, more sinned against than sinning.'

Leaving the Ghetto area, I now head towards Fondamenta degli Ormesini, which I cross over, and take the short passage along the Calle.d.Malvasia until I reach the Fondamenta della Sensa. Just before I get there, I cross a small bridge and there is a wonderful small café ahead of me where I can have a coffee. While I am drinking my coffee, I marvel at the beautiful Rio della Sensa canal, which I have just crossed, and notice that there are at least six small bridges spanning its path and again think how lucky I am to be here at this moment savouring these views. Fondamenta della Sensa is one of three streets which run parallel along the three main canals of Cannaregio, providing yet another access route from the Northern Lagoon to the Grand Canal. I only wish I could speak Venetian as there were several interesting locals of a respectable age who I feel sure could have kept me drinking coffee all day while listening to their tales.

Fully refreshed, I leave this gem of a café and walk along the canal in the direction of the Campo del Mori, which I turn left into, and notice how short and triangular in shape this campo is, nevertheless a very interesting and historical place to be. Campo del Mori certainly deserves some recognition today, as it originally was the home of Jacopo Tintoretto (1518–1594) who, amazingly, only left Venice once in his entire lifetime. His house stands to the right and is easily recognised by the stone figure of a merchant wearing a rather large turban. Incidentally, the Venice in Peril Fund, an organisation that I have recently joined, has restored the stone effigy and I shall explain more about this in a short while. Above the door is a number 3398, which signifies the Venetian house numbering system for post etc. Postmen recognise the number within each district rather than the street name as we would at home. Not so complicated, you might think, but nevertheless a daunting task when you consider that there are over 29,000 house numbers to find.

Tourists can be confused by the fact that there are also three other stone effigies close by which in appearance are similar to the one at Tintoretto's home. These three, however, are of the three Mori brothers, who were silk traders from the Peloponnese who settled in Venice in the early 12th century and built the Palazzo Mastrelli. The Campo name is said to originate from the Arab community that traded here and is someway related to the three brothers, who were named Rioba, Sandi and Afani. Rioba's stone effigy has, in fact, been given an iron nose for some reason or other and is the one bearing a heavy load on his back. Having photographed this campo, I now face the uncommonly attractive church of Madonna Dell 'Orto, which holds many treasures inside.

Madonna dell 'Orto is of Gothic design and was founded in the mid 14th century and dedicated to St Christopher, patron saint of travellers, to protect the boatmen who ferried passengers to the islands in the Northern Lagoon. The church façade is of red brick with a wonderful stone statue of St Christopher over the main portal and with statues of the 12 Apostles on either side. There are two superb arched windows below the statues of each of the Apostles and a large circular window above the front door, all in all, a perfect subject to paint, especially if you can get part of the campanile in as well. Incidentally, the campanile, which was completed in 1503, can clearly be seen from the Northern Lagoon approach. Although the church itself was originally dedicated to St Christopher, my research tells me that this was changed when the church was reconstructed in the mid 15th century, following the discovery, in a nearby vegetable garden, of a statue of the Virgin Mary, which was said to have had miraculous powers. But even though the church name of St Christopher may have been superseded by 'The Madonna' at a later date, there is, in fact, a 15th–century, newly restored statue of St Christopher, which is on display above the main door. Visitors are expected to pay an entrance fee of 2.50 euros when entering the church. However, I have decided to purchase a Chorus Pass for 8.00 euros, which enables me to visit a further 15 churches in Venice and is valid for one whole year. On entering the church, I am reminded of the fact that this was indeed the church that Tintoretto used and, as befitting of a master artist, there are several pieces of his works on display, such as the *'The Last Judgement'* and *'The Making of the Golden Calf'*, which he painted as a young man and are displayed on the main choir walls. It is said that Tintoretto was extremely secretive of the processes he used and he would forbid anyone to watch while he was painting. It is difficult to understand this when you think just how many works of art he completed and the period of time he actually spent painting them, but then perhaps that is why he reached the summit of excellence. At the far end of the church, to the right, there is a memorial tomb for this great master, which serves as his final resting place, which he shares with his sons.

Before I leave Madonna dell 'Orto, I should mention just how much work the 'Venice in Peril' fund actually does in an attempt to keep the treasures of Venice preserved and intact for the future. Having read and heard about this organisation for some time, I have to confess that it was not until this month that I fully realised just how much work they have actually completed since their formation following the disastrous floods of 1966. By visiting Madonna dell 'Orto for the first time this year, I have discovered that they have played a major part in its restoration programme, and it is not until you actually see just what has been achieved do you realise just how important their work is for Venice. Known by its present name since 1971, 'Venice in Peril' has worked continuously on many major restoration programmes and is currently working on several other important projects. I was also taken aback by one specific project completed in April of this year known as the San Giobbe House. This previously derelict and uninhabitable house has been renovated and returned to its original appearance, and now provides accommodation for working Venetians. Not spectacular, one might think, until one realises that this was not a restoration programme to allow investors to capitalise on, as this building is not for sale and will remain part of the heritage of Venice. Looking ahead at my outline plans for this journal, I have now discovered just how many buildings I will visit that 'Venice in Peril' have actually contributed in some way to restoring, so forgive me if I mention their name more than once in the coming months ahead.

I now leave Madonna dell 'Orto and make my way back across the Campo dell Mori. I then cross over the bridge and walk back down Calle Larga until I reach Fondamenta della Misericordia. Then, turning left, I walk alongside this pleasant canal and notice on my right a very attractive high brick wall which runs parallel with this waterway. Looking ahead to the end of this corbelled brick wall, there stands a statue of the Virgin Mary and Child on the corner where the wall turns at a right angle. It is then that I notice that the wall is protecting a convent, which I think is named Mary di Servi. This feature would certainly make a wonderful sketch and I hope I am fortunate enough to capture the reflecting light bouncing off of the canal. About a 100m ahead of me, on my right, stands the church of San Marziale, which unfortunately, I now discover is closed. My research, however, tells me that this church was built on the ruins of a medieval church, and today displays a large Baroque façade, having been rebuilt between 1693 and 1721. The rococo frescoes by Sebastiano Ricci are the main tourist attraction (which I have yet to see) and there is also a ceiling painting titled *'The Glory of Saint Martial'* which adorns the main chapel. According to legend, in 1286 a boat ran aground close to here, near to the church, whilst transporting an image of the Virgin Mary. The Doge, at that period, upon hearing of this incident immediately commanded that the image was to be permanently displayed inside the church, and it has remained here ever since.

Having now passed San Marziale I have reached an area, which houses the Scuola Nuova D. Misericordia and has the Palazzo Lezze to its left. Lezze unfortunately seems completely overpowered by the presence of the Scuola, which is a great shame as part of the side elevation, which I can see, is extremely attractive with small arched windows gracing the piani nobile which in turn is festooned with what appears to be fresh flower arrangements. When I look along the façade I realise just how large most Venetian palazzos really are, when viewed on the Grand Canal for example I obviously don't appreciate their actual scale, and looking at Palazzo Legge it's a great shame that I am unable to photograph this building from the other side of the canal, unfortunately there is no pedestrian access to perform this task.

My attention is now focused on the adjoining Scuola, which again appears to be closed to public entry at this time as the very large and ornate main doors are securely locked. However, as these doors are a wonderful example of Venetian craftsmanship I photograph them for future reference. The external appearance of the Scuola reminds me slightly of a Victorian industrial warehouse, with its austere brick finish, but I feel sure that the interior is quite the opposite. I guess I may have formed a negative opinion regarding the external appearance of the Scuola simply because of the wonderful Baroque Palazzo Lezze, which is completely overshadowed by the Scuola's presence. Sometimes I wonder just what went through the minds of those early Venetian planners when I see this occur. Fortunately, that doesn't happen to often.

I now leave this area to cross a small bridge which will take me on to the Fondamenta S. Felice. When crossing the bridge, I can't fail to notice the exquisite, yet dynamic façade of the Palazzo Papafava to my left, as it really does stand out amongst the surrounding buildings, sadly not one I intend to visit today. Papafava has some really attractive Gothic arches and balconies, which are well worth photographing, and I will most surely sketch this back in my studio at a later date. You will have noticed, reading this journal, that I never fail to find new material to work on and inspire my imagination and I constantly use the expression 'at a later date', I really do feel that Venice has no equal for my artistic needs.

Once across the small bridge, I turn right into the Fondamenta S. Felice, which will lead me to the Fondamenta d. Chiesa and eventually to the Strada Nova, but before I get there I intend to stop at a restaurant for lunch and my guidebook tells me that there are several close by which serve traditional Venetian food. It is only 12.20pm so I have plenty of time for a break. Let's hope I find a restaurant that is open. As luck would have it, I didn't have to wait long. As I was walking along Fondamenta San Felice, I noticed a nicely appointed restaurant which was open, but didn't realise that I should have booked my lunch earlier. Then, having explained to the waiter that I will not linger all afternoon, they accommodated me in a small niche of the restaurant where I quickly order a recommended dish of pasta, fish and what appeared to be red cabbage, which was delicious. This was washed down with a couple of glasses of white wine known locally as 'super Soave', which I thought complimented the food. I am a firm believer in eating what is recommended by the host, as it invariably saves the embarrassment of 'specifying the unknown'. Having finished my lunch with a nice cappuccino served with a selection of macaroons, I paid my bill, not the cheapest restaurant I've eaten in, but nonetheless well worth the visit. To the gourmet traveller, I can only recommend the 'full works' as a treat when you find a restaurant that is obviously popular, and take at least a couple of hours to savour not only the food but the people sitting around you. But, as I keep reminding myself, the journal is about discovering Venice, and my timescales are fairly restrictive for extended lunches, and even rest periods, to savour the Veneto wines.

Back to the journal itinerary again, and I am now walking along the Fondamenta d. Chiesa, which provides me once again with some nice material to sketch. I particularly like the view facing the small bridge with the numerous arched buildings along its concourse. I have now arrived at Strada Nova, which provides the main route for pedestrians to the Rialto; this well trodden street, built in 1871, connects the Campo S. Apostoli to the Campo San Felice. There are numerous shops along the route. However, today it is relatively quiet, but during certain festive occasions this area becomes alive and buzzing with scores of market stalls. In passing the Treghetto crossing point at San Sofia, I notice several gondoliers who are grouped together outside one of the cafes and wonder just how much work is available for these men as the winter season approaches. I seemed to have read somewhere that many of them put their gondolas into hibernation and take on whatever work there is going locally until the tourist season gets under way again in the spring.

I now reach the next church on my route, which is the Santi Apostoli, and suddenly realise that again I am not going to get the opportunity to enter as it is shuttered up with a builder's hoarding. The good news is that it is currently being renovated. When I included San Apostoli in my original itinerary, I wasn't aware of these works taking place. Not an immediate problem, as today I am only interested in the external view of this wonderful building, which I intend to paint in watercolour at a later date. Viewed from the Campo, San Apostoli is a very attractive building, and has a small dome, which is above the entrance, although slightly overshadowed by the adjoining building and tower. On either side of the church, stand two red plaster rendered buildings of varying heights which are linked to the church, and on the far left the tower is also adjoined to one of the red buildings, which itself has a small shop on the pavement level displaying a bright green blind with an advertising slogan. Can you imagine this jumble of structures being allowed in a rural city centre in England? Having said that, it doesn't detract in any way from the beauty of the church and its surrounding neighbours, and more importantly the campo has retained the same appearance since the 18th century.

Once the renovation work taking place within Santi Apostoli has been completed, I will hopefully be able to see first-hand the early Renaissance chapel in this 16th-century church, which was constructed by Mauro Codussi for the Corner family. The Corner Chapel, which is to the right of the nave, contains the tomb of Marco Corner, and was probably built by Tullio Lombardo. Incidentally, there is an inscription by Corner's daughter, Caterina Cornaro, Queen of Cyprus, who was buried here also, before she was eventually moved to the church of San Salvatore. The various altarpieces are by such notable artists as Veronese, Tiepolo and Diziani among others. It surprised me somewhat to learn that, in the 16th century, Protestants were actually buried alongside Santi Apostoli, and I guess for obvious reasons (being a Catholic community) they were later transferred to a cemetery on the Lido.

Returning to the Campo itself, there stands an austere and large two-storey building, the Scuola dell Angelo Custode, which was built by Andrea Tirali in 1713. In addition to this building there is also the Pre-Gothic Palazzo of the Doge, Marino Falieri. In 1806, German merchants, who resided in the Fondaco dei Tedescha, acquired the Scuola dell Angelo Custode and from 1813 it served as a German Evangelical Church.

Having photographed all that I see around me in the Campo dei Apostoli, I now make my way across the square to the Della S. Apostoli, which will lead me on to the Salizz Borgato and eventually to the tiny bridge which crosses a small canal. As I cross this small canal (which strangely isn't listed on my map), I notice the Palazzo Seriman to my right and I continue ahead until I reach Campo del Gesuiti. Within this campo, if you search enough, you will see both the insignias and inscriptions of notable craftsmen's guilds such as tailors (*sartori*), weavers (*tessitori*) and coopers (*botteri*), all of these artisan trades being very prominent in Cannaregio in times gone by.

The church of Santa Maria Assunta or, as it is now called, Gesuiti, sits just beyond the Oratorio dei Crociferi, which is now to my left as I face the Lagoon. Oratorio dei Crociferi commemorates the order of the Crociferi, who had close ties with the Holy Crusaders and were identified by the large grey cross, which they displayed on their outer tunics. The Oratorio is generally open between April and October, so today once again I am not going to see its interior. However, I know that it was originally the site of a hospice and church, which burned down and was later rebuilt in the 16th century. Inside there are wonderful paintings by Jacopo Palma, painted between 1583 and 1590, which tell the story of the Crociferi, and the work that was done for the pilgrims who stayed there (more of that later). Again, yet another amazing and beautiful building that has been carefully restored by the 'Venice in Peril' fund. Incidentally, Titian lived nearby, in Calle Larga dei Botteri, his house being sited across the Rio de Gesuiti. Unfortunately, this house was later rebuilt and his once elegant gardens have long since been removed.

The Gesuiti originally belonged to the order of Crociferi and was acquired by the Jesuits, who lived close by, in 1657. The church was built between 1715 and 1729 of Baroque design, the prime architect being Domenico Rossi whose brief it was to include a patterned floor from the plan of the Church of Gesu, which stands in Rome. The Baroque façade was the work of Fattoretto, who, it is said, worked well with Rossi and who eventually was responsible for the interior design. Inside the Gesuiti the visitor will be amazed just how much green, white and grey marble there is, and all sculptured to resemble wall decoration (hanging drapes). The craftsmanship displayed throughout the entire interior of this building is phenomenal and well worth sketching. I only hope my own work can do it justice. Obviously, the cost of building such a monument as this must have been substantial, even in the 18th century, and without the vast sums of money donated by the Manin family, who were the principle benefactors, this would not have been possible. In addition to the sumptuous marble decorations, there are also works of art by Tintoretto, *'Assumption of the Virgin'*, and Titian's *'Martyrdom of St. Lawrence'* to be found in the altarpieces. After 1773 the church/convent was taken from the Jesuits and became a public school, and in 1807 it was used as a barracks, but in 1814 it was eventually given back to the Jesuits.

Although closed at this moment, I have made my mind up to spend more time researching this magnificent building at a later date, as I personally consider it to be unrivalled in both beauty and excellence as a building within Cannaregio.

From the end of the Salizz de Specchieri, which is just beyond the Gesuiti, I get a wonderful view of the Lagoon and, looking to the right, I see the Island of San Michele, which I will discuss in a later chapter when I visit the surrounding islands of Venice.

My journey back to the interior region of Cannaregio will, in fact, retrace my earlier steps from Campo dei Apostoli, because I still have several other places to photograph as well as explore. Walking back, my thoughts return to an earlier conversation I had with the artist/musician Tony Green, in particular a question he asked me as to who I considered were my favourite artists. I can remember quickly replying, 'Living or dead?' and he said, 'Both'. I immediately said that I have many, but probably consider J M W Turner, Thomas Girtin, Canaletto, Edward Hopper, Roy Lichtenstein, Jack Vettriano and Ken Howard to be the ones I seem to favour and enjoy researching as well as viewing, the latter two artists, of course, being very prominent, extremely successful, and still producing wonderful work today. I can remember Tony looking at me and saying nothing, but I could sense that he obviously thought it strange in as much as my choice of artists was so diverse. I can well understand why he may have thought this selection strange. Most people do, but then that's the way I approach art and it is the 'diversity' of styles and techniques that I so enjoy. I digress from the task in hand, which is to concentrate on my travels in Cannaregio, I do, however, propose to mention more of my favourite artists in later chapters, but purely to comment on their work and why I like them.

The journey back to Campo dei Apostoli went quite quickly (thought processes have that effect on me) and when I eventually arrive there I immediately turn left into the C.llo d. Cason. Remarkably, within a few minutes, I will have walked from the extreme west of Cannaregio to its farthest eastern boundaries, but only, alas, have I glimpsed at a few of the treasures this *sestiere* has to offer. Time is moving on and I still have two more beautiful churches to visit, and as I walk along C.llo d. Cason, I now cross over a bridge, which spans the Rio del Santi Apostoli, where I stop to take a photograph of a majestic wellhead that faces me directly in front of the church of San Canciano. San Canciano wasn't one of the churches I had planned to visit today, but as some earlier buildings were closed I have decide to add this to my itinerary to explore. This very attractive little church has been recently restored, judging by its external condition, and when I enter from the left-hand door I am confronted by a wonderful black floor and a mounted crucifix of Christ, which stands guard over the access to the main aisle leading to a magnificent altar, which in turn is framed by a great arch. Although it is now 4.00pm, the sun is just still shining through the large circular window above the altar, which fills the church with daylight. There are several altars located on either side of the nave each finished in fine marble. As I intend to visit San Canciano again, I limit my time here for now and leave, but not without photographing the wonderfully decorative, restored brickwork and marble panels of its exterior walls.

Having turned left out of the front door of San Canciano, I continue along this street for a few metres and turn left into Campo Santa Maria Nova. In this campo, I find a great deal to photograph as this narrow square has an attractive wellhead and, beyond, an even more attractive Gothic building to admire. This small building must surely be of some historical interest, but one I haven't researched yet. I immediately notice, however, that this building has two wonderful windows, with a small statuette figure holding what appears to be a round object. My interest is aroused so I must return at a later date.

From Campo Santa Maria Nova I continue walking across a small bridge, which spans a minor canal, until I reach the church of Santa Maria dei Miracoli. This church is certainly well worth a visit and could be easily missed as it is tucked away in a maze of alleyways. Built in the 15th century by Pietro Lombardo and his two sons Antonio and Tullio, this Renaissance church is full of treasures. The elegant façade, which is built from a selection of decorative marbles, has lots of relief work depicting flowers, animals, mermaids and Triton, which run along the length of the pilasters. My research tells me that the majority of the marble used for this building was said to have been 'leftovers' from the Basilica San Marco. All I can say is that leftovers or not, the finished work has been tooled by master craftsmen. Miraculously, the church has had major renovation work over recent years, due to some structural defects which rendered it unsafe, funds for this work being raised by various groups under the control of the 'Save Venice Fund'. Having mentioned 'Venice in Peril' I should also mention the 'Save Venice Fund'. Again, formed following the disaster of 1966, this organisation falls under the umbrella of UNESCO to restore and protect Venice's threatened masterpieces. Based in the USA and Italy, this organisation to date has worked on over 200 restorations, which include the Accademia, Basilica San Marco, Doge's Palace and Santa Maria dei Miracoli, to name but a few. As with 'Venice in Peril', this organisation relies on donations and 'gifts' in order to achieve the success they have already achieved, and I really do commend their effort, enthusiasm and passion to keep Venice alive for generations to come.

Returning to the church, Santa Maria Miracoli is designed as a single-aisle nave with a barrel-vaulted ceiling topped by an elaborate dome. There are dozens of images of saints painted on the ceiling together with a wonderful cupola and screen on the altar showing masterful carvings; Lombardo also sculptured pieces on the balustrades close to the chancel, with fine marbles set into the cupola. Viewing the interior of the church is a real joy, as it is finished in pink and white marble, which looks great when the doors are opened and light penetrates the internal areas. The church was said to have been originally constructed simply to house a miraculous painting, namely the *'Vergine tra due Santi'* (The Virgin between two Saints), which was painted by Nicolo di Pietro. This image was said to have attracted many pilgrims of worship in the past. Finances for the construction of this church were originally provided by funds from the public. As the local population were anxious to retain and protect their miraculous image, they collected sufficient funds, which also enabled them to construct a convent connected to the church. This church is also an extremely popular choice for Venetians to get married in, and having visited it several times now I can understand why.

I would strongly recommend to everyone visiting Venice to seek out Santa Maria Miracoli, and explore its treasures and, for that matter, every one of the 16 highlighted in the Chorus of Venice Group, which I mentioned earlier in this chapter. All the proceeds from purchasing a group ticket contribute towards the opening up, maintenance, preservation and restoration of the churches of Venice. Having said that, there are scores of other churches which do not have an entrance fee and I consider a small donation (even simply by dedicating a single candle) is the very least that one can offer to help with conservation programmes that each and every church is confronted with.

It is now 4.40pm and I leave Santa Maria Miracoli (which I intend to return to in July when I shall have more time available to enjoy the finished artistry of this amazing church) and I walk east and cross over the bridge at the southern end of the church and make my way straight ahead to the Salizz S. Canciano, where I turn left again in order to reach the final building for my journal today, which is San Giovanni Crisostomo. The time now is 4.50pm, so I have some time to spare to enjoy yet another church before making my way back to Piazzale Roma.

My real reason for choosing San Giovanni Crisostomo today is that Antonio Vivaldi taught music here and lived next door. Having said that, it is also a church with character and style and well worth photographing and sketching. Vivaldi is by far my most favourite classical musician and composer and I listen to his work constantly whenever I am working in my studio, much to the delight of my dear wife, Avril, who keeps reminding me that although I like his music my neighbours may not be so keen. Yes, I do have the volume raised at times! Vivaldi had an incredible mental agility, which led to an interesting and productive life, and he had phenomenal success in Europe. He was said to be a 'quick fire' production line when composing his works, which is probably a fairly accurate way to describe his methods, when you consider he wrote over 500 concertos and 46 operas. I guess his real notoriety comes from his wonderful work *'The Four Seasons'* which he wrote in 1725, but I also like his less well-known works just as much. Given the opportunity, I jump at getting tickets for one of the local concerts throughout Venice, which are dedicated to his music, almost as much as I would going to see a live concert by Status Quo! That this son of a Venetian barber would, with unshrinking determination, eventually achieve such acclaim, is truly remarkable. One passage of extraordinary daring was when he trained the unwanted 'daughters' of courtesans to play his music in La Pieta. Some would say, and I would agree, that that was a monumental achievement, and I place him highly in my personal top ten heroes' list. In the July chapter, I intend to visit the church of La Pieta at the very end of my journey walking around the *sestiere* of Castello, where I hope to gain more interesting facts about Vivaldi, and his association with this remarkable building.

San Giovanni Crisostomo, which was designed by Mauro Codussi, was said to be his last great work of art and was built between 1479 and 1504. It has treasures inside by several masters, one being Bellini's *'St Jerome with St Christopher and St Augustine'*, which was possibly his last painting. Unfortunately, the interior of the church is a little dark to fully appreciate the majority of work displayed. However, the external appearance is really attractive with its terracotta colour and Istrian stone façade.

My journal and travels end here today and I am really pleased with the ground I have covered in Cannaregio and rejoice in the fantastic weather I have experienced during this November visit. Before I make my way back to my welcoming Bar San Lucia, for a refreshing drink, I thought I would walk that little bit further to the Rialto and take a leisurely ride back on the vaporetto. To get to the Rialto, I simply continue south down Salizz S. Giovanni Crisostomo to Campo S. Bartolomeo, which takes me nicely onto the Riva d. Ferro and the Rialto pontile. Having reached the pontile, I enjoy a few minutes watching the people around me until my vaporetto arrives, which it does within a few minutes. I have to confess that I feel a great deal of sympathy for these craft when they arrive at each pontile, as they move sluggishly into position, then are immediately swamped by passengers and, without any delay, are commanded to make their weary way back onto the Canal, and a few minutes later are made to repeat their burden yet again. Having said that, I jump aboard and it is noticeably empty for this time of the day. I settle back to enjoy my ride and gaze at the Palazzos once again. The immediate area around the Rialto Bridge still has lots of tourists milling around at this time of the day. They are either sitting in bars or viewing the sights from the Bridge, all enjoying the weather and the occasion.

I try to remember the names of each palazzo as we sail back to Ferrovia pontile, which is extremely difficult without the travel guidebook, and decide that I am ready for a rest even though it would be beneficial to note the palazzos which I haven't researched, for a later date, but today I just want to enjoy the ride. The vaporetto takes just over 20 minutes to arrive at Ferrovia and I alight and make my way to the final watering hole for today, Bar S. Lucia. The barman who served me on my last trip welcomes me and, surprisingly, recognises me, probably because I have called for a pint of draught Guinness and a spinach pastry. Can't be that many tourists who order that combination. The bar seems busier today than last month, but I still manage to get a table and my Guinness appears within minutes. Time to reflect on the day, check my notes, view a couple of photographs I took earlier and generally bring the travels of the day in Cannaregio together.

Although the itinerary I set for this visit was less taxing on the feet, it nevertheless took me across the width of Cannaregio, but, looking at my map, there is still a great deal more to explore at a later date. When I opened this chapter, I mentioned that Cannaregio was the most unspoilt *sestiere* of the six. My journey today seems to have proved this point, as I felt there were very few tourists around, making allowances for it being off-season. Local Venetians may argue that I have missed many interesting places, such as the Carmelite Monastery, St Alvise Convent and Parco Savorgnan, and perhaps could have spent more time photographing the northern part of the Lagoon. My reply is simple and taken from a quote by Sir Francis Drake which reads, 'There must be a beginning of any great matter, but the continuing until the end until it be thoroughly finished yields the true glory.' I think that summarises it nicely.

After having a delightful chat with Enrico, the owner of Bar San Lucia, and feeling fully refreshed, I make my way back to the bus terminal at Piazzale Roma, still enjoying this Indian summer weather and taking in all the activities that are taking place around me. It doesn't seem like nearly eight hours since I stepped off the bus on arrival, but it is, and, what's more, the good old No. 5 arrives on time again and, even better, I get a seat without any fuss.

A good flight home to Gatwick with no silly car park ticket antics today, I arrive back home around 11.00pm a little weary but full of memories of the past few hours in the 'Serenissima'.

Buonasera Venezia.

CHAPTER 4
DECEMBER: Santa Croce and San Polo
Neighbours of Change and Tragedy

The festive season will soon be upon us, and the shopping mania, which arrives each year, is now well underway. Over the years, I have to confess that the Christmas period has become far too commercial for my liking, and both time and change have introduced a new meaning to what was once a religious festival.

During the past month, I have been busy. Apart from undertaking my initial research for Chapter 4, I have completed painting my new set of six abstracts of the Venetian *sestieri*, which took me much longer than I had planned. To top it all, I am having great difficulty in getting my new work onto my website due to a problem with the photographic quality. I seem to be spending more of my time actually photographing my work than I am painting, which is ridiculous. In order to improve my photographic skills, I have decided to change my outlook on traditional methods of photography and settle for the simple techniques that are available using modern digital cameras that don't have complicated features. Let's hope that works!

In this chapter of my journal I intend to bring together two *sestieri* which have experienced considerable change by both catastrophic

December 2006

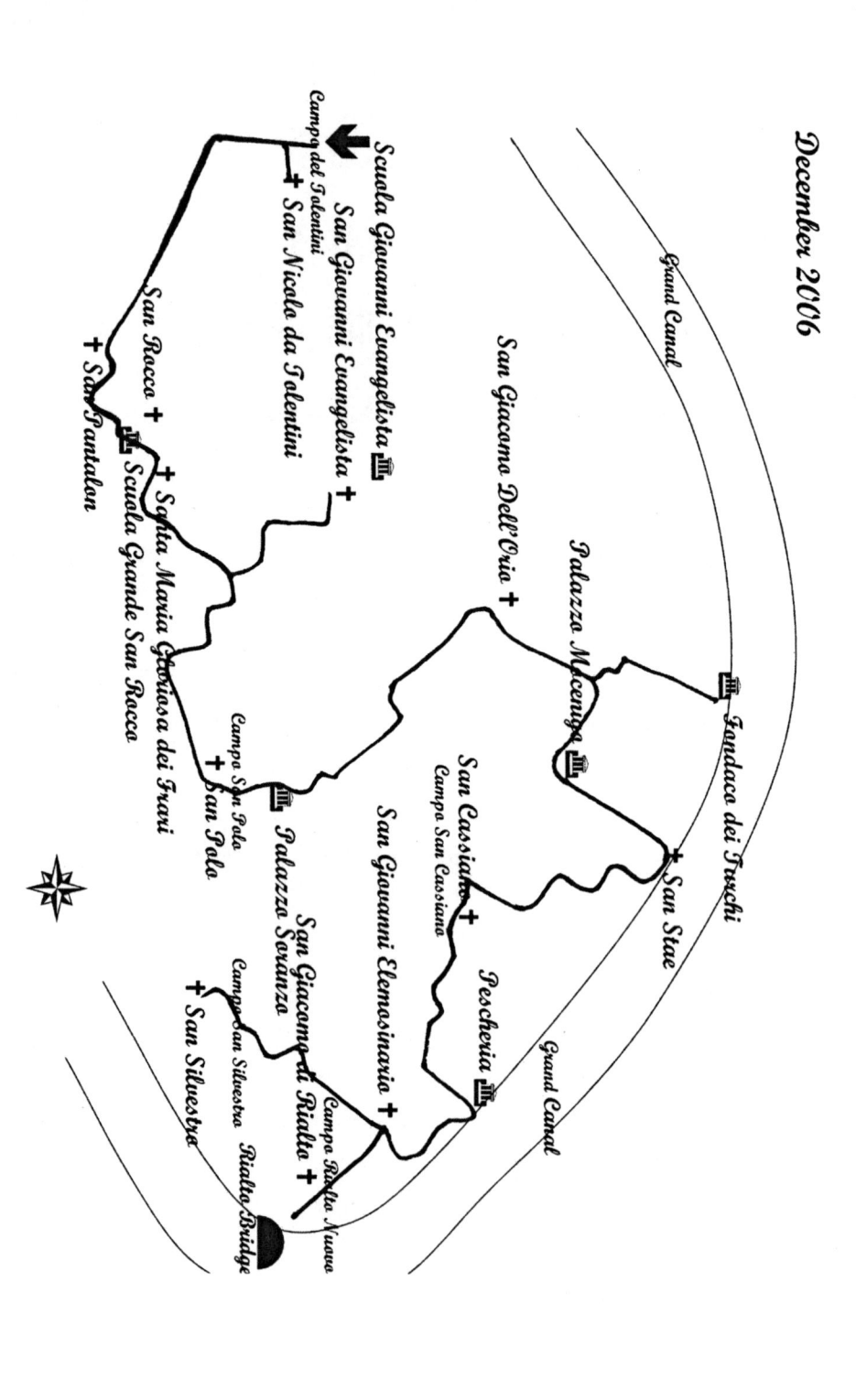

Map of Venice showing locations including:

- Grand Canal
- Fondaco dei Turchi
- San Stae
- Palazzo Mocenigo
- San Giacomo Dell'Orio
- Scuola Giovanni Evangelista
- Campo dei Talentini
- San Giovanni Evangelista
- San Nicola da Talentini
- San Rocca
- San Pantalon
- Scuola Maria Gloriosa dei Frari
- Scuola Grande San Rocca
- Campo San Polo
- San Polo
- San Cassiano
- Campo San Cassiana
- San Giovanni Elemosinaria
- Pescheria
- Palazzo Soranza
- San Giacomo di Rialto
- Campo Rialto Nuovo
- Campo San Silvestro
- San Silvestro
- Rialto Bridge

events and industrial evolution but, today, like Christmas, have still retained their identity if not all of their history. The districts of Santa Croce and San Polo are often linked together in various travel guides and other tourist publications even though they are deservedly completely independent of one another. By linking both, I can also design a route which will highlight neighbouring areas. The first, Santa Croce, has experienced fundamental change to meet 20th-century requirements, with the evolution of transportation and the introduction of decorative gardens, at the expense of removing some wonderful churches, and the second, San Polo, has experienced both tragedy and change inflicted by fire and war, resulting in disastrous fires that reduced most of the Rialto to ruins, and, much later, the sacking and redeployment of the Scuolas by Napoleon Bonaparte.

Geographically, Santa Croce and San Polo cover the west and mid-western territory of Venice and, like the San Marco *sestiere*, boast two bridges that cross the Grand Canal. Within the two *sestieri*, there is so much social, financial and industrial history to explore that I will attempt to bring each faction together in order to produce a complete picture of these districts as they are today. I will not be visiting the far west of Santa Croce, as it holds very little artistic value for my needs; by artistic value, I simply mean that most of this area has really evolved since the 20th century to accommodate the high traffic of tourists. The Bacino della Stazione Marittima, a dock for cruise liners, the Piazzale Roma, a bus terminal and the Garage Comunale, car parking facilities, are prime examples. However, there are several gardens, one being the Giardino Papadopoli, which, whilst offering a pleasant refuge for the Venetian public, was unfortunately created in 1810 by demolishing the church and monastery of Santa Croce, from where the *sestiere* got its name. In fact, Napoleon, aided by his stepson, in his second attempt to govern Venice, destroyed over 150 churches during his short reign of the 'Serenissima' in order to create parks, and, during this period of carnage, over 25,000 works of art were also destroyed during a period of unmerciful plundering, in addition to those that were stolen and taken out of the country. Without wishing to dismiss these facts too lightly, let us now focus on visiting some fantastic places of interest, en route, for the traveller to sketch or simply photograph, whilst circumnavigating these impressive districts. The prime landmarks today will include places like the Scuola Grande di San Rocco, (passing the Frari again), exploring Campo San Polo and its church, and then travelling north to Campo San Giacomo, again with its magnificent church. From there, I will be walking close to the Grand Canal area to Fondamenta D. Turchi (Natural History Museum), then visiting the churches of San Stae and San Cassiano, before making my way back along the main thoroughfare to San Silvestro, which is where my journey ends today, just south of the Rialto Bridge on the right bank of the Canal.

Given enough time, as this route is fairly time-consuming, with a great number of buildings to visit, I hope to see the interior of San Giovanni Elemosinario. Obviously, I shall be making a small detour of the Rialto area, having already visited it in an earlier chapter, but will no doubt find some more interesting facts to write about in this wonderful area. I shall be retracing my steps occasionally en route, but that is unavoidable, and, as always, there are many other historic and meaningful buildings, churches and streets to discover in both Santa Croce and San Polo, which I hope to explore on another day.

My travel bag today is similar to last month, which includes the essential map, from which I have previously planned and detailed my route, my camera and my digital recorder, which I use all the time to ensure that I capture the sounds and detail of my travels.

* December 7th 2006

It is still very mild for December, and a pleasant surprise not to have to scrape the frost from the windscreen of my car before leaving home at 4.45am in the morning, even though it is extremely dark and tipping down with rain.

Again, the pre-flight security screening at Gatwick is fast and efficient and there appear to be more travellers than last month checking through the Departure lounge. I decided to have a breakfast of bacon and egg, muffins and orange juice, which has set me up nicely for the fairly lengthy day ahead.

The 6.45am easyJet flight to Marco Polo airport was again on time and I was lucky enough to grab a seat by the window at the front of the plane, which meant a quick exit on arrival and also the opportunity to marvel at the magnificent sunrise this morning. Having spent several minutes flying through dark clouds, there suddenly appeared a horizontal beam of light which materialised when we were above 9,000m, followed by a vivid blue sky and rising sun. What a way to start the day.

Upon arrival at Marco Polo airport, I am really pleased to see that the weather is not only mild but also dry today, and not tipping down with rain as had been predicted by the weather forecast. For once, I was pleased to see that the forecast was wrong. We landed on time and I was through the Italian immigration checkpoint in minutes to purchase my ACTV travel pass for the day. As with my previous journeys to Marco Polo airport, the No. 5 bus is at the terminal bus stop waiting for passengers for the short trip to the 'Serenissima' and I discover that this bus is numbered 5D, which to my delight travels directly to Piazzale Roma, without deviating from the main road, as the No. 5 bus does, to accommodate more passenger stops. By doing this, I save about 10 minutes on my journey from the airport, which gives me that extra time to enjoy Venice. Pure magic. I am really looking forward to today's route, as there are several interesting places in both Santa Croce and San Polo that I have yet to see, so once off the bus at Piazzale Roma, the local time now 10.50am, I begin my journey. I head west towards the Giardino Papadopoli, just 20m from the bus terminal, to reach this small but attractive park. To get there, I simply walk down the steps from the bus terminal, cross the small bridge, which spans the Rio Nuove canal, and the park is directly facing me. An iron gate signifies the entrance to the park, which is permanently open to accommodate the busy traffic of pedestrians who use this route as a short cut.

As with all of my routes, I am armed with my map (Touring Club Italiano – Venice), in order that I can navigate with relative ease whilst still enjoying everything around me. Once through the park, I pass the Hotel Sofitel, which is to my left, and I am now facing a small bridge, which I cross over (Ponte Tolentini) and follow the path directly ahead. The water level today in the small canal seems unusually high and, what's more, sunshine is grinning through to make the water sparkle. At the end of the Fondamenta Tolentini, I cross another bridge on-to the Fondamenta Minotto, which I follow with the canal on my right. To my left is a small church tower and I now arrive at Salizz S. Pantalon, where there are two bridges adjacent to one another. I pass a local restaurant, which provides a selection of local dishes and has an amazing selection of eight-course meals for around 40 euros. That may seem a lot of money, but the fare on offer seems superb, a gastronomic delight if you have the time to savour it, and from the menu on display I think the host is probably English speaking. After passing the restaurant, I continue to the next small bridge, which is on my right, and cross the Rio d. Malcanton. Once across, I am now on the Calle Vinanti and it is here that I notice an attractive building directly ahead of me, which stands just beyond a small brick bridge. This relatively small junction of the canal will make a very attractive sketch, especially the sculptured Gothic windows belonging to a red, rendered house close by. Standing on the small brick bridge, to my left is the Palazzo Marcello, which I don't know much about other than it is built of red brick with Gothic windows on all floors to its main façade.

Leaving Palazzo Marcello, on my left I continue west down the Salizz S. Pantalon, passing several small shops, all prepared for the Christmas period. Whilst observing the architecture around me, I notice a stone/plaster image of the Madonna and Child set into a brick wall, which surely has some historic interest, but unfortunately I can't date it. Another local restaurant comes into view, which offers a three-course meal for only 11 euros: absolute value for money. I have often used local restaurants like this one, which always prove to be good, especially when the food is accompanied by the local wine. A little further along, I notice the Palazzo Arnaldi. Not much is known about this building other than it is in desperate need of some urgent care and attention. It is sad to think that this was once a substantial residence probably owned by a noted patrician of Venice. Facing me at a distance is the bell tower of Saint Pantalon church, which has an attractive balcony on the top of the tower just below its small dome.

I continue down the Calle dei Pretti, along what I can best describe as a very narrow shopping street, strangely enough having several opticians shops in its concourse, and arrive at a small wooden bridge with a weathered balustrade, which I photograph and then cross. On the other side is a sign directing me to the Frari, which I have visited many times before to paint as well as explore, and I now know that I am close to my first stopping point, which will be the Scuola Grande San Rocco. Still following Calle dei Pretti, I turn left down a very narrow street, which again literally becomes a single lane thoroughfare as it barely gives pedestrians enough room to pass one another. As a guide marker, I take note of a small bar, easily recognisable by the three lanterns outside advertising my favourite tipple, Guinness. I turn left again into a very narrow street, which then leads me to another small bridge called the Ponte Siroco, and again notice a sign reading 'Frari'. I am now in the tiny Campo San Rocco. It is important to record these small passageways as there are several in this area and it's very easy to become totally disorientated, as I have found out in the past!

Within Campo San Rocco there are two street traders erecting their stall to sell some Christmas gifts and they are certainly experts in working in small areas; this must be one of the tiniest campos in Venice. Offering my seasonal greetings to the traders, I now walk under a small passageway which has a well seasoned wooden ceiling, with each beam having its own story to tell from centuries gone by. Once through the delightful passageway, I now see the white façade and splendid artistry of the Scuola Grande San Rocco building.

Now seems an appropriate time to briefly explain why, when and how the Scuolas of Venice came into being, as they played an enormous part in Venetian history. I will be visiting and reporting on several throughout my journal and today I will be visiting a Scuola, which, in my opinion, is a very special one. Scuolas were of two types, firstly the *Grandi,* such as San Rocco, St Mary of Charity, St Marks, St Theodore, St John the Evangelist and the Misericordia, and secondly the *Minori,* which numbered around 400 in total at any one time. They were each run by lay brotherhoods who took care of the interests of both the arts and the professions, in addition to playing a major role in looking after foreign workers who needed assistance, and finally, but equally important, they tended the poor and sick. The Brotherhood of San Rocco were originally dedicated to Saint Roch (San Rocco), to assist the sick during the times of the plague, and were recognised as early as 1478. St Roch was a French-born medical student who made a pilgrimage to Italy in 1315, and who dedicated himself to helping those suffering with the plague. Having done so, he returned home and was completely ignored by his wealthy family and eventually died in prison aged only 32. Respectfully, his body was returned to Venice in 1485, where it was reverently entombed. There are numerous pictures of St Roch displayed throughout Venice, usually depicting him with a sore on his thigh, which legend states was licked clean by a dog who also brought him food when he himself became a victim of the plague.

The Brotherhood tried to demonstrate that they would purge the world of sin by various means and, in time, interacted with other groups, such as the Dominicans, to form the Scuola Grande, which in turn was financed by the wealthiest groups, to fund the construction of several buildings and provide medical aid and assistance in times of plague and war. Within this powerful brotherhood, there was a plethora of skills and professions available to administer their work, such as: doctors, lawyers, merchants, etc. The lesser Scuolas (*Minori*) also became very active but they were funded by less wealthy patrons, such as craftsmen of various disciplines and guilds who functioned from more modest buildings. The Scuola was an amazingly powerful group who were highly recognised and who held some station in Venice. However, they was never allowed to govern and were watched over carefully by the Council of Ten, which I will explain in the next chapter.

After the Great Plague of 1576, St Roch's church became a place of pilgrimage every year for each appointed Doge, and this same festival is still enacted on the 16th August each year, when a canopy is erected in St Roch Square (Campo San Rocco) between the Scuola Grande and the Church. There is a magnificent painting by Canaletto of this ceremony, in London's National Gallery, depicting this festival in all its splendour; however, Canaletto has used his artistic licence to overstate the actual size of the Campo, which becomes apparent when you visit the Scuola. I personally feel that great masters such as Canaletto should be allowed to exercise their artistic options whenever they deem it necessary and in this particular painting I really do feel that Canaletto has succeeded in capturing the moment perfectly.

Construction of the Scuola Grande Rocco was started in 1489 by Bartolomeo Bon, then continued by Antonio Scarpagnino in 1527, and finally completed by Giangiacomo dei Grigi in 1560. Funding for this work was provided from very generous donations by notable Venetians in an attempt to protect them from the plague should it return!

When viewed from the exterior, the Scuola is a remarkable piece of architectural design, with its lovingly restored Renaissance façade, proving just how talented Venetian craftsmen were of that era. Internally, the Scuola is a maze of artistic elegance, as it is primarily a gallery displaying the work of Tintoretto, work he undertook from the early age of 29 and continued for the next 25 years, producing a treasure trove of masterpieces for all to admire. There are two Great Halls to visit, the first one is situated on the ground floor, which really does set the tone for the Great Upper Hall, reached by ascending either one of the magnificent staircases, which themselves are majestic works of art. There is also a smaller hall on the first floor, Sala dell' Alberg, which was used by the Brotherhood for their various assemblies. The walls and ceilings of the Great Upper Hall are completely covered with outstanding masterpieces of art, mostly by Tintoretto, but there are some paintings by Titian, Tiepolo and Giorgione in addition to various other works by Marchiori, Negri and Zanchi, not forgetting some wooden sculptures by Pianta.

To explain this palace of art treasures in a few paragraphs is simply impossible for me do. As I consider it to be a constant source of surprise and delight each time I visit, it simply has to be explored first hand. Whenever I visit, there are scores of tourists and art lovers taking advantage of the framed mirrors that are made available to view the artwork on the ceiling of the Great Upper Hall, and today the Scuola staff are reinstating what I can only describe as floor-mounted gold-framed lanterns around the panelled walls, which really does finish off the internal decorations. It would be irreverent of me not to name some of the art treasures on display along the centre of the ceiling of the Great Upper Hall. Therefore one can see *'The Miracle of the Bronze*

Serpent', 'Moses Strikes Water from the Rocks', 'Jacob's Ladder' and 'Jonah Emerges from the Whale', to name but a few of Tintoretto's works. In the Albergo Hall there is also Tintoretto's *'Crucifixion'*, with a portrait of the great master (man with a beard) looking at the statue of Christ (he is standing just above the man digging around a stone).

As is the case with so many of the Venetian buildings that I visit, I find it difficult to prise myself away from the Scuola Grande San Rocco, but I have to, and I look forward to returning in the future, as there is always so much to see and all for as little as the 7 euros entrance fee. It's quite remarkable that the majority of Scuolas were dissolved in the 18th century, following the fall of the Republic, and utilised as hospitals or galleries. However, two still remain as original charitable bodies and continue to run for the purpose they were originally intended for.

I exit the Scuola San Rocco and photograph its façade, yet again hoping to capture another detail I may have overlooked in the past. I then choose to listen to two street musicians who are performing by the steps leading to the main entrance. These musicians are fine performers, as so many are in Venice. Their music is certainly enhanced by the wonderful acoustics which reverberate in this small square. Well worth a coin in the hat and a great interlude before I enter the church of Saint Roch, which is literally a few metres across the campo.

The church of Saint Roch, like the Scuola, simply cannot be overlooked on my tour, and the fact that it is united in history as well as design makes the visit more meaningful. Built originally at the same time as the Scuola, the church was eventually reconstructed in 1725 by Giovanni Scalfarotto. The amazing Renaissance façade was created between 1765 and 1771, by Bernardino Maccaruzzi, and is entirely in keeping with the style of the Scuola. The statues on the façade are all by one sculptor, G. Marchiori. The interior nave has a flat ceiling, and my research informs me that Tintoretto painted the original organ doors. On the main altar is situated the urn with St Roch's body, and like the Scuola opposite there is a wealth of art on display again by Tintoretto and other notable artists. The most prominent pieces by Tintoretto depict scenes from the life of St Roch, one being *'St Roch Curing the Plague Victims'*. Many other equally majestic artists on display include Giuseppe Angeli, Sebastiano Ricci, Pordenone and Fumiani. When I leave the church and walk down the five curved steps by the main entrance to continue my journey, I can't help thinking just how fortunate tourists, journeymen, artists and native Venetians are in having so much artistic wealth and history compressed into one small campo. Fantastic. I leave the Campo San Rocco and walk directly ahead along the Salizz S. Rocco for a few metres; I then turn left and I find myself in the eastern elevation of the Frari, which I visited in September and is a location which I often stop to paint or sketch in the spring and summer seasons. As I pass the Frari, I remember another eerie story of its history, which refers to a wooden coffin, which is hung high up in the transept and holds the murdered body of a Venetian nobleman. I wonder if the current workforce, who are restoring the Frari at present, will eventually make this artefact more prominent for all to see. Only time will tell. The restoration work on the Frari is obviously in full swing, as the informative builders' hoardings displayed on the lower perimeter walls would suggest, and as I circumnavigate the building and pass the cafes and shops to its right, I make my way to the small bridge in front of the Frari's main entrance, resisting the temptation to explore it once again. Once over the bridge, I turn left into the Rio terra S. Toma, walk a few metres, then turn immediately right into C. Magazen, go past a weathered wooden buttress overhang, which leads to Calle dell Olio, and carry on to the next building to visit, which is the church of San Giovanni Evagelista and its neighbouring Scuola Grande.

On arrival at this location, I walk through the beautifully ornate open arch, which stands supreme in the Campiello S. Giovanni, and my mind travels back to Campo San Rocco, as yet again the church and Scuola Grande stand opposite one another, hidden from time in a small campo. Unfortunately, when I arrived, unlike St Roch, the church of San Giovanni Evangelista was closed for some reason, which is disappointing, and strangely enough there was the 'standard issue' flood protection barrier in place directly in front of the main door. I realise that these barriers play an important role in times of the Acqua Alta, but today there are no warnings imminent, so I am quite confused, and in my limited Italian attempt to ask why this is so to a member of the Scuola staff, who when asked simply shrugged her shoulders and dismissed the question immediately. Not having visited this church before, I have limited research at hand, but will once again put it on my return list to 'explore' for another day. Likewise, I had not intended to visit the Scuola San Giovanni Evangelista, as two Scuola Grande's in one day would be mind-blowing, so for now I can only give a brief resume on what research I have made in the past.

The Renaissance exterior to the campo was designed by Pietro Lombardo and has an interesting marble finish on its walls. There is an eagle lunette above the portal of the arch, which I had earlier walked through, which traditionally is the symbol of St. John the Evangelist. The Gothic interior of the church was renovated in

1759, while the 14th-century Scuola was rebuilt in 1512. Originally there were paintings by Jacopo Bellini and Capaccio, but some were moved to the Accademia during the French occupation.

The Scuola is both of Gothic and Renaissance style, with a portal designed originally by Mauro Codussi. Inside the Scuola there is a double stairway, as there was in San Rocco, again built by Codussi, which rises to the Main Hall. At the top of the staircases there are several paintings by Domenico Tintoretto on display in the Upper Hall. Records inform me that the Scuola was presented with the 'Relic of the True Cross', which was considered to be its finest gift. Listed in the Scuola are a set of wooden poles with mother of pearl insets. These poles support a processional canopy which is carried by members of the Scuola on various processions through the City. These poles were restored, cleaned and maintained by 'Venice in Peril', displaying yet another important undertaking of a project to preserve the history of Venice and its artefacts. Not wishing to undermine or understate the historic value and beauty of these two buildings, I will make every effort to revisit them both and explore the treasures they have to offer at a later date, and I would urge every tourist to do so when in Venice.

I now leave this small campo but not before noticing the remarkable stone insets which dress the Campiello De La Scuola, framed by the red brickwork, again another sketching opportunity for the artist.

My next stop will be the Campo San Polo and, in order to get there, I have to back-track my steps to the Frari to pick up the journal trail once more. As I reach the Frari, I am reminded what time of day it is as its bells are ringing aloud, as it is now 12.00. What a wonderful place to be at this moment in time: the bells are ringing and the weather is perfect for strolling (a crispness in the air and dry), so now is the time for a short break and a cup of coffee. I make a quick stop at a bar, which I have mentioned before, located directly facing the small bridge in front of the Frari. Whilst I am enjoying my coffee, I remember reading somewhere that about a hundred years ago one of these small shops, which was in fact a coffee house, became internationally famous for having a performing tomcat called Nini, so much so that dignitaries as well as royalty would visit this shop just to see the cat perform. Eventually, both poets and artists were said to have considered using Nini in their works, but only a small statue was eventually cast to remember him by. Alas, the cat is long gone as is his statue, but I believe there are still some photographic records kept by one of the shopkeepers to record this tale. I've always wondered if it was the same shop that I am now standing in ...... E un mistero!

Fully refreshed from enjoying a coffee and a biscuit, I now move on, making my way to the Rio Terra, where I leave the shop, turn directly left and walk up a narrow alleyway until I reach Rio Cassetti, and then turn right into the Rio Terra. Along the Rio Terra I notice a delightful bar on the right selling *nouvo* wine. Guess it's the first crop of Veneto wine this year, and just across the road there is an attractive wooden beamed archway which leads to the Corte Amaltea (not shown on the map). I now turn right into C2' Saoneri and walk to the end of this small passage, which, incidentally, has a fine art and model boat shop to visit at some time. I then turn left into Salizz S. Polo, cross over the Ponte S. Polo and I notice the church of San Polo, which is on my left, and check the time, which is only 12.35pm. I have now arrived at Campo San Polo, which is the second-largest square in Venice, St Marks being the largest, and I instantly notice that there are many period-style buildings surrounding this remarkable campo.

With my back to the church, I observe that the buildings to my left appear to be much older than the rest and I remember reading that this *sestiere* was named after both the church and campo.

There are now three palazzos in Campo San Polo: Palazzo Mafetti, Palazzo Soranzo and Palazzo Corner Mocenigo. Apparently, there once was a fourth, called Palazzo Gargonzi, which was pulled down in the 19th century. Palazzo Mafetti sits on the northern side of the square and was built by Domenico Rossi. It looks in a very poor condition with its windows boarded up, and is definitely in need of some major restoration. Palazzo Soranzo once had a small canal running in front of its façade, which, I am told, is shown in a painting by Caneletto, but the canal was filled in to enlarge the square. Soranzo can also claim to be a building where Casanova, who was at one time 'adopted' by a wealthy Venetian politician who lived in the Palazzo, worked as a musician. Palazzo Corner Mocenigo has its main façade facing the Rio San Polo and is one of the largest Renaissance palaces in Venice. Alongside the Corner Mocenigo sits the print shop called the Tipograpfia Tasso, which was built by the engineer Giovanni Bonvenati. Campo San Polo was noted for the market events and the spectacular shows that it hosted. One such show was the public ball to celebrate the marriage of Andrea Vendramin in 1507. As well as becoming a shrine for worship, many religious services were held here, and lastly, but not to be overlooked, it was used as an arena, once again, for bull fighting!

The church of San Polo still retains its original front door, having a red brick exterior that looks in remarkably good condition, and was founded by Doge Pietro Tradonico in the year 837. However, control of the church went to the Frari in 1810, following the fall of the Republic. The church has some incredible artwork by many excellent artists including Tintoretto *('Last Supper')* and Tiepolo *('Stations of the Cross')*. The detached campanile was built in 1362 and has some macabre effigies of lions (depicted eating a snake and playing with a human head) at the base of the tower.

Before I leave the campo, I must record how delightful the scattering of trees are around this square. Even though their leaves are missing, it is so nice to see them standing in this area, which complement the buildings that are positioned around them. It is also easy to imagine just what life was like several centuries ago in the square, with street musicians, peddlers, market stalls and other entertainment spread across this generous expanse. Just the place to sit and ponder under the shade of a tree. But, as it is now 1.15pm I have decided that lunch awaits me, so I will backtrack across the Campo to Salizz S. Polo where I noticed earlier that there was a rather inviting little restaurant with its green blinds acting as a colourful backdrop to the immediate area in which it is located. As with most trattorias, you cannot expect the elegance and style of an expensive restaurant, but this small unit certainly proved to be exceptionally good value for money (a set meal for 16 euros) and a very pleasant and comfortable place to be. My meal consisted of a seafood starter (collection of shrimp and calamari), followed by a pork chop with salad and finished with a slice of cake. To wash this down I had a couple of glasses of local white wine, and the complete meal came to 20.50 euros. What is more, I had some good company and conversation with a couple of American tourists from Detroit who, I feel sure, would have been interested in my watercolours had I had some to show them. Such is the plight of the artist.

Fully refreshed and raring to get on with my journey, I leave the trattoria, say farewell to my colonial cousins and head back across the Campo San Polo until I reach the far corner, which leads me into the Calle Bernado and eventually to the Calle del Scaleter. A quick glance at my watch tells me it is now 2.15pm. At the end of the Calle del Scaleter, I take a sharp left, then turn immediately right into Terra Parrucchetta and now face Campo di San Agostin on my left. Continuing along, I now cross the Ponte Del Parrucchetta, walking in the direction of the Calle Tintor, a narrow walkway with shops either side. Once at the end of the Calle Tintor, I see quite clearly, directly in front of me, the church of San Giacomo dell' Orio. One observation I should make is that the majority of locals I have passed in the last five minutes all have a very dark, almost glowing olive complexion, more so than any group of people I have seen today, and I wonder if they are a select group of indigenous Venetians from this particular area.

The church of San Giacomo dell' Orio really is an attractive building, a perfect subject to sketch or paint, as it encompasses an incredible number of earth colours and many horizontal and vertical lines to build a picture from its complex shape and size. To access the Church, I have to walk almost 300 degrees around its perimeter until I arrive at a small arched doorway in the corner of a tiny square. The door is opposite a small bridge. The church was founded in the 9th century in this area once called Luprio (which Orio derives from), and was later rebuilt around 1225. It has a mix of architectural styles and materials: the façade is said to be Romanesque, with an ancient square plan bell tower also dating from the 13th century. Inside the church, I sense a feeling of tranquil grandeur immediately as I look at the ceiling. You simply cannot miss the wonderful wooden keel-shaped roof, which was built in the mid 14th century. The footprint of the church is of a cross plan design, with two aisles and a transept.

The main altarpiece is a rare piece of work by Lorenzo Lotto depicting the Virgin and Child with saints (16th century). Other masterpieces include an ancient marble font, and works by Jacopo Palma, one being *'Miracle of the Loaves and Fishes'*, as well as another altarpiece by Picolo Veonese representing *'St Lawrence, Gerolamo and Prospero'*.

Having savoured the delights of this wonderful church and its surrounding area, I now make my way back to Campo San Giacomo Dell 'Orio, and my immediate thoughts are that although these remarkable churches are made available to the public to visit, many of them, this last one included, do not provide brochures in English for visitors to purchase. They do, however, provide some information on printed cards which you may borrow for your visit, but only if you ask for one. Although I do research on the web, I personally prefer to visit each location knowing it would be possible to obtain more local information from the host building in the form of a brochure, which would serve as a record of each visit to archive and cherish. I once mentioned this anomaly to a friend of mine, who simply answered by saying, 'Learn the language and buy your books in Venetian bookshops, information is all there!' Unfortunately I can't argue with that statement.

Leaving Campo San Giacomo Dell 'Orio, I travel along the Calle Larga, which leads me directly towards the Grand Canal and my next stop, which is the Fondaco dei Turchi (Natural History Museum). At the end of Calle Larga, I turn left, then right onto the Fondaco dei Turchi, where the museum is situated on the Canal front. Before reaching the museum, I notice a great deal of renovation work taking place around this area, and a short conversation with an English-speaking tourist reveals that the museum is closed. It is a great shame, as the research undertaken beforehand led me to believe it would be a very interesting place to visit, especially as I haven't explored this building before.

My research tells me that the Fondaco dei Turchi was originally a house for the Pesaro family, built by Giacomo Palmieri, which they gifted to the Baron of Ferrara in 1381. It eventually became a warehouse, which was used by Turkish merchants in 1621, and who traded there until 1838. Like the Jews, the Turks were considered to be enemies of the Venetians, even though they enjoyed the income they received from them, so many restrictions were placed on them and they were confined to this area by building protective gates and nailing down their windows! Eventually the Turks left the building and it remained empty and derelict until the Venetian authorities purchased it in 1865, primarily as the Correr Museum, then in 1923 as the Natural History Museum. Today the Museum caters for the natural sciences, and is the holder of the records for the Lagoon. Amazingly, inside the Museum, there apparently is a 5000-litre water tank containing seawater, which replicates the Lagoon and its aquatic plant life. There is also a pre-Roman boat on display that was discovered in the Lagoon. During the Republican era, it was once a popular place for holding dances, which the Venetians loved. A campaign by John Ruskin in the 1880s to restore the building proved successful, but unfortunately the restoration work was considered to be finished to a poor standard. Armed with this limited research, I will surely return to visit the Fondaco dei Turchi on another day. As the time now is still only 3.10pm, I intend to add another church to my itinerary to compensate for not visiting the Museum.

I now head back along the Fondaco dei Turchi and back on to the Calle del Tintor, which, I might add, has several good trattorias, some of which I have used in the past. When I reach the

Salizada San Stae, I turn left into this main street and continue along until I eventually reach the Church church of San Stae. Today there is a great deal of pavement restoration work taking place as I amble along, and, believe me, I have to be extremely careful where I walk to avoid the obstacles which confront me every few metres. Managing to avoid the temporary hazards and barriers ahead, I now pass the Palazzo Moncinego on my right, which now serves as a study centre for the History of Textiles and Costumes, yet another place to record for a visit another day. It is always useful to collect a list of buildings to visit, in case the weather should become inclement and walking does not become the chosen option. I now arrive at the church of San Stae.

For most tourists, San Stae is a useful vaporetto pontile staging to alight and explore the central districts of Venice, and is a location for one of the most delightful churches to visit. The church of San Stae was a parish church as far back as 1127 and, like most buildings of that age, was in need of some restoration by the 17th century. In view of this, it was redesigned by Giovanni Grassi, following instructions from the then Doge, Alvise Mocenigo, who, incidentally, is buried in a tomb in the centre of the nave, which is of white marble but has some macabre cartoons around its edge, namely, two skeletons with scythes on each side and skull and cross bones on both top and bottom. The graceful Baroque façade, designed by Domenico Rossi and finished in marble, compliments the Palladian architecture, and viewed from the Grand Canal provides a triumphant boldness so characteristic of this style of architecture. The central aisle has a vaulted ceiling with three chapels on each side of the nave; the ceiling has a large coping around its sides, supported by several heavy broad columns, which run parallel with the nave. There are some impressive large semicircular windows, which my research informs me, allow the sun to shine in and then be reflected by the white internal decoration. Today is not the best day to observe this, so, unfortunately, I can't experience this first hand. The altarpiece to the right is an amazing piece of work by Niccolo Bambini, and in the presbytery there is a unique cycle of works by Venetian artists of the 18th century, who were commissioned to complete works for Andrea Stazio. These include *'St James led to his Martyrdom'*, by Giambattisa Piazzetta, and *'The Martyrdom of St. Bartholomew'*, by Giambattista Tiepolo. In the sacristy there are several paintings left from the original church and various decorations on canvas, which form a cornice with portraits of eight parish priests, along the walls. If you are clever enough to spot it, there is also a bust of Antonio Foscarini, who was wrongly accused and exiled for treason. Before leaving the church of San Stae, I have to thank the kind lady at the reception counter, who patiently sits throughout the day in her enclosed compartment, because she allowed me to take a guide brochure outside and photograph it, as it was in English script (some churches provide this facility on request), as once again there was no brochure to be purchased. Another observation I should also make is that although the Chorus ticket does provide the opportunity to visit such wonderful churches, not all of the personnel who greet you at the reception kiosks are as pleasant and as helpful as the lady of San Stae.

The time now is 4.10pm and, as I leave the stunning church of San Stae, I pass the campo, follow the Fondamenta Pesaro, which crosses a small iron bridge, Ponte Giovanni, and then turn left down a very narrow street, which leads to the Galleria International of Modern Art, where I turn right again into the Fondamenta Pesaro. Again, it is worth recording the modern art gallery for future reference, which as an artist I will certainly visit on another occasion, when time permits. I am now walking alongside a small canal and to my right is Palazzo Agnusdio, which has a delightful small bridge that leads into a small doorway with a marvellous semi-circular effigy above the door. To the right of the door is a Gothic arch, which is partly boarded with a metal grill above. This location will provide me with several sketching projects, so I make sure I get it on camera. Having recorded the area, I continue, still on the Fondamenta Pesaro, until I reach the Calle de Ravano, which I turn left into and continue walking with the Grand Canal to my left (although not visible) until I reach a small bridge over the Rio della Due Torri, which I now cross. Once across, I continue ahead until I get to the Calle d.Regina, which I turn right into and follow for some way. At the third turning on the left, which I take, I walk straight ahead, crossing the Ponte Andrea, which eventually leads me into the Campo San Cassiano.

Today I have deliberately bypassed visiting the church of *Santa Maria Mater Domini*, which sits just south of the church of San Stae, the reason being that time is of the essence, however, I feel I should include this church in my journal. The church of Santa Maria Mater Domini can normally be reached simply by walking from San Stae back to Calle dei Tintor and continuing east for another 150m towards a small but attractive campo where the church is situated, which, although hidden within the snaking canals of Venice, displays some fine Gothic architecture as well as a 13th century house of interest called the Cassa Zave. There are also some delightful bars and a very interesting blacksmith's workshop, which all surround a 14th-century 'wellhead'. The church of Santa Maria Mater Domini was founded in the 11th century, but rebuilt in the early 16th century by either Giovanni Buora or Mauro Codussi (my research is unclear on which of them it was, but they were both accredited Renaissance architects) and the building was finally consecrated in 1540. The campanile was rebuilt in 1740. Like many other historical Venetian buildings, the church has fortunately had some major restoration work, which was undertaken by 'Venice in Peril', primarily to the roof, guttering and the eaves. The Istrian stone has also been waterproofed, and the windows repaired, but the façade has been left untouched for now. Internally the church is based on a Greek cross floor plan, which has four corner chapels and a graceful dome. The interior finish is a crisp white and grey, which is enhanced with works of art by Vincenzo Catena *'Vision of Santa Christina'* (1521), a lesser-known artist and successful merchant. Given the time, this church is well worth a visit (as they all are) and its adjoining campo will provide many interesting subjects to paint.

Returning to my route again, I am now standing in Campo San Cassiano, which was once the site of the first public opera house in Europe, which first opened in 1636 and was eventually demolished in 1812. Research informs me that Campo San Cassiano was notorious for prostitutes in earlier centuries, which does not surprise me as it is fairly close to the Rialto quarter and on the boundary of San Polo. The church of San Cassiano was originally built in the 9th century and funded by a group of wealthy Venetians. It was greatly restored in the 19th century and has a barn-like appearance which some consider far less attractive than its 13th century campanile. There are several works by Tintoretto inside, one in the sacristy, *'The Crucifixtion'* (1508), with two others in the main chapel, *'The Resurrection'* and *'The Descent into Limbo'* both of which are said to be poorly restored. As this church was not on my main itinerary for today, I resist the temptation to explore it, and walk diagonally across the campo until I reach the Calle dei Christi, where I turn left into Calle dei Botteri. After walking about 20m, I turn into Calle Scrimia, which eventually leads me to campo Beccaire, where I am reunited with a familiar sight, which is of course the Pescheria.

Although this fish market has ceased trading for several hours, the time now being 5.00pm, there is still that smell of the sea around and one or two porters are cleaning down their stalls ready for the market tomorrow. The temperature has now dropped considerably and the light is fading, so I get a move on in the general direction of the Rialto Bridge. Passing behind the Fabbriche Nuove, I now turn right in the direction of the Ruga d. Orefici and, once there, I walk along this busy market street for a few metres until I reach the last church to visit today, which is the church of *San Giovanni Elemosinario*.

This church is sometimes difficult to locate as it is hidden by a complex of buildings and shops and sits literally between two market stalls. San Giovanni Elemosinario is a small church by Venetian standards and, again, on plan its footprint replicates a Greek cross inside a square. The original church dated back to ancient times, before 1071, according to my research, but was unfortunately destroyed in the Rialto fire of 1514, as were so many other fine buildings in this area. The church we see today was eventually rebuilt in 1531 by Antonio Abboni, who, incidentally, was also responsible for some major work in the reconstruction of the market area. Many years ago, part of the area in front of the church was utilised by the clergy, who rented it out to various traders, which provided them with additional income. The interior of the church gives me the feeling of mystery, remoteness and secrecy, not simply because I am viewing it on a late winter afternoon, but because what I see appears solemn and dramatic. Having said that, I do experience some emotional warmth knowing that this diminutive church has no doubt provided a religious retreat for Venetians throughout the centuries and will continue to do so. Looking up at the central dome with its peripheral vaults, then casting my eyes around the walls, I wish I could transform what is a fairly plain church, in decorative terms, into a more deserving appearance. There are, however, many art treasures to enjoy. On the organ doors there is a remarkable painting by Marco Vecellio, and frescoes on the central dome which, at one time, were thought to be lost, but were eventually revealed when some restoration work took place. On the great altar, you can marvel at the famous altarpiece by Tiziano titled '*St. John the Almsgiver*', as well as savouring a work by Leonardo Corona, '*Crucifixion of St. Andrew*'. A frescoed tomb was also discovered during restoration, which lies in the middle of the nave. I have to confess that I didn't find the person sitting at the reception entrance very helpful at first when I asked for some information regarding the church, even though he was English-speaking. However, like the lady at San Stae, he did allow me to photograph the brief summary of the church which was available on a card, before I finally left.

As I walked out of the church, I literally walked straight into the centre of the market and was surprised just how populated and busy this area was, considering the time of the year. Moving on along the Ruga Vecchia S. Giovanni to the Rio terra San Silvestro, which led to the Campo San Silvestro, my thoughts were now trained on the vaporetto journey I would be taking back to Ferrovia pontile. When I arrived at the San Silvestro pontile, after crossing the campo, I looked back at the Rialto Bridge and enjoyed the early evening darkness, with the various lights reflecting in the Canal.

I waited about five minutes for the vaporetto to arrive and, when it did, it was fairly full, as you can imagine at this time of the day. Once aboard, I settled for a standing position in the centre of the vessel where I had hoped to get a good view of the palazzos on the Grand Canal, which should be illuminated in the early evening. My trip back to Ferrovia was quite eventful for two reasons: the first, because there was some congestion on the Canal just beyond the Rialto Bridge, which created a heavy verbal exchange between the vaporetto crew and several bargemen. I was standing literally a metre from the cabin in which the pilot was stationed and, believe me, whatever was wrong certainly hit a sensitive note with this guy. The second incident was much more interesting. It started when two vaporetto inspectors boarded the craft and went about their work checking that each passenger had a validated ticket. All was well until they discovered that two tourists were travelling without tickets. I have only ever come across these inspectors once before and I remember how they dealt with a similar situation, and today was equally as entertaining. When the tourists were discovered to be travelling without tickets, they attempted to plead ignorance, but the inspector dealing with the situation simply shrugged off any excuse they had to offer and demanded that they pay the penalty for their misdemeanour. I'm not quite sure what the exact penalty was, but I did see what appeared to be two 50 euro notes being handed over with some vociferous comments being exchanged between both parties. I have to compliment the two inspectors in the way they handled the situation and in the manner in which the second inspector managed to check all the remaining passengers' tickets before we arrived at the next pontile. Obviously they needed to check everyone before passengers disembarked and I wondered to myself just how much lost income this mode of transport must suffer during the course of a year, and then I thought of the many reminders that inform everyone of the high penalties imposed for not having a ticket.

Excitement over, I still have time to gaze into some of the palazzo windows, at least those which probably remain the palaces they once were, and marvel even from a distance at the ornate chandeliers and artwork that adorn these beautiful buildings. However, not all look so graceful internally in the evening light, as some palazzos may have ornate façades but the interiors are no different to the average office complex you would see in any city, in any country. I am, however, still of the opinion that it is important to maintain as much as possible of Venetian architecture, even if it means 'doctoring' some interiors in order that they may serve a useful purpose to the community.

It is 5.55pm when I arrive at Ferrovia, which still leaves me sufficient time to visit Bar S. Lucia on the Rio terra Lista di Spagua for my well-deserved tipple before heading home. On my short walk to Bar S. Lucia I can't help but notice that the Christmas spirit is fairly well marketed in the shops as I pass, and the street traders also have made every effort to advertise their merchandise, but I don't get the same suffocated effect from tinsel and holly as I do in the UK. Venetians do enjoy their Christmas and treat it as a family festival. Thousands of native Venetians return to the 'Serenissima' from all corners of the world at this time of the year to be with their families and attend church services, so I am told, and the majority still understand and remember the religious significance.

Even though I am only a third-generation Italian, I still remember Christmas as a child and, as a young man, when my mother and grandmother would prepare hundreds of ravioli (tortellies) a couple of days before for lunch on Christmas Day, each delicious parcel of spinach, cheese and cabbage being crowned with 'bunja' (a tomato-based salsa). This recipe a closely kept secret which had been handed down from generation to generation for centuries. To compliment the tortellies, there were plates of chicken, veal and pork and some selected vegetables, and everyone simply served themselves, feasting until almost full. Almost full, but still enough room for the Panettone, served on its own or with double cream. I can remember there always being wine on the table, not just at Christmas, and my grandfather would empty some into the thick 'minastra' (stews) at meal times. The wine incidentally wouldn't be served in fragile goblets, as we do today, but in glass tumblers of all shapes and sizes, and it wouldn't be purchased at the local store; it would be home-brewed from grapes which were harvested from small vineyards in their villages nestled in the northern Tuscany mountains, and brought to the UK. by the lorry, van, or car every year.

When I arrive at the Bar S. Lucia, I order my Guinness and ricotta spinach (wonderful when heated up) and I have approximately 25 minutes to enjoy my refreshments, review the day's journey and have a chat with Enrico, the owner of the bar. He recognises me now when I order my Guinness, and between the two of us we are able to exchange pleasantries. I inform him that I will be bringing my eldest daughter, Louise, with me, on my next visit in January. It will be her first trip to Venice and hopefully we shall be able to spend a little more time in the bar before rushing off to the bus depot.

With 12 minutes left to get to Piazzale Roma bus depot, I speedily make my way back along to the Scalzi Bridge, cross over it and walk past the Santa Chiara Hotel, arriving at the bus stop a minute before the bus arrives. Again, it is on time. The bus trip takes about 25 minutes, despite stopping several times on the way to the airport, and I arrive at Marco Polo with plenty of time to spare. Booking in with easyJet was slightly later today, as the Bristol flight checkout was still underway when I arrived. This didn't affect the departure time in any way, but it did mean that my ice-cream counter in the departure lounge was closed. Good for the diet, not for the soul!

The flight home had a full compliment of passengers and, even after some problems with passenger numbers, we still arrived at Gatwick 25 minutes early, which is always nice at this time of the evening. During the flight, I had the opportunity to make a few notes to supplement my digital recording, and at the same time start to plan my next trip in January. I have decided to get both the first and second drafts of the December chapter completed by Christmas, in order that I can spend some quality time in my studio getting some sketches of my Venetian walks and my new abstract portfolio completed before my next trip, which will be in 2007. My, how time flies when you are enjoying yourself!

Buonasera Venezia, Buon Natale

Fig.1   Santa Maria Gloriosa dei Frari

Fig.2 Grand Canal

Fig 3 Piazza San Marco

Fig.4 Bar S. Lucia

Fig.5 Santa Chiara Hotel

Fig.6   Santa Maria Formosa

Fig.7 Rio Bacino Orseolo

Fig.8   Palazzo Salviati

Fig.9   Santa Maria e Donato

Fig.10   Santa Maria Assunta & Santa Fosca

Fig.11   Fondamenta San Mauro

Fig.12 Rio dei Frari

Fig.13   Santa Maria della Salute

Fig.14 Squaro San Travaso

Fig.15 Campo Manin

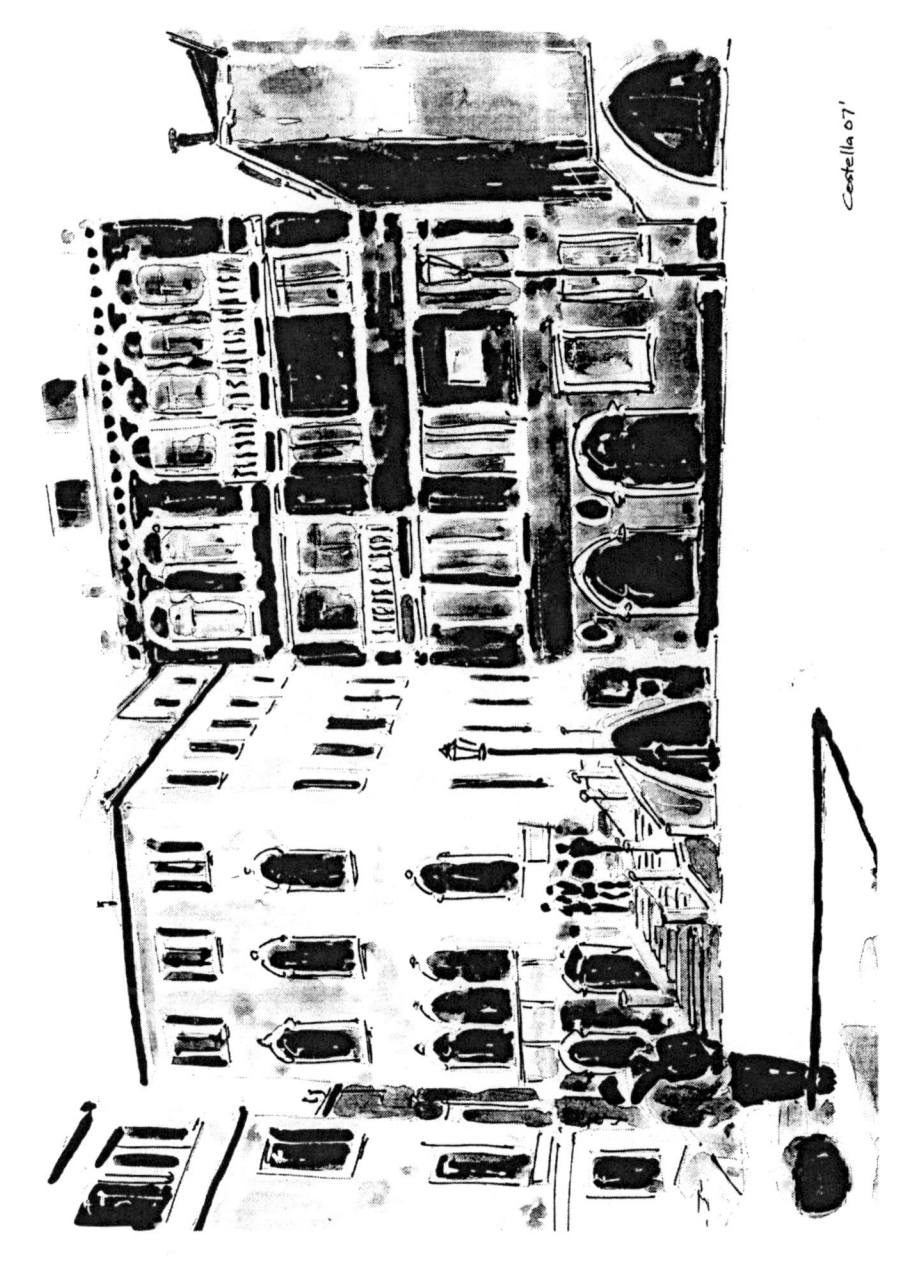

Fig.16 The Rialto Bridge

CHAPTER 5
JANUARY: Piazza San Marco

'From the Malamocco rises the Citadel'

A new year means new resolutions to make; resolutions that usually mean well, when first made, but are often forgotten within weeks. In 2007 I have decided that, in order to keep my enthusiasm fresh, I shall follow two paths. The first path is simply to record my successes and failures; in doing so I hope to recover from indiscretions. The second path is slightly easier: those resolutions that I really like and find easy to achieve, I will simply devote more time to. With that in mind, my first resolution for this year is to ensure that I keep ahead of my journal, complete it on time and within budget. The nicest resolutions are always the easiest to keep!

In a similar fashion the early Malamocco settlers of the 9th century, after agreeing formal proposals and with a fixed determination, decided to move to the Rialtine Islands, thus fulfilling a significant resolution which would have a major impact on the evolution of Venice. Malamocco was an area on the eastern shore of the Lido where those early island settlers decided to leave in order to build their first stronghold, which was considered far safer to protect from future invasions, that first stronghold being

January 2007

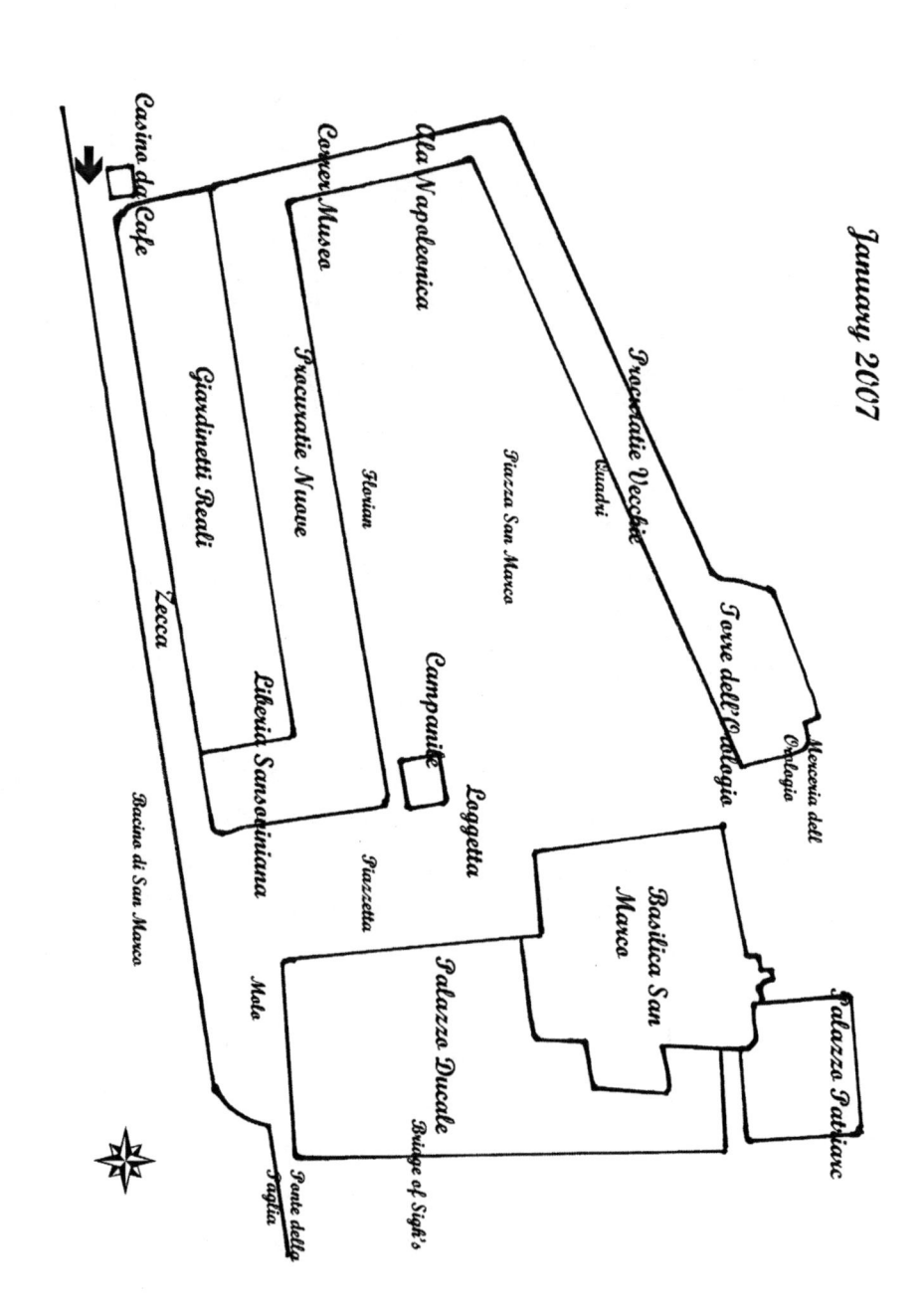

Map of Piazza San Marco, Venice:

- Casino del Cafe
- Procuratie Vecchie
- Ala Napoleonica
- Correr Museo
- Procuratie Nuove
- Florian
- Giardinetti Reali
- Piazza San Marco
- Quadri
- Torre dell'Orologio
- Merceria dell'Orologio
- Zecca
- Libreria Sansoviniana
- Campanile
- Loggetta
- Piazzetta
- Molo
- Basilica San Marco
- Palazzo Ducale
- Palazzo Patriarc
- Bridge of Sighs
- Ponte della Paglia
- Bacino di San Marco

the area we now know as Piazza San Marco.

It was here that the Palazzo Ducale (The Doge's Palace) was built and it was from here also that the seat of the Doge was to reign supreme for almost a millennium. At about the same time, the remains of St Mark were stolen from Alexandria and brought to the island hidden in a barrel of pork (to avoid being discovered by the Muslims) and from then onwards he was to become the patron saint of Venice, St Mark being chosen as a Christian saint in defiance of Byzantine domination at that period. The Piazza San Marco was then the hub of activity in this new city and provided a direct link to the Rialto 'Islands' (as they were then called) and the busy seaport close to the Bacino San Marco. Water covered a large part of the Piazza in those early days, but nevertheless this important commercial area became a significant landmark historically in the development of the Venetian Constitution. Between the 10th and the 13th century Venice became a major trading port and significant changes were made to the Piazza. By the end of the 12th century, the Palazzo Ducale was enlarged, a brick herringbone pavement was laid and the canal and dock, which isolated the Palazzo were filled in. The size of the Piazza at that time was similar to today, and gradually, from this period onwards. The shape and design of this magnificent square, which we are now accustomed to, was beginning to form.

My journey today is probably the least energetic of them all, yet one of the most interesting for both tourists and artists alike. Until now, I have deliberately avoided highlighting Piazza San Marco in my journal other than to take a quick glimpse whilst crossing its historical paving, but now is the time to really enjoy the magnitude and splendour of its surroundings. Personally, I enjoy the Piazza best at this time of the year, with or without the

Acqua Alta, especially if the weather conditions are 'pleasantly seasonal'. I have experienced the Piazza when snow has fallen and the surrounding rooftops have a layer of white snow making a wonderful contrast to the earth colours of the buildings, and for purely selfish reasons I enjoy January because the multitude of tourists who are normally here is reduced considerably. I find there is also a special presence here in the early evening when the ornately sculptured quayside lights are illuminated and reflect in the waters of the Lagoon. Although the itinerary for today is relatively easy, no street maps required (unless you take the option of walking back to Piazzale Roma this evening instead of using the vaporetto), I still plan to visit many of the Piazza's wonderful buildings. Therefore my trusted travel guide will be an important item for the rucksack.

My journey, as always, starts from Piazzale Roma, where I take the vaporetto to the San Marco pontile, and, within half an hour or so of boarding this craft, I will be passing the Salute and gazing across the Lagoon towards the Lido. Once I arrive at my destination, I shall walk past the Royal Gardens, arriving at the Zecca, which overlooks the two columns of San Marco and San Teodoro, which both stand guard over the entrance to the Piazza and Piazzetta (the area immediately in front of the Palazzo Ducale walking from the waterfront). Within minutes, I will be facing both the Palazzo Ducale and the Campanile, which stand proudly amid their historic neighbours. Once in the centre of the Piazza, I will be confronted with the Procuratie Nuove, the Ala Napoleonica (Museo Correr), the Procuratie Vecchie, the Torre dell Orologia and, last, but no means least, the Basilica San Marco. So much history in such a small area. Too much, some may say, for a day trip. I agree, if you haven't been before, but still possible, which I intend to prove and enjoy today. As I previously stated, the routes I use may be enjoyed equally as well if used collectively or individually when staying for longer periods in Venice.

The biggest problem I have today will be limiting the amount of information I enter into my journal for each historic building I visit, especially the unparalleled beauty of both the Basilica and the Palazzo Ducale, which would take several chapters alone to explain in any real detail, so I hope that my short resume of events will not discredit all that is around me and will simply suffice to encourage artists and travellers alike to visit Piazza San Marco themselves. To supplement my tour today, I intend to include some major personalities, which have significantly contributed to the history of Venice, such as the governing Doges and the conquering Bonaparte.

My travel bag today contains my trusted travel book, camera, digital recorder and sketchbook (which I have brought over with me simply to review and itemise some future projects I have in mind) and, lastly, an additional sweater, as I think it might get considerably colder as the day moves on! Today is also a very special day for me as I will be accompanied by my eldest daughter, Louise, this being her first visit, so I hope she will find this trip as interesting and enjoyable as I know I shall.

* January 11th 2007

A slightly different start today, as I have some company on my journey to the airport. Louise has stayed overnight and the early morning discussion is centred around breakfast. The main topic of conversation at the airport strangely enough is not about food for the day but about the itinerary planned and our general expectations, being mindful of the mild weather forecast, which I diligently sourced the day before.

Our flight again was on time and, not surprisingly, there was a reduced number of passengers due mainly, I guess, to the winter season; all good news as far as I am concerned because that means that Piazza San Marco will be relatively empty when we arrive. Still not a great deal of snow on the Alps when we fly over, so I imagine that the winter skiing activities may be disappointing for many who travel to Europe this year.

Upon arrival at Marco Polo airport, we quickly make our way through immigration and purchase our ACTV tickets for the day and walk briskly to the awaiting number 5D bus, which will take us to Piazzale Roma. Before entering the bus, I stopped to assist a young couple, who were obviously unsure how to get to Venice as this was their first visit to the 'Serenissima', and, as fortune would have it, they were going to a hotel just minutes from where Louise and I were heading, so I was able to direct them.

Whilst the bus journey was fast and efficient, weather conditions today are not the best as there is very low cloud, which restricts visibility to about 300m, therefore hiding most of the Lagoon and the wonderful skyline of the city as we make our way across the bridge. The young couple travelling with us were keen to know what they were missing, so I became their personal guide on the bus, and on our journey on the vaporetto along the Grand Canal, until we reached the San Marco pontile. Having said our farewells and aiming the couple towards their hotel, Louise and I begin our exploration of Piazza San Marco by walking alongside the *Giardinetti Reali* (Royal Gardens). Before we set off, I should point out the Casino de Café, which is a small pavilion erected at the pontile end of the gardens, which is now used as the main Tourist

Office. This building is particularly attractive and provides good sketching material. The gardens we now walk past were designed and built by Eugene Beauhamais (Napoleon's nephew) during the French occupation, as Napoleon expressed a wish to see the Lagoon in panoramic view from the windows of the Procuratie Nuove. Unfortunately, in doing so, he demolished four historic buildings (the Granai di Terranova) which stood beside the Zecca and which was said to be the largest grain store in Europe. Today there are few market stalls on display along this concourse. In the tourist season there are many, so today we can enjoy and appreciate this stretch of walkway which is normally filled with souvenir stalls.

At the end of the gardens, we arrive at the *Zeccha* (formerly the City Mint), which is now occupied by the *Biblioteca Nazionale Marciana*, a research library that holds more than 900,000 books and 13,000 manuscripts. The Mint was founded in the 9th century and originally situated near the Rialto Bridge but was later re-sited in its present location. The building we see today was designed by Jacopo Sansovino and constructed between 1537 and 1545, and was built of stone and iron to make it fireproof, replacing the original Mint dating from the 13th century. Legend has it that the slaves of Cyprus buying their own freedom financed the construction of this building.

The Venetian gold ducat was minted here before it became the zecchino, and was used throughout European exchanges as it was considered to be the safest monetary system of its day. First used in Venice in 1284, the ducat was easy to mint and featured the Doge kneeling before St Mark. My research informs me that it was also the longest continuously struck coin the world has ever known (examples can be seen in the Museo Correr). The Mint continued to function until 1870. Before moving on, I should also mention the *Libreria Sansoviniana* (Biblioteca Marciana), as this building is attached to the former Zeccha and is, I believe, to all intents and purposes one and the same building now.

Libreria Sansoviniana is a very attractive Renaissance structure, which was built by Sansovino but was never completed during his lifetime; in fact, it was not finished until 1591. During its construction, in 1545 part of the building collapsed and Sansovino was imprisoned by the Council and only released after several pleas from noted artists and guilds. He was told to finance the repair work and change the design slightly in order to avoid future structural problems. The 16-arcaded bays with frescoes were attributed to Sansovino whereas the remaining five-arcaded bays were by Scamozzi (those which extend to the Molo). The original building, which was constructed on a site originally providing hostels, a bakery and slaughter house, was built from the bequest of Cardinal Bessarion, who eventually left all his literary treasures to the Republic in 1468. Entry into the library is through the Museo Archeologico, where you arrive at the Main Hall. This room holds wonderful paintings by Veronese, Tintoretto and Schiavone, among others. From the Main Hall there is an Ante Room which displays Titian's *'Allegory of Wisdom'* painted on the central panel of the ceiling. Napoleon made the Libreria part of the Royal Palace after the fall of the Republic and moved most of its original treasures to the Palazzo Ducale. One other notable artefact, which I think is most interesting, is the famous 'notebook' by Benvenuto della Volpaia (1486–1532) who was was a maker of clocks and instruments and also an inventor of machines. He was a good friend of Michelangelo, and acted as an intermediary between the Pope and his inventor friend. The library is well worth visiting at some time, but today my busy schedule does not allow me to do so.

Whilst I am enjoying the architecture around me, I should also mention that the area in which I am currently standing (between the Zecca and the PalazzoDucale) is known as the Molo, which serves as an arena for the Columns of San Marco and San Teodoro. These historic red and grey Egyptian granite columns originated from Constantinople, arrived in Venice in 1172 and were erected by Nicolo Barattieri, who, incidentally, was the designer of the very first Rialto Bridge. Originally there were three columns shipped to San Marco, but unfortunately one of them became dislodged from the barge which was transporting them, and fell into the Lagoon, where it still remains to this day. Of the two remaining columns, the one we see on the far west has a marble statue of St Theodore, who was the patron saint of Venice before St Mark. The other one has the Winged Lion of St Mark on its pedestal, which was restored by the British Museum in 1990 and is thought originally to be of Middle East descent, being made around 300 BC, and once formed a larger bronze piece. There are many interesting historical facts relating to these columns, some quite horrific; one being that these columns mark the spot where criminals were executed, either by hanging, decapitation or being buried alive. Another is that Ventians are said never to walk between them because they think it unlucky. I prefer to think of this area as being the hub of entertainment, as it was in past times, when there were several gaming tables in use between each column during the 12th century, as well as market stalls selling their wares. Whilst on the subject of tall objects, I can also see the Three Masts positioned directly in front of the Basilica, which were first erected in 1480 to accommodate the banner of St Mark, which, incidentally, is raised on specific feast days, the colour of the flag now being red, and with the tricolour of the Italian National flag. Alassandro Leopardi designed the pedestals, which are formed at the base of each mast, with the centre mast depicting the effigy of Doge Leonardo Loredan (1501–1521).

My watch indicates that it is still only 11.55am, and I haven't explored any of the buildings which grace the Piazza and the Piazzetta, but I still feel energised by simply being surrounded by so much history. Louise was impressed with the Grand Canal journey and I know that she will be amazed when we explore some of the buildings, which follow.

Walking from the Columns, I intend to travel clockwise around the Piazza so the next monument we see is the *Campanile*. The Campanile is probably one of the most popular tourist attractions in Venice as it really does stand majestically in the Piazza, almost as if it were standing guard over its neighbours. In fact, the original tower, completed in 1173, was built to serve as a lighthouse for sailors in the Lagoon when the Piazzetta was part of the city's harbour, and so careful were early Venetians to protect their city that they forbade foreigners from climbing the tower at high tide, which would have allowed them to record the navigable passages through the Lagoon. From the top of the tower, which is approximately 100m high, in fact the highest building in the square, one can see the entire city (but strangely enough not any one canal). Unfortunately, the Campanile is closed to tourists today and will remain so until February, but as visibility is extremely poor now, it is probably a good time for it to be closed.

The tower has five bells, which at one time were used for several purposes. For example, *'Marangona'*, the largest of them, would denote the start and end of the working day, whilst *'Malefico'*, the smallest bell, would give notice of an execution. *'Noona'* would signify it was noon, *'Mezza Terza'* would summon senators to the Palazzo Ducale and, finally, *'Trottiera'* would announce the Great Council was in session. Galileo was said to have demonstrated his new telescope to Doge Leonardo Dona in 1609 from its balcony, and, horrifyingly, it was used as a hoist for prisoners left to die in public view. Workers from the Arsenale used it to perform stunts like the 'Flight of the Angel', whereby they would slide from the top of the tower to the Palazzo Ducale during Carnevale.

The original tower was struck by lightning several times, as portrayed in a Caneletto painting, following which the first lighting conductor was installed in the late 18th century. Probably the most famous event to befall the tower was when it collapsed suddenly on 14th July in 1902. There had been several indications that the structure was unsafe, and remarkably its fall was recorded on film. Fortunately, the City Council immediately reacted to this disaster, met and quickly agreed that it had to be rebuilt to its original design, 'as and where it was', and reconstruction commenced in 1903. The foundations were laid between 1904 and 1905, and brickwork was begun in 1906 and completed in 1908, at the same time as the stonework commenced. The belfry was finished in 1910, as was the installation of the bells, and the metallic angels we see today were raised and set in place in 1912. During this period, the Logetta (the base of the Campanile) was reconstructed using the original design by Jacopo Sansovino as well as using most of the original materials, which thankfully were salvaged. Having said that, there were, however, new architectural and ornamental pieces sculptured for the Logetta by some of the finest marble workers and stonemasons available, ensuring that the repair was finished to its original glory. In the past, the Logetta was used as a meeting reception and also served as a guardroom for Arsenale workers, who, upon request from the Council, patrolled the area during certain festivities and events.

Moving away from the Campanile, we walk to the centre of the Piazza, avoiding flocks of hungry pigeons, to gain a greater understanding of the spectacle that surrounds us, and strangely enough most tourists refer to this area as a square, when in fact the Piazza is a giant trapezoid. I would like briefly to mention the *Piazza* and *Piazzetta Pavement* at this point, even though it seems to be covered by pigeons, who seemingly are encouraged to flock there in their thousands, as there are several stalls selling seed for the purpose of feeding them. Originally the Piazza was laid in bricks to a herringbone pattern, and in certain areas there were coloured bricks to signify where processional routes were observed and market traders could set up their stalls. In about 1723, these bricks were replaced with a more detailed arrangement of white Istrian stone, which was also designed to take the surface water away into a lower drainage channel. Both Jacopo Sansovino and Vincenzo Scamozzi were major players in designing and managing this programme of works, albeit at different periods, and they were both singularly recognised as being the 'State Architects'. The intricate detail of the paving stone was also designed to facilitate Piazza activities as well as being decorative, in some ways similar to the previous design but with a far more complex pattern. In accommodating the new drainage system, the level of the Piazza was raised by almost a metre to its present-day level. By 1890 the pavement was again renewed, mainly because of the wear and tear it had been subjected to, and every attempt was made to ensure that the original stone pattern was retained. Whilst the drainage system can handle heavy rain, it cannot cope with the Acqua Alta 'high water' and therefore this entire area floods when water rises up through the water channels during certain tides.

I am now facing the *Procuratie Nuove,* which is adjoined to the Libreria Sansoviniana and which runs due west from the Campanile. This attractive Renaissance-style building was designed and constructed between 1582 and 1640, the first part by Scamozzi and finally completed by Longhena, and was built on the original site of the Orseolo Hospice. It was once used as lodgings for the Procurators of Venice, who resisted living there because they considered that their own palazzos were considerably more luxurious than the apartments provided here. Napoleon's stepson commandeered this building during the French occupancy for use as a royal palace. During this period, he demolished the church of San Geminiano so as to link this building to the Procuratie Vecchie (on the opposite side of the Piazza) in order to accommodate space for a ballroom to be built, which when completed was aptly named the Ala Napoleonica. Like the Procuratie Vecchie, part of the return wing of the Nuove abutting the San Geminiano Church was also demolished to enable this work to be undertaken. Today the first and second floor form part of the Museo Correr, which I intend to visit shortly. The arcade running below Nuove is extremely famous for several reasons, one being that it is featured in many works by Caneletto and another that it provides a unique shopping colonnade, one tenant being the famous *Café Florian*. Opened in 1720, Café Florian was originally called the Caffee della Venezia Trionfonte, and only later took the name of its owner. Its tables of wood, and marble walls decorated with frescoes with gold inlay, are majestic, and the interior has a number of small rooms depicting an assortment of ethnic motifs. As an early coffee house, it was used for business as well as pleasure and became internationally known for its excellent service and attracted many visitors, as indeed it does today. In the 'open season' there are tables set out on the Piazza, with a group of accomplished musicians playing, which really is a fantastic spectacle, and, well worth a visit inside too.

My next appointment is actually visiting the Museo Correr, but as it is just after noon and close to lunch time Louise and I have decided to take a short break before entering the building. Not wishing to travel too far from the Piazza, we make our way across the square, past the Baccino Orseolo, and find a small trattoria where we can have lunch. Normally I would go for the local dish but we both agree that the pizzas look good so we decide that pizza, salad and a chicken wrap are the order of the day, and the lunch break will give us some time to reflect on our journey so far. Whilst having lunch, I decide to text my dear wife, Avril, simply to say we arrived safely and are enjoying ourselves, a task which would normally take me several minutes. Handled by Louise, a lengthy message took seconds for her to complete, and after settling our bill we make our way back to the Piazza. On the way back, I realised that Louise was intent on looking at every piece of glass and jewellery displayed in the shops, so I decided that we would walk back to Piazzale Roma at the end of our day, which would allow her to do some window-shopping.

It is now 1.20pm as we enter the *Museo Correr*, which is located by walking through the arched opening in the centre of the Ala Napoleonica. I am really looking forward to exploring this museum again, as it covers both the art and cultural history of Venice throughout the ages. As I mentioned earlier, this building occupies the site where the church of San Geminiano previously stood, which was used by an ancient order that had rebuilt their church in the 16th century.

Before I start to explore this wonderful museum, I should briefly mention some facts relating to *Napoleon Bonaparte* and Venice, especially as I now enter a building which is attributed to his short, but nevertheless commanding reign over the city. Surprisingly enough, Napoleon made his first and only visit to Venice on the 29th November 1807 and left on the 8th December 1807, and research informs me that he hated the city, which comes as a surprise since he clearly made every effort to change its culture in order to bring it in line with his master plan. A brief resume of events during his period in Venice doesn't make spectacular reading but does, sadly, display his political and military impact on the city, which proved to be quite devastating and which regrettably was administered in a ruthless fashion. He entered the city via the monastery of Santa Chiara, this being fairly close to Piazzale Roma, and then sailed down the Grand Canal that same day to Piazza San Marco where he disembarked, having refused an invitation to attend dinner in celebration of his victories. One of his first decrees was to provide a suitable cemetery for the Island, which, when finished, was named San Cristoforo. It lasted for about 30 years, until full, following which, San Michele was constructed. He then considered several other building projects, which meant demolishing many beautiful Renaissance buildings, and, although many works of art were saved when his programme of works commenced, many other treasures and works of art were destroyed. On the 2nd December (the third anniversary of his coronation), after inspecting the Arsenale and the Lido for defence purposes, he launched two corvettes destined for the French Navy, and then followed a regatta on the Grand Canal, and later attended a banquet in his honour. On the 3rd December he was said to have observed Venetians walking knee deep in water on the Piazza, from his apartment windows, before going on to Murano to inspect the glass factories. The next two days, the 4th and 5th December, were spent touring the Lagoon, first being transported to S. Giorgio Maggiore, then on to Torcello, Burano and S.Erasmo. On the morning of Tuesday 8th December 1807 he departed from the 'Serenissima' never to return, and the rest, as they say, is history.

We are now in the reception of the Museo Correr, having climbed an impressive staircase, and I have decided to purchase an entrance pass (Musei Civici Veneziani), which will allow me to enter several of Venice's museums collectively for only 18 euros, the pass being valid for six months. From the reception, we now enter the Ante Chamber, which then leads to the Napoleonic Gallery, which, when viewed from the outside, links the Museo Correr to both the Procuratie Nuove and the Procuratie Vecchie. From here we enter the 'infamous' Ballroom, and immediately realise just how elegant this room is, being an original design by Lorenzo Santi. Several statues grace the area, such as the masterpieces by Antonio Canova (1757–1822), two of them being *'Orpheus'* and *'Eurydice'*, both incidentally carved in Vincenza stone. In one of the adjoining corridors, visitors can view a remarkable marble statue of Napoleon dressed as a Roman Emperor! Walking back into the Napoleonic Gallery via the Ante Chamber, we arrive at an area filled with wonderful plaster casts by Canova, which also displays a model of his tomb; the real one stands majestic in the Frari.

Moving on, we arrive at the Throne Room, which holds many works by noted artists such as Giovanni Canal and Giovanni

Berilacqua. From here, we go through to the Banqueting Hall, which again displays incredible pieces by Canova, such as his statue named *'Cherub'*, together with frescoes by other masters. Having now moved on to another interlinking room, I see what is probably my most favourite statue in this area, which is the *'Venere Italia'* by Canova. It may only be a plaster model (the original is in Florence), but to my mind this object is of surpassing beauty, a real gem. By now, we have turned left and are heading towards a group of about 13 additional rooms inside the Procuratie Nuove which display, among other things, a vast collection of coins, a library of books, historic documents, fantastic artwork and a fine collection of weapons and armour. As there is so much to see here, I can only highlight my favourites on display in the remaining areas of the first floor.

Coins have always held a fascination for me, so having such a vast collection to look at is really good news, and what a collection there is. If I were to hazard a guess, I would say that there is almost every type and denomination of coin minted in Venice from its begining to the fall of the Republic, and, what's more, they all look in remarkably good condition. To supplement the coins, there are several tools and machinery items on display, which were used to mint coins in the 18th century. Moving on from the coins, there is an interesting array of information relating to the Arsenale, with various paintings and historic views of this area together with data about the various guilds related to the craftsmen who constructed such a vast number of historic vessels, when Venice once had a naval force to be reckoned with.

Finally on this floor is the Armoury, which really does have a comprehensive collection of weapons and armour on display. Having quickly looked around this area, we make our way back to Room 14, then ascend the staircase to the second floor and find that there are still another 15 rooms full of treasures to see. As I have already viewed the Gothic, Venetian, German and Flemish artwork before on this floor, Louise is happy for me to briefly wander through each room, and view some of my favourites by Carpaccio, Bellini and Vivarini and especially the Italian Bronzes. In addition to this, there is some 16th-century majolica work on display, and the Manin Library to enjoy, as well as a collection of games and information on social events of days long since gone. I guess my favourite piece of artwork on this floor has to be the very famous *Two Venetian Ladies* by Vittore Carpaccio, which clearly gives so much information about the social history of Venice in the late 15th century. These two elegant ladies, who were at first thought to be courtesans, provide an illustrated journal of their age, especially when viewed with the upper part of the original panel, which is displayed in the J. Paul Getty Museum in America.

As it is some time since I visited the Museo Correr, I totally underestimated just how much was on display and therefore just how long one can spend here to fully appreciate the treasures on view. However, today is purely to give Louise an overview of what Venice has to offer, and therefore we move on with our journey.

We now leave the museum and make our way back to the Piazza and take time to view the *Procuratie Vecchie* on our left (north of the square), as we walk towards the Basilica. Procuratie Vecchie, which was originally the home of the Procurators of San Marco (financial agents). These agents worked in the court of law and were also administrators of all government-owned property. There were never more than nine Procurators at any one time and these were considered to be the second in line to the Doge, who was probably a former Procurator himself. The original building on this site, which was destroyed by fire, dates from the 12th century, and was eventually replaced in the 16th century by the one we see now. Construction was started by Codussi, then handed on to Bartolomeo Bon and finally completed by Sansovino in 1532. Again, like its opposite neighbour Procuratie Vecchie, it is a magnificent piece of architecture, which graces almost the entire length of the Piazza. Today it is privately occupied and consists of apartments on the upper floors, with leased retail units on the ground floor, all of which are tastefully enhanced by its elegant arcade. A really famous coffee house in this arcade is the *Quadri*, which opened in 1775. Quadri was said to be the first coffee house in Venice to serve Turkish coffee and was a great favourite with the Austrians during their time of occupation. In fact, research tells me that there was a great deal of rivalry on the Piazza between the Venetians, who tended to favour 'Florians', and their opposite counterparts who favoured the Quadri. Whatever, Quadri has a similar ambience and history to Florians and nothing is more delightful when sitting at one of their tables in the Piazza drinking coffee and listening to their musicians play.

Next door to the Procuratie Vecchie is the *Torre dell Orologio* (Clock Tower), which was built between 1496 and 1506, again in Renaissance design and constructed by Mauro Codussi, with additional work later completed in 1755 by Giorgio Massari. The builders and designers of the clock mechanism took three years to complete this piece, and legend has it that when they completed their task, they were deliberately made blind so that they could not build a similar one! The clock itself has three displays to record the phases of the moon, the zodiac, and tides for navigational purposes. The Clock Tower's roof terrace has two bronze statuettes depicting two men known as the 'The Moors', who traditionally strike the bell every hour. There is a charming statue of the Madonna standing between two small pillars under an arch supported by a small balcony, this being positioned just above the clock itself. The Torre dell Orologio has a wonderful archway on the ground floor leading to the *Merceria*, which is the prime street linking San Marco to the Rialto.

With so much Venetian history still to marvel at, my thoughts at this moment return to those courageous early settlers in the early 9th century who, by sheer endeavour, were in some way responsible for all that I now enjoy today. Their desperate plight from the Malamocco must have been horrendous, knowing what dangers were in store for them had they remained, and I am reminded of a quotation from George Bernard Shaw which reads, 'He who has never hoped, can never despair.'

It is now 2.30pm and I want to focus on the two spectacular buildings still remaining on my itinerary today. The first is the sensational Basilica San Marco and the second is the equally stunning Palazzo Ducale. Obviously, to do these outstanding buildings justice, each must be visited on its own merit. As I have time to visit just one briefly today, I have decided to explore the Basilica San Marco and, as a supplement to the journal, provide a brief resume from my previous visits to the Palazzo Ducale, which will include a short history of the Doge.

So here we are, at last, at the main doorway to the *Basilica San Marco*. As I am carrying a knapsack, I have to deposit this in a building to the left of the Basilica, where it is retained until I return. Louise is lucky she has only a small shoulder bag, which she can take with her.

A basilica was first built on this location in the 9th century as a shrine to St Mark. It was then replaced in the 11th century, but that building was dismantled and rebuilt to the current design we now see (well not quite all of it, as I shall explain). The Basilica is built to a Greek cross plan beneath five huge domes, which were added in 1094. Jacopo Sansovino later strengthened the building during renovation from 1529 onwards. The façade displays mosaics from several different periods and there are some wonderful crafted and extremely picturesque Romanesque carvings above the entrance, which date from the 13th century. The only surviving mosaic from the early days is the Porta di San't Alipio, which is on the far left of the façade. In the very early days, the area directly in front of the church accommodated an orchard, vineyard and vegetable garden! Each of the Basilica's beautiful and majestic external arches is a major work of art depicting religious scenes of the life and death of Christ, each still retaining its stunning mosaic colours, which illuminate the stone and marble around them. There are also arches which contain the signs of the zodiac and scenes from the history of St Mark; especially interesting is the one on the right that depicts his body being smuggled out of Alexandria. To describe the detail of the arches on the main façade is almost impossible. One has to stand and view this masterpiece with a pair of binoculars to fully appreciate its beauty. Often I have just stood in one position for 20 minutes, usually to the annoyance of my fellow tourists, completely comatised by what I see. Apart from the ornate workmanship on show, such as the pinnacles, statues and decoration; I cannot begin to imagine how many different variations of marble there are in the pilasters, columns and arches.

Above the doorway stand replicas of the original *Horses of St Mark (The Quadriga)*; the originals are now safely displayed inside within the *Museo Marciano*. The oriental design was produced to reflect just how important the Byzantine culture was in this period, and the Basilica, it was said, had been modelled on two basilicass that stood in Constantinople. The original domes of the Basilica were covered with larger wooden cupolas (than what is on view today), each having a lead dressing. This was carried out during the Basilica's restoration period between the 11th and 15th centuries. The original brickwork was covered with the new distinctive marble façade, and columns with capitals were introduced, which completely transformed the original design. Many of the artefacts which adorn the façade were, in fact, the spoils of war, which Venetian merchants had taken from their enemies; features such as pilasters from Acre and the *'Tetrachs'* (a handsome sculpture of the 4th century depicting the four rulers of the Roman Empire, numerous legends being associated with this group of men).

Venetians constantly designed buildings in the Byzantine fashion throughout the 12th and 13th centuries, which incorporated an extensive amount of mosaic work (just wait till we get inside), and Venetian craftsmen became very good at mosaic work from this period on. Many cartoons and sketches by Tintoretto, Titian, Veronese and other great artists demonstrated just how good they were in using this art form in later years. There are areas of the façade that perhaps have not been sympathetically restored over the years; for example, parts on the north and south have been replaced with grey stone instead of marble. Standing resolute on the corner of the main façade is the *Pietra del Bando* (Proclamation Stone) which, interestingly enough, was said to have partly protected the Basilica from further damage when the campanile collapsed, even though the stone was split. It was from this stone that all proclamations and penal sentences imposed by the Republic were announced.

Now it's time to actually enter the Basilica. Entrance is free to the public but there is a charge of 1.50 euros if you want to go on the Loggia. Worth every penny, believe me. The internal geometry of the Basilica on plan shows that it has three longitudinal naves and three transverse naves. The riches and craftsmanship inside are amazing, as it is a real treasure trove, and access to these treasures is achieved by walking through the narthex (the area between the front portal and the interior). This transitional area is decorated with a formidable mosaic floor (12th century) as well as an array of mosaic coloured domes and arches depicting scenes from the Old Testament.

Before entering the Basilica itself, I have the opportunity to visit the Museo Marciano, which is accessed via a staircase from the narthex and leads to the Loggia dei Cavalli, where we can view the entire piazza from above the main door of the Basilica, which also provides an elevated view of the building's interior. Whilst in this area, we can also view the replica Horses of San Marco close up, as well as studying the external façade cladding in more detail. Moving back into the interior of the building, and the Museo, allows us to gaze at the artefacts and exhibits on display, including manuscripts, mosaics and tapestries.

Up to now, I have not mentioned the interior mosaic work of the Basilica, which I can only describe as phenomenal. The craftsmanship and sheer volume on display is outstanding. Research tells me that there is over 4,000m² of intricate and stunning mosaic work on display. Looking up at the central dome, one can see the scale, beauty and the quality of this astonishing mosaic work, and it is only when you study this work close up that you realise just how much craftsmanship, effort and labour was required to achieve this finish. The majority of the interior finish was completed by the 13th century, but many other works have been added since.

Each of the five great domes of the Basilica are named as well as having geographical positions, *St John*, facing north, *St Leonard*, facing south, *Emmanuel*, facing east, *Pentecost* facing west and last but by no means least *Ascension* in the centre, each one depicting biblical scenes from the New Testament.

I should also mention the *pavimento* (internal pavement), as it deserves some recognition, being decorated throughout with complex and colourful mosaic patterns as well as scenes depicting animals and birds.

Coming back down the extremely steep staircase (the riser of each step being incredibly high) from the Museo back into the heart of the Basilica, we make our way through the main aisle and gaze up at the domes from the ground level whilst making our way towards the *Golden Sanctuary*. Situated behind the High Altar is the *Pala D'Oro* (Gold Altarpiece), which was made in the 10th century by medieval goldsmiths. This magnificent revered and cherished piece of work is adorned with precious stones, gold and enamelled plaques, again depicting biblical scenes such as the Crucifixion, the Resurrection and the Ascension. Unfortunately, Napoleon was said to have taken many of the precious stones from this area. The Sanctuary door is by Sansovino and depicts portraits of both himself and Titian. There is a small charge of 1.50 euros to see this work of art close up, and to my mind it is money well spent.

The Baptistery (Church of the Cherubs), although closed, contains the tomb of Doge Andrea Dandolo 1343–1354. Also buried here is Jacopo Sansovino, whose remains lie by the altarpiece, close to the font, which he designed. The *Treasury*, which is open to the public, is situated in the south transept and is said to have been part of the original Palazzo Ducale. Inside the Treasury, you can see the many cherished objects brought back from the foreign Crusades, such as chalices, semi-precious stones and religious artefacts, that survived the pillaging and ransacking following the fall of the Republic and, strangely enough, in more recent times, the sale of semi-precious jewels. Look out for the 7th century Episcopal chair that is on display. We now leave this area and make our way back to the main entrance door, still appreciating the splendour that is all around as well as above us. Just before leaving the Basilica, I mention to Louise that the smaller of the two pergolas, which stand either side of the *Rood Screen* (right-hand side), is in fact the one where the newly elected Doge would have been presented to the public before entering the piazza; this leads me nicely into my short introduction to the Doge, before I talk about the Palazzo Ducale.

Throughout the earlier chapters of my journal, I have constantly referred to the Doges of Venice and now is an opportune time to explain in more detail just what an important contribution they have made to Venice over the centuries, up until the fall of the Republic. The Doge was a prominent member of society, graced with gifted intelligence, who served as the chief magistrate and leader of the Republic of Venice, and could be compared to the more recent Italian title of Duce. *The Doge* was first introduced around the 6th century, replacing the Tribunes that led the early settlements in the Venetian Lagoon, and their original titles were similar to that of an emperor, i.e. for life, and passed down through the family, thereby creating a dynasty rather than a republic. In 1172 the election of Doge was committed to a Council of 40, and the inheritance factor was no longer considered valid. In 1297 members of the general public were excluded from the Council so that only a small, select group represented this auspicious Council. The economic, environmental and social support administered by this hierarchy appeared to provide a stable government regime as new regulations were introduced, a hierarchy which remained until 1797. This newly imposed resolution reminded me of a quotation by Paul Valery (1871–1945) which reads, 'Politics is the art of preventing people from taking part in affairs which properly concern them'. Before I continue with more historical facts regarding past Doges, now is a good time to understand the original Venetian Constitution (if only I could)!

Firstly, there was the *Great Council*, made up of about 2,000 people from a limited number of families, mostly from the noblest and wealthiest Venetian stock. They were instrumental in setting up the extremely powerful *Council of Ten,* which was initially set up as a temporary unit to bring some stability to Venice following a failed coup in 1310 by Bajamonte Tiepolo, the Council of Ten being responsible for the security of the Republic. This Council of Ten built up an army of spies to watch over future plots against the Republic, plots by both exiles and Venetians alike. This powerful group of Venetians assisted in streamlining the government's decision-making process, and were elected by the Great Council for a term of one year only, and could not be re-elected until two years had passed (every other year). No two single-family members could serve on the council at the same time. From this new Constitution there evolved the process, in 1268, for the election of the Doge which read as follows:

From the Great Council 30 were chosen by lot

The 30 were reduced by lot to 9

The 9 named 40

The 40 were reduced by lot to 12

The 12 named 25

The 25 were reduced by lot to 9

The 9 named 45

The 45 were reduced by lot to 11

The 11 named 41

The 41 nominated the Doge, for approval by the Assembly

Now that I have made that perfectly clear (if only), perhaps a short history relating to the Doge would be timely. There were almost 100 of them elected from their inception in 697 until the fall of the Republic in 1797. Whilst they were considered to be the prime figurehead in Venice during their term, they were constantly under strict surveillance and had many restrictions imposed upon them. For instance, they could not own property in a foreign land, and could only open dispatches when officials were present, but they were allowed to continue trading independently, as their salary was considered to be minuscule. Their office was for life, unless they committed a misdemeanour (some **did**), but the majority of them were seldom elected to office until they were advanced in years. Let's look at a few, the figures in brackets indicate their term of office.

In the year 1000, *Doge Pietro Orseolo* II (991–1008) took a fleet of ships down the Adriatic to eradicate the threat of pirates. His flagship bore the banner of St Mark (Winged Lion) for the first time. Successfully beating the pirates, the Doge was given the title 'Duke of Dalmatia', which proved profitable for Venice. In commemoration of the victories over the Dalmatians, on each Ascension Day the Doge and Bishop of Castello, with other notables, would sail out to the Lido, and on to the Adriatic. Once there, prayers were said. Later, in the 16th century, this feast day was made more prominent and consisted of throwing a gold ring into the sea.

Doge Pietro Candiano IV (959–976) was elected Doge after previously being a pirate. This was in order to stifle his mercenary exploits. After trying to manipulate Venetian administration, he was confronted with a major riot, which resulted in the Basilica San Marco being almost destroyed by fire. Whilst attempting to flee from the rioters, he was killed by the mob!

Doge Otto Orseolo (1008–1026) was the youngest Doge to be elected, at the age of 16, following his father, but unfortunately he was later exiled to Constantinople for a misdemeanour.

Doge Vitale Michiel II (1156–1172) was responsible for setting up the six *sesteri* (districts) in order to collect money to fight the Byzantines when they confiscated property from the Venetians. The fleet set sail in 1171 to Constantinople to negotiate with the Byzantine Emperor, but it was to no avail. Doge Vitale Michiel returned to Venice with the two columns that now stand on the Piazza, but was killed by a mob riot brought about by his failure against the Byzantines.

Doge Sebastiano Ziani (1172–1178) was responsible for setting up guilds for craftsman, artisans and shopkeepers (introducing weights and measure standards). He was also responsible for hosting a major meeting between the then Pope, Alexander, and

Emperor Fredrick I, to unify and consolidate relationships with the Byzantines (1177).

Doge Pietro Gradenigo (1289–1311) was in office when Marco Polo returned home in 1295; he was one of the most controversial Doges, having made numerous reforms to the Great Council. An attempted coup was planned during his reign, which eventually resulted in the formation of the Venetian Constitution. Another coup was attempted, in 1354, by *Doge Marino Falier,* which, as I have explained in an earlier chapter, was suppressed, resulting in the Doge being beheaded in the Palazzo Ducale.

Doge Francesco Foscari (1423–1457) was renowned for his military and war campaigns against Milan, which lasted almost two decades.

Doge Andrea Gritti (1521–1523) was equally renowned for being a distinguished diplomat and military tactician; he was responsible for concluding a treaty with Charles V, thereby ending Venice's active involvement in the Italian Wars.

Doge Pietro Grimani (1741–1752) was responsible for constructing huge sea walls (Murazzi) for the sea defences of the city. The walls were made of Istrian stone and were some 14m wide and 4m high. Work continued with this mammoth task until 1786.

Finally, I must mention *Doge Lodovico Manin* (1789–1797), who staged the most elaborate celebrations ever when he was appointed, even though he was purported to be a modest person. Manin, unfortunately, will always be remembered as the last Doge in office, following the French occupation on the 15th May 1797. After 1,000 years of elected Doges, Manin abdicated as the French entered the city.

Having attempted to paint a brief picture of the Doge and the Venetian Constitution, it is time to talk about the final building on today's itinerary, *Palazzo Ducale*. Again, the traveller must visit this wonderful building to really appreciate its beauty, as I have done several times in the past, but, for now, a short narrative will hopefully whet the appetite.

The Palazzo Ducale has been rebuilt many times in the past due to fire, and construction of the present building started in 1340. The pink Verona marble façade with its majestic capitals supporting Istrian stone arcades was rebuilt in the Gothic style. Particularly nice is the balconied window facing the Lagoon, which dates from around 1404 and was designed by Pierpaolo and Paolo delle Masegne, the crown of the balcony, however, being built much later. Research tells me that the design of the Palazzo is attributed to Filippo Calendario, whilst Giovanni and Bartolomeo Buon were responsible for the *Porta della Carta*, which is situated on the Piazzetta side of the building. The Porta della Carta (ceremonial entrance) got its name from the area where scribes worked and kept their archives (*carta* meaning paper), and on display is an excellent sculpture of Doge Francesco Foscari kneeling before the Lion of St Mark. The oldest part of the building is the façade overlooking the waterfront, which is festooned with 14th- and 15th- century capitals, as is the Piazzetta side, some of the latter, however, having long been replaced. The Gothic design, which is finished with a delightful variation of decorative sculptured work, was originally painted and gilded, with the Piazzetta façade having an extremely attractive balcony with a wonderful piece of sculpture depicting *The Statue of Justice* standing high above its sheltered arch. Each of the façade's mentioned have an amazing portico supported by robust columns that provide a spectacular vista for travellers when approaching Venice from the Bacino de San Marco, a view which I shall always remember from my first visit.

The current public entrance to the Palazzo Ducale, (called the *Porta del Frumen)* is accessed by walking beneath the portico on the waterfront side, and it is here where our exploration begins. Before entering the Palazzo, you are asked to store your hand luggage in a secure area by security staff. Don't be surprised to see other tourists retaining theirs. I can never fully understand why this happens! The interior of the Palazzo is made up of four floors, each floor having a wealth of treasures to see. There are splendid halls to see, highly embellished walls and ceilings and fascinating chambers, each chamber preserving centuries of history. I have decided not to enter each area in chronological order as this is simply impossible for me to record. Instead I hope to provide an interesting commentary, without, hopefully, undermining this incredible building and each area of interest, and simply record my visit floor by floor, even though I will be moving backwards and forwards to capture as much as I can.

The ground floor area of the Palazzo accommodates the grandiose courtyard with its ceremonial staircase, which was built in 1485. Within the courtyard sits the *Scala dei Giganti*. This giant staircase has figures of *Neptune* and *Mars* prominently positioned at either side of the summit. Close to the stairs is an archway dedicated to Doge Francesco Foscari (1423–1457) which is finished in bands of Istrian stone and red Venetian marble. There are also other statues within the courtyard, namely those of *Adam and Eve*, which sit opposite, facing the staircase. Beyond the staircase is the 16th century Senators Courtyard (close to the Palazzo's entrance). There I pass under the arcade which leads to the *Scala dei Censori* (the Censors' staircase) from where visitors can walk to the upper floors. Still on the ground floor, to the left of the visitors' entrance, is the *Museo dell Opera*, which was once the offices for the maintenance and upkeep of the building. Today, documents and artefacts are stored here. Within the Museo are six rooms which display some original capitals and columns depicting parables both historic and mythical which I found very interesting architecturally but difficult to understand in political or religious terms. The artefacts on display were part of a major restoration plan, started in the latter part of the 20th century, which involved the removal and preservation of many columns and capitals thought to be fragile and valuable and in need of immediate attention, all of which were replaced with replicas. Each of these six rooms deserves a visit, as they do provide the visitor with an overview of just how talented the craftsmen who worked on these original pieces really were, and there is an amazing amount of biblical reference and social history depicted in the sculptured stone. One particular capital on display in Room 3 was once described by John Ruskin as being 'the most beautiful in Europe', which depicts Adam and Eve at the time of the Creation.

From this area, I now move up the first two flights of the Scala dei Censori, which takes me to the Loggia overlooking the Courtyard, which runs around three sides of the Palazzo. This area is now used by the Venetian Heritage Group and Museum Authorities. Originally these areas were used by the Venetian government and there are several *'bocche di leone'*, which were special letterboxes provided for Venetians to post accusations of an unyielding nature regarding their fellow neighbours, which would, if found to be of a criminal or religious nature, incite immediate action from government officials! Still on the Loggia floor, I now see the *Scala d'Oro*, or Golden Staircase, which is architecturally accredited to Jacopo Sansovino, whilst the décor is attributed to both Alessandro Vittoria and Giambattista Franco. On the second flight of the Scala d'Oro (first floor), I now arrive at the Doge's Apartments, the Chamber of Government and the Prisons.

Although rebuilt in the late 15th century, following a fire, the *Doge's Apartments* offer a variety of interesting rooms which clearly advertise the prestigious role this elected leader enjoyed, well, almost every one of them. The *Sala dello Scudo* is the first of the rooms to visit, and on display there are large globes and wall maps, which served to prove to visiting guests or audiences that Venice was powerful and knowledgeable globally. The historic maps on display are works by Francesco Grisellini and probably date to 1762. I can only imagine just how impressed early onlookers would have been when confronted with these globes, which not only show the earth's surface but also lunar spheres. Moving on, I enter the *Sala Grimani*, whose name was significant in the old Republic as there had been three Doges from this powerful family. In addition to the magnificent ceiling in this room, there is also a wonderful fireplace on show. Complementing the ceiling are large panelled friezes by Andrea Vicento depicting a plethora of academic, religious and historical events. Next to see, is the *Sala Erizzo*, which is a slightly larger room, showing the Erizzo family coat of arms clearly displayed; Doge Erizzo was known for his military achievements. I now pass the *Sala Pruli* with its fine stuccowork, which takes me on to the *Sala dei Filosofi*. Originally this room housed many works by Veronese, which were removed in the 20th century for one reason or other, but nevertheless there is some nice stucco work to admire, as well as a fresco by Titian above the door. The next two adjoining rooms, *Sala Corner* and *Sala dei Ritratti*, have some very nice paintings on display, my favourite being *'Madonna and Child Enthroned'* by Alvisi Vivarini. Finally, I arrive at the *Sala degli Scudieri*, which once was the room for the Equerries, appointed by the Doge, who were on call 24 hours a day. Just imagine how active this area was in times of strife. The doors from this room lead back to the landing of the Scala d'Oro.

I now leave the Doges' Apartments and head in the direction of the *Chambers of Government*, which occupy the major footprint of the first floor, the most significant rooms being the *Sala del Maggior Consiglio* and the *Sala del Scrutino*. Rooms on this concourse housed the legislative, judicial and executive members of the government and are extravagantly decorated to impress all who enter them. I'll come back to these two rooms in a while, for now I am climbing the staircase again and move into the *Sala delle Quatto Porte*, with its amazing décor by Andrea Palladio and Giovanni Rusconi. The barrel-vaulted ceiling is a masterpiece of white stucco and gilding, and there are frescoes by Tintoretto in addition to numerous other works by past masters.   Next, I make my way to the *Sala Dell Anticollegio* and the *Sala del Collegio*, which, as you would expect, are also decorated magnificently, again displaying masterpieces by Tintoretto, Veronese and Aspetti, my favourite piece being *Mars and Neptune* with the Campanile cleverly displayed in the distance. The ceiling work in the Sala del Collegio really does require lots of studying time to fully appreciate the craft and skill that is on display.

It is time now to move on to the *Sala del Consiglio dei Dieci* (Council of Ten), an impressive room, which accommodated this hierarchal and powerful group of men; I think this room is my favourite in all the Palazzo, if one is allowed to have a favourite amongst so much beauty. Both the ceiling and the frieze are breathtaking, and when reconstruction work by Scarpagnino was completed, Ponchino, Zalotti and Veronese concentrated on the artwork. Amongst some of the masterpieces here are *'An Aged Oriental Man', 'A Young Woman'* and *'Adoration of the Magi'*. Unfortunately, the central panel of the ceiling is not the original, as this is now housed in the Louvre. The next room to view is the *Sala della Bussola*, which although wonderfully decorated is quite an imposing area. I use the word 'imposing' as I have read several accounts of judicial execution, which at times was said to be horrendous.

From here I travel to the *Armoury*, which can boast an equally attractive group of decorative rooms, which, as the name would indicate, hold a collection of weapons, armour and tools of torture! Then, from the Armoury rooms, I enter the *Liago* (a corridor), which has a very attractive ceiling with painted and gilded beams.

It is now time to walk back down to the first floor again, and I make my way to the magnificent, and I mean magnificent, *Sala del Maggior Consiglio*, which is by far the most majestic, commanding and authorative chamber in the building, which was used by the Maggior Consiglio, who were a body of the younger men of the Venetian Republic who had some say in the running of the city. Every time I enter this room (or more aptly hall) I am overwhelmed by its size, a room that was built in the 14th century and has some remarkable paintings dating from 1365 on display. It really is difficult to describe this space and not undermine just how wonderful it is. It could hold as many as 2,400 patriarchs, which gives you some idea of its size. Although the room was partly damaged by fire in 1577, it was decided to retain the original features and commission new artists to decorate both the ceiling and walls, a monumental task even for the master artists of the day. There are many works by Tintoretto, Veronese and Bassano, to name but a few. The enormous panelled ceiling was completed in 1584 while the walls were thought to have been completed some 20 years later, which I can well understand, as the sheer volume of artwork on display is overwhelming. Again, I do have some favourites, the main one being *'Paradise'* by Tintoretto, which stands mighty and majestic and encompasses the entire end wall (with the raised podium); he worked on this masterpiece between 1588 and 1594. Then there is *'The Triumph of Venice'* by Veronese (1582), which is sited in the centre of the ceiling at the same end as Tintoretto's *'Paradise'*. One simply cannot leave this room without spending some time studying the frieze, which depicts a large number of portraits of Doges, painted by Tintoretto's son, Domenico, which, although thought to be purely imaginary images, do add to the historical interest, especially the one that is shown simply as a black curtain, which represents the Doge Marino Falier (1354–1355), who, as I mentioned earlier, was beheaded for his conspiracy against the Venetian Republic

There is one room left which I would like to mention, called the *Sala della Scrutino*, which was formerly used for voting purposes whenever constitutional issues occured. In this room, we have outstanding paintings of Venetian naval victories and, again, almost all of the works are accredited to Tintoretto, Veronese and their pupils. This room, like the previous one, also has a frieze which serves to display the remainder of portraits representing former Doges.

Even though I didn't actually visit the Palazzo Ducale today, its presence is clearly in my mind as I write this short narrative. Hopefully, I have been able to convey just how splendid a building this is, and a building which must be seen to be believed. Louise has been promised a tour on her next visit and, as the time is now 4.15pm, it is time to head back to Piazzale Roma. I mentioned earlier that I would be walking back and the walk would be more of a sightseeing cum window-shopping tour for Louise. This can be done on a day trip quite easily, but make sure you have a map just in case. Remember what I said about missing your flight in Chapter 1? If you are not that confident, then I recommend that you jump on the next available vaporetto from San Marco to Ferrovia. As I intend to walk back, I have simply outlined my return route back to Bar S. Lucia below in broad terms, which will eventually get me there by about 6.00pm and in time for some welcome refreshment.

Having left the Palazzo Ducale area, I am looking forward to grabbing a coffee soon, and the route I take back will enable Louise to see some of the Rialto and the Ghetto area as well as scores of jewellery and glass shops. This can be achieved quite easily in an hour, but should you get lost on the way, then simply follow the street signs arrowed either 'Piazzale Roma' or 'Ferrovia'.

- Merc d. Orologio (Clock Tower)
- Merceria S. Zulian
- Merceria calle san Salvador
- Via 2 Aprille (San Bartolomeo)
- Ponte Rialto (Rialto Bridge and shops)
- Saliz San Giovanni Crisostomo
- Campo dei Apostoli
- Strada Nova
- Rio terra della Maddalena
- Rio terra S. Leonardo
- Campo Ghetto
- Rio terra Lista di Spagna (Bar S. Lucia)

We arrive at Bar S. Lucia at 6.05pm. Not a bad guess. The bar is quite full this evening but there is still a table at the rear, which we grab, and it is nice to be welcomed back by our host, Enrico, who has my Guinness and Louise's vodka and Coke on the table within a couple of minutes. While relaxing and recapping on our travels today, as well as enjoying a spinach ricotta, I reiterate the fact that Venice should be enjoyed at a leisurely pace, which I think we succeeded in doing today. Having said that, Loiuse pointed out, as a first-time visitor, that she thought it was important to plan ahead, and although Venice can still be enjoyed by casually walking wherever your fancy takes you, the day visitor must be aware of the time constraints getting back to the airport.

Having rested, and feeling refreshed, we head back to the bus station at Piazzale Roma, which takes about 10 minutes, and arrive a few minutes before our No. 5 bus pulls in. The journey to Marco Polo takes about 20 minutes and we are one of the first to the checkin. Unfortunately, pre-booking is not possible on the return flights. Still time left to wander around the departure lounge. Unfortunately, the majority of shops close at 8.00pm, also, regrettably, the ice cream parlour, which I was looking forward to, so we sit comfortably until our flight is called. Chatting on the flight home, I reminded Louise that although Venice is a relatively small city, there is so much to see and, obviously, what we saw today was just an appetiser. But I was pleased to have been able to take her to so many wonderful sights and help her to understand some of its history and beauty and why I enjoy the 'Serenissima' so much. The flight home was comfortable and I am already planning an interim trip before my scheduled February one (which, incidentally, will be the *Carnevale* period) as I want to spend a whole day wandering around the *Ca'Rezzonico* and the *Peggy Guggenheim Museum*. Can't wait.

Buonasera Venezia

CHAPTER 6
FEBRUARY: The Eastern District

'From the Age of Decadence to the Age of War'

St Valentines Day, to many, means a time of romance, pageantry and celebration, but in more recent times it has been infamously associated with massacres and warfare. Attempting to bring all these characteristics together seems appropriate for my next chapter and my visit to Venice this month, as I intend to capture the atmosphere of *'Carnevale'* and at the same time discover how past Venetians prepared themselves for war. In doing so, my journey today will cover many different aspects of Venetian history and will take me from the Piazza San Marco on a short trail that very few tourists seem to take, but one which I consider to be both scenic and extremely interesting.

Last month, I provided quite an extensive overview of the Piazza San Marco, and, therefore, although I shall spend some time at this location again today, enjoying the carnival atmosphere, I intend only to talk about Carnevale as it presents itself in the Piazza, and, of course, some of its history and theatre.

My travels today will take me along the 'Lagoon promenade' to what is known as the *Eastern District* (part of the Castello *sesteire* which will feature in the July chapter), as this area is the principal

February 2007

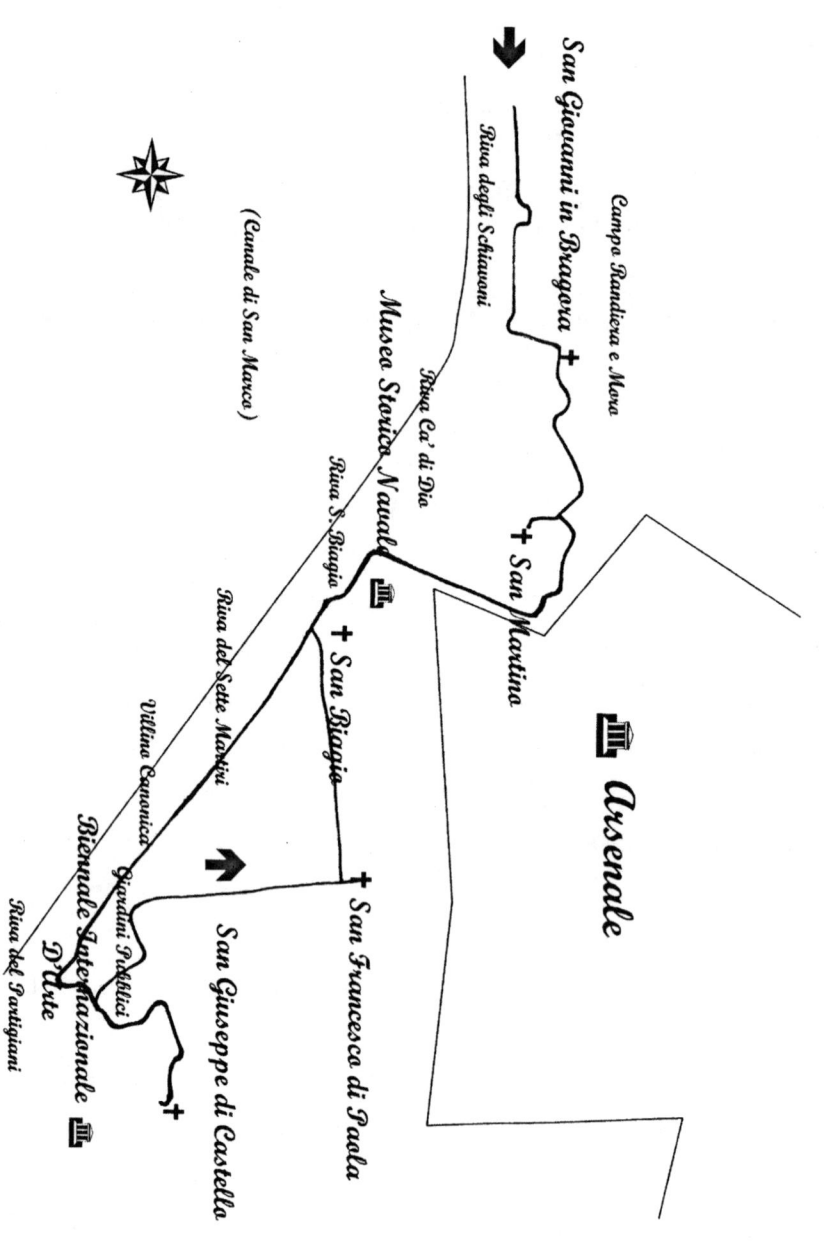

Campo Bandiera e Mora

San Giovanni in Bragora

Riva degli Schiavoni

Riva Ca' di Dio

Musea Storico Navale

(Canale di San Marco)

Riva S. Biagio

+ San Martino

Riva del Sette Martiri

+ San Biagio

Villina Canonica

Arsenale

Giardini Pubblici

Biennale Internazionale D'Arte

+ San Francesca di Paola

San Giuseppe di Castello

Riva del Partigiani

site of the former Venetian naval dockyards and arsenal, which is known as the *Arsenale*. From the Arsenale, I will be taking a relatively short walk through the public gardens and, at the same time, find time en route to highlight some appealing and picturesque churches and monuments. As the actual walking part of my journey today will probably take no more than three hours, I have provisionally planned my itinerary to include a trip to the top of the *Campanile*, which was closed last month, to photograph the celebrations below on the Piazza, before I eventually make my way back to Piazzale Roma. Most of my research for today will have been completed prior to my visit, as I intend to enjoy whatever celebrations are in hand, and my travelling pack will simply consist of my small digital camera, digital recorder and map.

* **February 14th 2007**

The weather at 4.45am on this Surrey winter morning is extremely damp; it is pouring down with rain as I set off again for wonderful Venice. Once through the security checks at Gatwick, I make my way as usual to the breakfast area in the departure lounge before getting my 6.45am flight to Marco Polo airport. Whilst waiting for my flight, I get the opportunity to read an article about the Seige of Venice in 1848, which is very interesting and informative in as much as this and a future chapter will highlight the short but courageous lives of both Daniele Manin and Giuseppe Garibaldi.

The outgoing flight was on time again and, armed with my reading material, the 1 hour 40 minute flight seemed to pass remarkably quickly. When I arrive at the ticket office in the airport, I discover that my ACTV day pass will now cost me 13 euros. Still a bargain, considering one can travel almost everywhere on it throughout the day. Incidentally, whilst spending many hours researching for my journal, I have come across an entry form for a national competition to redesign the ACTV pontiles in Venice. Whilst the entry criteria seem daunting, I just might investigate further (more details in the April chapter).

The normally incident-free journey from the airport to Piazzale Roma was hampered slightly today due to some form of political demonstration by locals who were driving in convey back and forwards across the Ponte della Liberta. Fortunately, this only put another 10 minutes on the journey. On arrival at the bus depot, I directed some English tourists to the ACTV pontile, where they boarded their vaporetto, which incidentally was also the one I was travelling on, and I managed to get seats at the rear of the vessel, which gave them a good vantage point for photographs on their journey to the Rialto. Even though I had seen several people in costumes on the trip along the Canal, I was amazed at how many people there were in costume around the pontile area alone. Carnevale was definitely in full flight. As I walked along the Riva degli Schia Schiavoni towards the Molo, there were dozens of costumed characters, mostly in pairs, parading along this quayside just in front of the Giardini Reali (Royal Gardens) wearing costumes depicting 18th- century characters. Although I have witnessed Carnevale several times now, it still amazes me just how much effort, time and expense people put into reproducing this spectacle, and just how much enjoyment they have, not to mention the pleasure they give to the thousands of spectators who descend upon Venice at this time of the year. Fortunately, my journey today will not only allow me to travel along most of the southern Lagoon 'promenade' and enjoy the scenery, but will also give me ample time to enjoy the festivities in the Piazza later, when I return.

From my vantage point at the Molo, I can't help but notice the many street traders positioned along the Riva Schiavoni and columns of tourists making their way to the Piazza from the opposite direction. But, for now, I simply glimpse at the Piazzetta and walk past on my way to the lower eastern region of Castello. The view looking down towards the three 'promenades', which follow the contour of the lower part of the Lagoon, is a colourful sight on most days, but today, as I stroll along taking photographs, there is a real theatre flavour, with so many 'performers' posing and re-enacting those heady and promiscuous bygone times. Apart from the general tourists, there are also many professional photographers at work who seem to attract the best of the play actors, which is a real bonus to people like me who can take advantage of a snapshot while they are working on their 'studio' poses. Standing on the Ponte d. Paglia (the first bridge after the Palazzo Ducale), several performers are positioned with their backs to the Ponte d. Sospiri (Bridge of Sighs), which really does add a Renaissance flavour to the finished photograph, a scene which most tourists, like myself, will treasure.

As I reach the end of the Riva de Schiavoni, I now turn left into the Calle del Dose, which will lead to the first church on my itinerary for today, which is the San Giovanni in Bragora. Along the concourse of this calle are several small restaurants, which serve some very nice meals. A set meal, for instance, will cost around 25 euros, which is extremely good value considering the location. Having now reached Campo Bandiera e Moro, I am facing the former Palazzo Gritti, which is now the Hotel Residensa, and which has an extremely well renovated façade. I suspect that it has recently been renovated as there is still a fair amount of scaffolding around this building and work on the roof still appears to be unfinished. The façade is finished in Istrian stone and has a very attractive five-arched mullioned window on the piano nobile, a fine example of Gothic architecture.

The campo itself has a number of attractive buildings all varied in design, which compliment the austere if somewhat unassuming façade of the church of *San Giovanni in Bragora*. This well preserved church, which was rebuilt in 1475 by Michelle Cadussi, is on the site of the original church built in the 8th century, which was founded by the Bishop of Odenzo. The church is dedicated to Saint Giovanni Battista and Bragona, named either after '*bragola*', meaning 'market square', or '*bragolare*', meaning 'fishing'. The façade of the church is probably the only original piece of construction, and has a red brick finish with a central door positioned under a Gothic arch. This is framed by arches either side which stand above two small doors. When I say the church is unassuming, I should add that it does have a rather attractive three-bell tower, which stands to the right of the façade, hidden slightly by the curve of the main church walls. The church comes alive once I am inside, as I immediately notice the Gothic basilica design footprint, which has three naves, three apses and a wonderful ceiling with exposed beams designed like a ship's hull. This ceiling design really does release a mysterious opulence which I can't describe. Columns from the original church are on show and there are some notable paintings to view, especially the '*Battesimo di Cristo*' by Cuna da Conegliano (1492–1494). Other artists with work on display include Vivarini and Lugano. I also discovered that Vivaldi was born in one of the houses in the Campo. Unfortunately, I can't find out which one at present.

Time to leave Campo Bandiera e Moro, so I make my way back and join the Calle Crosera, which takes me on to the Calle Erizzo. This short walk takes me past some very interesting small shops and a trattoria, before I reach a small bridge, which I cross and which will eventually lead me to the church of San Martino, looking out for the sign reading 'Vincenzo Gagluardi' as a guide. Again, when I first view San Martino from the exterior it reminds me very much of the last church, as it also has a similar brick façade. Having said that, the main entrance is beautifully sculptured in stone together with several other small fashioned pieces above the head of each brick pier. San Martino was originally designed by Sansovino, and enlarged later in 1540. Inside, it has a really beautiful Renaissance altar, built by Tullio Lombardo, which is situated in the left aisle and was built in 1484. This altar originally belonged to the church of San Sepolero di Gerusolemane, from where it was removed when the church was demolished in 1807 by Napoleon to create more room for the Arsenale. San Marino is named after Saint Martin, who has an annual festival held in November in his honour. Domenico Bruni originally painted the ornate ceiling decoration, and the remains of Doge Francesco Erizzo (1631–1646) are buried in the middle aisle. Before leaving the church of San Martino, I must add that this church is not normally open for visitors in the morning, so be mindful of this fact. I now head west along the Fondamenta di Fronte, which will take me to the *Arsenale,* I notice that it is still only 12.15pm and there is still lots to see and plenty of time to see everything.

Access to the interior of the Arsenale is forbidden (other than on some special excursions) as it is still a **N**aval institution, but that doesn't disguise the fact that this iconic fortification has a very distinguished past. The entrance gateway to the Arsenale is classical Renaissance with some Byzantine sculpture added, and was built by Antonio Gambello in the mid-15th century. Above the doorway there is a wonderful tympanum with a sculpture of the Lion of St Mark and, below, positioned in the main gateway area, stand four magnificent lions, which were taken by Venetians as spoils of war. To the right of the gateway, on either side of the Rio dell Arsenale, stand two powerful-looking watchtowers, finished in red brick and stone, which guard the entrance to the dockyard, and immediately in front of them stands an ageing wooden bridge. The entire area surrounding the Arsenale is so picturesque and the view from the Ponte de Arsenale del Paradiso (what a name), looking back along the Rio dell Arsenale canal towards the Lagoon, makes a romantic but powerful statement for every visitor today, as it must have done in days gone by.

The Arsenale really evolved in the 12th century as a repair and stores depot for the Venetian Republic, as there were many other shipyards in operation. In the 14th century the government of Venice decided to increase the number of galleys it built, and eventually the Arsenale became the biggest shipbuilding yard in Europe, if not the world. The Arsenale workers (*Arsenalotti*) generally consisted of small but specialised teams of tradesmen and artisans who collectively became a militant force who were not afraid to voice their opinions. On one occasion, they rioted, in 1569, when they forced their way into the Palazzo Ducale and demanded an audience with the Doge himself, which they succeed in getting, as this colony of workers were held in high esteem by the government and were awarded many social privileges because of their value to the economy, defence and support of Venice. Apart from their prime task of building, maintaining and servicing galleys and the like, they were often called upon to act as firefighters when needs arose, as well as being a unified body who acted as guards of honour for the Doge. Many books have been written about the power, glory and social standing of the Arsenale and its workers, and while researching material for my journal I discovered several observations from visitors between the 13th and 17th centuries, which I think summarise this incredible community.

Pero Tafur (13th-century Traveller and Adventurer) wrote: 'this was the most advanced arsenal in the world, with the most up to date navigational aides, there were 80 galleys moored in addition to other vessels'. He also gave a remarkable description of the 'call to arms', which reads:

'Once the Council Bell was rung, within one hour the square was full of men who received pay and went into the Arsenale. Upon entering the Arsenale there are great streets either side of the canal and out came a galley towed by a boat. From the windows of houses either side of this canal (10 houses in total) each galley was handed cordage, bread, arms, ballistae and mortars, in fact everything that was required. When the galley had reached the end of the street all the men required were on board together with the full complement of oars, and each galley was fully equipped and armed from end to end, all within six hours.'

William Thomas (16th-century Traveller, Art Critic and Writer) wrote:

'There were at least 200 galleys that could be furnished and out to sea in a short period of time ... Having the staple amount of timber they could build a galley, complete, every day of the year ... 16,000 people work in the Arsenale every day, enabling them to have their masts, cables, sails, anchors, rudders and oars etc pre-made and stored.'

John Evelyn (17th-century Diarist, Scholar and Gardener) wrote:

'The foundry where they cast their iron is 450 paces long and has 13 furnaces, forges were continuously at work ... One canon weighing thousands of pounds was being cast and eventually completed during the royal visit [reference to the visit of Henry III of France] ... There are arms and stores to equip 800,000 men, and one gallery is 200 yards long for cables ... There is a continuous supply of fresh water available, and they have placed 2 rhinoceros's horns in the well to keep the water from poisoning.'

What a spectacular sight this must have been to Venetians and visitors alike when the Republic was in its prime, and as my interest is still aroused with ships and naval history, what better place to visit next than the *Museo Storico Navale* (Naval Museum). This building is literally a stone's throw from the Arsenale, so I cross the wooden bridge and make my way down the Fondamenta dell Arsenale in the direction of the Lagoon. Within five minutes, I arrive at Campo S. Biagio, where I will explore the treasures of the Naval Museum. The museum building was once a 15th-century granary used to bake '*biscotti* and bread' for the Venetian Navy. Most of the 25,000 items on display in the museum were originally secured in the Arsenale, Casa dei Modelli, where models and other important artefacts were stored. Unfortunately, many of the finely crafted models disappeared when the French sacked the island in 1797.

As I enter the Museo Storico Navale, which was founded as recently as 1919, I am very impressed by the relatively small entrance fee of 1.55 euros, which, for the number of treasures on display, is fantastic value. There are numerous rooms both large and small inside the museum to explore, located on several floors, each area specialising in naval memorabilia, and I intend to visit them all. From the entrance lobby, which has an enormous 16th-century galley lantern on display, I take note of a notice which informs visitors of what they are about to see and also explains that the models on display were actually used for shipbuilding, as apposed to simply working from scaled drawings. The notice also reminds each visitor that the collection includes not only Venetian ships and boats but also the craft built here for both the French and Austrian navies during their time of occupation. In addition to this, there is also a large collection of model fishing vessels from China and the Far East to see on the top floor. I should also explain that this building is a maze of rooms, so in order to gain some understanding of its orientation I am simply circumnavigating the building in an ad hoc fashion.

The first area of the museum I arrive at is the *Cannons' Room*, where there is an enormous cannon, weighing 90lbs, which was designed by Cosino Cenni. This cannon sat mid-deck on a Tuscan galley of 1643. There are many wooden models depicting various islands and foreign fortresses, each sculptured in a papier-mâché material, and framed and displayed on the walls. These were considered to be extremely secret in their day, as they held a wealth of information regarding naval fortifications. Moving on, I now enter the *Armaments' Room*, which houses small weapons etc. There are large muskets on show from the 16th century which have a 25-mm bore and served as small cannons which rested on the ship's deck and were used for close combat, mainly to damage the masts of enemy ships. Again, there are plenty of maps showing enemy fortifications around Europe as well as a 13th-century mortar war weapon used in the Genoa War. By contrast, when I enter the next room, still on the ground floor, named *Twentieth-*

century Weapons, there are machine guns, a mini-submarine, small boats and a collection of early radar instruments to view close up. Continuing still further, I arrive at the *Model Vessel Room*, which for me as an artist is really fascinating as there are many scaled models of various galleys that were built here throughout the 14th and 18th centuries including one that wasn't, *HMS Victory*. Yes, our very own, the only difference being that its hull is finished simply as varnished wood and not the familiar colour we see in Portsmouth today. Besides the *Victory*, one other model really does stand out, which is a 16th-century Dutch galley, modelled to perfection by talented craftsmen. Incidentally, I'm not sure what scale these models are, in fact. They must vary considerably from craft to craft but each one is fairly substantial in size. Walking back to my starting point, I get to the *Main Staircase*, where there is a very large globe, dating from the 15th century, surrounded by several ships' ornaments also of the 15th century. These are in turn overshadowed by tapestries depicting naval battles and a wall plaque of the coat of arms for the ceremonial vessel owned by the Morosini family.

Having climbed the stairs to the first floor, I now enter the *Map and Instrument Room*, where there are cabinets displaying 18th-century navigational equipment and associated instruments. To complement this equipment, there are some interesting books containing ancient maps used by early explorers. One, in particular, grabbed my attention: it was by P.Corneli (1692) and consisted of charts of the New World. Moving on and upwards, I now ascend the staircase to the *Second Floor* and, after glancing over several artefacts in the first room, make my way to the second room, which has models of the Arsenale showing the eastern entrance, which, from its condition, was apparently under repair at the time.

As I leave this room, I move into a much larger room where the model vessels are on a massive scale. Seeing is believing. There are three cabinets which house 16th-century models all around 2m in length, and range from the *Fusta*, which was a combat vessel with 24 benches for oarsmen, to the *Friscata*, an 18-bench frigate used for close-range warfare, and lastly to the *Briganto* class, which was a 28-benched look-out vessel. Perhaps the most spectacular model in this room is of the 16th-century *trireme*, which was a colossal warship of its time. There were three rows of oarsmen who sat either side on the 16 benches, each bench using a 56-kg oar. This warship was armed with a large battering ram and had six sails.

There really is so much to see in this museum and I have only glimpsed at its treasures, but my most memorable vessel on display was a Venetian Galley in *Room 15*. This model seemed to be on an even larger scale than the rest and its finely crafted detail depicted a warship, which when built to operational size was 50m in length by 12m in width; it had 49 canons on one deck and was pulled by 343 oarsmen. The total crew displacement was 700! As I walk back down the staircase, I take note, on the second-floor landing, of the artefacts dedicated to Admiral Morosini, who defeated the Turks in the 17th century. Morosini became Doge of Venice in 1688 and fortuitously lived through the extensive plague epidemic, which crippled the Navy of that day.

Before finally leaving this gem of a building, I try to imagine just how vibrant and active the Arsenale area must have been in its heyday, and how proud the Venetians must have been to call themselves 'masters of the sea'. Today the Arsenale that is on view to the public still sends a powerful message to visitors about the once magnificent Venetian fleet and still retains most of its architectural history for all to enjoy. The time is now 1.30pm as

I leave the museum and begin my walk along the Riva Biagio towards my next destination, which will be the Giardini Pubblici (Public Gardens).

The sun is particularly noticeable as I stroll along the surprisingly empty quayside, in the direction of the Giardini Pubblici, as it reflects on the Lagoon whilst I look across to the Lido. This is a good time to take a photograph, looking back towards the Molo with the Campanile, Palazzo Ducale, Salute and San Giorgio Maggiore in view, which I can capture in one frame from this perspective: a worthy challenge to sketch back in my studio. Even though I have taken scores of photographs from this angle and painted many watercolours from this view, today there is that extra sparkle in the water, which unfolds a magical fascination. Having crossed the small bridge over the Rio della Tana, I am now walking along the Riva dei Sette Martiri, and the next memorable building that comes into view is the Villino Canonica. This really is a very attractive building, which sits proudly on the Riva with its tympanum above the doorway and small balcony above. On either side of the main door there are inlaid framed marble panels which contrast perfectly with the buff titanium-coloured rendered walls. All areas of the rendered walls are again framed with red brick, which to my mind gives the whole façade a very Venetian look. I should also mention the impressive arched loggia in the adjoining garden to Villino Canonica, which is set back and surrounded by a group of tall mature trees. This unassuming but very interesting loggia will certainly provide me with some sketching material back home.

From the Canonica, I continue walking along the Riva del Partigiani and cross over the next bridge, which leads me to the entrance to the *Giardini Pubblici* (Public Gardens). Interestingly enough, the *Giardini Esposizione* vaporetto pontile, directly facing the Garden entrance, is a recognised stop for the No. 1 vaporetto, which travels all the way back to Piazzale Roma (handy if you are short on time for your return journey). As I walk into the Public Gardens. I immediately notice a group of bronze and stone statues discreetly positioned near the entrance, where several groups of elderly locals are sitting and chatting, while a brigade of young students from a local school make their way to the vaporetto. I suspect that the locals use the gardens often; I certainly would, as they provide a fantastic view across the Lagoon. Disappointingly, I can't see much grassed area around this particular spot; I certainly think it could do with some colour, as the general appearance is somewhat austere-looking. Having said that, the tree-lined Viale Garibaldi, which is immediately to the left of the entrance, is quite impressive. With that in mind, I shall return and walk this passageway once I have found San Giuseppe Di Castello.

Continuing my walk diagonally across the gardens, I travel under a small archway, which leads into the Riva Teira S. Isepo and which will take me into a small campo. This particular area appears to be extremely run down and has scores of billboards, wall posters and graffiti covering the walls of the surrounding buildings. I can only assume that this particular area of Castello is the poorer part, judging by the general appearance, and probably the least visited by tourists. At the far end of the campo is a small bridge facing me, with the church of *San Giuseppe Di Castello* to my right. Judging by the exterior condition, I suspect that this historical church is closed down, as the main entrance appears to be boarded up, which is a great shame, as I don't like to see buildings slip into decay. Therefore I really do hope that it is on some organisation's list to restore. As I can't enter the church at this time, I'll refer to my research, which tells me that it is 16th century and once formed part of a convent and monastery in the past. It has a single nave, a chorus and a frescoed ceiling. On the left side of the nave is a monument to Doge Marino Grimani, which was designed by Vincenzo Scamozzi. Also housed in the church is another monument to the Procurator Grimani (in the chancel), which is attributed to Alessandro Vittoria. The entire façade of this sorrowful-looking church is in desperate need of some major restoration, as the rendering is clearly falling away from its brickwork, and the once decorative stonework has been ravaged by years of neglect. It breaks my heart to see such a monument waste away. Above the doorway there is a small sculpture depicting a biblical scene, which is framed by a triangular tympana and has two attractive arched windows on either side. Although condition-wise this church is extremely run-down, it still commands an amazing presence and certainly deserves some loving care and attention.

Standing on the small bridge which crosses the Rio de San Giuseppe, looking both east and west, I photograph the reflections of the surrounding buildings in the waterway of the canal, which are so colourful, in addition to capturing the tower of San Anna in the distance. Amazingly, there is a painting by Canaletto called *'View of San Guissepe di Castello'*, which he completed in 1740, showing the church as it was at that time, with paviour's working on the surrounding pavement area. There is also a colourful impressionistic painting of this particular view by John Singer Sergeant.

It is time to backtrack across the campo and part of the gardens in order that I can walk along the Viale Garibaldi, which I mentioned earlier, so, once having arrived back at the main entrance, I turn right before walking along this tree-lined avenue that will eventually take me to the Via Giuseppe Garibaldi. Walking down this concourse reminds me of the many countryside roads in France that Napoleon had built, with tall trees for shade for his returning armies. Sitting to my right is a strange-looking conservatory-type building which is almost derelict; in fact, it has metal acro-props supporting the internal structure, obviously a building of some historical note and one that I must investigate on another day. When I arrive at the end of the Via Garibaldi I am confronted by a large memorial, sculptured in bronze, which as its name would infer is of the Italian patriot and soldier *Giuseppe Garibaldi* (1807 – 1882). Although Garibaldi was not Venetian, he is respected by the islanders as well as by most Italians, and in view of this perhaps I should mention the part he played in the eventual unification of Italy, as I will be writing about Daniele Manin (1804 – 1857) in the June chapter, because of his major role in the Siege of Venice in 1848.

Garibaldi led many military campaigns, described by some as a passage of 'extraordinary daring', which brought about a unified Italy. He was born in 1807 in Nice (which was once an Italian city, before it was taken by the French) and he became a sailor of some merit who rose to the rank of captain. In 1833 Garibaldi was to meet Giuseppe Mazzini, who was a passionate exponent of liberal republicans and social reform and who became a major influence in Garibaldi's political and social life. Having failed in the war waged with Genoa, Garibaldi went into exile in South America where he formed an Italian Legion in 1843, taking the black flag as his banner and adopting the now famous uniform of the 'Red Shirts'. Having been favoured by the newly elected Pope Pius IX, who also was an exponent of the unification of

Italy, Garibaldi with his small army assisted in some revolutionary action in Palermo. Following this uprising, Garibaldi returned to South America, where he was instrumental in raising an army and a fleet for the Uruguayan government against Argentina. He returned to Italy during the Revolution of 1848, offering his services to Charles Albert of Sardinia. During this episode of revolution, Mazzini persuaded Garibaldi to command the defence of Rome, and, together with his wife Anita, he played an important part in the forthcoming battles. But, sadly, the city fell in 1849, following which he fled to the north pursued by the Austrians and the French. Unfortunately, Anita died by his side whilst his army was retreating. In 1850 he managed to reach New York where he settled for a while, before travelling to Europe as a merchant sailor.

Once again, Garibaldi returned to Italy, in 1854, and in 1859 he formed a volunteer unit to fight in the Austian-Piedmontese War. In 1860 he formed a group of 1,000 volunteer 'Red Shirts' who supported the uprising at Palermo and, with his passion for liberation, eventually defeated a 3,000-strong French force at Calatafimi, where he declared himself ruler of Sicily. Being supportive of Victor Emmanuel II, he acknowledged him to be the King of Italy (in title only) and retired, without accepting any reward for his services. It was at this period that Garibaldi set up the famous *International Legion*, bringing together many European forces to finally achieve the liberation of Italy. During these developing years, he offered his services to Abraham Lincoln to fight in the American Civil War (1861), but was courteously fobbed off due to certain demands he made on the President. Finally, in 1866 Garibaldi took up arms again, with the support of the Italian government, during the Austrian–Prussian War, in the hope of taking Venice from the Austrians, which climaxed in the third Italian war of independence. Venice finally was free from Austrian rule and became part of Italy after an armistice was eventually signed. Apart from a few other skirmishes, in one of which he was taken prisoner, Garibaldi eventually gave up his militant liberal views for the sake of Italian unification, and his popularity, his military skills and the fact that he could raise an army from the 'common people' eventually made him the hero of his nation. He died on a remote Italian island in 1882.

Before finally leaving the Giardini Pubblici, I am reminded of an additional place to visit when I am next in Castello, which will be in a later chapter when I walk the inner regions of this *sestiere*, this being the *Venice Biennale* (International Contemporary Art), which is permanently held at the *Biennale Internazionale D'Arte*, located on the east side of the Public Gardens. This event has taken place on every uneven numbered year since 1895, and this year will be held between the 10th June and 21st November, an event I really do enjoy attending.

Back to my itinerary once again, I now leave the Public Gardens, by walking through some impressive iron gates, and facing me is the church of *San Francesco de Paola*, which unfortunately is closed due to the time of day. This is unfortunate, as it is a church which I have found extremely difficult to research due to the minimal amount of information made available, at least in English. With this in mind, I have decided to return to the church before I complete my journal, in an attempt to see what the interior is like. I feel sure that I will not be disappointed.

I am now walking down the Via Giuseppe Garibaldi in the direction of the Lagoon, which gives me the opportunity again to take some very nice photographs of the bridge I crossed earlier, which also gives me a magnificent view of the Salute in the distance. This seemingly major thoroughfare is packed with shops and provides the locals with all their needs in this easterly pocket of the 'Serenissima'. Once I get to the end of this street, I am now back on the Riva S. Bagio where I turn right and make my way back to Piazza San Marco. This walk is fantastic on any day, but today there is a crispness in the air which makes it special for me, and, what's more, there are very few tourists about at this point. That will of course change once I get back to the Molo, where the pageant of Carnevale should be in full swing. It takes a good 15 minutes to stroll back to the Molo, and when I arrive, although the crowds are substantial, there is no queue at the entrance to the Campanile, so I take full advantage of this fact and decide to enter. Having paid my 6 euros to travel by lift to the top of the Campanile, I take advantage of this location to eat a panini and have a soft drink which I brought earlier, in order that I can get the most out of the day without having to stop for lunch. Having said that, I still have plans for some proper food once I get back to the airport.

Once at the top of the Campanile, I realise that this was a good idea because, with the weather being so nice today, I can get some splendid views of the Piazza below, which during Carnevale is very colourful, so while I am here I shall take some photographs of the views from each of the four sides of the viewing balcony. From the east elevation, I get a wonderful view of the entire Riva degli Schiavoni as far down as the Arsenale, where I was earlier, and beyond to the Giardini Pubblica. Just below me I see the rooftop of the Basilica San Marco, displaying its copper and lead roof dressing, and the many access routes for maintaining this wonderful structure. Moving to my left slightly (NW), I can see the island of San Michele and, beyond that, as far as Murano, which I intend to feature with other surrounding Islands in the March chapter. Whilst standing in this viewing balcony, I get a chance to photograph the famous Campanile bells that I mentioned in the last chapter, and I think about the number of times they must have rung in their historic past, to inform Venetians of impending danger, as well as governmental and social declarations. Moving further round to my left, I am now looking directly north and I can see literally thousands of Venice's red- tiled roofs, which are protecting their vulnerable structures below, and I realise just how densely populated this small island really is.

Although there are scores of churches and belltowers to see from this position, I still find it difficult to identify each one, even now, without the aid of my map, and despite the fact that I have viewed Venice from this position several times before, it still amazes me that I cannot see, let alone identify, one internal canal from this high vantage point. Moving around to my left again, I am now looking due south-west and I get the opportunity to take some really nice shots of the Salute and Customs House, which is especially picturesque with the sun being quite low and reflecting on the waters of the Lagoon. This group of photographs will certainly get me painting again, once I return home, and maybe give me some inspiration for the pieces which I intend to enter in the RA Summer Collection. I change my viewing position to the west side of the viewing balcony and immediately below is the Piazza, which is heaving with tourists and locals enjoying themselves watching the circus acts on the temporary staging built especially for Carnevale. This staged area at the Ala Napoleon end of the Piazza takes up a fair proportion of the pavement area, with its parade platform extending towards the Basilica, even so, it still allows plenty of room for the incidental entertainers to play-act and perform. From this viewpoint, I really do get a splendid view of the Dorsoduro *sestiere*, which will feature in a later chapter, and even beyond that into the Canale di Fusina.

Moving around to the south elevation of the Campanile, I have the beautiful island of San Giorgio Maggiore facing me, with its superb church (a feature to record in every artist's sketchbook or photo album). In April I propose to visit this small island together with La Giudecca and the Lido and spend a whole chapter exploring their treasures and enjoying the work of Palladio and Longhena as well as many great artists, first hand. Looking beyond San Giorgio Maggiore, I can clearly see the Lido and the definitive navigational 'bricolas' (navigational baulks or buoys) that stretch across the southern Lagoon. Having spent an enjoyable period of time eating, photographing and, more importantly, enjoying the view from this historical tower, I take the lift back down and arrive on terra firma just in time to see the climax of the acrobats' performance on stage, before the costume parade for the day begins. While I walk around the Piazza to get a better viewing position, I notice hundreds of people wearing masks, small children who have been dressed in costumes for the day, clowns performing everywhere, confetti being thrown at random and inevitably a large contingent of police to marshal what is going on, as best they can. As in every major city in the world where there are attentive crowds like today, it is essential to keep your wits about you, as there will be many 'characters' around to relieve you of your possessions!

Although there was a period when Carnevale remained virtually stagnant for many years, following the fall of the Republic in 1797, it was thankfully resurrected in the 1970s, and most Venetians have taken this spectacle to their heart once again, as all who visit Venice during the celebrations can see. Many of the costumed characters that you see 'performing' in popular tourist areas, irrespective of inclement weather conditions, are in the main financed by the city. Around the city there are several palazzos which stage masquerades and, if you are lucky enough to be offered a ticket, they are usually very expensive. I haven't personally attended any such events although I have some interesting footage on CD of these festivities. There are street performers everywhere throughout the Carnevale fortnight of festivities, and a copy of the complete programme can generally be accessed through the 'visitvenice.co.uk' site so that tourists can, if they wish, plan their stay according to their needs.

Carnevale really began in the 12th century, following the Republic's defeat of Ulrico, when the tradition of slaughtering a bull and 12 pigs in Piazza San Marco on Shrove Tuesday started in celebration of this victory. It wasn't until 1268 that the famous masks, which I will explain shortly, came into use. The real heyday of Carnevale was in the 18th century, when rich noblemen from all around the world came on their 'grand tours' and revelled in all the pleasures that were available, and there were many to choose from. During this period, it would appear that every form of 'promiscuity' was permitted, and the fact that everyone wore masks levelled this debauchery to all social classes. Revellers would travel the city completely incognito, usually wearing the 'bautta', a black silk hood, and a 'tabarro', a large cloak, together with a three-cornered hat with a mask.

Before I enjoy the 2007 version of Carnevale, perhaps a look into the past might be interesting, as it will provide some infamous background information. In modern terms, the carnival lasts for about two weeks, but in the 18th century it lasted for several months and was known then as the 'Venetian Season'. Festivities in that period in Venice were official (of a fashion), and feasting and entertainment took place in the public square on *'giovedi grasso'* (Carnival Thursday), when feats of amazing acrobatics were performed. One amazing feat was for an acrobat to descend a rope from the belltower of San Marco. During the festivities the general public, as well as the patriarchs, would marvel at the acrobats, firework displays, tightrope walkers, puppeteers and street entertainers, all supposedly under the control of the State. Harmless, one might say, in the early days leading up to the 18th century, but during the period that followed the decline of Venice, Carnevale appeared to explode and consequently sparked off an inordinate programme of 'pleasure', and everything was about to change. In this abnormal climate of pleasure, both carnal and gambling pursuits became a prime occupation, which, as I mentioned before, attracted the rich young nobles to Venice. This period has been fully documented in the paintings of Francesco Guardi and the diaries of Giacomo Casanova.

During this age of decadence, there was a boom in the theatre as well as an epidemic of gambling fever. Women were said to have been big losers during this gambling period, which caused an enormous number of 'courtesans' to evolve (far more than at any previous period in Venetian history). The government made every effort to close the gambling houses (the Ridotto) but this only caused hundreds of private emporiums to emerge, supposedly undercover. Venereal disease was rife and syphilis, better known then as the 'French disease', accounted for 20% of the Venetian population being admitted to hospital.

Giacomo Casanova was probably the most notorious character of the day, and he was an obvious victim to be infected by the

'French disease', but miraculously he recovered, whereas most simply rotted away and died. Giacomo was born in 1725 in Venice, and died in semi exile in Bohemia in 1798. His promiscuous lifestyle made him a legend amongst the decadent society of Europe, for he was not only an adventurer and womaniser, but also a writer in his spare time! There have been many stories told of his exploits, some hilarious others scandalous, as he used all his charm and guile to gain the company of women and often used threats, aggression and intimidation to achieve his goals. It is not known just how many children he fathered, nor is it known just how much debt he acquired. What is known about this libertine is mainly information gained from his own biography, which runs to 12 volumes and is simply titled 'History of My Life'. In leading this very promiscuous lifestyle, he made many enemies from all walks of life, and it was said that he became a marked man by the Venetian Council when his misdemeanours were reported in the 'Bocca di Leone'. The fact that he was imprisoned in 1755 for his amourous adventures with both nuns and married women, and his eventual escape from the 'piombi' (prison cell), made him a cult hero, but, in doing so, he spent a great deal of his remaining life in exile. History will remember him as the 'Spirit of the Age' whilst most Venetians today simply view him with some embarrassment but consider his legend to be a rewarding tourist attraction.

Equally promiscuous during the heyday of decadence were the courtesans, and many stories have evolved from their activities. In fact, during the 18th century, there was a guide published for 'clients', which provided a shortlist of addresses where these women could be found. One noted courtesan, albeit of an earlier decade, often mentioned when researching Venetian society, is *Veronica Franco*. Veronica was born in Venice and was the daughter of a courtesan, Paola Francassa, from whom she learned her profession in the mid-16th century. Apart from being a stunning beauty of her time, she was also well educated, having had private tutors. She eventually became a literary advisor in the 1570s, joining Domenico Venier's literary group. During this period she was also considered to be an extremely talented and accomplished musician. Originally married to a doctor, whom she divorced, she had six children all from different men. One of her former 'patrons' was said to be Henry III, King of France, whom she mentions in one of 50 'familiar letters', which she published in 1580. I imagine they caused quite a stir at the time. During her literary career, she wrote and published many poems as well as letters, which seemingly elevated her to a higher plateau than her peers. Once her courtesan days were over, and considered to be a wealthy woman, she attempted to become a moralist and tried to discourage mothers intent on raising their daughters to become courtesans from doing so. In 1580 Veronica was arrested by the Inquisition, on charges of witchcraft, charges which she eventually proved to be false, but by then her career was over and she had lost her wealthy patrons. In defending her innocence, she lost most of her fortune and worldly possessions, just at a time when the plague was killing thousands (1575–1577) and society was at its worst. She died aged only 45, in poverty, in a section of Venice known for destitute prostitutes.

Perhaps now is the right time to explain more about the tradition of the mask, as it plays an important part, even today, in the tradition of Carnevale, as well as being a prime revenue commodity for Venetian shopkeepers and traders alike. Masks are an essential part of Carnevale and have been worn since the 11th century, becoming well established by the mid 15th century, when the *Guild of Mascereri* was recognised from that period onwards. The original mask was typically worn over a black hood together with a tricorn (three-cornered hat). This was complimented with a long black cape to provide the maximum amount of disguise (the bautta). The original laws regarding the wearing of masks date from the 13th century, and specific laws were introduced when masks were seemingly worn throughout the year. The patriarchs of the city, usually rich merchants and adventurers who risked their lives when at sea bringing trade to Venice, decided to create a certain lifestyle which disregarded rules and allowed them to a 'freedom to act' mentality that required some sort of disguise. It was from this impropriety that the mask came into being in Venice and remained intact until the fall of the Republic. By wearing the mask, certain deeds were overlooked or forgotten, and government rules dictated its use on certain occasions. In fact, at one time it was compulsory to wear a mask when visiting the state casino (the Ridotto).

Let me now explain some types of masks together with the fashionable accessories such as *Fans* and *Beauty Spots* that once accompanied the costume and helped create this entire theatre of mystery. I will begin with the mask, the *'Volto'*, which allowed the wearer to eat and drink without removing it, and was usually worn with the *bautta* (the dark hood) under a tricorn hat. This was considered to be the most common of disguises and was worn by the majority of Venetians. Next is the *Moretta, or Muta*, which was worn only by women, and its aim was to simply conceal the eyes and mouth, at the same time allowing ample cleavage to be displayed in their dress. The Moretta was small and oval in shape and usually covered in black lace, and was held to the face by a button, which was fixed on the inner part of the mask and kept in place by gripping the button with the teeth. This made the woman wearer completely mute and without expression and only responsive once her face was exposed. From my list of quotations, which I particularly like, the one that comes immediately to mind, written by Saint Jerome (374–419), is: 'The face is the mirror of the mind, and eyes without speaking confess the secrets of the heart'.

Homosexuality was very common in Venice, like most other cities, and the *Gnaga* was used by male prostitutes in order to disguise their faces to look like women. They also wore dresses and full women's attire. Apparently, the Venetian government in the 1500s were exceedingly concerned about the growth of homosexuality, so much so that they allowed women prostitutes to stand half-naked at windows in front of their own homes to encourage more men to use 'their' services rather than their male equivalent. Probably the most well known mask we remember today is the *Plague Doctor*, its origins going back to the 14th century, when doctors actually used them during periods of the plague. It was thought that this type of mask could be sealed to the clothing and the long 'beak' filled with peppers and herbs would resist any infection. Worn as a decorative piece, it was considered to be a symbol of resistance. I can't think why! Masks were also used in modern theatre from the 16th to the 18th century, but usually confined to the most gross of characters that were being portrayed. Such notable characters include *Pontalone, The Captain, Zanni, The Doctor, Harlequin* and *Palcinella*. Today the sale of masks is considered to be an essential source of income for Venetian traders, and most on display are designed in a more decorative and attractive style, which I can see all around me today.

The reason why fans and beauty spots were important to the costume, especially during the decadent periods of Venetian history, was simply for their use as accessories to flirt with, as they gave off several signals. Fans, for example, were known, not surprisingly, as the 'language of the fan'. By the dropping or positioning of the fan, the male admirer would understand each signal as a code of practice. Fans were considered to be an essential item of dress by upper-class women and were used for cooling, shielding the face and swatting flies and mosquitoes! In the 18th century all upper class women paid extortionate prices for their fans, which were made in Burano. Finally, the ritual of beauty spots was considered to be an accepted form of promiscuous sign language adopted by women of all classes. A spot below the left eye was said to be a sign of passion, whereas a spot in the lower left jawbone was said to be debonair. Women wearing a spot above the left side of the lips were said to be flirty, and, finally, a spot worn at the left edge of the mouth was considered to be the 'killer'!

Today Carnevale seemingly takes on a slightly different theme, having declined gradually from its heyday, and been completely ignored during the 1930s, when Mussolini banned it. In the late 1970s a group of Venetians who were acknowledged as being devotees of Venetian history decided to revive the carnival atmosphere and tradition and, more theatrically, the reintroduction of the 'masked celebrations'. The theme next year (2007) will include the tricentenary of writer and playwright Carlo Goldini, who was said to have encouraged the Carnevale to be a 'festival for everybody'. This year, Piazza San Marco will host music from all parts of the world, and this extravaganza will feature a variety of bands doing 'battle', bands with a Latin American theme, marching bands, Italian groups and even Scottish bagpipers!

The circus display called 'Magic of Fire', part of which is being performed while I am here today, is quite spectacular, with its climax including an acrobatic young lady 'exercising' on lace curtains 10m above the stage!

Before I leave, to make my way back to Piazzale Roma, I still have time to watch and photograph the costume parade on the Piazza, and what a spectacle that is for tourists and locals alike. There must be at least 100 different people from many nationalities who have spent a small fortune in obtaining these period costumes who will parade themselves on the catwalk for all to photograph and enjoy. Their make-up must have taken hours to complete let alone the effort they have made to get to the Piazza from all over the island. It irritates me slightly when I read derogatory revues about the pageant of Carnevale, when I think just how much effort has gone into staging and participating in this event. I realise that some of the 'outfits' worn may be considered alien for historical Venice, I realise that tourist 'gizmos' are sold on every street corner, but if in doing so it plays some part in keeping this island solvent, then long live Carnevale!

Looking at my watch I realise that it is now 5.15pm so, having enjoyed the festivities on the Piazza (I wish I could have stayed longer), I must now make my way to the pontile stage at San Marco for the vaporetto journey back to my favourite bar for some refreshment. Making my way back alongside the Royal Gardens, I didn't take into account the number of other people who also wanted to catch the same vaporetto. Fortunately there is room for me on board, albeit standing room only. I shouldn't have been surprised to see a crowded vaporetto – people have to get home – but I was surprised to see how many costumed people were travelling back along the Canal at this time of the day. Two young oriental ladies dressed in immaculate Venetian costumes particularly took my eye as they patiently stood for the entire journey back to Ferrovia, being pushed and shoved as people boarded and disembarked along the entire length of the Grand Canal. When we eventually arrived at Ferrovia pontile, they unassumingly walked off the vaporetto and went straight into the railway station, and I thought, surely not journeying still further today. That summarised the magic of Carnevale for me, and how much it is enjoyed today. As it is just 6.15pm, I have decided to briefly visit the Scalzi church and dedicate a candle, and once there I realise that mass is being said, so I have to creep around the rear of the church on tip-toe.

Having completed my business in the church, I hastily make my way to Bar S. Lucia, and after having a quick drink and chat with Enrico, the owner, I make my way back to the bus depot to catch the 7.10pm bus to the airport. I always try to remember to look back at the 'Serenissima' when travelling on the bus back across the Ponte della Liberta, and today is no exception. My thoughts wander to the Piazza and I can imagine how vibrant it must look this evening with the night-lights set against the colour of the costumes.

I arrive at the airport and there is a small queue waiting at the check-in. Once I have my boarding pass, I make my way to the pizza bar where I order 'the works' with a large coffee. By now, I have quite an appetite and, considering that I only had a snack lunch, I feel no guilt whatsoever about feasting. Having enjoyed my meal, I make my way through security control (surprisingly, not having to remove my shoes on this occasion) and into the departure lounge, where I am disappointed for the first time today: the ice cream bar is closed! Feeling somewhat deprived, I make do with a chocolate bar instead and settle down to read my book, before my 9.45pm flight. Unfortunately, my plane was late arriving at Marco Polo, but that didn't really worry me because I had my book for company. Once the plane had arrived, we were on board and away in no time. The flight home was quite amusing because the senior steward was certainly a smart act. Apart from being efficient, he had a wicked sense of humour, which I considered being rather refreshing for a journey at that time of the night – perhaps others didn't. At Gatwick I was one of the first off the plane (I always try to get a front seat) and I quickly walked through customs (no baggage, remember) and I was home before 1.00am. Yes, it was a long day, but what sweet memories, especially when some confetti fell to the floor when I removed my jumper before retiring to bed.

Meraviglioso Carnevale, Buona notte Venezia.

CHAPTER 7
MARCH: Murano, Burano and Torcello
'In Search of the Northern Archipelago'

I am now halfway through my journal and, on reflection, am quite pleased that I have managed to visit and record so many interesting places in the 'Serenissima' to date. Having used the vaporetto as my prime mode of transport around Venice in previous chapters, I am now going to use a similar variety of transport vessels to get me to the Northern Islands of the Lagoon. In doing so, I hope to acknowledge, enjoy and understand the Lagoon more fully in its own right, as an essential part of Venetian history. The Lagoon, as well as being a prime food supplier, a defence barrier and an access link to every island within its waters, has now, more than ever before, become a considerable problem to the well-being of all it once provided for and protected in the past. This wonderful expanse of water is now frequently suffering from the ever-changing climatic conditions, which now threaten the very existence of all it protects, and I will attempt to explain briefly next month what major concerns there are.

As with Venice itself, I never tire from visiting its surrounding islands, and this chapter will give me the opportunity to photograph and sketch some very attractive buildings, as well as focus in on

March 2007

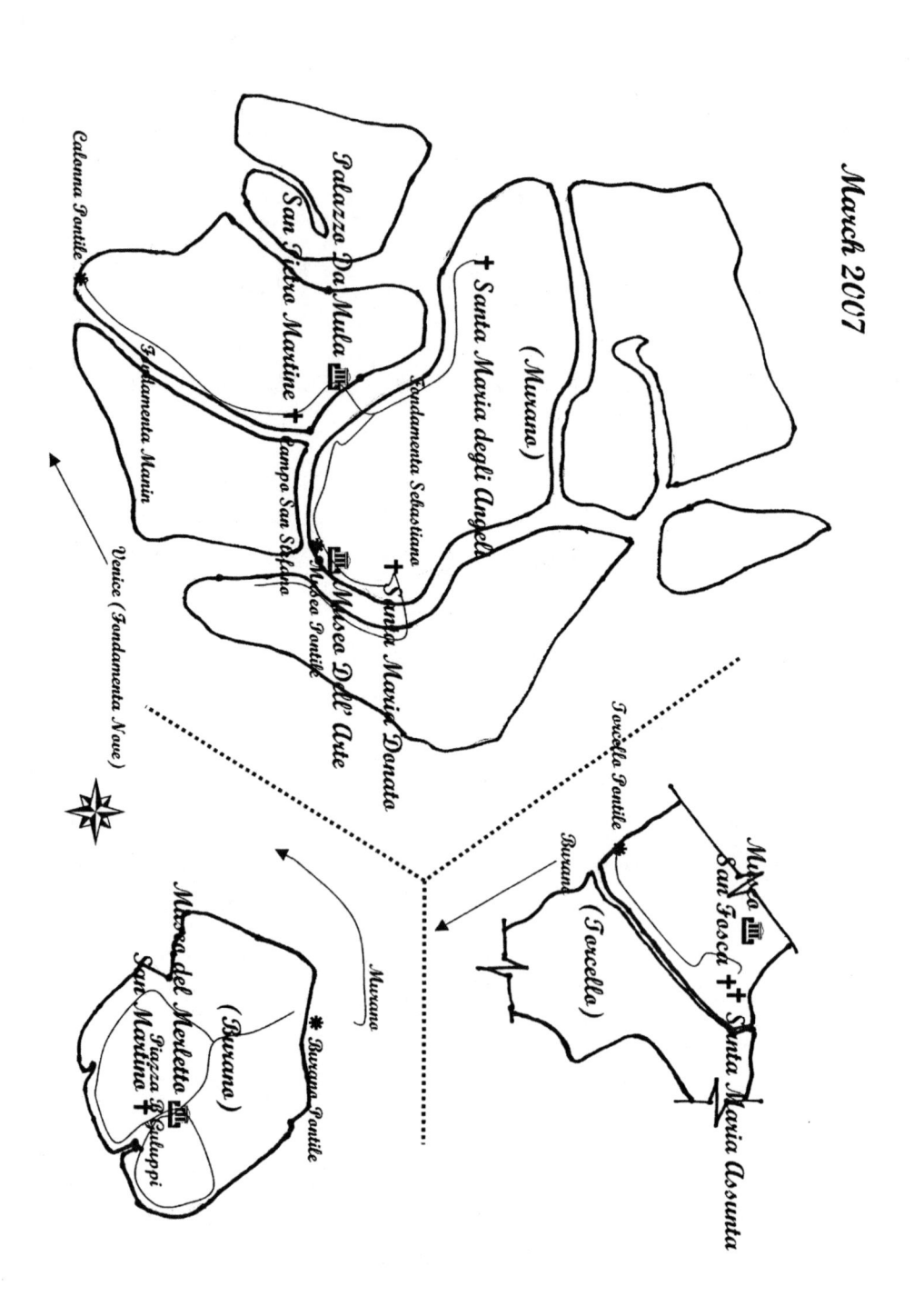

some local history on all the three islands of Murano, Burano and Torcello. All these three colourful islands, apart from retaining their own identities, have played, and to some extent still do play an important role in identifying the social and economic past of Venice itself. To visit all three islands in a single day, in a similar fashion to my previous chapters, is not really possible even though they are considered to be fairly close to one another, so in order to be able to explore each one properly, as I intend to do, I have decided to spend a second full day in Venice on this occasion. This will allow me to map out my journey as I travel, and spend more time visiting a number of buildings of interest. It will also prevent me from 'clock watching', especially waterbus timetables, during my periods on terra firma and give me an opportunity to 'eat locally'.

My first day will follow the same pattern as previous visits, whereby I arrive in Venice late morning, following which, I intend to travel to Murano and return to Venice that evening. When I arrive back to the mainland on day one from Murano, I will disembark from the *motonave* (the larger boats) at San Alvise pontile and hopefully visit some interesting places in northern Cannaregio, such as the Gesuiti, on my walk back to Piazzale Roma. Day two will see me up and out of my hotel nice and early to capture the hustle and bustle of an early Venetian morning, which I admit I miss on my normal day trips. As I have to get to the Fondamenta Nove pontile (north Cannaregio) to catch my waterbus for today's trip, I may walk there. It depends on the weather: if it is wintery then I'll use water transport. Once there, I intend to travel out to the islands of Burano and Torcello, and while there I will reserve a 'window of time' to enjoy some local lunch. As the geography of each island I visit on this trip is relatively easy to navigate, I haven't planned the itinerary for my routes in any specific order. I will, however, take my trusty map and travel guide with me to ensure that I capture most of the interesting places that are available to visit. My knapsack will be slightly heavier on this trip, as I need my two cameras, a sketchbook, digital recorder and binoculars as well as some overnight items.

***March 8th 2007**

Whenever I travel to Venice, I always check the 5-day weather forecast for the 'Serenissima' region, before leaving home, and I must admit that I was a little concerned about the Venetian weather today as I jumped into my awaiting taxi at 5.00am. The forecast said that it would be raining today but sunny tomorrow, so I packed some waterproof clothing just in case, which made my knapsack slightly heavier, but at least I would be dry. The taxi got me to the airport in good time for my flight and, as usual, I was through security and into the departure lounge quickly, where I grabbed my normal breakfast 'vitals'. The flight times to Venice change at the end of this month, so this will be the final 6.45am flight from Gatwick on easyJet, as the earliest flight from April will be the 7.45am out and 9.05pm for the return trip. That means that I get an hour less to spend in Venice on each day trip from now on, which in turn means that I shall have to re-plan the itinerary for future trips accordingly. To put this in perspective, it simply means that I will reach the Grand Canal by 12.00 midday and be back at the bus terminal by 6.50pm, which gives me almost seven hours to explore and enjoy.

My flight left Gatwick on time and it is interesting to see that there is more snow today on the Alps but still a great many 'brown patches' visible. Global warming or not, the skiing entrepreneurs must be feeling the pinch right now. The weather on arrival at Marco Polo airport was best described as being damp, but it had stopped raining. Having purchased my 48-hour transport ticket (25 euros) at the ticket office, I boarded the No. 5 bus and realised that I could not validate the ticket in the machine on the bus. Apparently this particular ticket can only be stamped on the waterbuses, which wasn't a problem, but is still a point worth remembering. The journey to Piazzale Roma was uneventful and I arrived at my destination by 10.40am (Italian time). When I got off the bus, I decided to register at the Santa Chiara Hotel, as I would probably not return from my travels today until the evening. Having done so, I made my way to the waterbus depot at Piazzale Roma to catch the No. 42 to Murano. I use the term 'waterbus', simply because the mode of water transport I intend to use today will be a mixture of both the vaporetto and the motonave, which sounds confusing, but isn't. What's important is getting the number right. The vaporetti, which I use most of the time, are the prime vessels for travelling within the island and the canals whereas the *motonavi* (plural of '*motornave*') are faster and generally larger boats used for longer routes to the surrounding islands. Just to confuse the issue even more, there are also *motoscafi* (plural of '*motoscafo*') boats, which are smaller, faster and sleeker in appearance, which operate in and around Venice. As I mentioned earlier, it's the boat number that is important, not the size and shape.

As my waterbus (No. 42) heads off from Piazzale Roma and makes its way along the Grand Canal, before turning left into the Cannaregio Canal, I notice that the church of St Germain and the Palazzo Labia are completely scaffolded on each façade, so I can only assume that there are some major works in operation.

The journey to Murano via the Fondamenta Nove took about 35 minutes and I was able to enjoy the boat ride across the Lagoon from the open seated rear of the waterbus, which enabled me to take some good photographs.

Before I arrive at Murano, it might be appropriate to explain some general facts about this small but important island. Murano is famous for its glass as well as once being a prime producer of salt for the Islands. In 1276 the island became self-governing, although still part of the Venetian Republic, and by the 16th century had a population of around 60,000. It minted its own coins from the 13th to the18th century, when it was considered to be one of the most important glass manufacturing locations in Europe. Palazzos were built here in the 15th century, when the island became more popular, as it had a modicum of arable land, which was made into orchards and vegetable fields. As glass was, and to some extent still is, Murano's main industry, it is essential to understand just how much this craft has contributed to its glorious history.

Legend tells us that glass was first discovered by the Phoenicians and first produced in Mesopotania when a ship loaded with nitre anchored on the coast of Phoenica in order that the crew could rest and eat. When cooking their meals, the ship's crew used small chunks of nitre (soda) to rest their cooking utensils on, and, whilst cooking, the nitre mixed with the local sand on the shore and a liquid, which was luminous resulted. Quite possible, as glass was originally made from nitre, silica (natural sand) and lime. From that early date (1500 BC), glass was produced throughout the Middle East and Europe in varying forms. In the 7th and 8th centuries a glass factory was in operation in Torcello, which was the first discovered on the Venetian Lagoon. From Torcello glass manufacture moved to Venice around the late 10th century, according to archived documentation held in the Byzantine monastery on San Giorgio Maggiore. However, glass was still manufactured in a variety of other local areas on the mainland.

In the late 13th century the Great Council of Venice decided to move the main glassworks to Murano from Venice as a safety precaution to avoid fires in the city, as the population had increased to around 130,000. The smaller furnaces that were allowed to remain were strictly controlled, and located in strategic areas. During that period, the early skills of foreign glassmakers were probably copied and adopted by Venetian travellers who visited the eastern Mediterranean, including Constantinople, and in the late 14th century, when Venetians had mastered glass production, it was eventually exported to parts of Europe, including England. In the 15th to the 16th century, Venetian glassmakers were in their zenith, or 'golden period', and experimented with different materials. They produced four main groups of glass:

- Enamelled glass, considered an exclusive product
- Crystalline glass for its transparency
- Aventurine glass for its gold flux
- Chalcedony glass for its colours

In the 17th to the 18th century, chandeliers and mirrors became successful commodities, mirrors, especially, as Venetians were the only people in Europe who could make them. Trade boomed until the 17th century, when France and Moravia emerged as principal glassmakers. This was also at the same time as trade routes were opened as new sea passages were being discovered, which diminished Venice's monopoly of commercial trade. The final collapse came with the fall of the Republic. Glassmakers were privileged citizens. They were allowed to wear swords, as they were the most prominent members of Murano society, enjoyed immunity from prosecution by the Venetian state, and their daughters were allowed to marry into affluent Venetian families. The down side was that they were not allowed to leave the Republic, thereby keeping all their manufacturing secrets in Venice. The Great Council were adamant that others would not replicate their goods. Some glassmakers did, however, 'wander' and got away with it. Others paid the penalty with their lives. In fact, there was a secret police force dedicated to the task of protecting the 'secrets' of glass, and they were known to administer penalties themselves, penalties which included having a hand cut off, or death by various macabre means.

During the Austrian rule, raw materials were restricted and taxation was increased, which eventually reduced the number of glassworks by half. In 1811 there were only 35 glassblowers, 19 of whom produced bead, with only six creating crystal, the later declining even further by 1860, when mosaic production developed again. The glass industry did survive, however, and glassblowers continued their skills during this period of occupation, and in the 1850s several sons of a glass manufacturer named Pietro Toso formed a new company called Fratelli Toso and revived the industry. In addition to this, an industrious lawyer called Antonio Salviati (his palazzo is mentioned in Chapter 2) set up a new firm in 1859, which made glass tiles, and mosaics (used to restore Venetian buildings), and he also opened up the European and American markets when he displayed his work at the World Expo in London. Throughout the glassmaking history of Murano, there have been a multitude of logistical, political and social laws imposed by government, mainly to disguise, conserve and, I guess, protect this noble art. But these masters of design and creativity have survived the storm, and produce remarkable treasures today for all those who can afford them or simply want to admire them.

Armed with this brief history, I now disembark from the waterbus at the Colonna pontile (Murano) and make my way along the Fondamenta Vetral, and to my right are some of the many historic glassworks which still remain on the island. Directly to my left are shops selling glassware items, as you would expect, each shop displaying an enormous range of goods to show interested customers. As I reach the intermediate point along this fondamenta, a small bridge that crosses the Rio del Vetral canal provides an ideal location to photograph the many wonderful Byzantine buildings that run along this attractive route. The majority of buildings on Murano have only two floors above ground level and all appear to be really well maintained. Nearing the end of the fondamenta, to my right, is the Campo San Stefano, which is an attractive but small square with a campanile and what appears to be a fairly modernistic and highly decorated cone shaped tree, surely not a relic from Christmas! Facing the campo and directly to my left is the church of San Pietro Martire, which I now intend to explore. This Dominican church was first built in the 1363, and rebuilt around 1415, following an earlier fire. Internally the church, with its Renaissance colonnades, has a magnificent altarpiece displaying winged marble statues; and is illuminated by 'borrowed' lighting, which highlight intimate parts of the church. There are a number of small murals, which are positioned between ornate arches, and, as you would expect, some fine pieces of artwork, including the painting of *Madonna & Child with St Mark*' by Giovanni Bellini, Veronese's *'St Agatha in Prison'* and *'St Gerome in Descent'*. The sacristy has a museum, which can be viewed for 1.50 euros and is well worth visiting if only to see the wonderful wooden carvings (*dossali*) inside. These Baroque-style carvings of historical and mythological beings are on each side of the altar in the vestry. Merged with these figures are scenes from the life of St John the Baptist.

As I leave San Pietro Martire, I notice the time is now 1.00pm, so I decide to grab a snack lunch in a local cafe by the Ponte Longo Bridge, which is directly to my left as I leave the church. Having decided to have a short break, my curiosity takes me to that decorative cone-shaped tree I mentioned earlier, as there is a small cafe in the campo. I decide to have a coffee and a heated pannini and sit outside the cafe, hoping to find out just what that tree is all about, and I discover that it is partly made of glass plates, which represent leaves, and serves as a showpiece for the glass manufacturers. Having enjoyed my short break, I make my way to the Ponte Longo, which gives me the opportunity to view the Canale degli Angeli, which is on my left, and to my right the Canale Grande Murano, the bridge location being the point of division for the two canals. Once over the bridge, I turn left and walk along the Fondamenta Sebastiano Vernier, and can't help but notice across the main canal the very attractive former Palazzo Da Mula, which now serves as Murano's Town Hall. This building is a real gem; on the piano nobile level there are two Gothic arched windows either side of a group of four smaller windows, each with their own balconies. There are two stone sculptured panels on the façade, with rose windows and a small statuette which sits on a recessed arch above the central balcony. Two large Gothic windows flank the main door, which really does complement the overall composition: a really well preserved and beautiful building.

As I walk further along, I come to the semi-derelict but nevertheless delightful church of Santa Maria Degli Angeli. The church is hidden beyond a small campo and access is achieved by walking through a small opening, which is formed by a brick wall linking two buildings. Today there appears to be some restorative work being undertaken and the church is certainly closed to the public. I am really not sure whether it is still used, judging by its external condition. The campanile, like the church itself, is also in need of major restoration, which I hope it will eventually get, as this 16th-century building certainly deserves some attention. Unfortunately, I am not able to get much research information on this church at present, but nevertheless it is well worth the walk to see this building, if only to understand what supportive role it must have played over the centuries for the local community. The small campo is obviously a popular meeting spot for this neighbourhood, as there are several groups of elderly people who appear to be enjoying each other's company.

I am now walking back along the route I came, passing the Ponte Longo bridge and continuing to the end of the Canal Grande, where I bear left into the Fondamenta Giustinian, which will take me to perhaps the most important building on the island, which is the church of Santa Maria e Donato. This wonderfully preserved building is on the site of a former 7th century-church of the same name. Whilst researching this church, I was amazed to read that the exterior restoration work was considered by some to be poor, as there had been some 'modifications' made which included new windows. My personal opinion is that I see a well preserved building which clearly identifies the degree of craftsmanship achieved by both past and present artisans, and better that these historic monuments are at least preserved rather than becoming ruins. The exterior of the building has several Istrian stone parapets on display, and the colour and design features of the exterior brickwork give a warm, solid and decorative appearance. Inside the church there is a spectacular 'ship's keel' roof, which looks down on the superbly restored mosaic floor, which although completed in the 1970s has still retained areas originally laid in the 12th century. There are three naves, separated by tall Greek columns, with an original pulpit, which was built in the 6th century, together with the relics of St Donato, which are kept within the High Altar. Today, due to my itinerary schedule, I cannot visit the interior of this church, as it doesn't reopen until 4.00pm, but having been inside on a previous occasion I can recommend everyone visiting the island to look inside. I have today taken several new photographs for my sketching book to complete at a later date.

On my way back to the Museo pontile, which is just a short distance from St Maria Donato, I intend to visit the glass museum, which is based in the former Palazzo Giustinian, which I have passed several times in the past but have never explored. Entry to the museum costs 5.5 euros and is well worth the price, as there are literally hundreds of pieces of glassware on display, covering many centuries. As one would expect, there are many very early pieces from the Egyptian period, which have miraculously survived the test of time, as well as a history of Murano glass production up to the 20th century. My favourite pieces have to be the exquisite garden designs replicating garden scenes, all in a variety of styles and to a scale such that most of it would cover an entire dining room table. These pieces were obviously made for the wealthy, as the workmanship and detail of each piece must have taken a great deal of labour and materials to complete. I also found the section explaining the history of glassmaking very interesting. Even though the majority of this display was presented in Italian, nonetheless it was fairly easy to follow the processes taken by early glassmakers to produce their wares. Having earlier researched the history of Murano glass, I was able to fully appreciate just how varied and intricate this fine art had developed through time and just how precious a commodity it had become to Venice.

It is now 3.30pm, and I leave the museum and make my way to the Museo pontile for my journey back to mainland Venice where I intend to supplement my Northern Islands itinerary by visiting the interior of the Gesuiti church (closed on my November trip) to enjoy its wonderful interior. At this time of the year there are remarkably few tourists around, so again I have the choice of seating when I board the watercraft back to Venice. As the weather has greatly improved and some sun is grinning through, I decide again to sit outside on my trip across the Lagoon and enjoy this expanse of waterway, at the same time capturing some photographs of San Michele as we pass. San Michele is a very small island, which I intend to visit at a later date as it has a very attractive church and an interesting cemetery, which must certainly have lots of history to share.

The journey across the Lagoon is particularly spectacular today because I have the opportunity to photograph the Dolomites, which I can clearly see in the distance, as the cloud formation is unusually high, making this mountain range visible. This opportunity doesn't happen often, so I intend to take full advantage of this spectacle; it really is a wonderful sight to behold, with its snow-covered peaks acting as a backcloth for the 'Serenissima'. The weathered watercraft is sailing along quite comfortably and my thoughts shift to the importance of these vessels (including the vaporetti) and the contribution they make to the Venetian way of life. Most tourist guides have nothing but praise for the reliable, punctual and, in a way, romantic watercraft that provide total transportation support along the canals and across the Lagoon. Before the advent of these vessels, the gondola, traghetti and a lesser-known passenger barge called a '*burchiello*' were the only means of transport for Venetians, certainly after the time when horses in the city were banned in the 14th century.

'Vaporetto' translated means 'little steamer', and whilst most vessels are powered by diesel today they still maintain their original name. Having mentioned, before, the numerous routes available to passengers and the type of craft, it might be helpful to explain the watercraft I use regularly. The good old No. 1 stops at every pontile along the Grand Canal, not good if you are hoping to get to the bus or railway station quickly, but excellent if you want to see and photograph everything along the Grand Canal. For a quicker journey, stopping at fewer pontiles, take the No. 82. In general terms the No. 42 and 52 travel clockwise around the Island whereas the No. 41 and 51 go anticlockwise (to be sure when journeying anywhere simply look at which direction the vessel approaches a pontile, it usually continues in the same bearing).

The Northern Islands can be reached from Fondamenta Nove 'LN' (North), which in turn seems to be linked to most of the southern routes. The night sevice 'N' runs to most places but at less frequent intervals. I think the ACTV services are great, so much so that I have entered a competition sponsored by Vela, which is part of the group listed, to redesign the ticket offices and pontiles. Yes, I have acquired the competition guidelines but, realistically, know that my submission will be scrapped. When I first heard of this initiative, I thought it would be nice to have a chance to release my artistic ideas within the island I so adore. Unfortunately, the entry criteria are somewhat restrictive. Having foolishly assumed that I would not need any architectural or engineering qualifications to design a simple proposal, I started to produce some sketches of what I thought would be suitable designs and colours for each pontile and ticket office. Having done so, I now realise that I should also have produced the construction designs, which are far beyond my capability, so my artistic thoughts will not be realised! I felt much better, however, after reading the 12-page competition entry document, especially the 'conditions for participating' section, which effectively stated that competitors must not be over 41 years of age! Is that an EEC Directive? I think not. Anyway, having created some nice sketches, I have sent my outline proposals to the competition committee. 'Mille grazie vaporetto, lungo may continuare'.

Short commercial over, back to the journal. My watercraft now arrives at Fondamenta Nove and the time is 4.15pm, which is perfect timing for the short walk to the last building I intend to visit today, and one that certainly wasn't originally on my Northern Islands itinerary, but is nevertheless an added value inclusion. From the Fondamenta Nove pontile, I turn right when I alight from the waterbus and walk a short distance along its concourse, where I turn left into Salizz dei Specchieri, which leads me directly to the Gesuiti church. As I arrive there, the main door is open and ready for visitors and I can't wait to see the interior of this wonderful building once again. If you remember, it was closed on my November visit. As I enter the church, I am immediately impressed by the central altarpiece, which stands majestically displaying its spiral marble columns, similar in design to the Scalzi church but different in colour. I can't help but notice the profusion of white, green and grey marble on display, which has been sculptured to represent material drapes. This church really is magnificent, and an absolute must to visit whenever you are in the Cannaregio *sestiere*, as is the Oratorio dei Crociferi, which is sited opposite the church.

Having fully enjoyed my visit to the Gesuiti once again, I realize that it is now 5.30pm, so I make my way back to the Piazzale Roma by taking the No. 41 vaporetto at Fondamenta Nove, which gets me back at 5.55pm, perfect timing for my usual nightcap at Bar S. Lucia, where this evening I can stay longer as I don't have to get back to the airport tonight. By now, my knapsack is becoming quite heavy, having carried the extra equipment around all day, and, to add to that, I am extremely thirsty. As I enter the bar, I am greeted by Enrico in his usual friendly manner, and note that my glass of Guinness is already being poured for me before I even sit down. What a service. I wish I could transfer this bar back home. When the beer arrives, I order a couple of spinach ricotta pastries and my supper is complete, well very nearly, that is, after a couple more 'Liffey Waters'. I usually record a few brief, but relative notes when I'm at the bar, just to make sure I haven't missed anything throughout the day, and whilst doing so I captured the attention of a Scottish guy, who had emigrated to Australia but happened to be on holiday in Venice. Beer, being a natural discussion subject for most men, led to a really interesting chat with this guy from Sydney, who was travelling all over Europe and who had visited several major cities in a relatively short period of time. I look upon Bar S. Lucia as being my local now, and I could quite easily visit it each day if I was a local, as there are always so many interesting people coming and going. After a short while, Enrico decided to put football on the bar television screen and we discuss European football. After a while, he suddenly realised that I am a Chelsea season-ticket holder. He then immediately calls Matti, one of his bar staff, over who is also a very keen Chelsea supporter, so I have no doubts that my future visits will focus around football.

After a couple of refreshing hours in Bar S. Lucia, I decide to make my way back to Santa Chiara Hotel for the evening, and review my plans for tomorrow. I am really looking forward to the trips to Burano and Torcello. Once in the hotel, it's a simple night cap, a coffee and some reading, before I retire reasonably early, as tomorrow I want to be up bright and early to enjoy a full day's journeying to the far north of the Lagoon.

'Buona notte, Venezia'.

* **March 9th 2007**

After a good night's rest and my itinerary for the day planned, I get up at 6.00am, shower, dress and then go for an early morning walk before breakfast. The morning temperature and general weather forecast for the day tells me that it is going to be perfect for my journey across the Lagoon, but, before that, I want to take in the Venetian morning before breakfast, so I leave the hotel and head towards the Fonadamenta S. Simeon Piccolo, where I turn right at the Scalzi bridge and head towards the Frari church (September chapter) and from there make my way back to the Giardino Papadopoli. The walk takes about 45 minutes at a reasonably slow pace, but I am able to enjoy the early morning hustle and bustle of people and watercraft on their journey to work. Once back at the Santa Chiara Hotel, I am ready for my breakfast, which, I hasten to add, is a culinary delight and will set me up for the day, well at least until lunch. Having settled my bill and had a very interesting conversation with the manager at reception on a number of subjects, notably my journal, local affairs and a special bookshop that I have to visit sometime, I make my way to the Piazzale Roma ACTV watercraft terminal. Once there, I board the No. 42, which will take me to Fondameta Nove again. Once I arrive, I leave the vaporetto and walk to my right, where I cross over a small bridge until I reach the motonavi pontile where I can catch the No. LN, which will take me to Burano.

Today is a double treat, as I will visit both Burano and Torcello, which means I get to travel to the north of the Lagoon and visit two very important historical islands of Venice. In order to get to Torcello, I will have to first travel to Burano and then change watercraft for the very short trip to the second of my scheduled islands. The frequency of motonavi to Burano is very good, generally every 30 minutes, and likewise the craft to Torcello is again at 30-minute intervals; the art is synchronising each trip. Having said that, the crews of each vessel are particularly helpful when asking directions and times, at least those who can speak English. When the LN motonave arrives at Fondamenta Nove I realise that I have to share the journey with two parties of teenage schoolchildren, so I expect a noisy crossing. I was wrong. The kids were reasonably well behaved and I managed to get a window seat, which proved to be very beneficial.

Crossing the Lagoon was an absolute joy. Not only was the passage smooth, but the scenery at times was quite spectacular, and the 50-minute journey was a perfect start to the day. The motonave called at Murano Faro, Mazzorbo and then Burano on its journey, and is a very comfortable craft, which is larger than the vaporetto, and has a toilet on board. The Venetian Lagoon is a wonderful expanse of water linking the Adriatic Sea to this historic lake, and as it is a major contributor in the evolution of Venice

I intend to briefly provide some historical and current ecological facts in the April chapter when I visit the South Islands.

Today I am visiting the Northern Islands and the motonave is now docking at Burano pontile. The weather is great, sunshine and blue skies, and a cool breeze coming in from across the water. The time now is 9.40am as I disembark and make my way with the other passengers in the direction of Burano town centre, and I immediately sense a warm welcoming feeling from some locals who are casually sitting in a small open park area near the pontile. As Burano is quite a small island compared to Murano, I realise that I could probably circumnavigate it reasonably quickly, and therefore I intend to explore its interior in two stages. Firstly, I have decided to do a preliminary walk into the town centre, probably to Piazza Galuppi, and explore the church of San Martino. From there I will walk along the east side of the island and return to the pontile, all hopefully within one and a half hours. This will enable me to catch the late morning watercraft to Torcello, where I can explore all the treasures it has on view. By about 1.30pm I shall return to Burano and continue to explore the remainder of the island, and hopefully stop for a local traditional lunch, which I am looking forward to.

Burano has been inhabited since Roman times. The fleeing Lombards eventually took refuge in the mainland cities whereas the people of Altino settled on this island in the late 6th century. The island became fully occupied by the year 1000. This exodus and its outcome remind me of a quotation by Alfred Lord Tennyson (1809–1892) which reads: 'Our island home, is far beyond the wave, we will no longer roam.' Although Burano is only 9.5 km from Venice, the distance across the Lagoon was considered to be quite considerable in those early days, and even more comforting was the fact that it was semi-protected from the dreaded malaria disease (which is prevalent in a swampy terrain) because of the island's geographical position, which produced strong winds from the sea, thereby keeping away the mosquitoes. The island was originally divided into five islets, Terranova, San Moro, Giudecca, Mandraccio and San Martin, and is now one of the archipelago of islands linked by bridges. My research tells me that the present-day Burano is not the ancient one. Due to the erosion of the island, because of its location in respect to the sea, the ancient inhabitants who did live there moved in 959 to the present-day island between Mazzorbo and Torcello and named their new island Burano Nuovo. It is said that traditionally the womenfolk on the island painted their houses in vivid colours, to assist their fishermen husbands in finding the island when returning home in bad weather. The houses, incidentally, are of a standard design, being a simple square shape, in complete contrast to the Venetian style, even though Burano was once considered to be the capital of the Northern Islands.

In the 16th century Burano became famous for its lacemaking. So good was the quality of work that Louis XIV employed local lacemakers in order to learn their techniques. The original term used for handmade lace then was *'punto in aria'*. The Dogaressa Morosina Morosini, wife of the Doge Marino Grimani, set up lacemaking workshops at this time. In the 18th century lacemaking went into decline and, fortunately, was revised in 1872, when the school of lacemaking, known as the *'Scuola dei Merletti'*, was opened. This is now housed in the Palazzo del Podesta, which is an attractive 14th-century building. Burano 'point lace' is remarkably skilful and has seven stitches, which make up its design. One stitch apiece is completed by a single woman, who then hands it on to another, until the design is completed. A one square metre design can take as long as two months to complete. Today the fine lace produced from this island is extremely expensive, as one would expect. However, the tourist is constantly reminded that there are also inferior pieces of work made in the Orient on sale. Therefore I suggest that buyers consult the experts if they want genuine Burano lace.

Back to my travels. Having left the motonave, I am now following the paved pathway that runs diagonally across the small-grassed park area towards a group of small buildings, which will lead me to the town centre. Passing several small souvenir stalls, I continue along this walkway until I arrive at Fondamenta Cavanella, which I can only describe as being one of the most attractive small streets I have ever walked down. There is a small canal, which divides this street, with small craft shops on either side, and each house appears to be freshly painted in wonderfully rich bright colours that really do bring this attractive scene together. Continuing along this route, I arrive at a small bridge, which overlooks the southern part of the Lagoon, and I cross over the canal when I reach this point. Walking along this route, I have photographed several houses which have fishing nets systematically hung out to dry, each one having been painstakingly untangled and folded neatly ready for using again. The pavements are like the houses, kept beautifully clean and tidy, and there are local people outside their homes polishing the brass and copper and ensuring that their doors and window cills are spotless. To many, I feel sure, the sight of washing hanging on clothes lines generally portrays a community of impoverished and underprivileged tenants. In Burano I think quite the opposite, as this simple domestic task seems only to enlighten just what this small community is all about. Not only do they have a proud and interesting history, but they also wish to demonstrate that although they are now in the 21st century, tradition and lifestyles remain forever unchanged even in this more affluent society we live in today.

I now turn left and make my way along the Fondamenta della Pescheria for a hundred metres then turn left again into a campo, which leads me to the main thoroughfare, which is the Via B. Galuppi. I have to confess that I really don't think street names are important on this island, as it would be almost impossible to get lost, and for once I do not rely on my map (the same will apply in Torcello). There are several small restaurants en route to choose from, and I notice that there are also plenty of street pavement improvements underway; I would think that this work would be completed by the summer season. Incidentally, everywhere I walk I seem to notice the amazing tilting campanile, which is a good geographical reference point. At the end of Via B. Galuppi I arrive at Piazza Galuppi and the Church of San Martino. The piazza forms a really large square and, being the centrepiece of the island, has its usual complement of souvenir stalls for the tourists to enjoy. In addition to this, it is also the assembly point for festive and religious groups, and today is no exception as there appears to be an event taking place. I must confess that even the street traders do not appear to be as commercial as those in other towns I have visited; I really do like the feel of this island. The piazza and main thoroughfare are named after Baldassare Galuppi (1706–1785), who was a Venetian composer and was born on Burano. His father was both a violinist and barber on the island, and Baldassare, showing some talent, was given the opportunity to study under Antonio Lotti. He later went to Florence and played, in his first appointment, as a harpsichordist there in 1726. From 1728 he was composing operas, and in 1740 worked at the Ospedale dei Mendicanti at St Mark's. Having travelled to London, he spent two years there completing works for the Haymarket, after which he returned to Venice in 1743. He also spent several years in St Petersburg at the Court of Catherine the Great (1765–1768). On his return again to Venice in 1768, he was made choirmaster to the Ospedale. During his lifetime Baldassare wrote over 100 stage pieces and composed many cantatas and keyboard sonatas.

The entrance to the church of San Martino is through a doorway, which is situated in the far corner of the piazza, adjoining the Canonica, as it doesn't have a main entrance as such. The present church was reconstructed between the 16th and the 17th centuries and consecrated in 1645 by the Bishop of Torcello. It has undergone many restorations in the past: in 1867 the central nave was renewed; in 1874 both side naves and the cross vault of the transept were renewed. In 1913 the ceiling and organ were lost following a fire, the organ being completely replaced within one year of the fire. Unfortunately, the original organ, which was destroyed, was considered to have been a masterpiece of its time. Although the exterior of the church looks a little austere and plain, the interior is a magnificent work of art in the Baroque style, with a footprint in the shape of a Latin cross. Classic columns with ornate Corinthian capitals support the main arches and there is a barrel-vaulted ceiling covering the central nave, presbytery and choir stalls. There are six wonderful classical red marble columns and four oriental ones, which adorn the main altarpiece, which was built in 1673. The flooring consists of red and white stone squares, which give a warm appearance and, to my mind, complement the rows of seasoned wooden pews on either side of the central nave.

Starting from the left aisle, I pass a series of magnificent altarpieces of St Anthony and St Joseph, which stand alongside artwork by Francesco Fontebasso, namely *'Adoration by the Shepherds'*. At the far end of the aisle is the altar of the Sacred Heart, where I can see the Eucharist in a tabernacle; this piece was completed by a local Burano sculptor named Remigio Barbaro. Beyond the altar are pieces attributed to Carpaccio and Bellini. From this altarpiece, I can now enter the vestry and, from behind the altar in this area, view a glorious painting called *'St. Mark Throned'*, by an artist with the equally artistic name of Girolanio da Santa Croce, which he painted in 1541. The surrounding choir stalls were once in an ancient church in Torcello, which unfortunately was destroyed long ago by fire.

I now cross to the altar on the far left of the church and arrive at the left chapel, which contains a sarcophagus that holds the remains of three saints, and was given to the church in 1630. This gift was made in thanks of a solemn promise made by the Burano citizens as their island had avoided the plague epidemic in the early 17th century. Interestingly enough, there is a large painting by Antonio Zanchi (1690) in this chapel called *'The Miracle of the Children who Drag the Urn Ashore'*, which depicts an historic legend reminding everyone of the time when the sarcophagus containing the bodies of the three saints of Burano suddenly floated to the shores of the island. The local population vainly attempted to drag this heavy artefact onto the beach and failed, when suddenly some children of the island ('their innocence supplanted strength') eventually succeeded in doing so. As I walk back to the main door of the church still within the left aisle, there are altarpieces of the Madonna of the Rosary together with an early work by Giovanni Tiepolo (1696–1770), *'The Crucifixion'*. Finally, before

I leave this very beautiful church, I arrive at the altar of St Rocco, a masterpiece created by Palma the Younger (1544–1628).

As I exit the church, to my left is the Oratory to St Barbara (of Egypt) who was martyred by her own father in the 4th century, and there is an interesting story of the complicated journey to find her final resting place. Her body was first transferred to Constantinople and then, in the 11th century, it was brought back to San Marco in Venice. From there it was transferred again to St John the Evangelist in Torcello where it remained until the French destroyed part of the church in 1811. It was during this period that St Barbara was finally laid to rest here in Burano.

I mentioned earlier the tilting campanile of San Martino which can be seen from most parts of the island, and to gain a better view of this structure I have walked around the back of the church to the far side. Although the campanile has been restored many times in the past, it still looks in need of some major preservation work today, especially as it leans by 1.83m, which is mainly caused by subsidence. Walking back to the Piazza B. Galuppi, I now focus my attention on the bronze memorial to Baldessare in the square, and take time to look around me at the houses, shops and people who are fortunate enough to live on this beautiful island. The quality of life amongst the local people must be outstanding, judging by their facial expressions and the pace at which everything moves. I really do believe that this island is set in a time capsule, which is seldom moved by the pressures of this day and age.

It is time to leave Burano for a short period while I move on to Torcello, but I intend to be back for lunch, so I make my way back to the Burano pontile, following a similar route to the one I used earlier. When I arrive back at the pontile, there is a small group of people waiting to catch the Traghetto T, which will transport us all to the island of Torcello. So much done already, and it is still only 11.10am. The Traghetto T vessel travels backwards and forwards between Burano and Torcello every 30 minutes, and again provides a comfortable service for this short journey, which takes about 12 minutes. On a day like today, it is a pleasure to travel on the Lagoon as the weather is fantastic, clear blue skies again allowing me to take some marvellous photographs.

On arrival at the Torcello pontile, I alight and begin the short walk along a newly laid herringbone brick pavement, which will take me to the heart of this small but significant historic island. Whilst walking, I remember having previously read about this island and its earliest inhabitants the Romans, who were here in the 2nd century, and of the remains that have been unearthed by excavations. In the past, however, it was not properly inhabited until the 5th century. In the 7th century, the Bishop of Altino took the entire population of his town to Torcello, thereby annexing them and removing them from Byzantine rule forever. In time, the population from the surrounding islands united to form one Venetian state. Torcello now houses the Lagoon's oldest buildings and was considered to be the richest and most important of the island group in the 10th century. The decline of Torcello occurred progressively between the 12th and 16th centuries, during which time malarial disease became prevalent due to the increased volume of swampland that had been reclaimed, resulting in the inhabitants moving to either Murano or Venice itself. Deserted today, other than for a handful of residents, all that remains is a group of religious buildings symbolising the advent of Christian belief.

Ahead of me I can see the campanile and part of the church and basilica, which are slightly hidden by the small community of buildings along the brick pavement concourse, which runs parallel with a small canal. The canal, strangely enough, looks fairly static and I can only assume that there is some form of lock system further along the canal, which regulates the flow of water. Around me I can see arable land, which I feel sure is managed and farmed today as it was many years ago. There appears to be some work being done on the pavement further ahead and a diversion notice leads me, in a circular route, to my destination, passing a small farmhouse and a couple of restaurants. I arrive at the church area by crossing a small bridge and immediately realise just how peaceful and, in some ways, remote this sanctuary of Torcello really is, and probably has been for hundreds of years. Like Burano, I expected to see some souvenir stalls close by to these imposing historic buildings, but thought to myself once again how uncommercial and respectful these traders appeared to be as they restricted themselves in order not to undermine the occasion. The entire area surrounding and fronting these historic buildings had an atmosphere of peace and tranquillity, which I suspect remains constant, as there are not many visitors assembled here at any one time due to the remoteness of the island. Most of the ground area is grassed, though slightly worn with the flow of traffic, but each visitor seems to have a healthy respect for conserving this rural location. As I previously mentioned, there are basically four buildings to visit, all within close proximity to one another, and the general public can purchase a ticket for 8 euros which will allow them to explore each one in any order they prefer. I have decided to visit the Museum first, then the Basilica, then the Church and, finally, to walk, yes walk, to the top of the Campanile. Having purchased my ticket from the basilica shop, which is to the left of the church, I make my way across the grassed area to the small museum, which is isolated from the other three buildings.

To the right of the museum entrance there is a red brick wall, which has many stone relief panels on display as well as other artefacts positioned on the ground. These would normally grace the interior of most museums. The museum itself was probably a domestic building in the past – unfortunately, I have no history – but is nevertheless is an attractive structure, having some Gothic windows and a very attractive bell tower. Inside, the visitor can walk around two floors and sample relics of Greek/Roman antiquity, and view archaeological finds from the estuary from early Veneto and Etruscan periods, together with bronze remains, as well as many items from the Middle Ages up until the 16th century, which include items for the manufacture of glass. Having walked around this well presented and preserved archchaeological museum building, I now make my way back over to the Basilica to enjoy the history and occasion of this iconic structure.

Work started on the original basilica in 639 when the inhabitants of Altino escaped their invaders, and is said to be the first church of Venice, but, unfortunately, only some lower parts of the façade remain. Then, in the mid-9th century, various parts were extended and, finally, the building we see today, which is the Santa Maria Assunta built by Orso Orseolo, was constructed in the 11th century on the same site as the original one. The main façade is primarily constructed of brick, which has been sculptured by ornate arches. The basilica is linked to the church by a porch, which was later extended to the main hall. When I walk into the interior of this building, I immediately notice that there is plenty of light coming from both the high central nave as well as the lower south-side nave. What appear to be large reinforced wooden beams span the width of the basilica in Byzantine style, reinforcing the ancient structure. The central nave is annexed from the side naves by marble columns on each side, whilst several other smaller columns divide off the presbytery. There is a magnificent mosaic floor designed in a multitude of patterns, with some parts of this floor dating back to 1008, the remainder being laid in the 13th century. The right-side nave has two altars, one being 16th century, which has a Veronese painting titled *'The Slaughter of the Innocents'* in situ, the other constructed in the 17th century.

Moving into the presbytery (the far altar in the centre), which was built in the 15th century, I notice at once the wonderful 'iconostasis' of the Madonna and Child with the twelve Apostles, which bridges the entire presbytery. Immediately behind the iconostasis is a large 15th-century wooden crucifix, centrally placed for all to see from any angle within the basilica. There are also some stunning 11th-century Venetian/Byzantine marble panels showing biblical scenes together with a variety of animals, which, it is said, were transferred from the Basilica San Marco in the 14th century. Amazingly, there is a bishop's seat built into the brick design of the central apse, which is at the top of a stairwell and which, in turn, has a circular brick seating arena modelled to follow the semicircular construction of this iconic area. Although the interior of the basilica has not the wealth of paintings and frescoes that one might see in Venice, the mosaic work is spectacular and more than compensates for this. As I leave this building, I really do feel a sense of time and achievement that these early pioneers of Christianity must have experienced.

I now make my way to the church of Saint Fosca, which is adjoined to the basilica and was built in the 12th century, again on the site of a former church. Miraculously, this church escaped demolition by the French in 1811 and, like its neighbour, is built of brick and stone. The front elevation has a series of graceful arches supported by delicate columns, which in turn support a small trapezoid wall fronting a spherical vault, which is positioned on the top of the building. As I mentioned earlier, the majority of the structure is finished in brick, but there is some rendering to the external parts of the cupola. Internally, the church is as interesting as its neighbour, but strangely enough the original marble altar, built in the 17th century, was moved into the sacristy and replaced in 1970 by a new one. Apart from that, the tapestries which adorn the walls, depicting the martyrdom of St Fosca, certainly are original, but to my mind in need of some major restoration. There are a number of marble decorations running along the cornice and into the presbytery. In the main aisle there are similar supporting wooden beams to those of the Basilica, which bridge the width of the church, together with a small crucifix, again in the centre of this expanse. Whilst the interior of St Fosca could be said to be quite 'minimal' (not sure if that is the ecclesiastical word), it is furnished with 14th-century frescoes depicting the Crucifixion, another illustrating Saints grouped together, and one dedicated solely to St Christopher. One artefact of interest is the sarcophagus in honour of a local surgeon named Gaggio who died in 1426, and there are also three tombstones, set in the floor, of former priests of the island together with one of the daughters of a former Torcello magistrate, which are dated between the 17th and 18th centuries. Most of the interior finish is in brick, which does give it a slightly rustic appearance. However, there is a wonderful wooden-trusted circular ceiling which, I think, stands below the external cupola. I now leave this ancient church, to make my way back into the Basilica entrance in order to gain access through to the Campanile.

Access to the Campanile is through a secure door, which is manned by appointed staff; they sensibly keep check on the number of visitors at any one time exploring this tower. The main reason for this is that the visitor has to walk to the summit of the tower, which incidentally is 50m high, and the access route has a limited amount of space to pass other tourists. Strangely enough, the chap at the door told me that priority should be given to people making their way down! Having walked to the top, I think it is fairly exhausting and priority should be with people walking up, as there is no 'tread and riser' like a normal staircase; it is simply a series of sloping ramps which platform every 90° to the left. But, believe me, the view from the top is sensational once you eventually get there. The campanile recently underwent a major restoration in 1997. Up to then it had many rebuilds following structure failures due to subsidence, and is slightly shorter now than its original size. However, as I mentioned earlier, the view from the top is fantastic. On a clear day like today, with a good lens on my camera, I can clearly identify the building profile of Venice from one elevation as well as a very graphic view of Murano. Walking around the bell-tower, I can see the many fishing grounds within the Lagoon (in fact, the 360° view of the Lagoon itself is a wonderful sight) as well as panoramic views of Torcello itself. I now realise just how sparsely populated this island is, as there are just a few small houses to be seen, the rest being open land with a few small canals running through. Making my way back down the campanile was considerably easier than going up, and once down I made my way fairly quickly back to the Torcello pontile as I did notice, when

I was looking from the top of the campanile, that the Traghetto watercraft had just arrived from Burano.

With a minute to spare, I arrive back and board the watercraft, which in all fairness did sound its ships horn to inform those making their way back to the pontile that it was about to depart. Some lucky visitors sprinted back and were successful, but others would have to wait for the next craft to arrive 30 minutes later. Although the time is still only 1.45pm, I feel that I have been lost in a time capsule today, as there has been so much interesting history to absorb. Torcello like Burano is an enchanting island to visit and I recommend that everyone visiting Venice finds time to visit these northern islands. During the 10-minute trip back to Burano, I make a note to myself to return again to these islands, as they are so picturesque and the journey out to them is terrific. Having said that, I have still to explore the remainder of Burano and seek out a good restaurant for lunch. Having reached Burano, I leave the pontile and walk back into the town centre, first to eat and then to explore more of the islands, streets and lanes.

Earlier this morning I noticed several restaurants on the Fondamenta San Mauro which looked inviting, so I have to choose one. When I arrive at San Mauro I decide on a restaurant called the Ristorante Al Vecio Pipa, which is located adjacent to a very picturesque small bridge over the canal, and has seating both inside and outside, I go for the seating inside as it is air-conditioned. Inside the restaurant there is ample seating space and I choose a table by the window so that I can enjoy what's going on outside on this beautiful spring day. After being courteously shown to my table, I immediately notice just how well appointed this restaurant really is. Apart from the very comfortable seating and decor, the whole ambience of the interior is inviting. When the menu arrives,

I am pleased to see that there is quite a comprehensive selection to choose from, as well as set meals, all of which are printed in English. I discover that the waiter serving me, named Michael, is actually the owner, and apart from being extremely helpful when choosing my food, he also assists me with the wine selection. And what a feast it turned out to be! The first course consisted of local mussels with pasta in a white wine sauce; which was followed by veal Milanese with a mixed salad and, finally, an apple dish in pastry with cold custard and cream. The food was delicious, and the local wine excellent, as were my coffee and glass of Grappa, and I spent over one and a half hours just sitting, relaxing, talking, and considering myself very fortunate to be here enjoying the day. The cost of the meal was very reasonable considering the quality of food and the service provided, and I would thoroughly recommend this restaurant. When I eventually finished my meal and continued my travels, I made my mind up that Ristorante Al Vechio Pipa would be my first choice whenever I travel to Burano, and I look forward to my next visit later in the year, when I hope to enjoy the great food and good service once again. From the restaurant, I now decide to walk back to the central Piazza and make my way along a canal that leads to the north part of the island. Having strolled the full length of this narrow fondamenta, I am now facing the island of Torcello once again (though further east), and I have a reasonably good view of the waterway system that separates these two islands. I noted that the motoscafo No. LN that had brought me from Fondamenta Nove travelled on to Treporti, which is the next and very last stop on this particular route. My research tells me that there are still some fortifications standing at Treporti to visit which date back to the fall of the Republic. That's going to be my reason for revisiting

Burano! Another reason for revisiting will be to see the collection of controversial 'modern' housing units that have been built on the even smaller adjoining island of Mazzorbo. Having walked some of my lunch off and had a good look at the remaining east side of the island, I decide to head back to the Burano pontile and take the motonave back to Venice. When I arrive back at my starting point, I have a short wait for the No. LN to arrive, during which time I gaze across the Canale di Burano to Torcello and remember how exhausting it was climbing to the top of the campanile!

The motonave journey back to Venice allowed me to rest my weary feet once again for about 40 minutes, and I thought again just how important these vessels really are to the economy of the 'Serenissima'. Upon my arrival back at Fondamenta Nove, the time is 5.15pm, and having had a very pleasant cruise back across the Lagoon, I now make my way to the appropriate pontile to catch either the No. 41 or 51 back to Piazzale Roma and my final call for today, which is Bar S. Lucia. Once back at Piazzale Roma, I head towards my favourite bar, which will allow me about 40 minutes for a night cap. While there, I am pleased to see Jason, the Irish barman, once again. I haven't had a chat with him since last October due to the shift patterns they work at the bar. After a quick chat with Enrico and Jason, I make my way back to the bus terminal and arrive at Marco Polo airport at 7.35pm, making my way through security and into the departure lounge by 7.55pm, a record time, and just in time for my last treat of the day, an ice-cream ... magic. Whilst waiting for my flight back home, and in between reading my book, I couldn't help thinking about my travels during the past two days and how I can best record the Northern Islands in just one chapter. But one chapter it is, so I hope I have done it justice. During the flight home I manage to get the front seat again, which I shared with a couple of Celtic supporters who had spent the past three days enjoying Italy, after their team were unfortunately knocked out of the Champions League. The banter and humour coming from these two lads made my journey home pass very quickly, but my thoughts still remained in Venice, as I simply couldn't totally switch off from the fond memories of the past couple of days, which I have recorded in my mind as well as in my camera. Writing this chapter constantly reminds me of this trip, especially Burano, and I hope to share a lot of these memories with Avril, and hopefully return to these islands very soon.

Buonasera. Venezia.

CHAPTER 8
APRIL: The Southern Islands
'Time and Tide in Competition with the Lagoon'

Last month, I thoroughly enjoyed my travels to the Northern Islands and became totally besotted with the serenity and history that each destination revealed, especially Burano. Having travelled on the Lagoon so many times before, in both fair weather and foul, I have always enjoyed each adventure within this protected and scenic mass of water for several different reasons, the main one simply being that I generally try to create a sense of time and occasion for certain historical events that have occurred over the centuries.

Throughout Venetian history, the Lagoon has played a phenomenal role in providing food, segregating communities and protecting the population from invasion. But just how protected and vulnerable are Venetians today in times of climatic and ecological change?

In this chapter, I will attempt to explore the formidable problems that haunt the Lagoon and what impact these problems will have on the people of Venice in the 21st century, as well as its surrounding islands, and try to understand just how this may affect its staple income of tourism, in addition to exploring three of

April 2007

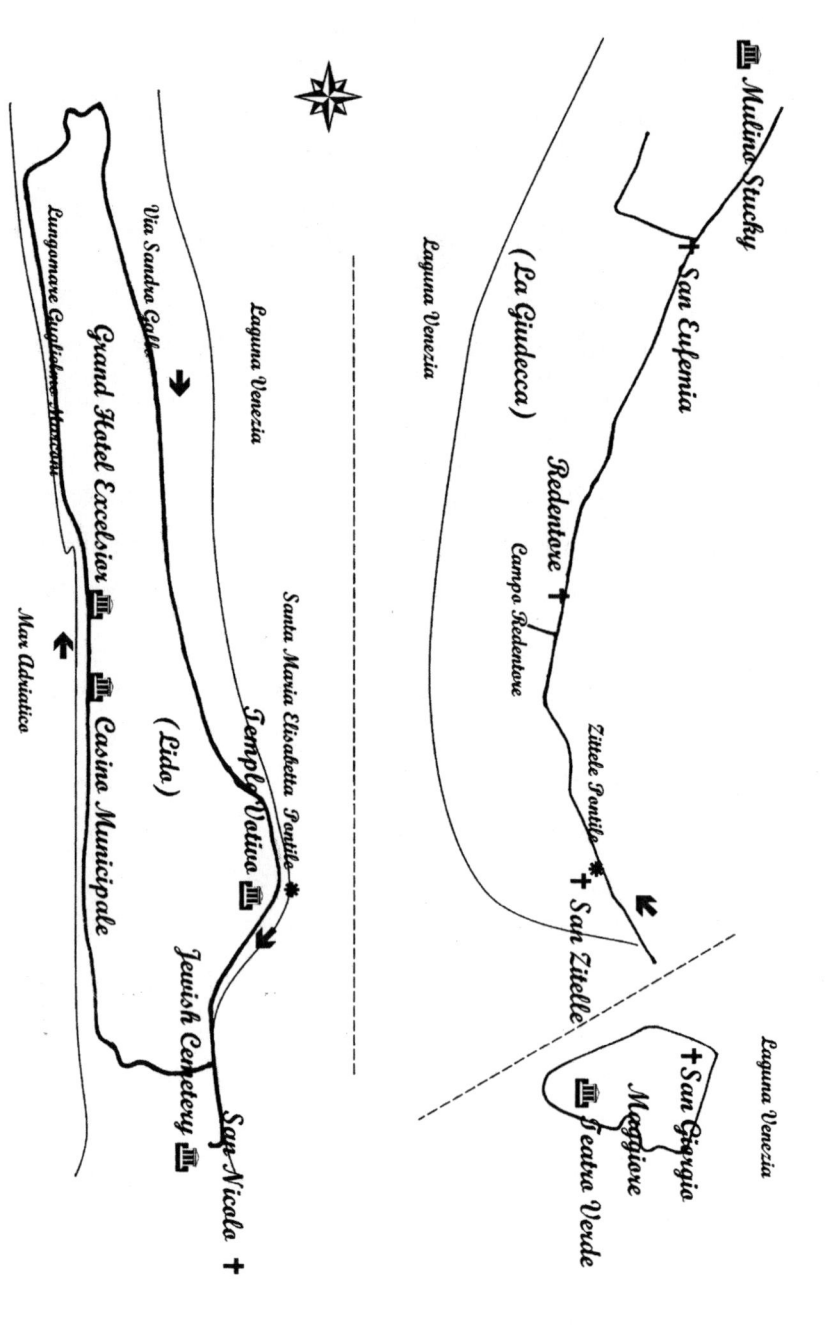

the most prominent islands in the southern part of the Lagoon. Up until now, for the purpose of the journal, I have avoided travelling to the Giudecca, San Giorgio Maggiore and the Lido, simply because I consider that all three of these locations deserve some recognition of their own. Arguably, one might say that the tiny atoll of San Giorgio Maggiore is hardly an island which constitutes a special feature; my view is that, as it contains a substantial piece of Palladian architecture, it is worthy of its single status. My route around the Giudecca will take me along the northern perimeter of the island, where I will visit wonderful churches like the Redentore, Le Zitelle and San Cosima, two of which stand magnificently on the water's edge. In addition to this, I will attempt to explain how this island mass has transformed itself from an industrial expanse in the western region to a more modern residential area which offers more realistically priced accommodation for Venetian residents as well as other nationalities who have decided to live here.

Firstly though, I intend to spend a full day on the Lido with a hired bicycle, in order to circumnavigate most of this popular summer resort, where I intend to visit its beaches and historic cemetery and, strangely enough, marvel at its more contemporary structures which have evolved in the 20th century. Obviously, like last month, I will need two days to explore these islands in detail and, due to other commitments, I shall be making two-day trips rather than staying overnight, which means that my time exploring will be restricted to approximately 7.5 hours for each day from my time of arrival. This restriction in time, due to the recently changed flight departure times, isn't going to spoil any of my future day trips; it just means that I will probably have to avoid the 'long lunches' which I have grown accustomed to.

But, to be perfectly honest, 7 hours of walking, photographing and recording my travels in one day is ample time, as it can be quite exhausting, especially when I have a heavy knapsack to carry. In normal circumstances, I would make directly for my predetermined destination, then set up my easel and sketch or paint for a couple of hours before moving on. Slightly different when I need to record detailed routes for the journal.

As I intend to be cycling on the Lido for at least 10 km, and probably walking for about 11 km on the Giudecca, my knapsack will be kept to a minimum, basically a digital camera, recorder and notebook, leaving me with some room for snacks and drinks, especially if the days are warm and sunny. I can't wait to start.

* April 12th 2007

As I have previously mentioned, today's journey to Venice will be completed in a shorter window of time than previous months because of new flight timetables, so my outgoing flight is at 7.45am today. I reach Gatwick on a clear and relatively mild morning at 6.15am, make my way through security control, which strangely enough is not too busy, and grab myself a strong black coffee and a snack once I am in the departure lounge. It is now 7.00am, so I get my head into my new book, whilst eating an egg and bacon muffin, and simply lose myself in time, reading about the days before the fall of the Venetian Republic, so much so that I have to walk quite quickly to the flight departure lounge and arrive just in time as the last few passengers are boarding the plane. Being a single passenger certainly has its advantages, because I was able to choose from any of the first six rows of seating, which is great because I can be one of the first off the plane at Marco Polo airport when we arrive, and that is an advantage if you have no luggage to collect before leaving the terminal building.

Although my flight was delayed by 40 minutes due to some traffic control problems in France, the journey out was very comfortable and I arrived in Venice at 11.05am (Italian time). Having passed security control, I was in the arrival lounge quite quickly, had purchased my ACTV day ticket by 11.25am and hastily made my way to board the No. 5 bus seconds before it pulled away (that saved me a 30-minute wait before the next one was due to leave). By 11.45am I was off the bus and making my way to Santa Chiara Hotel, where I presented the duty manager with a watercolour that I had painted some time ago of the hotel, which I promised him on my last trip. From the hotel I make my way to the Piazzale Roma pontile to catch the No. 61 vaporetto, which will take me to the Lido. There are other routes to choose from but this particular watercraft does the journey in only 34 minutes.

I shall be using waterbuses often during this visit, whilst travelling around the southern part of the Lagoon, which is great because it gives me the opportunity to see the mainland from a different perspective as well as gaze beyond this mass of water to the distant Adriatic. I cannot describe just how much I enjoy travelling on the Lagoon whenever I am here, and just how lucky I feel Venetians and their neighbours are in having this highway on their doorstep. It must be wonderful to own a small launch and travel in and around this vast lagoon. Whenever I travel on or over a substantial mass of water, I often think of the quotation by Arthur C. Clarke which reads: 'How inappropriate to call this planet Earth, when it is clearly Ocean.'. Whilst on the subject of the Lagoon, I should really take time out to briefly explain, as best

I can, just how important this expanse of water is to Venice and its inhabitants, and just how delicate it is proving to be to achieve the right balance in order to protect both the 'Serenissima' and the ecological framework which surrounds it.

The Lagoon, whilst serving as a passageway to trade, commerce, safety and even life itself to Venetians for over 1,500 years, is fast becoming Venice's greatest enemy, and raised considerable cause for concern in the 20th century, as it still does today. I frequently speak of the delights of being transported across this lake on my travels around the Venetian islands, and occasionally mention the Acqua Alta, but most of the 16 million visitors to Venice each year are simply not aware of the frequency of flooding, which is increasing year by year. Italians have applied several legislative acts in the past to ensure that Venice is reasonably protected and that restoration work to its magnificent buildings is ongoing, but most experts seem to be of the opinion that the only practical solution regarding this problem of rising sea levels is to block the incoming tides from the Adriatic. The floods are generally caused by sudden storms coupled with certain winds that simply force the waters of the Adriatic into the Lagoon. When I speak to local Venetians they tell me that the population is diminishing partly due to the cost of living but mainly due to the imminent and overwhelming peril that threatens the island in addition to the regularity of flooding, which as I mentioned earlier is increasing each year.

Venice stands in the centre of a tidal lagoon, which is about 50km long and 19km wide, and although the Lido plus a group of substantial sea walls help in some way to protect the Lagoon from the Adriatic. Further steps must be taken to ensure that the catastrophic floods of 1966 never occur again. Finding the balance to restrain the perilous tides, without damaging the fragile ecosystem, has become an awkward dilemma for the Venetians authorities, and is proving to be a monumental project and one that, all parties agree, needs to be resolved sooner rather than later. There appears to be this reluctant alliance between each conservation group to resolve these worrying issues, even though their goals are the same, and I think some critical judgement should be made by both factions to achieve a fast solution.

The Lagoon has both fresh and seawater systems, the freshwater being provided by the numerous rivers from mainland Italy which enter into the northern part, and the sea and river currents which merge, resulting in clay and sand deposits creating salt flats. Apart from the income received from salt over the past centuries, this particular ecosystem today provides abundant food for many bird species as well as providing much vegetable matter for the fish to feed on. Some areas are noted wetlands and form an important sanctuary for bird life, which as an amateur ornithologist is a subject close to my heart. I understand that this wetland sanctuary provides a habitat for bearded tits, marsh harriers, sandpipers, sedge warblers, reed bunting, redshanks, curlews, bitterns, dunlins, cormorants, mallards, terns, swans, spoonbills and herring gulls, as well as many land-based birds such as blackbirds, swifts, swallows, house sparrows and the great tit. Parts of the river estuary also provide some protection and homes for many birds, as there is an abundance of rush beds for them to visit. The muddy parts of the Lagoon, which are generally under water other than at tide times, contain plenty of algae. Likewise there are also small islets, which provide lots of vegetation. This vegetation is a neat patchwork of different communities of maritime plants, each adapted to a different degree of submergence and drainage, and the mud can be an important feed ground for waders.

Fish farming is also practised within the Lagoon (and is also at risk), and interestingly enough, many ancient forms of netting are still being used. Fishermen have created banked areas known as *vallicultura*, which form a group of water channels, to attract and retain fish throughout the season. These innovative areas are generally compartmentalised to allow breeding ponds. Another innovative fishing practice is the Lavoriero, which acts as a lock where fish enter and are graded for size and species after being filtered from other elements, which are drawn into the water channels.

Sea levels have also risen dramatically since the ice age, thereby affecting the Lagoon. Venice and its islands have only survived due to constant work over many hundreds of years. Incidentally, the average water depth in the Lagoon is less than a metre; there are, however, man-made channels cut into the seabed to allow shipping to function. This channel navigation programme, implemented over the centuries, meant that more commercial shipping traffic was made possible to feed the then growing economy. To accommodate this, a scheme was devised in the 15th century to ensure that Venice remained an island, as natural processes would have linked the island we know today with the mainland. During this experimental period, work began to create great sea walls (*Marazzi*), thereby keeping the Adriatic out, at the same time, offering the sanctuary of a harbour. These great walls also forced the tides to flow in a more concentrated fashion, thereby keeping the shipping channels free.

In the 20th century, still further problems arose when the Lagoon was developed to accommodate the industrial havoc of Marghera. This dramatically affected the salt marshes and surrounding areas. The ecological effects of this action has resulted in the Lagoon losing 20% of its plant life, about 50% of the bird species have disappeared, and there has been a sizeable amount of water pollution from waste products flowing in from the rivers.

Apart from the ecological problems I have mentioned, the Acqua Alta occurs more frequently now and it is no longer unusual to find partial flooding almost everywhere in Venice during the winter periods. Although Venice is sinking gradually and is well below the water level recorded in the 18th century, the sea levels are more worrying, especially when certain wind conditions become more prevalent. The disastrous storm conditions of 1966 caused the water level to rise by almost 2m, which resulted in an environmental catastrophe for the city. It did, however, open the eyes of the world to Venice's misfortune and will, hopefully, in time achieve a final solution. Some sinking is inevitable, but fortune has it that Venice is built on a solid clay base which provides a reasonable foundation for the millions of wooden piles that collectively support the city we know and love. The rising sea levels are obviously recorded meticulously in order to gain an accurate assessment of any impending crisis, and as a frequent visitor I have experienced substantial flooding (between 25–100cm) on several occasions, and when this does occur it can affect over 90% of the island.

There are many ambitious projects currently in place, to check, stabilise and protect the ecological system within the Lagoon, and these projects are primarily aimed at reducing erosion, revitalising the salt marshes and reducing pollution, all of which is largely dependent on substantial grants and funds raised by various caring organisations. Two prime areas of investigation, currently being considered, focus on the reopening of certain Lagoon areas and filling in many navigational channels.

More significant is the major barrier project work *(Mose)*, which has proved to be extremely controversial in as much as there are serious doubts as to the outcome of such a monumental undertaking. On the one hand, there are the environmentalists, who quite rightly feel that once the barrier is completed the Lagoon will be considerably harmed by the effect it will have on the ecosystem, whilst, on the other hand, there are groups who dispute that water quality problems will occur, as they feel that the Lagoon could be flushed out more often by using the barrier system; they also have concerns regarding the overall cost-effectiveness of such a scheme. The barrier, or barriers, as there will be over 70 moving steel panels spread across the three inlets of the Lagoon, will be opened and closed around five or six times a year, mainly during the winter months, and this in turn will affect tidal flushing, which eventually will impact on the amount of sediment that is removed.

Whatever the solution, whether it is the barrier scheme as a planned preventative project, or to spend the equivalent budget on continual restoration, Venice is in an extremely fragile environmental situation at present. There is no agreed solution to stop the inevitable climatic changes that will come due to global warming, but it is comforting to know that Venice at least has been targeted for some considerable remedial action to protect its amazing heritage. I hope that this brief resume of the problems confronting the Lagoon has opened readers' eyes to the concerns facing Venice, and the continuous endeavour to stabilise what has become an enormous problem.

Moving on, I now board the No. 61 waterbus and position myself mid-decks in order to enjoy the late-morning sunshine and sea breeze on my journey to the Lido. The weather today is perfect from my point of view: temperatures around 19C, blue skies and hardly any wind. As we pull away from the pontile, I remember that this vessel actually travels in the direction of Tronchetto, before turning left into the Canal di S. Chiara, and then travels under the road bridge, after which it cruises along the Canal Scomenzera before it joins the Canal di Fusina. This particular canal then merges with the Canal della Giudecca before opening up again to the Lagoon. Once past Canal di S. Marco, from the vaporetto I can see that there are several tower cranes amid the Mulino Stucky (a complex which I look forward to visiting on my next trip, as it was a former industrial unit which has developed into a new residential area on the Giudecca). The vaporetto I am travelling on stops at S.Marta, S.Basilio and Zattere before crossing over the Canal di San Marco, where it stops at Giardini Exposizione before moving on to S. Elena and finally across to the Lido. This journey appears far less crowded than other vessels, and really does provide wonderful views of the north of the Giudecca as well as panoramic scenes of the Venetian mainland from the Lagoon. I probably have a hundred different photographs of this particular journey, which has provided me in the past with a wealth of material for landscape backdrops of S. Maria Salute, S. Giorgio Maggiore and the many other spectacular building adjacent to the Molo.

My watercraft, having navigated the narrow channel passage to the Lido, now arrives at the pontile of S. Maria Elisabetta after an extremely pleasant cruise, which only took 34 minutes from Piazzale Roma. It is now 12.55pm, and once I have disembarked I make my way to the Gran Viale (the main road opposite the pontile), where I hope to rent my cycle. The cycle-hire shop is located down a narrow passageway to the left, just off of the Gran

Viale. There is a large sign signifying bike hire, so it is very easy to find. As the main tourist season is yet to begin, when I enter the shop I am the only customer requiring attention, so I am kitted out with my cycle in a couple of minutes and out of the shop and on the road very quickly. Having been provided with a map of the island by the cycle shop, I make my way in the direction of the Riviera S. M. Elisabetta (simply head towards the ACTV pontile and turn left). From previous trips to the Lido, I know not to expect many ancient buildings or mysterious passageways leading to small campos, which I usually encounter on my travels. What I will see, however, is a vast stretch of Adriatic beach, which has a creditable modernist history, and I also get the opportunity to cycle for several kilometres on a level plateau, and enjoy the breeze from the sea. The Lido is approximately 12km long and has a population of about 20,000 (mainly Italians), and I intend to circumnavigate most of its coastline and main roads, which run parallel with each side of the coast. The Lido is made up of three districts: to the north end (where I start my journey) it is known as simply the *Lido*, the centre is the *Malamocco*, and the south end is known as the *Alkevoni*.

Historically, the Lido can boast that, in 1202, it was used as the staging post for many thousands of Crusaders waiting to go forth on the Fourth Crusade (they were there simply because they had to wait until they could pay the Venetians for the ships they had ordered to take them to the East). The island was also used as a transit stage for the German Emperor Federick Barbarosa in 1177, which followed several years of conflict after he had crowned himself Holy Roman Emperor of Rome, for which the reigning Pope initially banned him from entering Venice itself!

As I cycle along the Riviera San Nicolo, I notice just how many parked vehicles there are, and remember that the Lido is the only island in the Lagoon with roads, other than the short stretch of tarmac from the Ponte della Liberta to Piazzale Roma bus terminal. Having cycled for a few minutes, I now reach the Franciscan Monastery of San Nicolo, which stands slightly off of the main road. The present San Nicolo structure dates back to the 17th century, and architecturally has two Byzantine capitals, situated at the entrance, which are remnants from the original building on this site. Above the doorway is a plaque depicting the achievements of a member of the Contarini family, recording three of his military and naval victories. The main façade of the monastery is relatively plain compared to others of that date, with straightforward bonded courses of weathered brickwork, and the side elevation is even less ornate, having simply been painted.

From past research, I remember that this part of the Lido is the only quarter of the island that has some cultural history, part of which can be seen across the Porto di Lido where you can view the fortress of San Andrea on the island of Le Vignole, which was built by Michele Sanmicheli between 1435 and 1449. At the rear of San Nicolo lies the Jewish Cemetery, which was given to the Jews in 1386 for the burial of their dead once their relationship with the Venetians had become more civilised. This concession had come about when Jews from all parts of Europe made their way to Venice as it developed into an important trading and financial city. The cemetery has become quite decayed today: gravestones overgrown with grass, and tombstones fallen or leaning against other monuments, and every one of the Istrian stone facings is sadly covered in lichen and ravaged by the elements of both the sea and the wind. Originally the cemetery grounds were said to be vineyards belonging to the monastery and were given over to the Jewish people by the Benedictine monks. As the Jewish population gradually declined through the restrictions imposed upon them on the mainland, so also was the cemetery reduced in size, and was almost abandoned by the end of the 1700s. During the 19th century a new cemetery was opened in an adjacent area, once the Lido became more inhabited, at which time many former graves were discovered. Following this discovery, many tombstones were collected and repositioned in the old cemetery. Unfortunately, the original stone locations were lost, so that the original sittings are not accurate. There are, however, many inscriptions and sculptured images which signify varying Jewish references in both Hebrew and Venetian dialect, and one striking memorial depicts a tree of life rising from a vase. Another famous grave is said to be that of Rabbi Leone da Modena, who was a teacher and writer, and who, it is said, was addicted to gambling. He eventually died in poverty in 1648.

I leave the Jewish cemetery, return to Riviera San Nicolo and head back in a westerly direction, passing the ferry terminal on my right. When I reach the Via Marco Polo, I turn left and cycle to Strada dieto l' Ospizio Marino, which will eventually get me to the Adriatic coastline of the island. Today the pollen from certain trees is falling like snowflakes and there is a mass of what look like cotton balls on the pavements and roads, so I can't wait to get past this avalanche of floss. Having pushed my cycle to the limits to get past this seasonal discharge of nature, I am relieved to find myself on the Lungomare d' Annunzio, with the wonderful beaches of the Lido to my left. These white sandy beaches are absolutely amazing as they stretch for several kilometres, but unfortunately a great many are exclusively owned by the hotels, which I guess the general public cannot use.

In the 19th century the island became renowned for being the first 'lido' as we know the word. The title probably originated about the same time as Lord Byron was challenged for a wager to take part in a marathon swim, which he accepted. The swim, incidentally, was from the Lido to Santa Chiara, and Byron succeeded in winning his bet in just four hours. This famous race took place in 1818 on the 25th June and really did open up the Lido to many tourists, especially followers of this famous poet and Romantic. Interestingly, George Lord Byron left England in 1816 for the last time and travelled throughout Europe on his journey to Venice, stopping at Geneva, and then on to Verona, Vinceza and Padua. He eventually arrived in Venice and booked into the Hotel of Great Britain. His entourage consisted of an enormous coach, large enough to accommodate a bed, a travelling library and scores of household goods! Having stayed at the hotel for a short period, he eventually moved to private rooms over the shop of a draper in the Frezzeria (just west of Piazza San Marco), and eventually took out a lease on the Palazzo Mocenigo (on the Grand Canal). It was during this period that the Austrians occupied Venice, which Byron deplored. He did, however, form a strong allegiance with the monks of San Lazzaro. San Lazzaro is one of the smaller islands in the Lagoon and is neighbour to La Grazia, San Servolo, Lazzaretto and Sacca Sessola, all of which lie in a stretch of the Lagoon between the Giudecca and the Lido. I hope to visit some of these islands later this year. Byron stabled his horses on the Lido and would row out to the isle on a regular basis to ride. The character and history of Lord Byron's days in the 'Serenissima' are well documented, and, although I am not a great reader of his works, I am told that he lived a full and extravagant life, had numerous love affairs, was always in debt and loved Italy dearly until his early death in 1824 at the age of 36.

As I continue my cycle ride I pass several notable villas and one in particular catches my eye called Villa Margherita. This villa, which faces the Adriatic, is well protected by an attractive but serviceable pair of large iron gates and has terra cotta painted walls with ornate balconies. Today, the villa's natural earth colours are wonderfully supplemented by the aqua blue roller blinds which are regimentally pulled down to protect each room from the sun throughout the summer months. Moving on still further down the Lungomare Guglialino Marconi, I reach the midway point along this coastline and finally arrive at the Piazzale dei Casino, which houses the Casino Municipale as well as the Palazzo dell Mostra D. Cinema. I am fortunate today as the streets are relatively empty, with few tourists on the island. In September this particular area really comes alive when the Venice Film Festival comes to town. Looking directly at the Casino, with my back to the sea, I can see a mass of white stonework with shuttered windows on the façade, and very little else to complement this building other than its Fascist architecture made fashionable in the early 20th century and encouraged by Benito Mussolini, which to my mind works reasonably well with a period of art that I enjoy, that being Art Deco. The Palazzo dell Mostra stands alongside the Casino, which is probably the heart of the Venice Film Festival. This event, which delights the film world every year, will reach its 62nd birthday in September, and the vista around the area I am now standing in will be transformed considerably. This spectacle is actually the oldest film festival in the world, which began in 1932 as the Exposizione Internationale deArte Biennale (festival of contemporary art), the principle awards being the 'Golden Lion' (best film) and the 'Volpi Cup' (best actor and actress).

While I am in this location, I cross the empty road and take the opportunity to photograph the thousands of beach canopies that are positioned neatly along this almost never-ending stretch of white sandy beach. Approximately 300m further along the road from where I am standing is the very attractive and majestic-looking Grand Hotel Excelsior, which from the road elevation has some interesting external domes, circular towers and graceful Gothic windows which seem to disappear into the distance. On the opposite side of the road, across from the main entrance to the hotel, there are some steps which lead to a balconied platform area overlooking one of the few attractive canals of the Lido. This particular area is where all the celebrities and dignitaries arrive on watercraft from the mainland for the Festival.

By now I am in need of some light refreshment, so I stop to grab a refreshing drink in one of the many cafes that are situated along this scenic route, and spend a few minutes idly sitting in the shade simply gazing into the Adriatic. Once refreshed I continue cycling along the very quiet coast road of the Malamocco district until I reach the Murazzi, where I decide to turn right and make my way north across the island for the homeward ride along the Via Sandro Gallo. When I reach Rio Teta, I make my way across to the Lagoon side of the island and, after some fairly monotonous cycling, reach the Via Sandro Gallo. Ahead of me is a considerably long stretch of wide road, which will take me back to Piazzale San Elisabetta. I would imagine that this particular stretch of road could be quite hazardous at the peak of the tourist season; today it is empty, fortunately, so I can idly gaze around as I cycle, without having to concentrate totally on the road. Although I enjoy cycling on the Lido, I have to confess that there is little to excite my grey cells other than the occasional canal view, so I make my way back to the cycle-hire shop without stopping at any other point en route, that is, until my back wheel punctured about 3 kilometrtes from the shop. This slowed me up slightly, but I was determined enough not to get off the bike and walk!

Having arrived back at the bike shop at 2.45pm, I suddenly realised that, in the past two hours, I had probably cycled 16km or more, and the hire charge was only 5 euros, which I thought was very good value, as I had been able to see most of the coastline of the island. Had Avril been with me today, I would probably have hired a tandem for the pair of us, as I own one back home, and it has provided lots of fun for all my family over the past twenty years. So, having paid my bike hire charge and explained to the shop owner why my back wheel was wobbly, I stroll back to the pontile at Santa Maria Elisabetta, which literally takes only a few minutes, and I am in plenty of time to catch the 3.02pm No. 82 back across the Lagoon to San Zaccaria, where I hope to meet up with a fellow artist at work. As usual, my waterbus arrives on time and I take the upper-level deck, which is open-air, for the short journey back across the Lagoon to Venice, and my thoughts go back to Byron and his amazing swim across this channel of water, which was no mean feat, especially if you include the last phase of his epic swim, which included the entire length of the Grand Canal. Whenever I leave the Lido, I always feel that although I have enjoyed being close to the Adriatic, as well as strolling around a busy and fairly interesting Venetian island, it is a resort rather than an historical landmark, nevertheless a place which must be seen when travelling to Venice. The journey across the Lagoon was very pleasant, and in no time at all I had disembarked and was making my way to the Molo, where I hope to meet Danish artist Harald Hansen who I first met in this same spot about a year ago. Harald has lived in Venice since 1966 and today resides in Cannaregio, and each year between April and September he can be seen painting at various locations, such as the Porta del Frumento (Palazzo Ducale). When I reach the Molo I am in luck today as I immediately recognise his easel half-hidden behind one of the pilasters, which offer some shade, and notice he is talking about his work, and displaying some of the many quality prints he has, to an interested tourist. I mentioned Harald once before, who incidentally originates from Aarhus in Denmark, in an earlier chapter, but did perhaps not explain his work, which is known as *'stilizzato'* and is quite impressive. The piece he is working on can best be described as a contemporary perception of the Basilica San Marco, which is finished in a wonderful blue tone with vivid and articulate lines. The precision and sharpness of his work is quite amazing, and I personally think there are some undertones of a 'surrealist' style. Whatever, Harald's work is special, and is worth seeking out when in Venice.

Having concluded my chat with Harald, I have decided that it is probably too late in the day to visit either the Giudecca or San Giorgio Maggiore so I decide to take a slow walk back to Piazzale Roma and grab a pannini somewhere, as I haven't stopped for food since breakfast time and the time now is 4.05 pm. From the Piazza San Marco, I take my normal route back to the Scalzi Bridge, by making for the Bacino Orseolo and on to Campo S. Luca. Why this route? Well, it gives me time to grab a snack in relative peace where I can sit quietly for a while and watch the world go by. Although I am sitting inside whilst eating, I can hear music being played outside, so I investigate and see that there is one musician playing a violin, another a guitar and the third a double bass! When I leave the cafe there is quite a large musical audience gathered, and rightly so, because this live music is fantastic and would grace any music hall. It is 4.50pm and from Campo S. Luca I make my way over to the Calle dei Ferro and eventually the Rialto Bridge.

When I arrive at the Rialto, I realise that the tourist season is well underway even though the Lido was quiet, and I cross over the bridge fairly quickly as I want to revisit the church of *San Giacomo Di Rialto,* which I know will be open at this time. When I arrived at the church (situated at the rear of the market), I realised that most of the tourists were also there, so I went inside briefly. took some notes and left after a few minutes. I hope to return and explore more of this small church later in the year when it is less busy. San Giacomo stands on the site of the very first church built in Venice, in 421, and was the oldest church in the city for many centuries. The current church was built in the 11th century and was the only building to survive the disastrous fire of the Rialto area in 1514. Today's church is affectionately known by Venetians as *'San Giocometto'.* There have been major refurbishment works undertaken in the church from as far back as 1601, including some restoration work on masterpieces attributed to Titian.

Having marvelled yet again at this delightfully unassuming but very interesting church, and whilst standing to one side of Palazzo dei Camerlenghi, my thoughts again are focused on the works of J.M.W Turner, who has managed to capture and portray a host of Canal views around the Rialto area. Being an enthusiastic follower of Turner's works, especially his pencil and watercolour pieces, which I have had the honour of viewing personally in the Tate Britain, I normally make every effort to match his sketches with today's landscape, using photography. There is some conjecture regarding Turner's finished oils in as much as he has, on occasions, used his artistic licence to achieve what he considered to be a more complete picture of the Venetian landscape. From my limited time viewing his original 1840 sketches, I personally cannot fault any of his work in relation to detail, other than to say that he may have concentrated on particular buildings that appealed to him, rather than include every building on the Grand Canal, but then isn't that what artists do?

It never ceases to amaze me when I think of the quality, sense of movement and accuracy of Turner's sketches, when you consider that he worked in close proximity to his subjects, usually from unstable watercraft and sometimes in the centre of the Grand Canal. Amongst my favourite of Turner's sketches has to be his *'The Rialto Bridge from the North'* (1840), where he captures the movement of various watercraft both moored and sailing close to Fondaco dei Tedeschi and Palazzo dei Camerlenghi, which is precisely where I am now standing. Forgive me for digressing slightly and going into artist mode once again, but it is important that I get my head around my own sketches for the journal, as I am falling behind with this work, which I produce in my studio back home. As you can no doubt see from the remainder of my sketches that I have earmarked to illustrate at the end of this chapter, I still have lots of artwork left to complete. Therefore, just talking about the great master J.M.W Turner really does provide the stimulus to create new work.

I now leave the area adjacent to San Giacomo and make my way firstly to Campo Beccarie and then on to Campo Cassiano, as I continue on my walk back to the Scalzi Bridge. The route is clearly signposted 'Ferrovia' for all tourists to follow, and provides a scenic route back to Cannaregio. You can't go wrong!

By the time I reach Bar S. Lucia, it is 5.45pm, which leaves me just enough time to have a drink, talk some football with Enrico and Matti and get some outside photographs of the bar, which I hope to recreate in a monochrome ink and wash sketch for the journal. At this point in time, I am not quite sure how many ink sketches in total I will be able to illustrate, as I have scores of many wonderful locations already sketched. Having said that, I think my favourite Venetian bar and hotel should be featured somewhere. As my scheduled return flight to Gatwick is now 9.05pm, I leave the bar and make my way to the bus terminal to catch the 6.40pm bus, which will get me to Marco Polo airport in good time. Although, as I previously mentioned, I have one and a half hours less to explore Venice on each day trip, I still consider that there is so much for the journeyman to see and enjoy in a day, and if the journey is well planned in advance it is remarkable just how much distance can be travelled on foot and by water transport. My flight home was bang on time. I was home making myself a drink by 10.45pm (UK time) and reminiscing about my enjoyable cycle ride on the Lido and meeting Francesco Da Mosto, and planning my next visit to San Giorgio Maggiore and the Giudecca to complete this chapter.

Buonasera, Venezia

* May 8th 2007

Today I intend to complete the Southern Islands chapter, and, yes, we are in May now, but I did say it would take two days to complete this chapter, so having spent the past three weeks or so since my last visit to Venice sketching and painting scenes for both the journal and my web site gallery, I am full of enthusiasm to return to the 'Serenissima' once again. The trip today will focus on the wonderful churches on both San Giorgio Maggiore and the Giudecca, as well as a good walk along the length of the Giudecca and, hopefully, I'll see some of the restoration work which has taken place since my last visit to the island.

As with my previous visit to the Lido, I make my way to Gatwick nice and early for the 7.45am flight to Marco Polo airport, full of enthusiasm once again, as I am looking forward to concluding my travels to the Southern Islands of the Lagoon. The weather forecast in the UK is set for being wet, windy and cool, whereas the forecast for Venice is sunny and dry. We shall see.

When I arrive at the South Terminal Gatwick, it is, as one would expect, very busy. However, my flight is on time and I have a very pleasant journey out to Venice, arriving at 10.40am Italian time. As usual, I make my way through arrivals, purchase my ACTV day ticket, board the No. 5 bus and arrive at Piazzale Roma bus terminal by 11.20am. The weather forecast was absolutely correct: the temperature is 20C and it is dry and sunny. It is also very busy, as it is now the beginning of the tourist season, which Venice relies upon and expects. Having made my way over to the vaporetto pontile, I board the No. 82 after a short wait, and once aboard I can sit back and enjoy my next journey, which is, firstly, to the Giudecca to explore a beautiful church and the local habitat, then later to San Giorgio Maggiore to marvel at another magnificent church, and ascend its campanile to enjoy the panoramic view from the top. The Lagoon is a hive of activity at this time of the day, especially as the vaporetto makes its way towards Tronchetto, where I notice many tourists arriving on coaches for a trip around the Lagoon, which I guess will probably end at San. Zaccaria, and my thoughts return to the very first time I experienced Venice on the 'football special', where I was also transported to Venice by waterbus from this point. As the vaporetto turns left, after calling at Tronchetto on its way to Sacca Fisola, I notice that at least three very large cruise liners are moored close by, all of which have navigated their way through the narrow passageway from the Adriatic, bringing tourists who will spend money, but also creating a menacing wake which affects the ecological balance. I seem to remember reading somewhere that, each time a sizable cruise liner enters the Lagoon, certain residents on both the mainland and surrounding islands actually experience the vibration from these craft as they travel down the Canale della Giudecca. The vaporetto transporting me to the Giudecca calls at Sacca Fisola, Basilio, Zettere, Palanca, Redentore and eventually Zitelle, which is where I disembark.

The island of the Giudecca was formerly called the 'Vigano' or 'Spinalonga', meaning 'long spur', and was partly urbanised during the Middle Ages. It once had some sizable villas and large garden areas, but few have survived. Research tells me that the more modern name, Giudecca, could be derived from the Jewish word 'giudei', as many Jewish people either lived here or were imprisoned on the island, following which, in 1516, the Venetian Jews were made to leave and live within the Ghetto. In 1712 a college for Venetian noblemen was built on the island (previously a foundation which originated in 1609), forming the building known as Palazzo Cavalli, which is situated on the Fondamenta San Eufemia. The Venetian patriarchs abandoned the island in the 18th century; records show that in 1624 there were 18 noble families living here, but by 1761 none remained. This exodus of patriarchs was due to the change in social standards when industry became more prevalent; the Mulino Stucky flourmill is one example.

Several churches and monasteries, such as Santa Croce and S. Cosima e Damiano, were used as military bases for the French, following the fall of the Republic, and since that period the island was generally known for housing a large number of the less wealthy population. Most tourists tend to agree that the Giudecca is an amalgam of quiet suburbs with very little activity and is enjoyed for its solitude and calm. There are many apartment blocks coupled together with modern housing units, and in some areas you can even see some houseboats. In the 20th century, factories were introduced as well as shipyards and even a film studio. The spacious sidewalks and boulevards are a delight to walk down, as we shall discover today, and new avant garde housing schemes seem to have resurrected this island mass, according to local people I have spoken to, one reason being that the rents are much lower than on the mainland.

In the past, pilgrims travelling to the Holy Lands were welcomed and accommodated here and it is said that Michelangelo lived here in 1529 whilst he made his designs (unsuccessful though they were) for the Rialto Bridge. Today the island is popular with many notable architects, travellers, designers, artists, composers, and, according to one local I spoke to, one very special music celebrity who is known for his extravagant costumes as well as having been an icon in the pop music world for decades. I feel sure everyone knows who I mean; I certainly have several of his CDs.

As I leave the vaporetto at Zitelle, I turn left and walk about 200m and reach the former convent of Zitelle. This imposing building was built in 1558 by the Jesuit, Benedetto Palmio, who delivered sermons urging Venetians to fund a church for 'maidens', hoping to discourage the underprivileged young women from a 'life of damnation'. In 1599 his request was answered and the Venetian Zitelle Institute was formed. The façade of the building (which at one time contained a church, convent and orphanage) is finished in a light-coloured stone, which follows classical lines that I personally think are not too dissimilar to that of the Redentore which I shall be visiting later. Not surprisingly, the design is attributed to Andrea Palladio, who I shall mention in more detail later in this chapter. Although there is no evidence that Palladio was actually involved in the construction of the adjoining church, it is feasible that he was responsible for designing the entire complex of churches on the island. The builder of the church was a Jacopo Bozzetto, who constructed it in a square design, the façade having wonderful Corinthian columns either side of a imposing doorway which is highlighted by thermal windows, paired towers and a dome which is partially hidden beyond the front elevation.

Internally the appearance is pretty basic in Venetian terms, however, there is a wonderful painting of the *'Madonna and Child'* by Antonio Vassillacci, which also portrays Federico Contarini, who was a powerful procurator of his time. Like all Venetian churches, history abounds and the church of 'Santa Maria della Presentazione' (its real name) is no exception. Research informs me that, in 1583, the Zitelle convent held over 200 maidens within its walls, each inmate being a member of the newly formed Institute. The vetting procedure for entry was certainly demanding: it required that each girl must be a virgin and in good health, be aged between 12 and 18 and have a good physical appearance as well as being 'socially' and 'economically' acceptable, quite demanding criteria imposed upon the parents! The Institute complex, however, was further enlarged in the early 18th century and completed by Paolo Rossi in 1710. Judging by the amount of restoration work that followed this period, there must have been some very wealthy benefactors, as ongoing works continued during this period, especially following a fire in 1764. By the 19th century, many major changes were introduced into the Institute, whereby older women were accepted, but these entrance criteria soon reverted back to the original demands for some reason or another, allowing only young girls to be accepted. In 1901, the Nuns of Carburlotto, who remained there for some years, looked after the girls of the Institute. By the 1970s the 'residents' were all transported to the mainland and the Institute complex fell into complete disrepair. Major restoration work followed, by extending the building footprint; during these works considerable thought was given to preserving some of the original artisan skills whilst introducing some modern-day improvements.

Today what was once a sanctuary for the maidens of Venice is now a prestigious seminar and exhibition centre, which unfortunately is shut so I will simply make my way along the Fondamenta d. Zitelle and enjoy the walk. Fortunately for me, the walk along the Giudecca today is completely shaded and, what's more, there are very few people about, so my earlier synopsis appears to be right. Looking across the Canale Giudecca to the Salute and Piazza San Marco, I sense a feeling of complete isolation even though this passage of water is relatively short in terms of distance, but what a vista it presents.

While walking along, I notice that there are what appear to be several commercial watercraft delivering their wares. One, in particular, can best be described as a builder's merchant, with his cargo of cement bags, wood and scaffolding, I then notice that there is considerable work in progress on one of the attractive houses that line this area of the pavement. Continuing along, I pass a couple of bars with their parasols and seating arrangements lining the street, each table occupied by customers enjoying their food al fresco, seemingly unaffected by the splendid view across the Lagoon; they must be locals. Once past this group of tables, the street ahead is empty again and I notice a really wonderful building called the *Casa de Maria*, which has been tastefully restored. The façade of the building is of a terracotta brick, which is finely crafted into diamond shapes and complemented by impressive Gothic-shaped windows each having a semicircular balcony. I can't help but relate this façade to the Palazzo Ducal albeit considerably smaller. The facing design and ornate stonework are very similar and serve as a testimony to the Venetian craftsmen who undertook this work.

As I reach the Fondamenta della Croce, I notice some terracotta-rendered buildings, which probably provide housing for the locals, and amongst these buildings are the occasional shops, which have been respectfully designed to sit inconspicuously amongst the residential buildings. The view ahead of me on this particular stretch of pavement is extremely picturesque and really does tempt visitors to continue walking into the vanishing point of an imaginary picture. Looking at my watch, I notice that it is only 12.45am and I am amazed at just how much I have seen in such a short period of time. By now I have reached house number 78 and notice that a few more shops are reopening for business. When I reach the building numbered 87, I see that it has a sign on the wall, which reads Ostellove Venecia, and I peer through the glass doors and discover what appears to be a cinema, again carefully disguised to ensure that the façade does not compromise the historical value of its surroundings. Moving on, I pass another group of tables and parasols, with the bar discreetly hidden in the building façade, and again think how inviting these alfresco eating places are on a day like today. This one is relatively empty so I make a mental note to check it out when I return. Surprisingly enough, there are very few eating-places along this elevation of the Giudecca, but I have to say that those I have seen all appear to be very comfortable and their customers seem to be enjoying their food.

By now, I have reached the Ponte della Croce, which is a small bridge spanning the Rio della Croce, which once I have walked over, takes me onto the Fondamenta S. Giacome, and I know that I am quite near to one of my favourite churches, which is the Redentore, but to get to it I have to cross yet another small bridge. After a few minutes' walk, I arrive at the Redentore and immediately think just how lucky I am to be exploring this building with hardly anyone else in sight, a rarity when you consider just how many people there would be in a mainland church of this magnitude during the tourist season. The existing church was originally built following the plague of 1575–1576, which killed over 50,000 Venetians. This site was chosen, as it was to be near to the Church of St Mary of the Angels and the Capuchin Friars Hermitage. It was designed and built by Andrea Palladio (yes, I will spend some time talking about him soon), who was sensitive to the needs of the large volume of parishioners, who he knew would eventually attend its holy masses. With that in mind, he built the church to a longitudal layout to accommodate large numbers of people, and the first stone was laid in 1577, when the plague had finally disappeared. The church was eventually completed by Antonio da Ponte and consecrated by patriarch Lorenzo Priuli in 1592, sadly after the great Palladio had died.

This beautiful building was styled on Roman architecture to a longitudinal plan, as I previously mentioned, and the temple façade stands as a front mantle which coordinates sensitively with the higher rooftops of the nave and side chapels, beyond which are the dome and lantern. The white stone façade appears to be almost layered to enrich and stylise the nave and chapels within, and the wide steps which lead to the large central temple doors, are framed by pilasters and columns. Triangular pediments are prominent at either side of the main façade, each elegantly sculptured.

The interior of this glorious church is full of treasures, and its design is purpose-built to a narrow specification, with its longitudinal nave accommodating the side chapels, connected to one another, which eventually lead to the domed crossing. There are semicircular apses on either side of the main altar, which are screened by splendid columns. The vaults and walls have stuccowork painted white and there are many sculptured stone details, each altarpiece having been commissioned by the Venetian Senate, who chose the best artists available at that time. Once through the main door and into the entrance hall, I notice the painting by Paulo Piazza depicting the offering for liberation of the plague, together with a marble memorial in memory of the vow made by the state in 1567, to build this outstanding church. There are two holy water fonts, each with bronze statues, and two large lunettes by Pietro Muttoni, the lower one called *Il Vecchia*, depicting St Felix receiving the infant Jesus from the Madonna, and the one above, which represents the Doge in front of the Virgin Mary, surrounded by St Mark, St Francis and St Rocco, which was painted by Paolo Piazza. Turning to my right, I am faced with the first altarpiece, which depicts '*The Birth of Christ*' by Francesco Bassano (1586) and, moving on to the second chapel, I gaze appreciatively at Domenico Tintoretto's *'The Baptism of Christ'* (1588). The third chapel also has a masterpiece by Tintoretto, depicting *'The Flagellation of Christ'*, again completed in 1588. Crossing the main aisle, I reach the fourth chapel (third chapel on the left side), which displays *'The Transportation of Christ to the Sepulchre'* by Jacopo Palma il Giovane. The next chapel, returning back to the main entrance, displays *'Christ's Resurrection'* by Francesco Bassano, which he completed in 1587, and, finally, the last chapel I arrive at is another Tintoretto, *'Christ's Assention'*, which he painted in 1588.

As I move to the centre of the nave, I get a good view of the Baroque high altar, which dates from the late 17th century, and behind it, beyond the four tall columns, sit the monks' stalls, which have individual sacristies on either side of the choir area. One of these sacristies is open to the public, but not today unfortunately, but it does contain several pieces of art of some note. Having said that, I personally consider that every piece of historic artwork in Venice is a masterpiece anyway. Looking up at the ceiling, I can see a barrel-vaulted design with small windows to the rear. Likewise the chapels are rectangular in shape and, again, each is topped by similar vaulted ceilings. The lateral walls are curved in appearance, with a central door which allows a passageway to continue down from the central nave, and then angles around the far apse until it meets the sacristy and choir.

The presbytery in the middle apse holds the main altar and is closed off by the four columns, and the Friars' Chorus, which is not visible, is beyond the columns behind the main altar. Palladio cleverly designed the windows to fully illuminate the church as well as provide a scenographic dimension around the amazingly beautiful crucifix which is on display.

Every year since the church was first built, specifically on the third Sunday in July, (other than a short period following the fall of the Republic), Venetians celebrate the *'Festa del Redentore'*, which is a major event in the Venetian calendar. Apart from the religious thanksgiving, celebrations include a large firework display on the previous evening, and the construction of a temporary bridge of boats spanning from the Zattere to the Giudecca, which accommodates a large procession. Venetians decorate their boats, and the Canale San Marco fills with between 1,000 and 2,000 watercraft, with their owners patiently awaiting the fireworks. The display, set off from isolated pontoons, lasts for about an hour, and when the main festivities are over the young head for the Lido and sit on the beach till dawn!

As I leave the Redentore, I feel very humble about my own creative abilities when I witness the masterpieces that this church holds, and would thoroughly recommend that every visitor to Venice finds time to visit this glorious monument by Palladio. Although I feel that I may have cut short my visit to the Redentore, I also realise that I will shortly be enjoying probably Palladio's finest masterpiece, which is less than a few kilometres away.

My journey continues along the Fondamenta S. Giacome, where I pass a small bar, once again full of customers even though the outlying area is completely void of people. Having reached the Ponti della Croce, I cross over the Rio del Ponte Lungo and notice even more restoration underway on the surrounding houses. I then pass a bank, street number 180, a glassware shop and a fine arts gallery, all of which are again sympathetically disguised behind their historic façades. I am now walking on the Fondamenta di Ponte Piccolo, still heading west, and come across a small supermarket, which I suspect caters for the entire island, and a few metres further along what appears to be the flank wall of a monastery called Monastero Clarisse SS. Trinita, which has a beautifully sculptured plaque above the name plate. In the distance I can see the Mulino Stucky building as it protrudes from the quayside, but I still have some walking to do before I get there. As one would expect, the views across the canal to the mainland are stunning, as is the view of San Giorgio Maggiore looking back along the promenade that I have just walked along.

I have to say that the buildings along this part of the Fondamenta are generally more interesting for the visitor, as there appear to be more palazzos on view, each one having an attractive façade with ornate windows highlighting the piano nobile's incorporated in the building design. There are also several splendid Gothic archways leading to narrow calles, inviting the tourist to explore. Having explored these corridors in the past, I should warn the reader that not all roads lead to Rome! Mistakenly I assumed that each calle would take me to the far side of the island where I could gaze at other southern islands in the Lagoon such as San Lazzaro, wrong, only one or two do so, so consult the map (see Chapter 1) before venturing down these tempting passageways.

Moving on, as the time is now 1.30pm, I cross the Ponte Piccolo and, once across, see before me another bar with its inviting tables outside, and I have decided that I will call here for some lunch when I return. Just beyond the bar is a small bakery with lots of goodies on display in the window; the pastries and confectionery are so typical of the Venetians love of sweetmeats. As I continue my walk from the Fondamenta Eufemia to the Fondamenta S Biagio, I pass the Palanca pontile, which is virtually empty at this point in time. I now reach the former church of St. Eufemia. The church is currently boarded up, as there appears to be some major restoration work in hand, and from my poor Italian translation of the construction notice on the hoarding the former church has been closed for some time. Unfortunately, there is no one around for me to clarify this fact, but I shall attempt to research the work in progress, and only hope that this charming church, which was founded in the 9th century, will in fact be fully restored quite soon. Having carried out some earlier research on St Eufemia, I do know that the church has had major restoration works undertaken in the past, the last being in the 18th century which resulted in the façade being modified and the internal plaster in the nave and ceiling vaults being repaired. There were also original paintings depicting the life of St Eufemia inside as well as marble sculptures crafted in the 18th century by Gianmaria on the altarpiece. The small garden at the rear of the church is still quite visible from the neighbouring bridge, which spans the canal that runs along its side elevation, and I decide to photograph this area for future reference. Behind the church, at the end of the Fondamenta Rio S Eufemia, stands the former convent of San Cosina e Damiano, and adjacent to this stands another former and notable convent of its day, which was the Delle Convertite. Today I understand it is a penitentiary for convicted women (according to some historians, not dissimilar to its former life!)

As I haven't mentioned the convents of Venice so far, I feel I should correct this anomaly and briefly describe those which were built on the Giudecca, namely San Bagio Cataldo, San Croce della Giudecca, San Cosima e Damiano and finally Le Convertite. There were nuns living in the Lagoon from 640AD when the Benedictines settled in Torcello, and by the 17th century convents were systematically spread throughout the 'Serenissima'. In a similar fashion to the Zitelle, the convents accommodated single girls from the patriarchal families as well as the poor. However, not all of the women and girls entering these convents took the solemn vows of chastity. Basically, there were two categories of nuns, which created a social stigma on many occasions, one being the *'Choir'* nuns, who generally came from wealthy families and did take their formal vows, and the other, the *'Converse'* nuns who were regarded as the poorer inmates. The main body of nuns came from patriarch, or noble families, and were considered to be the upper echelon of this pious calling and were given special privileges, probably due to the income they brought to the convents. This elite group were invited to take more senior roles within each convent. For many centuries the lifestyles and behaviour of the majority of convents were questioned time and again, which resulted in the Venetian Council continually commissioning independent audits of their convents, focusing on sexual behaviour, financial insolvency and general management. The audits then concentrated invariably on all spiritual matters, to ensure that discipline and religious vows were adhered to, and historic records state that there were many cases of nuns being badly treated, as well as their 'piety rights' being completely abused. This resulted in most of the convents being converted into 'fully enclosed' units, over the centuries, and many restrictions were imposed, such as confidentiality standards, the barring of visitors (ensuring that there was no contact from the outside world) and complete silence and obedience. Amazingly, if any of these rules were abused in any manner or form, even by accident, then severe punishments were administered. Following the Napoleonic suppression, all religious buildings were either ransacked or impounded, and in 1810 all monasteries and convents were closed completely, and from the 40 or so recognised convents that remained in Venice, all of the 1,400 nuns who resided in them were banished into the community, some being far too old to support themselves. This must have been a sad and shocking reprisal for many innocent women to face. Having walked around the area once occupied by these two convents, I reach the former neo-Gothic designed flourmill called the Mulino Stucky. A mill has been functioning in this location since 1833. Once a prosperous hive of industry, Mulino Stucky was a mega-sized flour mill for its period, at one time employing as many as 1,500 people, from the early 20th century up until 1954, when it eventually shut down. Its former owner, Giovanni Stucky, a Swiss businessman, was tragically murdered in front of Santa Lucia railway station on the mainland by one of his employees in 1910, at a time when his business was at it's peak, and his surviving family did their best to keep the mill in production. Many people who I have spoken to believe that the actual mill building is a blight on the Venetian landscape, and I can only respond by saying 'What about Marghera? My personal views are more sympathetic, as I feel that the restoration and development work that is currently taking place has revitalised this previously dank industrial area and, from the little that I have been able to see of the restoration work in progress, the external brickwork of the Mulino Stucky is very enhancing. By brickwork, I simply mean that the mill as a structure is a mass of red bricks, but with a difference: the lines and design of the corbelled work have been really well crafted, and the ongoing restoration work is as good as most historic churches receive. Unfortunately, as the restoration and development works are not finished yet, access is denied to this area, but when it is complete it will accommodate a prestigious hotel, a congress centre, residential areas, a restaurant and a private marina.

As the time now is almost 2.00pm, I have decided to walk back to the bar near the Palanca pontile and grab a quick lunch before visiting my final destination for today, San Giorgio Maggiore. My arrival at the bar is well timed as I get served really quickly as tables have now become available. Sitting here is a real pleasure, the views are fantastic, and having enjoyed my short but extremely delicious lunch of pasta with a couple of glasses of local wine I make the short walk to Palanca pontile to catch either the No 41 or 82 vaporetto which will take me the short distance to the church of Palladio, and as it is still only 2.50pm I will have plenty of time to explore this magnificent church before making my way back to Venice. The vaporetto arrives almost as I arrive at Palanca and within 15 minutes I am disembarking from the watercraft and facing me is the magnificent church of San Giorgio Maggiore.

Before entering this monument to Palladio, perhaps now is the right time to briefly talk about this masterful architect. Palladio's real name is actually Andrea di Pietro della Gondola and he lived between 1508 and 1580, but of course he is known to the world as 'Palladio'. Born in Padua, he was an apprentice stonecutter at 13, before moving to Vincenzo at the age of 16, following which he quickly developed an incredible architectural flair after becoming an assistant in the Guild of Masons. This was before meeting his mentor, Gian Giorgio Trissino, who in fact gave him his name. Initially he was responsible for designing magnificent villas and palazzos for the wealthy, and was based in Vincenzo from where he often travelled to Rome to work on other prestigious designs. For reasons best known to the Venetian Council, I understand he was never allowed to build a single façade on the Grand Canal or inner canals and streets, probably due to his preference for classical design. He was, however, allowed to build churches, and what stunning churches they are. The Benedictines appreciated his classical designs and gave him the opportunity to build San Giorgio Maggiore, which stands as a monument to his stylised and immortal love of Roman architecture. The Palladian style, named after him, has been a major choice of many designers since his death, and some of the many distinct features that he created are exemplified in his columns, pediments and masks, and his style is said to span the architectural gap between Renaissance and Baroque. His designs became extremely fashionable around the world, especially in France, Britain and the Americas, and in 1570 he published four books on his architecture, which remain as an edict of his genius to this day, and he was ceremoniously nominated 'Illustrious Citizen of Venice' in that same year. From as early as 1545, he was refurbishing the Basilica in Vincenzo, by 1577 he had begun constructing the Redentore and, even as late as 1580, he was still preparing drawings for the interior of San Lucia church. His interior designs were said not only to please the eye, but allowed more effective use of space, and he explored classical ways to ensure that mould and mildew could not form on the internal infrastructure of his buildings. To achieve this, he used a combination of lime plasters, Venetian plasters and Marmorino plasters, (which were polished decorative plasters used by ancient Egyptians, and known for there durability and anti-mould/mildew properties), which Palladio brought back into use after many centuries. Without doubt, Palladio was one of the most influential architects in European history, and his work encouraged and influenced people such as Inigo Jones, Christopher Wren and Lord Burlington to name but a few. So now let's enjoy one of his creations, but, first, a brief resume of the island.

The small island of San Giorgio Maggiore, which sits to the east of the Giudecca and south of Venice itself standing guard over the entrance to the Grand Canal, was first inhabited by the Benedictines in 982 after it was decided that a monastery should be built there, and was originally called the 'Isle of Cypresses'. This minuscule island was originally given to Giovanni Morosini (who, incidentally, later became a Benedictine monk), upon his return to Venice, by the Doge Tribuno Memmo, who was a distant relation of his. Doge Agnolo Partecipazio, who served the Republic between 949 and 952, however, founded the first church, which was built to his own design.

The church of San Giorgio Maggiore was built between 1560 and 1580, but was not finished before Palladio died. Consequently, the façade was left to Vincenzo Scamozzi to complete, following the original design, in 1610. The church's façade is a combination of the pediment of a classical Roman temple in unison with the design of a Christian church, which to my mind works really well, but for its day it was revolutionary. Internally this colossus of a building is modelled on the Renaissance concept of a central plan with a cross to house all the magnificent side chapels and naves which in turn would accommodate large congregations. The ceiling is framed by columns and arches supporting a 50m dome, and the thermal windows (shaped like lunettes, as used in the ancient Roman baths) provide a wonderfully uniformed light to the side chapels and nave. This is also assisted by the fact that there is reflected light from the inner walls, which are finished in Istrian stone, and which have some fine stuccowork on display. Strikingly, the nave has slender vaults, and the pilasters have strips of brickwork covered with stucco; looking at the nave one can see that the stage-like presbytery and choir dominate this area.

Looking in more detail at the internal decoration, I start at the choir stalls, depicting the life of St Benedict, which were originally carved in the 1590s and which form a semi circular collection of richly coloured and ornate timber seating, beautifully carved, together with a centrepiece chest and plinth supporting an equally robust lectern. There is a plethora of art masterpieces everywhere, too numerous to name them all, but I have some favourites, such as Tintoretto's *'The Last Supper'* and *'Fall of Manna'*, which he painted when he was over 90 years old. There is also a wonderful painting of *'St Benedict, St Gregory, St Mauro and others'* by Tintoretto's son Domenico. In the right-hand side aisle, you can view the tomb of Lorenzo Veneir (a noted Venetian general who defeated the Turks in the 17th century) and at the same time gaze at an altarpiece (the first altar) and view the *'Nativity'* by Jacopo Bassano, together with the magnificent crucifix (in the second altar) by Michelozzo Michelozzi. Other splendid masterpieces include Carpaccio's altarpiece of *'St. George and the Dragon'*, which he completed in 1516, and Jacopo Bassano's *'The Adoration of the Shepherds'*. To appreciate the beauty and scale of this wonderful edifice by Palladio (often described as a 'basilica'), you really must explore it first hand, for like many treasures in Venice 'words can simply not explain'.

In addition to the church, there is also the adjoining monastery, which has two restored cloisters: 'Cloister of the Bay Trees', designed by Buora and built by his sons around 1540, and the 'Cloister of the Cypresses', which was designed by Palladio himself in 1579. Internally there is a refectory dating from 1560–1562, a large staircase built between 1641 and 43 and an extremely long dormitory, which was completed around 1494. Unfortunately, artwork by Veronese, which once graced the walls of this monastery, is now hung in the Louvre, as were many other treasures which were plundered by the French, following the fall of the Republic. The original monastery was rebuilt on orders from Doge Sebastiano Ziani (who later lived there) in the 12th century, and again in the 13th century, following an earthquake! Interestingly enough, in 1433 Cosimo de Medici took refuge here when he was banished from Florence and during his stay he commissioned many improvements. Because Cosimo took his 'bank' with him when exiled by his fellow Florentines, he was pardoned within a year and allowed to return to Florence. It's amazing what you could do with money even in the 15th century! Fortunately, in the 1950s Count Vittorio Cini purchased the monastery from the state and fully restored it, at the same time creating the Cini Foundation. His collection of books, furniture, porcelain and artwork are opened to the public for a limited period each year at the Palazzo Cini, which is just west of the Peggy Guggenheim Museum on the Grand Canal.

To the south of the island there is a small open-air theatre (1,300 seats) set in a large garden. The theatre was closed in the late 20th century but is now reopened and stages events designed by the *'Biennale'* (more about this bi-annual event in July), which consist of dramas, music and dance.

There is just one more treat left for me on this island today, and that is to travel to the top of San Giorgio Maggiore's campanile because I, personally, think you get the best view of Venice from the top of this monument. To access the campanile, you take the door to the left of the choir and, once through a corridor, you reach the lift, yes lift, where you are taken to the top in seconds. Certainly easier than the climb in Torcello! Once at the top of the campanile, the view is phenomenal, especially today, as I can just make out the Dolomites in the distance as well as having cracking views of San Servolo and the remaining Southern Islands. From the viewing platform, visitors also get a great view of the entire city of Venice (wonderful vista of Piazza San Marco) as far across as the mainland, not forgetting a magnificent view of the entrance to the Grand Canal – all this for just 3 euros. I could stay here all day just looking at this beautiful city from the campanile but I have to come down, as it is time for it to close.

Having thoroughly enjoyed my visit to San Giorgio Maggiore, once again I must make tracks back to Piazzale Roma, as it is now 5.15pm. I am always amazed just how time flies by, especially in the 'Serenissima'. Obviously, there are still other islands to visit here as there were in the north of the Lagoon, which I shall be doing in a later chapter. I personally find that one, two or even three visits to each of the prominent buildings in Venice (and there are hundreds) still isn't time enough to fully explore the treasures they hold; it is a never-ending story. Having decided to take the No. 82 vaporetto back, I am delighted to see that one is just arriving, so I quickly jump on board for the 20-minute journey to the mainland, and then my 10-minute walk to my favourite bar. I notice on the return trip that the cruise liners are still moored on the Canale di Fusina and I also observe the scores of tourists at Tronchetto, before I eventually arrive at my destination. After leaving the vaporetto at Piazzale Roma, I briskly walk back towards the Scalzi Bridge, which I cross over, and make my way to Bar S. Lucia. Today I want to show Enrico, the bar owner, my preliminary ink sketches of his bar so that he can choose which one I should allocate for the journal, and, as always, that pint of Guinness is being poured directly I enter the bar, and I must confess that today I am really looking forward to my night cap.

Sadly, I learn that Jason, one of the barmen, is returning to his hometown of Dublin at the weekend and I wish him every success for the future. Having rested my legs for a short while, I bid my farewells to everyone and make my way to the bus terminal. On my journey to the airport, I reminisce about my day on the Giudecca and find it difficult not to generalise when evaluating this island as a tourist venue. Apart from the stunningly beautiful churches that I visited, I suppose this sizable island does have a charm of its own, not forgetting its historical value as a evolutionary part of Venice. However, I think of it as purely a quiet residential habitat that tourists occasionally visit, simply for lunch and to enjoy the view of the Venetian mainland. I think it is essential to explore the 'inner parts' of the island to perhaps fully appreciate its serenity and, of course, one has to discover Palladio.

My flight back to Gatwick is very comfortable and on time, and I have the pleasure of sitting next to a couple who had spent several days exploring Venice themselves, so I was able to enjoy their views and interests, following their visit, which made the flight home pass very quickly. I arrived home and was indoors by 11.10pm, remarkably fresh from my journey but, more importantly, with my mind firmly focused on my next visit, which I am pleased to say is only a week away. That gives me enough time to share the trip with Avril and get down to some serious writing in the meantime.

Buonasera Venezia.

Fig. 17　Pescheria

Fig.18 Ponte dei Pugni

Fig.19 Santa Maria Miracoli

Fig.20 Scuola Grande di San Marco

Fig.21　Santi Giovanni E Paolo

Fig.22   Santa Pietro di Castello

Fig.23 Fondamenta Barbarigo

Fig.24   Campo San Angelo

Fig. 25   Rio del Vatral (Murano)

Fig.26 Rio Ognissanti

Fig.27 Rio del Gafaro

Fig.28   Cloister of Santissima Trinita (Frari)

*Fig.*29   Piazetta 'Basilica San Marco & Palazzo Ducale'

Fig.30 San Giorgio Maggiore

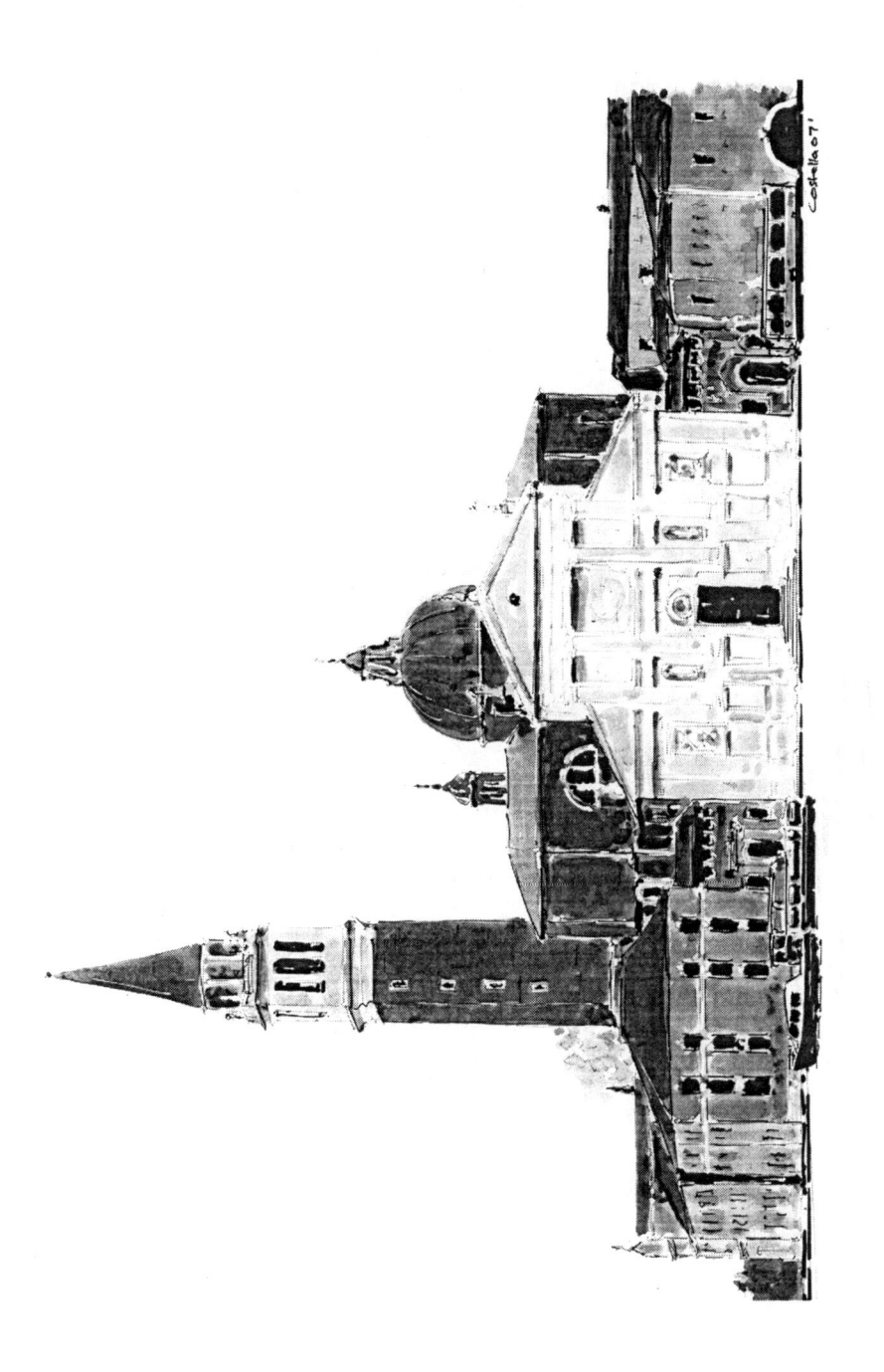

Fig.31 Ca' Pesaro

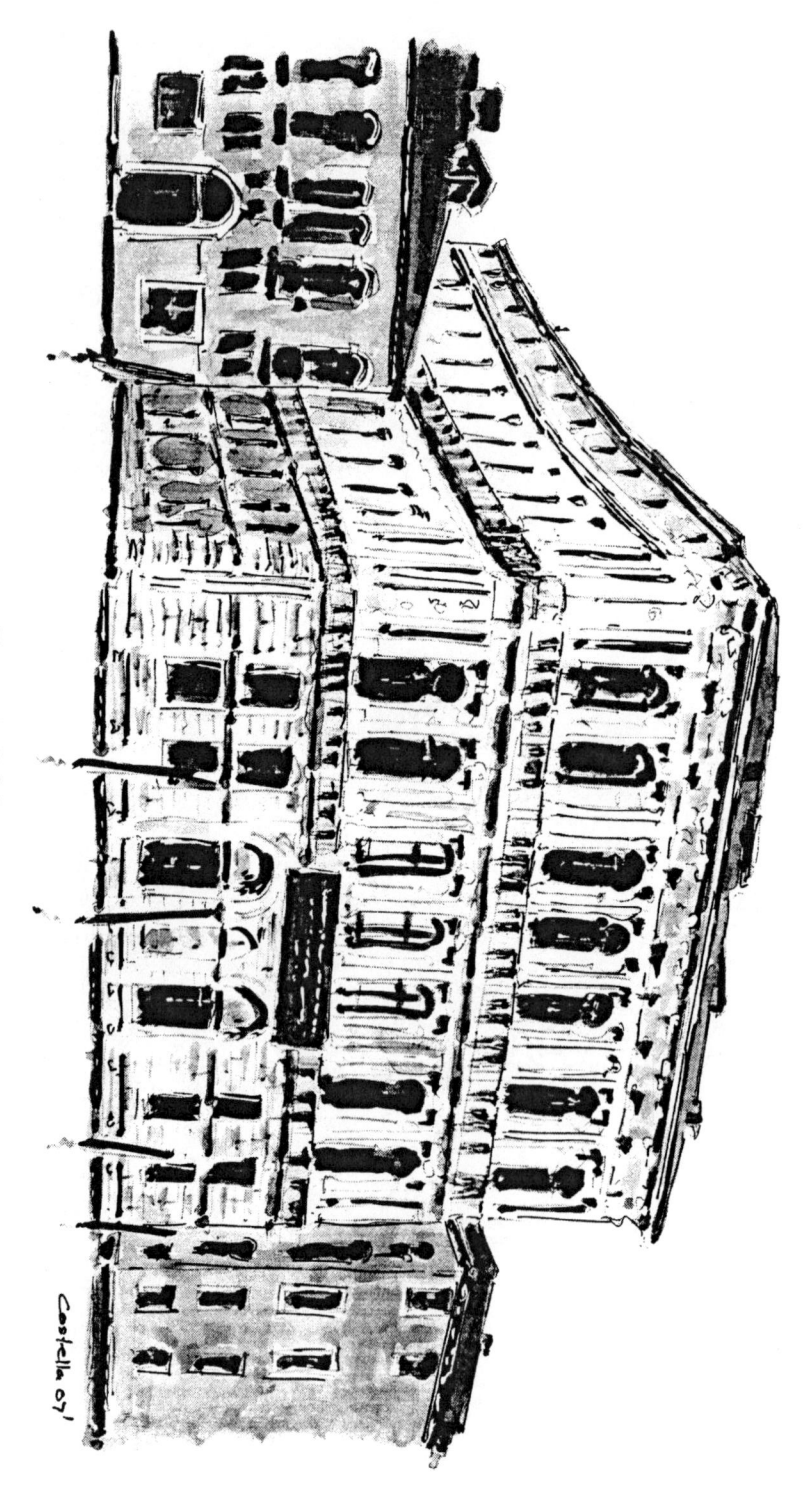

Fig.32   Ca' da Mosto

CHAPTER 9

MAY: Dorsoduro

'Piety, Enmity, Dexterity and the Plague'

In this chapter I am back on mainland Venice and will be concentrating on what is arguably the most interesting *sestiere* of them all, because of its diverse range of historical interest. Although almost every inch of the precious 'Serenissima' has wonderful tales to tell, and vistas to paint, Dorsoduro to my mind is special because it has such a heterogeneous concentration of significant attractions for the journeyman.

Throughout my walk today, I will be following a route that will encompass so many interesting places to visit it will be impossible to explore each one as fully as they deserve, so I will simply add a short commentary for those which I have unfortunately decided just to pass. This is in a similar fashion to the approach adopted in previous chapters, and will hopefully whet the appetite of the reader to revisit each route again, which is great if the reader is stopping over for a few days, remembering that the majority of my visits are undertaken in just one day. The itinerary for the walk, and the route itself, may seem demanding, but the mere fact that I will be travelling into areas where tourists are less prevalent, and seeking out some peaceful surroundings, will, I hope, prove

May 2007

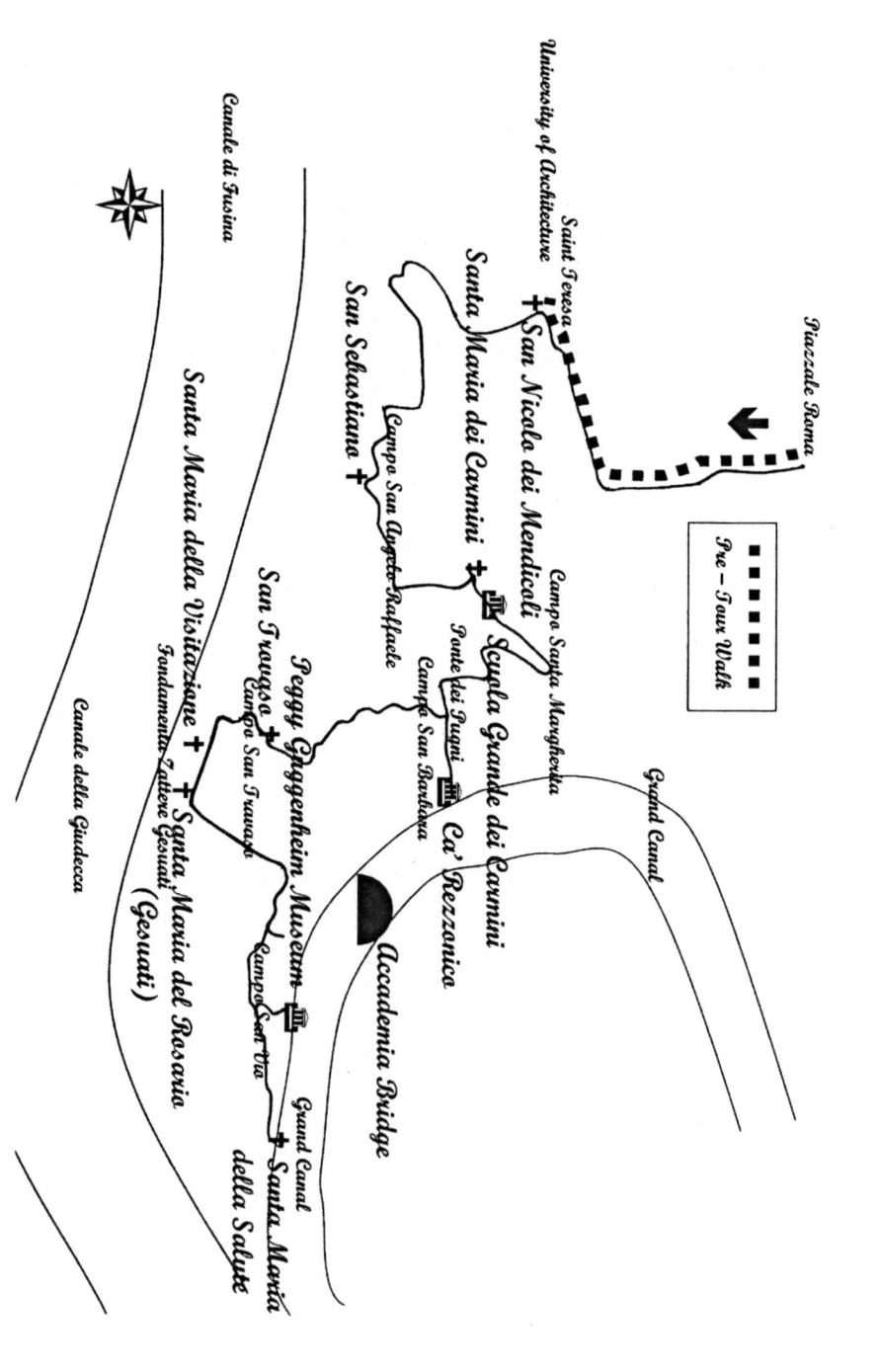

Pre – Tour Walk

Piazzale Roma

University of Architecture
Saint Teresa
San Nicolò dei Mendicoli
Santa Maria dei Carmini
San Sebastiano
Campo San Angelo Raffaele
Campo Santa Margherita
Scuola Grande dei Carmini
Ponte dei Pugni
Campo San Barbara
Ca' Rezzonico
Peggy Guggenheim Museum
San Trovaso
Campo San Trovaso
Santa Maria della Visitazione
Fondamenta Zattere Gesuati
Santa Maria del Rosario (Gesuati)
Campo San Vio
Accademia Bridge
Grand Canal
Santa Maria della Salute

Canale di Fusina
Santa Maria della Visitazione
Canale della Giudecca

extremely interesting. The sheer diversity of subject matter in this chapter, as the title would suggest, will capture the piety of the monastic presence, the enmity shown between rival factions, the dexterity of artwork that abounds in each gallery and, last but not least, the catastrophic impact that plague and pestilence had on Venice.

As a land-mass, Dorsoduro is not only slightly higher than other sestieri but is also more compact, an attribute which attracted settlers even before the Rialto, and, interestingly enough. the name translated means 'hard ridge'. Favoured in the early days by fishermen and sailors alike, this area became extremely popular by the early 19th century once the Accademia Bridge was built; it was looked upon favourably by wealthy visitors, especially the British, who attended the Anglican Church of St George situated in Campo San Vio. During this period the merchant shipping docks were constructed in the western section, where my journey begins.

* May 15th 2007

This morning is one of those mornings when I sense that whatever I plan or wherever I go, things will go well. The reason for my being so optimistic is simply because I rely on an alarm clock to get me up early and last night I forgot to set the alarm, but this morning I woke up exactly when I should. A simple task overlooked, but one that could have had a major impact on my day if I had missed my flight. I have carefully planned my itinerary for this trip to Venice and I know it will encompass a reasonably demanding walk, coupled with a plentiful selection of buildings to either explore or simply photograph. Having checked the weather forecast yesterday, I pack a cagoule together with my camera, recorder and map, and, of course, a good book to read on the plane, and set off for Gatwick with my immediate thoughts on breakfast. Gatwick seems busier than usual this morning but luckily the breakfast queue, although long, seemed to reduce in size fairly quickly, so I managed to get served quickly and was soon sitting at a comfortable table, with plenty of time to spare. After eating, I am delighted to see that my flight is boarding from Gate 9 today, so I only have a short walk from the departure lounge. My flight to Marco Polo airport is again on time and I also manage to get a front seat, which I shared with a group of golfers who were competing in a tournament somewhere near Venice, I guess. Most of my journey out was spent reading, and, after landing on time, within minutes I am through security, have purchased my ACTV ticket and am quickly making my way to the bus, which is just departing. The considerate driver, seeing me approaching, stops and allows me to board. I am now convinced that this really is going to be a good day. Incidentally, I should also mention the weather, which can be best described as perfect: clear blue sky, temperature around 18C and a nice breeze coming from somewhere, so much for the weather forecast! I have one call to make when I reach Piazzale Roma, before I start my journey, and that is to book a room for one night next month at the Santa Chiara Hotel, as I will be visiting Venice several times in June to paint as well as write. Having confirmed my hotel reservation and had a good chat with the hotel manager, I now begin my journey by turning right as I leave the hotel and make my way down the Fondamenta Cossetti, which will take me to the Fond Tre Ponti and eventually to Pagan Cazziola. My actual route today starts at San Nicolo dei Mendicoli, so I have a little walking to do before I reach this point, which is in the far western part of Dorsoduro.

As I near the end of Pagan Cazziola, having crossed a delightful small bridge, I turn right into Fondamenta delle Procuratie and, as I walk down this pleasant street with a small canal to my right, I can see over to my right the Chiesa San Maggiore, a red brick building with its own campanile gracing the skyline ahead, which one day I hope to visit, as this church is one of the few remaining churches that I have yet to explore. At the end of Procuratie, I cross over to Calle d. Madonna and turn left into Fondamenta dell Arziere, which in turn leads me to Fondamenta delle Terese and the start of my journey proper. From the map, you will see that I have passed the Church of St Teresa, which I also intend to visit in the future.

It is now 12.45pm and I am standing in front of San Nicolo dei Mendicoli, which I shall not be viewing today, although it has a marvellous history, like all the treasures of Venice. As I look at the façade of this attractive and quite unassuming church, I can't help but notice the Facolta Universitaria (University of Architecture) close by, and think to myself how fortunate these students are in having so many magnificent historical buildings around them to study. Having worked alongside architects for most of my working career, I was always interested when they discussed the art and science of buildings, and even more attentive when they used to reminisce about their field trips to distant lands, and I can't help thinking how many of them would have relished being a student in Venice.

San Nicolo Mendicoli is somewhat remotely located near the banks of the Canale Fusina, and this wonderful small canal flows past the south elevation of the church and turns towards the campanile situated on the east side. A church was originally founded on this site in the 7th century by the first settlers of the

Lagoon, and built by the 'Patavini' (inhabitants of Padua), thereby making it one of the oldest churches in Venice. It was originally dedicated to a Serbian Martyr named St Niceta and re-dedicated in the 12th century to St Nicholas of Myra. Today's church is best described as Veneto/Byzantine, with the central part of the façade dating back to the 12th century, and can also claim a fairly distinctive campanile and a 15th-century porch which sheltered beggars in the past (*Mendicoli* means 'beggars'). There have been several restoration projects undertaken within the church in the past, as early records would suggest, these works being in 1361 and 1580 while others are more recent, like the re-roofing project in the 1970s. Internally, the church has a central aisle, an apse (part of which dates back to the 12th century) and a vestibule at its western end. Gilded wooden carvings dating to the 16th century decorate the nave, and frescoes adorn the upper walls and ceiling depicting scenes from the life of Christ, which were painted by Alvise dal Frisco in the mid-16th century. It has a 16th-century organ and paintings from the school of Veronese, and Veronese's son actually painted the organ gallery. Unfortunately, as San Nicolo was prone to flooding, many treasures have been removed to other churches, and the floor level has been raised to avoid this problem recurring. I understand that priests had to paddle around the church whenever it flooded. It is also worth remembering that this church is only open 10.00am–12.00am Monday–Saturday.

Leaving San Nicolo, I now make my way back around the church until I reach Fondamenta Tron. I then pass the Hotel Tron and continue along the Calle Rielo, where I pass a delightful small harbour containing a number of craft, and continue ahead until I am almost at the Fondamenta Barbarigo. This really is a very attractive part of Dorsoduro and, judging by the number of people

I have seen so far, not overly populated with tourists; it really is a delight to be here. Whilst photographing the last church that I passed, I attracted the attention of one of the locals, who was very amicable and obviously wanted to try out his English on me, and we had quite a long chat about this particular area, which was very interesting. He reminded me of the fact that this area was once occupied by the Nicolottis, who were to make quite an impact on Venetian culture for several centuries; their story follows later on in this chapter. Apparently this chap had lived here for over 60 years, spending some of his early life as a young man in Paris, and, he said, it was in Paris where he learnt his English. I couldn't quite understand why that would be the case, but I have to say that, although I may have criticised some local Venetians in the past for their apparent dislike of anyone remotely looking like a tourist, I should remember not to generalise on this subject again, as the majority of the indigenous population are like this gentleman, both friendly and helpful.

Just before reaching the Fondamenta Barbarigo, I walk diagonally across an established patch of greenery and then walk ahead, enjoying the small shops along this fondamenta, until I reach a bridge, which I cross. I am now facing the church of San Angelo Raffaele. The vista beyond the church is quite unattractive, as all I can see ahead is some major restoration work in hand, with plastic screening protecting the entire face of a large building which stands directly opposite the Palazzo Ariani. Although San Angelo Raffaele is not on my itinerary today, it is open 8.00am–2.00am and 3.00pm–5.00pm weekdays, and one church which I shall visit later in the year. Moving on past this white-stone faced church and crossing Campo Angelo Raffaele, which has an inviting cafe in one corner, with a small bar close by, I stop to photograph some of the interesting houses surrounding this square. The short walk across the campo takes me to the church of San Sebastiano, which from an architectural plain is seen as a maze of split levels, rotundas and a campanile. Certainly, from the direction I am heading, the main door of this church, however, is located around the east side and sits opposite a small bridge over the Canale S. Sebastiano.

San Sebastiano has a wealth of history and is very special to me because of its association with one of the world's greatest artists, Paolo Veronese. The church itself was built in the 16th century, between 1505 and 1548, by Scarpagnino, to a Renaissance design. Dedicated to its martyr, St Sebastiano, and laid out in the form of a Latin cross, the church has a façade with a trapezoidal top with three statuettes above, and a central rose window with smaller Gothic designed windows on either side. Although the internal decoration came much later, what you see today is really special, as every inch of its ceiling and walls are covered with masterpieces. Designed as a single nave church, it has an atrium and a choir and a wonderfully decorated wooden ceiling with crafted panels. Veronese worked in this church, on and off, for the best part of his life and designed the complete interior. As you enter the church and turn right, you will immediately see an altarpiece by Titian depicting St Nicolas, which was built in the 16th century. Moving down to the third altar, there is a fine piece by Veronese called '*The Crucifixion*' and further along there is a monument to Bishop Livio Podacattaro by Jacopo Sansovino, also 16th century. In the centre apse, on the right hand wall, is Veronese's '*The Martyrdom of St Sebastian*'. To the left of the main aisle and through a corridor, is the sacristy, which has beautifully panelled walls about 2m high, and above the walls are magnificent pieces of art, entirely by Veronese, covering all of the ceiling and surrounding walls, depicting the life of San Sebastian. Moving back into the church itself, there is a bust of Veronese by Matteo Cornero (17th century) and, walking back along the left side of the aisle, there is an impressive organ, built by Francesco Florentino, which is cantilevered out onto a balcony. Again, the organ doors have magnificent paintings by the master, namely, *'The Presentation to the Temple'* and *'The Pool of Bethseda'*.

Paolo Veronese (1528–1588) was a Renaissance painter born in Verona and the son of a stonecutter. He was known as the supreme colourist (easy to understand why, when you marvel at the amount of colour variation in his work) and produced beautiful fresco work as well as his classic oil paintings. He arrived in Venice aged 25, and spent the rest of his life here, and, thankfully, because he was one of the few great artists who made sure that his paint colours would last indefinitely, the majority of his work is still as vibrant as it was when first painted. I discovered some charming characteristics when researching this outstanding artist, as he was said to be extremely generous, a socialite and a good family man. His generosity often went as far as only charging his clients and friends for the materials he used, not for his time. Veronese enjoyed riding with hounds, liked luxurious material items and always wore coloured velvet trousers. He worked with the artists and architects of the day, namely Palladio and Titian. He considered himself fortunate to head a family of artists, which included his brother Beneditto and sons, Carlo and Gabriele. Known for painting enormous scenes using wonderful colours to depict marble columns, costumes and extremely detailed 'feasts', he once got into some serious trouble, when asked to paint a scene of *'The Last Supper'*, in 1573, for the refectory of the Basilica di San Zanipolo. Veronese was summoned before the Inquisition, no less, to explain the sacrilegious content of its composition, and was asked to alter certain parts. Using his artistic licence and not wishing to alter what was a wonderful piece of work, as well as being a very large piece (5m x 12m), he simply renamed it *'The Feast in the House of Levi'* and his accusers accepted his decision. Another of his large pieces is the *'Wedding of Lana'* (1562–1563), commissioned for Palladio's refectory in San Giorgio Maggiore, which contains more than 100 figures, including Titian, Tintoretto and Veronese himself, and measures 10m wide. San Sebastiano really is Veronese's own church and I feel sure that he would wish no better resting place than the one provided for him here, in celebration of his work.

San Sabastiano really is a church to visit when in Venice, and as I leave I cross the small bridge by the main door and walk down Calle de Avogaria with its mass of hanging floral baskets on show. I am now heading towards another delightful bridge which, when crossed takes me past an impressive raised garden that has some ornate statuettes on the wall. I arrive at the Calle Lunga, which I follow for a few metres before turning left into Calle Pazienza. This part of the walk takes me along a narrow street and over another bridge, which crosses the Rio di San Barnaba, where I eventually arrive at Campo dei Carmini. Directly to my left is the Scuola Grande di Carmini, which I am looking forward to visiting, but first I need to see the church of San Maria dei Carmini, which is located and accessed from the campo itself. Facing the church, I get a distinct feel for Dutch architecture when looking at the façade, which is finished in brickwork with stone banding spanning its width. The upper part is designed with curved walls with statues positioned on each level. Having cycled extensively around the

Brabant region of Holland with my family in the past, I can't help feeling that I have seen similar external features before.

The church of San Maria dei Carmini was rebuilt in the 14th century following some nasty structural problems and, as you would expect, has had several major alterations to date, the most visual being the façade, which was rebuilt to a Renaissance style in the 16th century. There is a tall campanile that was saved from destruction despite a nasty tilt, which was corrected in 1688, but even today the perilous 'lean' can still be seen. The interior of the church is laid out like a basilica, with a large nave, with arches which display gilded wooden statues together with panelling covering the original Gothic features, and two aisles, all of which provide a magnificent setting for this richly decorated interior. Throughout the church there are illustrated paintings, by artists such as Andrea Celeste, Sebastiano Mazzoni and Pietro Liberi, depicting the history of the Carmelite Order, which was fairly active between the 16th and 18th century. Although the interior of the church is quite dark, it radiates some warmth from the variety of masterpieces on display, especially the works depicting the life of Christ, which can be seen between the nave and the choir. The centre apse of the high altar was built in 1633 and has stunning wooden stalls which were beautifully carved by Fruilian Raffaelli in 1688. The altars were rebuilt in the 17th century, and each adorned with masterpieces such as *'The Adoration of the Magi'* by Cima da Conegliano (1509), *'St Nicholas and Angels'* by Lorenzo Lotto (1529) and *'The Presentation of Christ'* by Jacopo Tintoretto (1543). One altar on the right-hand side of the aisle belonged to the Scuola (1594) which was given to them by the Carmelite monks. The altarpiece, called *'Virgin Bestowing the Scapular on St*

Simon Stock', was decorated by Pace Pace (yes, that's his correct name), a friend of Veronese.

Like all churches and basilicas I visit, I sometimes feel that the brief description I give of each interior usually undermines the treasures that lie within. Therefore, at the risk of repeating myself again: words are simply not enough; these masterpieces have to be seen. It is time now to leave the church and explore the Scuola.

As I walk the short distance back to the Scuola Grande dei Carmini, I have decided to explore the interior of this building in a fairly systematic route, which I feel will enable me to 'paint' a clearer picture of this grand Scuola. The Scuola was once the headquarters of the Carmelite lay fraternity who offered charity and help to the needy. Interestingly, the Carmini monastery had direct links with an early religious women's group, which was founded in the 14th century. This group had similar philosophies as the Scuola but were not favoured by their presence. The women of this group were productive in making 'scapulars' (worn by ecclesiastical ministers even today) but records show that this association went into decline in the 16th century. Construction of the Scuola started in 1594 and most of the remaining work was completed by 1638. Having said that, the façade took another six years. Then followed an untimely delay caused by the outbreak of plague, before it was eventually completed by Baldessare Longhena in 1670. Longhena built two façades on two levels: the first storey of the façade, where I entered, is of white Istrian stone with architrave windows and gabled porches, having Corinthian columns and pediments, which form a structured and symmetric appearance. The front elevation facing the church, however, has two levels of arched windows above two doorways with Istrian stone block work. Internally, the Scuola has three floors linked by an impressive staircase, which to my mind is the focal point of the building, known as the Sala Capitolare, which was decorated by Domenico Bruni between 1664 and 1674. Tiepolo was commissioned to decorate the ceiling in 1739 and replaced the former frescoes with nine spectacular canvases. The central canvas depicts the vision of St. Simeone on Mount Carmelo whilst the remaining eight depict various portraits of the Virgin Mary.

Access to the Scuola is from the street leading to Campo San Margherita, and once through the reception area you arrive in the Chapel. There you will see an altar, which sits to the left, depicting *'The Virgin of Carmel'* by Sante Piatti, having two small ornate doors either side, which lead to the Campo dei Carmini. Both the wooden bench seating in the chapel and the red and white marble floor have been restored at some time, but the two candleholders in gold wrought iron are completely original. Above and to the sides of both staircases there are paintings attributed to Nicolo Bambini (1651–1739) together with others by his son Giovanni. Moving on from the chapel, you can't help but notice the magnificent staircases with their white relief cornices which show detailed work of angels, cherubs, mermaids and eagles, all the work of Alvise Bossi, which he completed in 1728/9. To complement this work, there are also excellent frescoes by Sante Piatti. Moving on to the middle landing, one can marvel at the 18th-century Sacristy which, although quite small, contains rich walnut bench panels which are beautifully grained and preserved, all standing under a gracefully arched ceiling. The next room I enter is the Sala Capitolare, which I mentioned earlier, a room where the Chapter met and performed all major ceremonies. Longhena is said to have had a part in its design, and its ceiling is blessed with artwork such as *'The Virgin Bestowing the Scapular on St Simon Stock'*, *'Patience,*

Innocence and Chastity' and '*Sincerity*', all by Tiepolo, which I think are probably my favourite pieces in this room. Having said that, the walls are decorated with paintings by Antonio Zanchi, '*The Miracle of the Boy and the Well*' (1665), Gregorio Lazzarini's '*The Adoration of the Magi*' (1704) and many others, all of which are stunning.

Leaving the Sala Capitolare, I move into the Sala Dell Archivio, which was formerly used for archives and administration affairs. This room has an Istrian stone doorway of classical design and still retains an original wooden desk of the early period. Once again, walnut panels surround this room with benches built into the walls, each decorative figure skilfully carved and said to be the work of Giacomo Piazzetta. The ceiling framework is a wooden expanse of deep caissons with leaf and floral motifs, thought to be the work of Gaetano Zompini, whilst the artwork in place between the sculptured wood, which includes '*The Virgin Appearing to the Prophet Elijah on Mount Carmel*' and '*Samian Sibyl*', is by Giustino Menescardi and was completed between 1749 and 1753. The walls of this room are adorned with works also by Guistino Menescardi among others, and include his '*Abigails Offer*' and '*The Martydom of the Maccabees before their Mother*'.

The final room I am exploring today in this treasure trove is the Sala Dell Albergo, which was used as a shelter and reception room for the poor. The ceiling of this room is less embossed than the others but still has sculptured wood framing a wonderful painting of '*The Assumption of the Virgin*', and is surrounded by a series of oval works containing different prophets and evangelists each looking down from above. These works are by Alessandro Varotain, which he completed between 1634 and 1638. Each wall is covered again by 17th-century walnut panelling and has bench seating creatively carved with columns and capitals. Above the panelling the walls are covered with paintings including Ambrogio Bon's *'Adoration of the Shepherds'* (1697) and Antonio Balestra's *'Joseph's Dream'* to name but a couple, and, finally, the floor is a striking array of stars finished in red, black and white marble to a similar design as the Archivio.

Having savoured these two grandiose buildings, I must leave, as the time is 1.35pm and there is still much more to enjoy today and I am only halfway through my journey! When exiting the Scuola I turn left and feel the heat of the sun on my back as I head to my right and make my way diagonally across Campo S. Margherita, which is fairly busy at this time of the day, with its bars and shops catering for the tourists. I notice that the tall memorial flag pole, in the centre of the square, has a number of artists sitting on its steps making the most of the view beyond the campo, where two campaniles dominate the skyline, one of which I think is San Pantalon. As I make my way past the many bars and along the Rio Terra Canal, I can see ahead of me the Rio di Barnaba, which I crossed over earlier further down this canal, and shortly I shall reach what probably is the most infamous small bridge in Venice, the *Ponte dei Pugni*. This small insignificant bridge which I now stand on was for several hundred years the demarcation zone, or arena, for hundreds of confrontational battles which would decide territorial rights for two specific clans. These often merciless battles were staged between two groups of Venetians, the *Castellanis* who lived in the three sestieri of Castello, San Marco and part of the Dorsoduro, and the *Nicolottis*, who resided in Cannaregio, San Polo and Santa Croce.

The name of the bridge itself translates to 'Bridge of Fists', and you may notice that there appear to be two sets of footprints set in the stone on the bridge itself, which were the starting points for the contests that followed. Originally Venice was divided into two factions, following the election of two Ducal Councils around about 1032. These two factions, named after churches, the Nicollottis, from San Nicolo dei Mendicoli (western part of the city), and the Castellanis, from San Pietro di Castello (eastern part of the city), started their feud long before the families settled in the Lagoon, as the enmity between the families began when they lived in Jesolo and Eraclea, respectively, long before they were forced to move to the Lagoon and settle in the same location. The government encouraged this rivalry for a long time, hoping that it would keep any revolutionary uprisings in check. At the same time, they could call upon these men, who were considered to be a fighting force, in the event of any conflict against the enemies of Venice. Wearing their own definitive colours, red for the Castellanis and black for the Nicollottis, public games were held between the two groups, which featured fistfights, gymnastic pyramids and bull chases and inevitably ended in knife fights and open warfare. More often than not, what started as a controlled battle would end up as a knife-wielding slaughter, especially when the free wine came into effect. In later years, the fistfights became more controlled and specialised. However, defensive tactics were not deemed acceptable, as the crowd would rather see a bloodied face from a courageous fighter. The battles often involved up to 300 men on each side and often finished with the general public fighting as well.

Early reference to these mock battles (*battagliola*) were recorded in 1369, and those that took place on bridges in 1421; each event was watched by literally thousands of spectators, (seated on roofs, in barges and in all the surrounding streets) and often resulted in men being maimed and killed. Sharp sticks or robust cane (both hardened by soaking in oil) were familiar weapons, and fights of this nature were known as 'wars of the sticks'. Consequently, bridges were covered in sawdust and canals beneath the bridges were cleared of any debris. Once the specific bridge was won in battle, the respective family insignia would be painted on it until the next fracas took place. In 1705 the government intervened after some bloody battles, prohibiting any future gatherings near bridges, and severe punishments were imposed if these new laws were not observed. Finally, the 'battles' became only competitions and a truce was vowed in a gesture of unity against Austrian rule. Looking around me, I can well imagine just how many spectators would arrive for these notorious battles, as there is plenty of room to view from where I am standing. But, as I sheepishly move on, I have to admit that I would far prefer watching a football match today than watching the hostilities that took place here in the past, although one might argue that the spectator involvement hasn't really changed!

After crossing and moving away from the Ponte dei Pugni, I turn left and arrive directly in Campo San Barnaba, which has a marvellous church with a Palladian-style façade. The church of San Barnaba is not on my list to visit today, but one I will include in future itineraries. That's the problem I have with Venice: I can't just walk past any building of interest. But this one will have to wait. Dismissing San Barnaba wasn't easy, but I have to confess I am nearing probably one of the most interesting and educational buildings on this beautiful island and I can't wait to see and explore the Ca' Rezzonico.

Access to the Ca' Rezzonico is achieved from the rear of the building, as opposed to the Grand Canal side, so I simply walk past

San Barnaba church on the opposite side of the small canal, having crossed back over the Rio di San Barnaba where, after a short walk, I simply turn left into the courtyard of the Ca' Rezzonico, where visitors purchase their tickets. As I already have a group ticket to visit several museums in Venice, which I purchased when I visited the Correr Museum with Louise in January, I simply present my ticket and walk straight in, and as the time is now 1.55pm I will allow myself an hour and a half inside.

Ca' Rezzonico was designed and built by Ballassare Longhena, and eventually completed by Giorgio Massari between 1649 and1756, and was originally the Palazzo of Filippo Bon, who demolished two smaller houses which were formerly on this site. Unfortunately, the façade can only be viewed from the Grand Canal. Interestingly enough, Longhena's original design was based on a plan introduced to Venice by Sansovino, which incorporated an internal courtyard. The second floor was completed by 1752, and four years later the façade followed, which was built in marble in a heavily rusticated symmetrical pattern so characteristic of the Baroque style of its day. The two piano nobiles have large arched windows with carved heads and figures which are separated by a series of columns, and each floor has a delightful terraced balcony, and the mezzanine attic is defined by a series of oval-shaped windows. The building costs escalated so much that it eventually ruined Filippo Bon, but it was not until 1750 that the Palazzo was purchased by the Rezzonico family.

Originally the Palazzo had an enormous ballroom, with marble balustrades which was created by Massari, and when finished extended the entire length of the building, but although no longer there, the frescoed ceilings by Crosato, Tiepolo, Guarana and Diziani still remain in the magnificent state rooms, located on each of the piano nobile floors. By the 19th century, the Rezzonico family also became bankrupt and many owners followed, one being the poet Robert Browning, who lived here with his son, the painter, Robert Barrett Browning in the 1880s. The Ca' Rezzonico was finally purchased by the City of Venice in 1935 after its last extravagant owner, Count Lionello de Minerbi, also experienced financial difficulties. Building restoration work began in earnest by stripping the interior and returning to bare walls and ceilings other than some original frescoes, which were thankfully retained, as the aim was to reinstate the building to a genuine 18th century palazzo by retaining authentic furniture, paintings and décor. More extensive work to upgrade the building took place between 1970 and 2001, following which the museum then opened to the public with its new name *'Museum of 18th century Venice'*. Today the building is used to display its magnificent collection of 18th-century art, which includes entire rooms salvaged from other palazzos, including many tapestries, lacquer works and not forgetting some fabulous works by Canaletto. The best way I can describe this wonderful building is to walk through it and attempt to explain some of the exquisite detail that is on display.

The first-floor *Ballroom* is a wonderfully extravagant and decorative room measuring 24m x 15m, which was originally created by Massari himself in the 18th century. The walls are decorated in such a manner as to increase the overall perspective, which is attributed to Pietro Visconti. There is a large fresco on the ceiling by Crosato showing Apollo in a carriage reaching to all 'corners' of the world, together with two stunning chandeliers, which are survivors from the original furnishings. This room has an amazing amount of light penetrating from the triple-aspect setting, which illuminates each piece of the precious artwork on display.

Moving on to *The Nuptial Allegory Room*, this is more solemn looking, with its red damask wall covering and dark wooden panelling covering the lower parts of each wall. There is a large ceiling fresco, painted by Giambattista Tiepolo, his son Giandomenico and Gerolamo Mengozzi, which is by far the main attraction in this room, and one I personally like is called the *'Nuptial Allegory'*, which depicts Apollo in his chariot with the wedding couple surrounded by various figures of virtue, namely, The Three Graces, Wisdom and Fame. Like the Ballroom, there are several classic pieces of furniture on show, notably some gilt, carved armchairs and ornate Venetian wall mirrors. One other notable piece of artwork, portraying Pope Clement XIII, sits on an easel. This Pope was previously known as Carlo Rezzonico and was a younger brother of a former owner of the Palazzo. Just beyond the Nuptial Allegory Room, there is a small but brilliantly ornate Chapel with original gilt stuccowork on a soft white panelled backing.

I now enter *The Pastel Room*, which again has a marvellous ceiling fresco, which I was told was restored as recently as 2003, and depicts the *'Triumph of Poetry'*, which is said to have been completed in recognition of the writer and poet Quintiliano Rezzonico. I really like the display of portraits in this room, especially those completed by an accomplished female artist of the 18th century, Rosalba Carriera. Her work has a wonderful softness of character, which I feel portrays her subjects so sensitively, showing an expression of warmth from her sitters. There are two pieces, in particular, that express her work succinctly: they are the *'Portrait of Sister Maria Caterina'* and *'Portrait of a Gentleman in*

Red'. One other stunning portrait that catches my eye in this room is the *'Portrait of Cecilia Guardi Tiepolo'*, painted by Tiepollo's son, Lorenzo, of his own mother. Once again, this room has been tastefully furnished, with elegant items from other period Venetian buildings.

Not being a great tapestry person, I sometimes avoid entering rooms whenever these particular works of art are displayed, but I was glad I visited *The Tapestry Room* in this building, because of the interesting decoration that was on show. Like the majority of rooms in this splendid building, one has to view each fresco individually and examine the minute detail on show to really appreciate just how masterful each artist was in recreating these colourful allegories for all to admire, and this room is no exception. Jacopo Guarana's *'The Triumph of the Virtues'* is a more recently restored masterpiece, which is finished in a delicate pastel effect, creating a soft but extremely colourful scene, which almost shouts for the viewer to study in great detail. I must confess that the tapestries themselves are also mesmerising, as all three on display in this room tell such interesting stories. Each tapestry is filled with detailed episodes of events with King Solomon and the Queen of Sheba, which is enthusiastically explained in the digital commentary that is available. You cannot fail to miss the yellow lacquered door with beautifully detailed Chinese decoration, especially the intricate coloured flowers and pink ribbons which frame the oriental scenes. Unfortunately, the visitor only gets to see one side of this remarkable door, but I expect the other side to be of equal beauty.

The next room I enter is *The Throne Room*, which as its name would imply is quite a stately affair. I am immediately knocked back by the warmth of its rich velvet decor, which acts as a perfect backdrop for the grandiose furniture, each piece richly gilded, as one would have seen it in its original 18th century glory. My research informs me that the furniture is attributed to Antonio Corradini, who worked in Venice in the early part of the 18th century and was responsible for decorating the *Bucintoro* (the Doge's personal ceremonial barge). Corradini was also responsible for crafting the enormous frame which displays the equally outstanding portrait of Pietro Barbarigo, which is also hung in this room and was painted around 1770 by Bernadino Castelli.

As I leave the Throne Room, I am quite excited about the next room to view, as it is attributed to yet another great artist which Venice has produced. *The Tiepolo Room* is filled with works from this great artist and contains portraits such as '*Old Man with a Crown*', and two oval pieces, '*St Martin of Tours*' and '*St Blaise*', both of which sit either side of a wonderfully coloured and richly inlaid walnut bureau with original Venetian mirrors. In contrast to the artwork, is the green cloth card table, unusually designed with eight carved legs, four at each end. Linking this room with the Library is a short 'passageway' housing cabinets displaying fine porcelain, such as the coffee and tea service by Geminiano Cozzi, and the cups, saucers and plates by Giovanni Vezzi, each piece beautifully decorated with various coats of arms, landscapes and other rural scenes.

From the *Passage*, I now enter *The Library*, which has many masterpieces on display by Bellucci, Molinari and Lazzarini to name but a few, but the sculptured marble head of a woman, by Antonio Corradini, depicting a beautiful face shrouded by a veil ('*Veiled Woman*') is absolutely stunning.

Being conscious of the time, I quickly move on to the last room on the first floor, *The Brustolon Room*, which has a host of magnificent wood carvings by Andrea Brustolon together with paintings by Bellucci Langetti and Palazzo to name but a few. Brustolon's work, however, takes precedence especially his sculptured carving *'Allegory of Strength'*, which is a console vase stand depicting characters such as Heracles and Hydra supporting three Negro slaves who in turn are holding a large stand which supports a vase. A remarkable piece of work.

Leaving the Brustolon Room, I am now standing in *The Portego*, which is the final area on the first floor, providing a wide corridor with marble busts and sculptures by Orazio Marinali together with an altarpiece titled *'Mary Magdelene at The Foot of The Cross'*, painted by Giambattista Langetti. From the Portego, I climb the staircase to the second floor, which houses many paintings within the *Upper Portego*. My favourites, of course, are the Canalettos, namely, *'View of Rio dei Mendicoli'* and *'The Grand Canal from Ca' Balbi towards the Rialto'*. To the right of the Upper Portego are groups of rooms dedicated to Tiepolo frescoes, namely those from the villa in Ziango (near Murano), which have recently been restored, in addition to several scenes from the life of *Punchinello*.

Punchinello, or as we would know him, as Punch, is a classical character that originated in the Commedia dell 'Arte and became famous in Neapolitan puppetry. He is normally depicted with a long nose, resembling a beak, usually has a black mask and wears a long white cloak. His temperament is usually known for being mean, vicious and crafty and his character generally portrays someone who is stupid and unaware of what is going on … reminds me of a certain politician. Can't think who! As I hastily move on, passing through various small rooms such as the *Chapel, Centaurs,* and *Satyrs,* I arrive at the exquisite setting of *The Harpsicord Room* where, as you would expect, stands an 18th-century harpsichord on display, surrounded by furniture and doors depicting scenes of rural bliss, each one painted by a past master. Still making my way through the second floor, I walk past one area know as the *Passage* and eventually reach *The Parlour Room*. In this room, I can enjoy the work of Francesco Guardi, among others, and I pay particular attention to a couple of his works, namely, '*The Parlour of Nuns at San Zaccaria*' and '*The Ridotto at Palazzo Dandolo in San Moise*' both of which are well known pieces. Guardi, like Canaletto, gives a wonderful insight into the life and times of 18th-century Venice, and between the pair of them they have painted my most favourite scenes of the 'Serenissima'. Reluctantly, I have to move on and I now arrive in *The Longhi Room,* which is equally magnificent, as this room holds some incredible masterpieces, which include '*The Fortune Teller*'. Remaining on the second floor, I quickly walk through rooms wonderfully furnished and reach an area where they have reconstructed a chemist's shop of the 18th century, I now finally arrive at '*The Egidio Martini Picture Gallery*'. This gallery is fantastic, as it has over 300 pieces of artwork on display and is a museum of its own.

Ca' Rezzonico really is an excellent building to visit, as there is so much to see and enjoy for the visitor, even if those visiting have no previous knowledge of Venetian art or history, as the carefully recreated rooms provide a colourful, informative and interesting voyage into the 18th century.

What a day so far. The time is still only 3.35pm and I have visited some outstanding buildings, albeit briefly, and there is still much more to follow. As I leave the Ca' Rezzonico, I make my way back towards San Barnaba and the weather outside is still great for walking. I cross over the small bridge which leads back into Campo S. Barnaba, then cross the campo and arrive at another bridge, which crosses the Rio Malpaga, and then continue along this route until I arrive at Calle Eremite. From here I turn right, then almost immediately left, which will take me in the direction of the Palazzo Brandolin, where there are some nice little shops, and an infants' school judging by the noise coming from a concealed playground behind a very high brick wall. When I arrive at Calle Chiesa, I bear left and walk to the end, where I am now facing the Rio di San Trovaso. After turning right, I walk a few more metres and arrive at the church of San Trovaso, which is facing the very attractive Palazzo Nini, with its two floors of attractive Gothic windows set in the façade, which is finished in red and yellow stock brickwork. Although I shall not be visiting San Trovaso today, it also has some really interesting history, and while here I observe the fact that the square the church stands in has been raised above street level to protect the filtered rainwater for the well. Earlier today I crossed the Ponte dei Pugni and mentioned the feud between the Castellanis and the Nicolloti. Well, this church served as the only neutral ground for these fighting clans. In order to maintain some modicum of safety, San Trovaso was built with two almost identical classical façades each with separate entrance doors, one overlooking the canal the other the square, in other words one for each clan. This arrangement served the community well and provided a reasonable solution to a very sensitive problem; I can't imagine just how difficult it must have been to officiate in any one of the lengthy services that were conducted here!

The church itself was built in 1590 and stands on the site of the original building which was constructed in the 10th century.

It is built to a Latin cross plan, with a single nave and side chapels. San Trovaso is a wonderful example of a Palladian church, and is dedicated to St Gervais and St. Protais (Trovaso is an abbreviation of Gervasi and Provasio). The spacious interior houses some Tintoretto and Giambono works among others, the most notable Tintoretto pieces being *'The Temptation of St Anthony'* and *'The Last Supper'*, and two larger pieces at each side of the choir, *'The Expulsion from the Temple'* and *'The Adoration of the Magi'*, both begun by Tintoretto but eventually completed by his son Domenico. The marble altar built in the 15th century has some wonderfully carved angels in the foreground.

I should also mention, while in this area, that the adjoining Squero di S. Trovaso is the oldest boatyard in the city that builds gondolas. The building itself is reminiscent of a Tyrolean house and dates back to the 17th century. Business is not quite so hectic nowadays as there are only about 500 gondolas in Venice today, whereas there were 10,000 in the 16th century.

The time is now 4.05pm and, with the church to my right, I now make my way across Campo San Trovaso and past the church's second entrance, cross over another small bridge, which leads me to the Calle de Magazen, which I follow around to the right, and find myself now on the Fondamenta Zattere Lungo. Once I turn left and cross the Rio terra A Foscarini, I am now on the Fondamenta Zattere ai Gesuati. The weather is still fabulous, so much so that I now look for the shaded areas to walk, as I didn't bring my hat and I still have some walking to do before the sun disappears. The first church I reach, situated on my left, is the lesser known but still glorious San Maria Della Visitazione, with its outstanding 16th-century ceiling. But today I am more interested in the next church, a few metres along, which is known to the locals as the

Gesuati. Not to be mistaken for the Gesuiti in Cannaregio, the Santa Maria della Rosario is a very different church. Built between 1726 and 1743 for the Dominicans by architect Giorgio Massari, replacing the smaller church that stood nearby, this church was funded by many Venetian benefactors. There were several noted artists who contributed to the interior design, namely, Tiepolo and Morlaiter. Originally there were Jesuits on this site, in the 13th century, but they were later suppressed and the Dominican order took over. The Gesuati, as it is known today, was consecrated in 1743. The exterior can be described as being fairly tall, standing 27metres high, and has four imposing columns with decorative capitals. The front portal is crescent in shape and focuses the eye on the two large elegant doors; at the rear are two small belltowers, which stand in front of the dome, and I think there is some resemblance in shape to Palladio's Redentore. Internally, there is a vaulted ceiling divided into 16 sections, and the floor is a mass of black, red and white marble. Upon entering the church, you immediately notice the two holy water fonts designed by Massari, which are finished in a Siena yellow, and a glorious crucifix at the start of the nave, which was made by Ceroni in 1746.

As I walk down the right aisle of the church, I immediately notice Morlaiter's statue of *'Abraham'*, finished in Orsera stone, then further along, the first chapel, which depicts three Dominican saints, namely, *'St Catherine of Sienna, Agnes of Montepulciano and St Rose of Lima'*, which was painted by Tiepolo in 1748. The next altarpiece details a piece by Massari titled *'Jesus heals the Blind Man'*. Moving along, I come to the chapel of St Dominic, which has both marble and canvas materials as a decorative feature. The canvas of this saint was painted by Giambattisa Piazzetta in 1743. Next door to the chapel are six confessional boxes, which lead on to the next chapel, also dedicated to three Dominican saints, namely, *'St Ludovic Bertrand, St Vincent Ferrer and St Hyacinth.* Once past this amazingly pious chapel, I reach the presbytery, with its ornate balustrade, and further on, beyond some doors, is the Sacristy, which has beautifully carved large choir stalls. Above the main altar are splendid frescoes by Tiepolo, one in the central area being *'David Blowing the Horn'*, which he completed in 1739. Moving across the nave to the left aisle, there is a relief sculpture by Morlaiter depicting the *'Baptism of Christ'*. The chapels on this elevation are in symmetry to the other side and include a masterpiece by Jacopo Tintoretto (brought here by the Dominicans) together with chapels dedicated to the *'Madonna of the Rosary'* and yet more Dominican saints. Before leaving this imposing church, I should mention the impressive ceiling by Tiepolo, which characterises the Holy Rosary and other pious acts being performed. It also depicts previous Doges and Patriarchs observing the various scenes together with the lesser mortals of Venetian society.

Having spent a short but very interesting time exploring the Gesuiti, I now leave the church, the time being 4.30pm, and I still have a reasonable walk to get to the two remaining major Venetian buildings I have chosen to record on my journey today. Turning left out of the church door, I go directly left again and head along the Rio terra Foscani, which will take me in the direction of the galleries of the Accademia, but before reaching them I turn right into Calle Nuove, a narrow passageway with cafes and art shops, and this eventually leads me onto the Fondamenta Veneir, where I turn left into San Cristoforo. After walking a few more metres, I arrive at the Palazzo Veneir dei Leoni, better known today as the *Peggy Guggenheim Collection* of modern art, which translated means

'Museum of 20th century Art'. When entering the graceful and serene gardens of this building, I suggest that every visitor spends some time enjoying the artefacts in these grounds, which decorate this wonderful area, before moving into the main building. Prior to offering a brief resume about Peggy Guggenheim, I should mention something about the Palazzo Veneir dei Leoni, which claims a noted list of previous owners, such as the Loredans, Valiers and Contarinis, as well as a German sculptor whose name escapes me at the moment. The building was originally designed by Lorenzo Boschetti in 1749 and was originally intended to be on a monumental scale, which stretched back to the fondamenta at the rear of the grounds. The preliminary drawings were said to have been influenced by Sansovino and Longhena, but unfortunately never materialised. The Palazzo was also meant to be fairly tall, with an Istrian stone façade, but unfortunately building works coincided with the fall of the Republic and therefore the ensuing economic crisis put a halt to further construction, and what we see today is a single floor only, which clearly has been remodelled to appear as a finished building, but it nevertheless plays an important part in the evolution of the Grand Canal.

As I shall not have time to visit this building today, perhaps I should explain what there is to see inside, but first a little about Peggy Guggenheim. She was born in 1898 to wealthy American parents in New York City and inherited a fortune at the age of 21. Peggy became part of the art fraternity when working in a bookstore, and later went to live in Paris where she became friendly with artists and writers alike. When in Paris, she became good friends with Natalie Barney, Romaine Brocks and Djuna Barnes as well as Samuel Becket, in 1937. Her first marriage was to Samuel Beckett, a writer and sculptor ; they had two children, Sinbad and Pegeen. Then, in 1938, Peggy opened a gallery for modern art in London and collected many abstract and surrealist pieces; her collection included works by Picasso, Ernst, Miro, Magritte, Ray, Dali and Klee. In 1942 she returned to New York where she opened a second gallery called Art of This Century, and is said to have enhanced the careers of both Jackson Pollock and Max Ernst. She later married Ernst. After the World War II, she returned to Europe where she founded her Venetian Gallery, which now can claim to have at least 180 masterpieces on show. In the 1960s Peggy Guggenheim stopped collecting art but allowed her collection to be loaned out to many European and American galleries. Peggy died in 1979 in Padua, but is buried in the gardens of her palazzo in Venice beside her beloved dogs, and she left her entire collection to her uncle, Solomon R. Guggenheim, primarily for his Foundation as well as her own gallery in Venice. A small selection of the wonderful artwork you will find inside this veritable palazzo include a 1948 Bronze *'The Angel of the City'* by Marino Marini, *'Men in the City'* by Fernand Leger (1919), a mechanical and richly coloured depiction of modern art, *'Landscape with Red Spots'* by Vasily Kandinsky (1913), which has a concentration of primary colours radiating from a central red spot, *'Dutch Interior'* by Joan Miro (1928), using red beige and blue colours (all those I enjoy using in my own abstracts), *'Birth of Liquid Desires'* by Salvador Dali (1931), hallucinatory figures beautifully painted, and last but by no means least, *'Alchemy'* by Jackson Pollock (1947), an unusual mixture of different mediums, including string. These are just a few of the many works that are on display within the gallery, and each room of Peggy's house presents a marvellous journey through the history of modern art. I thoroughly recommend a visit, as there is a wealth of art to enjoy in wonderful surroundings.

Walking back to Calle San Cristofo, I can imagine just how much joy Peggy Guggenheim must have experienced living in this particular area, even more so when I turn left and cross the Ponte Cristofo, which brings me to the small but delightful Campo Barbaro. This campo, although small, has an extremely attractive grassed area with some established rose bushes and small trees, and I wonder if this little green enclave was here when Peggy lived nearby. If it was, I feel sure she would have passed this area many times and enjoyed the serenity of this little oasis. Continuing ahead along the Calle Bastion, I now cross a small bridge where I can clearly see to my left the Pontile St Maria d. Giglio (on the Grand Canal) and realise I am near to the final building on my itinerary for today. All that is left is for me to walk the length of the Calle Abazia, which is just a few metres, and cross the small bridge at the end, where I arrive at the Campo dell Salute and, of course, the majestic Santa Maria della Salute.

This incredible church is probably the most sketched and painted building in all of Venice, as it dominates such a commanding view at the very mouth of the Grand Canal. I have sketched and painted this remarkable church so many times in so many varying mediums that I feel I know every curve and straight line of its exterior. Probably the most interesting skyline is that taken from the Accademia Bridge. Although I haven't actually painted the Salute from the bridge itself, I have been very fortunate in getting scores of photographs at varying times of the day, throughout the seasons, which transform the silhouette, the shadows, the colour and the reflected light on the Canal. Today, however, tourists will be very disappointed, as the entire dome of the church has been scaffolded out, for what I can only assume is major restoration work.

The Salute, as it is reverently known as, is an awesome sight when cruising along the Grand Canal, and its history encompasses every aspect of Venetian culture, religion and architecture. The reason for its construction, which has given so much ecclesiastical pleasure as well as aesthetic value to millions of visitors for almost three and a half centuries, was due to an epidemic of the plague, which affected all of Europe. In 1630, when a third of the Venetian population had been killed by the plague and the city was in the blackest abyss of despair, the Venetian Senate vowed to create a sacred and indissoluble union with their Maker by building a church in honour of the Virgin Mary, who was said to have miraculous powers which could overcome the plague, if He would stop this crippling disease. This particular outbreak is sometimes referred to as the 'Italian Plague' and lasted from 1629 to1631; Venice was a casualty and suffered mostly between 1630 and1631. Bubonic Plague claimed the lives of 280,000 people and was the last of the pandemic plagues, which began with the Black Death. According to history, German and French troops carried the plague into Mantua in 1629, and Venetian troops infected with the disease retreated into northern and central Italy, spreading the infection. The Republic of Venice was infected in 1630 and casualties recorded amounted to 46,000 people out of a population of 140,000, and historians believe that this was the start of the economic decline and political power that Venice had enjoyed for centuries.

The disease (Bubonic Plague) is a product of rodents and fleas; infection is caused when infected fleas bite humans after the fleas had bitten rodents. Plague bacteria multiply inside the fleas, sticking together in their stomachs, causing them to starve. The flea greedily bites a host and continues to feed even though it cannot sate its hunger; it then vomits blood, containing the infection, back into the bite wound. The weather in Venice at that period of time was hot and humid, providing an excellent breeding ground for millions of fleas and rodents throughout this densely populated city. When eventually, the plague casualties began to reduce, probably due to much cooler weather arriving, the Venetian authorities honoured their promise to their Maker by building the Salute. A competition was held to select an architect, and of the 11 submissions two were short-listed, Longhena and Rubertini. Baldassare Longhena was chosen, and it is felt by some that the completed church follows similar lines to the footprint of the Redentore, although I have my own views on this subject. Construction was delayed because of substantial works being necessary for the foundations (conflicting numbers are given for the foundation piles required, 100,000–1,000,000) – whatever, a substantial amount of timber when added together with the 4 metre-long wooden 'footings', which acted as a platform for the base of the stonework. The building is largely constructed of brick 'marmorino' (a brick covered in marble dust) with marble facing, and is designed to an octagonal floor plan incorporating two domes and two campaniles. The main dome is meant to represent the crown of Mary. The exterior is lavishly Baroque, and the detail of each of the octagonal façades provides a wonderful opportunity for pencil and ink sketches, especially the ornate buttresses which support the main dome, which, incidentally, is made of wood to reduce the weight.

Internally the floor plan is of a central octagonal nave standing directly under the main dome, and is said to be similar to the Roman-style Basilica of St Vitale located in Ravenna. Sixteen side galleries surround the nave as well as a series of chapels; there is also a domed presbytery and a monks' choir. The presbytery high altar features a sculpture of the Madonna and Child saving the population of Venice from the plague. Most of the interior walls are faced with grey stone and some white plaster, and there is a most spectacular marble floor decorated in a wonderful mosaic, which depicts the 32 pieces (roses) of the Virgin Mary's rosary. The marble floor in the central nave is protected from walking on, so the visitor simply encircles this area, but if you have some binoculars it's worth looking up at the central dome, as there are some attractive red columns which are decorative rather than supportive. There are a number of artworks by Tintoretto and Salviati, although Tintoretto's great work *'Mariage at Cana'* is actually in the Great Sacristy. Many of the great masterpieces are unfortunately located beyond the main altar, where visitors are not allowed to enter, which include several works by Titian, one being a collection of saints, namely St Mark, St Sebastian and St Roch.

On the 21st November each year, a procession (Festa della Madonna della Salute) crosses the Grand Canal on a specially constructed pontoon for a thanksgiving ceremony in celebration of the end of the plague epidemic. Having simply walked around the circumference of this remarkable monument and church and having respectfully lit, in honour of my family, one of the many candles that grace each altar piece, I leave the brilliantly beautiful and elegant Salute.

The time is now 5.20pm and I have not eaten since breakfast at Gatwick, so I am ravenous, to say the least, and my tired legs are due a rest. Fortunately, as I am walking down the steps of the Salute, a vaporetto is just arriving (No. 1) which will take me across the Canal to the St Maria d. Giglio pontile, where I can catch the faster No. 82 vaporetto and enjoy my journey back to

Piazzale Roma and some welcome refreshment at Bar S. Lucia. By the time I arrive at Enrico's bar, I have only 40 minutes to enjoy a rest, grab a spinach gnocchi and have a drink, before catching the 6.40pm bus back to the airport, where I have decided to eat. Today, for a change, I sit outside the bar, and as I watch the world go by I notice Enrico crossing the street in front of his bar, and then stationing himself in a small ice cream kiosk opposite. On enquiring, I discover that he owns the kiosk and, by the amount of customers he gets, I suspect the ice cream is delicious, but not the perfect complement to Guinness, so I will have to wait for another day to sample a large cone!

After taking a steady walk back to Piazzale Roma bus station (incidentally, I am glad that I brought my cagoule, after all, as it suddenly, without any warning, poured down before I got to the bus stop), I arrive just in time, as my bus is about to depart. No spare seat on this occasion. However, the journey back to the airport only takes 20 minutes, and I am in the airport and checked in by 7.30pm. Whilst checking in at easyJet, I have one eye on the pizza parlour to my right, so after collecting my boarding pass I enjoy a good supper before making my way to the departure lounge. Unfortunately, my flight is delayed tonight, but the time passes very quickly as I have an interesting conversation with a group of American tourists who are returning to the USA the following morning, after spending 31 days touring all around Europe. When I eventually arrive back home, I must confess to being a little tired. However, my thoughts are still very much in Dosorduro and the amazing journey I made in just one day, and fortunately I can have a good lay-in tomorrow!

Buonasera Venezia

CHAPTER 10
JUNE: San Marco
'Merchants, Music and Revolution'

'Flaming June' is a phrase we English like to use whenever the weather is particularly hot in this month. However, to Venetians, flaming January would be an appropriate expression for the San Marco sestiere, which I am about to explore. There are two specific areas of San Marco which I shall be visiting today, both of which succumbed to fire in the month of January, albeit many years apart. The first incident was when the Rialto area was completely destroyed by fire in 1514, which I briefly mentioned in an earlier chapter, the second incident, in 1996, being La Fenice (Opera House), which was almost completely ruined by flame. Each incident in its own way had a major impact on Venetian society, and in the normal Venetian manner they passionately restored the areas to their former glory without any hesitation.

Although I shall only be passing the Rialto briefly today, I will be using the Merceria (a prime pedestrian route) in the early stages of my journey, experiencing the many trading and merchant activities which have been prevalent here for many centuries. The particular path I have chosen for my journey today is quite a relaxed one, even in the month of June when tourism is starting

June 2007

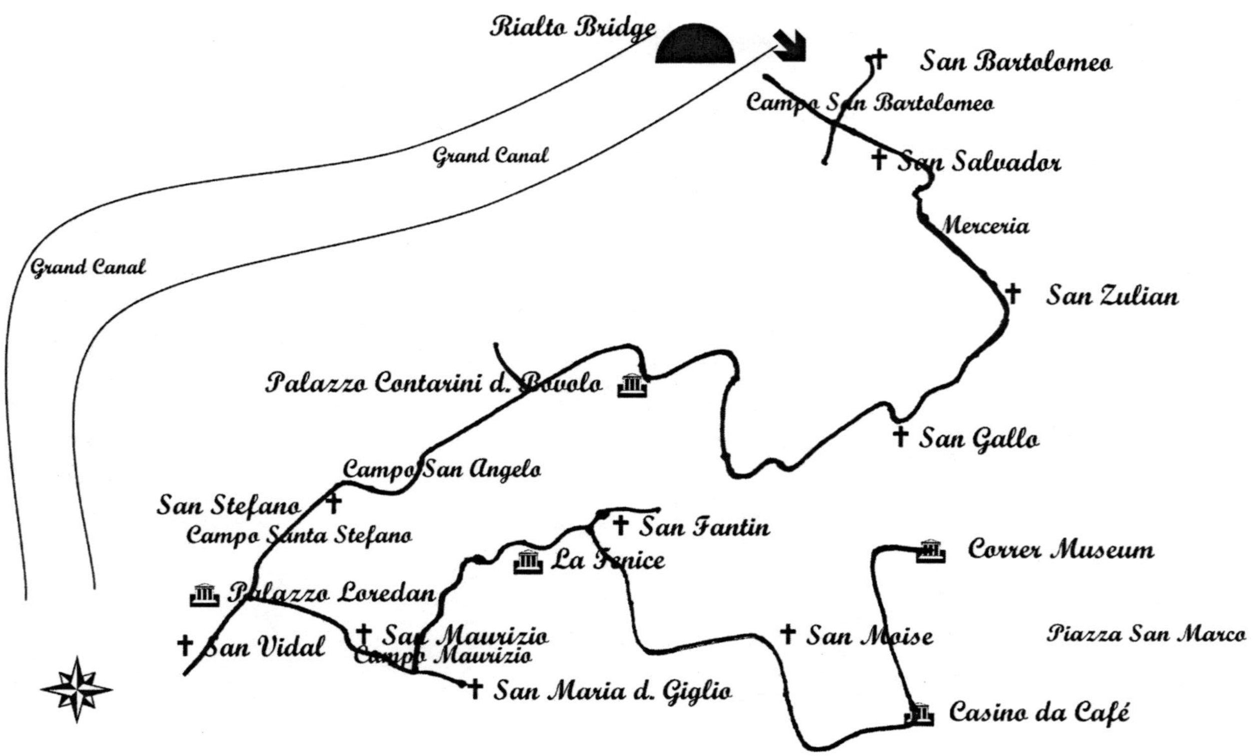
Rialto Bridge
San Bartolomeo
Campo San Bartolomeo
San Salvador
Grand Canal
Merceria
Grand Canal
San Zulian
Palazzo Contarini d. Bovolo
San Gallo
Campo San Angelo
San Stefano
San Fantin
Campo Santa Stefano
Correr Museum
La Fenice
Palazzo Loredan
San Maurizio
San Vidal
Campo Maurizio
San Moise
Piazza San Marco
San Maria d. Giglio
Casino da Café

to peak, and I intend to take the reader to a few remote passages to explore and enjoy as well as seeing a feast of wonderful churches and buildings to either photograph or sketch. Along this relatively short route, which will probably take about two and a half hours, there will be many opportunities to actually visit some churches and other buildings. Again it is dependent on whether the traveller is staying overnight or returning the same day, which is what I shall be doing. Whatever, at the end of today's journey it will be impossible to remember every precious treasure that is there is to be discovered, especially all the priceless artefacts that are on public view.

Approximately midway through today's itinerary I will descend upon Campo Manin and take some time to explain more about this Venetian hero and his quest for independence from the Austrians, who had earlier occupied the 'Serenissima'. There are several of the larger campos to enjoy today, especially Campo San Stefano, which, apart from its historical significance, has a wealth of eating venues to choose from. Probably the highlight of my journey today will be to revisit La Fenice once again. This glorious opera house has provided Venetians and the world with a world-class auditorium, and has hosted some formidable classical artists over the centuries. As well as being impressive in operatic terms, La Fenice is of outstanding architectural interest, having been almost completely rebuilt to its former elegance.

I must confess that the journey today, being relatively short, also gives me the opportunity to visit the Correr Museum once again, allowing me to drool over an exhibition of art by John Singer Sargent, a decision I made when planning the route. The reader, however, could use the extra time exploring the buildings on the route to fully utilise the precious time spent in Venice.

* June 12th 2007

Before leaving home for Gatwick this morning, I make sure that I have packed my cagoule, as the weather report for Venice today reads extremely wet. Other than that, I am travelling fairly light as I intend to simply voice-record my route, without worrying about too much photography and sketching. I must also confess to having spent a couple of days last week in Venice simply enjoying some of the Biennale events together with sketching some scenes for the journal without having to physically record my travels. Having said that, I probably visited all of the sestieri in turn, and had lunch in both Burano and the Giudecca, and those two days alone could have filled a chapter.

Back to today. Gatwick is, as you can well imagine, very busy this morning, but that did not delay my 7.45am flight and, by 11.30am Italian time, I was getting off the bus at Piazzale Roma, having purchased my ACTV ticket at the airport, and making my way to the vaporetto pontile. In order to get to my starting point for today's journey, I have decided to take the No. 82 vaporetto to the Rialto, which will save me some time, as I intend to get the most out of my day before returning home this evening. The weather this morning is slightly overcast and there is a fine drizzle of rain, but it is warm with humidity as high as 83%, which means an umbrella rather than the cagoule. Last week I got bitten several times by flying insects one evening, so today I have some insect-repellent wipes, just in case; these come in handy on the flight home, as I shall explain later.

The trusty old vaporetto arrives at the Rialto after a 15-minute ride, and as I disembark I turn right and head towards Larga Mazzini, which will eventually lead me to the Merceria, which I know will be filled with tourists shopping or window gazing. This incredible union of streets seems to be the main attraction with tourists, especially those who are here for one day only, having just arrived in Venice on one of the large cruise ships. These tourists are taken via Tronchetto to Piazza San Marco and left to explore what they can in the few hours they are here, and for some reason or other, once they have spent some time looking at the treasures around the Piazza, they head along the Merceria towards the Rialto. Once at the Rialto, they inevitably make for the Pescheria and then return to the Piazza. Good for the Venetian traders, as they rely on this income, but not so good if you are hoping to use the 'textile route' (an expression used for the Merceria which has remained over the centuries) as a normal thoroughfare.

Hopefully our journey today will be far more interesting than purely window gazing and will take a shorter period of time to achieve. As I near the start of the Merceria, which I shall feature soon, I arrive at the church of San Salvador, which, although closed at present, does offer a wealth of treasures inside to admire. Pope Alexander III first consecrated this church in 1177, shortly after his reconciliation with Frederick Barbarossa. The present building was first constructed around 1508 by Giorgio Spavento and completed by three other notable architects, namely, Tullio Lombardo, Vincenzo Scamozzi and Jacopo Sansovino. Looking at the white Istrian stone façade, which was added by Giuseppe Sardi, I see the Palladian-style design with triangular tympanum and a relatively small but grandiose portal with multiple steps. Internally the church becomes a Renaissance dream, with works of art such as Sansovino's tomb for Francesco Venier on the south wall, and Titian's *Annunciation* altarpiece on the high altar. There are many other works, which include paintings on the organ doors by Vecellio, and statues of St Roch and St Sebastian by

Vittoria. In the sacristy there are frescoes by Camillo Capelli and in the right transept is the tomb of Caterina Cornaro (1550), the former Queen of Cyprus, which was created by Bernadino Contino. It is unfortunate that this church is not open at present, but there are still many more to see today, which, in my opinion, are some of Venice's finest buildings. I am amazed at the total footprint of ground area that was allocated to San Salvador and the former adjoining convent, as it is huge in relation to most other ecclesiastical buildings, which surprises me somewhat when I think of just how little room there was to build on this small island.

Now having joined the Merceria, I start to follow its trail and I am amazed just how many people are actually shopping, considering the quality of the upmarket designer shops there are along this concourse, which literally cuts across the city centre of Venice. Even before the onslaught of tourists, this thoroughfare served as a prime route connecting the Piazza San Marco with the busy Rialto area. This internal trade link served the Venetians well, and is divided into three separate streets, each having its own identity. From the Piazza, the first stretch is called Merceria dell Oroloio, which then leads to the Merceria di Zulian and eventually links with Merceria di San Salvador, where I am at this present moment. The name Merceria derives from the word '*mercer*', meaning a dealer in costly textiles, and an appropriate name considering the wealth of textile trading there was throughout Venetian history. Eastern textile traders were common in Venice, as trading links with the Orient and the East proved to be profitable, especially the Persian silk market. Venice, with Genoa and Florence, were the major centres of textile trade and practically dominated the textile markets of the world. Silk, being the major textile commodity to arrive in Venice, was spun in great volumes by Italian women in all three major cities, and there are some interesting stories which relate to the entrepreneurial achievements of this group of fine artisans. One such story relates to a widow named Maria Brancaleoni who, in 1570, offered a patent to the Venetian government which clearly described a machine of her own invention that could spin both silk and flax. This machine reputedly could spin four times faster than any single woman could achieve, but the idea was not utilised by the Government as they were concerned that such a machine would affect the employment of the poorer women of the city – a noble thought but would the same principle apply today, I wonder!

Silk was used by the State as a currency in its own right, the raw silk being brought from China and India and made into fine brocades, which commanded huge prices throughout the civilised world. There were demanding laws imposed by the Government on the import of raw silk, but that did not stop the 'silk worms' eventually being smuggled into the Republic, thereby effectively cutting out the source supplier and the revenue taxes that were collected.

Strangely enough, even in the decadent and prosperous age of Venice, it would be common to see the patriarchs using the markets of the Merceria as well as the poorer population, and noblemen shopping side by side with servants was a fairly common sight. Today is no different: one can still see the wealthy mixing with the less fortunate. However, I suspect the majority of sales gained from the more fashionable designer shops that are everywhere on the Merceria, would suggest that most customers are of a higher income bracket.

As I continue my journey along the Merceria, I turn right then left along the Marzaria S. Salvador, which eventually leads me into Merceria San Zulian. At the end of this concourse, I arrive at a small bridge, called Dei Bareteri, where I turn right into the Calle Fiubera, but before crossing the small campo in front of the church of San Zulian (sometimes referred to as Guiliamo), I decide to briefly look inside this remote but engaging little church. The façade of San Zulian is finished in Istrian stone and is slightly overshadowed by the very attractive main doorway, which is framed by a wide sculptured arch that has two columns supporting a statue of the physician Tommaso Rangone. Rangone was the generous benefactor who financed the rebuilding of this church in the 16th century. The church itself was built by Jacopo Sansovino, but due to his untimely death before it was completed it was finished by Alessandro Vittoria in 1570. After entering the church, I can immediately see that there is some major restoration work in progress, especially in the sanctuary and apse, as there are scaffolding and dustsheets everywhere. The small entrance floor to the church is a mixture of coloured marble set into a concentric design, and today, with the steady rain coming down, I was amazed to see the main door secured open to the elements. Internally, what is currently on display is still worth studying, such as the ornately gilded woodwork and a magnificent marble altar just left of the high altar, which is screened off. The central part of the ceiling depicts *'St. Julian in Glory'* by Palma the Younger, and the altar to the right of the nave has a beautiful work of art by Paolo Veronese depicting *'Pieta with St Roch, St Jerome and St Mark'*. In the small chapel at the left of the chancel there are a group of terra cotta figures by Girolamo Campagna, of the Virgin Mary and Mary Magdalene. The church of San Zulian was not on my itinerary today, but I am glad I did look inside, albeit briefly. It certainly is worth a revisit on another day, when the current restoration work is finished.

Coming out of the church, I turn right and head for the Ponte Dei Ferali, again noticing just how many designer shops there are. Once at the bridge, I cross over and arrive at the Calle Fiubera. This interesting narrow street, which is virtually deserted, has a nice bakery shop, restaurants and small gift shops, and makes a pleasant change from the busy Merceria, and, looking at my watch, I see that it is only 12.30. Ahead of me, running diagonally across Fiubera, is the long Calle dei Fabbri and, when I reach this intersection, I turn right, walk for a short distance and then turn left into S. Gallo (this diversion will take me off the main tourist route), where I continue crossing a couple of small bridges on my way. Once over Campo Rusolo, I see another small bridge, which is very familiar, as it crosses the Rio Orseolo, an area that I have painted and walked past many times on my preferred route to the Rialto. Standing on this busy little bridge, looking along both sides, I can see many gondolas being manoeuvred along this narrow canal, and my mind goes back to a past confrontation I had with a gondolier whilst I was sketching in this area some time ago. As this area is a prime gondola staging-post for tourists –it literally backs onto Piazza San Marco –there appears to be an assumption that artists shouldn't consider sketching from this very interesting and picturesque scene. On this particular occasion, although my Italian was poor, I think the complaining gondolier actually realised that I wasn't moving from the remote spot where I was standing until I had finished my sketch.

Once across the Rio Orseolo, I now move into the Calle Tron and once again I am confronted with a plethora of interesting small shops to view, but I have more pressing things to do. At the end of Calle Tron, I bear right into Frezzeria and eventually pass Corte dei Pignoli, before reaching the Calle dei Fuseri. I am now right in the centre of the tourist route once again, as there are even more designer shops to see, which are only interrupted by a bridge crossing the Rio Fuseri. For the shopper, this route must seem like the yellow brick road to heaven. Not being a great shopper myself, I make some steady progress along this concourse, which will eventually lead me to arguably one of the most attractive exposed staircases in all of Venice. I refer, of course, to the 'Bovolo', which forms part of the Palazzo Contarini. I must be careful to make sure that I don't miss my turning when seeking this wonderful monument, as this little gem is tucked away in the Corte Contarini dei Bovolo, which, without the helpful signs available, would be almost impossible to find.

Access to the Bovolo is gained by walking down a very narrow passageway which has been decked out with scaffolding for a considerable amount of time. Once through this temporary tunnel of steel, the Bovolo suddenly appears to your right and is certainly well worth the effort getting there. Although access is denied to this 'snail like' tower today, the architectural features are something to be admired. I seemed to have read somewhere that it is proportionally out of scale, but to my amateur eye it stands magnificent. Either Giovanni Candi or Giorgio Spavento built the Palazzo Contarini, in 1499. No one is quite sure who it was, but it has both Renaissance and Byzantine influence in its design. There have been many alterations made to the building over the years, such as the arches on the piano nobile and the stonework at water level, but the building is still in need of some restoration. The façade itself can be seen from the San Luca canal where the

Gothic round arches of this palazzo can be clearly admired. The famous staircase, or tower, which I am standing near, got the name Bovolo from its shape (the Venetian for snail is '*bovolo*') and is of a helicoidal shape, with round rampant arches finished on the top by a dome. In 1717 Elizabetta Contarini married a trader from Bergamo named Giovanni Minelli who was one of the former patriarchs who actually paid 100,000 ducats to gain this title. In 1803 the palazzo was sold to Arnold Marseille, who later turned it into a hotel. Today it is owned by a charitable organisation. Bovolo is certainly well worth visiting and, hopefully, the staircase will eventually be open once again to explore – a treat well worth experiencing.

As I make my way back through the narrow passageway, I turn left and arrive at Campo Manin, which is named after one of Venice's former heroes. The campo itself is, as you would imagine, interesting and historical. Well, certainly three sides have some former heritage; the remaining elevation of the square, however, is more modern. In the 1960s the Casa di Risparmio di Venezia, as it is known, was constructed and, although an attractive building to modern-day standards, it does to my eye look a little out of character with its neighbouring buildings. On the far side of the campo, facing the wonderful monument of Daniele Manin, sits a 17th-century palazzo (red rendered walls), which is flanked by two attractive small bridges. This is a scene I have painted many times before.

Daniele Manin was born in Venice in 1804 from Jewish parent stock, but, as tradition would suggest, patriarchs sponsored his family, and his father, who adopted the name of Manin, later converted to the Christian faith. Manin studied law at Padua University and later practised in Venice, and was said to be a man of considerable learning. As a politician and a Venetian, Manin detested Austrian rule at that time and his patriotism inspired many Venetians to rebel. In 1847 he delivered a petition to the Austrian Emperor detailing the needs of his nation and was arrested and eventually charged with high treason, which infuriated the Venetian population. This emotive action, together with the advent of revolution in Italy at that period, forced the Austrian Governor to release Manin, at the same time inspiring revolutionists to take control of Venice, forcing the Austrians to evacuate the city.

Manin became a national hero and took the role of President of this new Republic for a short period of time. During this period, Venice was under siege, and for almost two years Manin resisted the ongoing onslaught of the city by the Austrians, who had re-formed and rearmed in considerable numbers. The siege of Venice, as history will confirm, was defended by Venetians with determination and courage, but, unfortunately, once the fortress at Marghera was lost, the brave defenders of the 'Serenissima' were faced with disaster. Marghera defences were an essential element in support of the siege, and, once they were broken, food became scarce, the all-important Venetian powder magazine blew up and cholera broke out. This sequence of events together with continuous shelling from Austrian batteries eventually brought an end to the Republic once again. The Austrians actually deployed hot-air balloons which unloaded explosive devices during this conflict. But, fortuitously, this first attempt at aerial warfare became a farce due to several anomalies which occurred, and even in times of desperate revolution it was said that Venetians found time to cheer and laugh at this 'failed' means of warfare. Cannaregio continued to bear the main battery attacks, as did parts of San

Polo as far south as the Zattere. In fact, the shell damage was also quite severe on the Grand Canal, where many palazzos were damaged. The siege proved to be far too great for the Venetians to withstand, and many people fled to the furthest regions of Castello, even though the Arsenale was probably a prime target for the Austrians. Throughout this horrific siege, Manin continuously made every attempt to keep the Venetians hopes alive for victory and continued independence, but eventually succumbed to the might of the Austrian attack. Conditions deteriorated to such an extent that Manin was forced to capitulate and, in August 1849, he negotiated terms with the Austrian general Radetzky. Radetzky demanded several terms of surrender one of which was the forced exile of 40 known Venetians who were responsible for the initial revolt.

On the 28th August 1849 Manin and his entire family left the Lagoon never to return. In fact, Manin's wife died from cholera within hours of being exiled. For the next eight years, Manin was the main spokesman for the unification of Italy and generated considerable support amongst the French during his time in exile in Paris. Eventually Manin abandoned his fight for republicanism and founded the National Italian Society in 1857. But, at the age of 53, he died in France following a long period of ill health. In 1868, two years after the Austrians had left Venice, his remains were returned to Venice, where he was given a public funeral. Venetians both then and today are full of admiration for Manin's honesty, his statesmanlike character and, above all, his love for Venice, which ultimately led to the unification of Italy as we know it today. Having read several accounts of the siege of Venice, I have only provided a brief resume of what was a tragic and remarkable event, and Manin was considered to be a true believer in unity. Where others were thought perhaps to be far more sceptical, Manin can, then, be hailed as a true Venetian hero of his age. I can't help thinking of a quotation by Hannah Arendt (1906–1975), which I think, summarises revolution quite succinctly. It reads 'The most radical revolutionary will become a conservative on the day after the revolution.'. True in many cases, but did that apply to Italy?

Leaving Campo Manin, I take the far left of the two bridges, which will take me on to the Spezia d Mandola d. Cortesia, where I continue until I reach the end of this street, which eventually brings me to Campo Stefano, the largest square in San Marco other than the Piazza itself. There are many pavement bars and restaurants surrounding this campo, and another monument stands in the centre of the square, which is dedicated to Nicolo Tommaseo, who for some reason is known to Venetians as 'Cagalibri'. Tommaseo was an Italian linguist, journalist and essayist as well as being the editor of a dictionary of Italian synonyms. His academic career took him around Europe, but he is probably better known by Venetians for being an outspoken liberalist and defender of the revolution; because of his association with Manin he was also exiled at the end of the siege, and ultimately made his way to Corfu.

The campo itself was once the arena for major bullfights, and one recorded incident carefully explains the havoc that took place here on these occasions. It would appear that a large stand collapsed during an ongoing contest in 1802 between man and bull which resulted in absolute carnage, following which all further contests were stopped. My real interest here today is to visit the church of Santo Stefano, but, before I do and because the time is only 1.10pm, I have decided to briefly take a look at Palazzo Loredan from the outside, which is at the south-west end of the square. This elongated palazzo has one short façade finished in stone with a much longer return with some elegant multi arched windows. This interesting palazzo is often overlooked by sightseers which is sad, as it has some remnants of an original Gothic design that can be seen from the Rio S. Vidal canal and is invariably upstaged by its neighbour, the former church of San Vitale, which now stages concerts and exhibitions. Palazzo Loredan was acquired by the Loredan family in 1536 and was built to a Renaissance design by Antonio Scarpagnino. There is a 15th-century wellhead in the entrance together with finely crafted arches which sit on Istrian stone capitals, the entrance hall itself having two arches to one side with three smaller arches in the centre. There are two main staircases, which converge into one to form one magnificent ascending passageway, which is tastefully decorated. The mezzanine ceiling decoration is 16th century and there are two large rooms on the piano nobile one of which is decorated with 18th-century stucco work, as well as fine works by Tintoretto, one being his *Madonna and Child with Four Senators*. Today the palazzo is home to the Institute of Science, who have been in residence since 1891.

Having taken a quick look at Palazzo Loredan, I head back across the square to the church of Santo Stefano, which sits at the far north end of this busy campo. The church was founded in 1294 by the Augustinian movement, and this particular church has been reconsecrated several times in the past, allegedly, because of blood being spilt within its walls! Santo Stefano is one of a minority of churches that were actually built over canals. This unusual building design occurred when the church was expanded in the 18th century. Looking from the campo, my personal opinion of the church is that it does not look particularly attractive, but that all changes once you enter this enchanting building. The exterior of the church is Gothic in design and was completed in 1374, having a façade which appears high and wide in the central section, incorporating a superb doorway decorated with a 'roping' design with leaves encompassing an arch that has an angel supporting God the Father. Internally the church is extremely well illuminated with natural light and appears very spacious and tall. There are diamond-patterned walls, in a similar fashion to the exterior of the Palazzo Ducale, and the ceiling resembles a ship's keel, which is really striking with its richly painted decorations, especially the rosettes. There are three wide naves separated by columns that have coloured capitals and pointed arches, creating an overall slender appearance. Looking from the main doorway there are five chapels to the left and four to the right, which were built in the 18th century, whilst the main altar dates from the early-17th century. There are many works of art to be enjoyed here, as you would expect, and probably my favourite are the works of Tintoretto in the main sacristy, *'The Washing of the Feet', 'The Agony in the Garden'* and *'The Last Supper',* all completed around 1579/80. Together with the paintings are objects of jewellery alongside classical pieces of work by Antonio Canova and Pietro Lombardo, which are all displayed in cabinets that form a gallery around the cloister. Within the Treasury are wooden chests, made of rich walnut, fronting panelled walls, which provide a magnificent contrast to the lighter walls and artwork above. To the left of this area is a Renaissance monument to Giacome Surian by Lombardo and his sons, which is decorated with shells. The interior of this church is magnificent; even when leaving, the visitor is presented with a really fine piece of craftsmanship on the internal side of the façade, displaying sculptured art, which decorates the walls above and to both sides of the main door, and is quite beautiful, as it complements the walls of the nave.

As I leave San Stefano, the time is 1.30pm and I think to myself how much I have enjoyed this church, as well as getting full value from my Chorus pass, which I originally purchased last November. Of the churches included in this pass I have visited at least 12 to date, and the beauty of this pass is that all the churches advertised are open from 10.00am till 5.00pm each day, and the total cost of the pass is only 8 euros.

Once out of the church, I turn left into the campo, walk a few metres and then turn left again into Calle d. Spezier, which will lead me to Campo San Maurizio and the next two churches on my chosen route, which are very different in appearance and purpose. After crossing over a small bridge that spans the Rio del Santissimo, I arrive at the church of San Maurizio, which is on my left. Visitors are in for a surprise when entering this former church; it is quite dissimilar to those I normally visit, but it is nevertheless really interesting to explore. As I enter the main door (admission is free), I am instantly confronted with a cabinet full of delightful musical instruments which were around during Vivaldi's time, each splendidly displayed and certainly worth viewing, as there is a wealth of historic value on show in each cabinet. This small but beautifully proportioned building is now used for exhibitions, and currently has many instruments on display, which include violins, cellos, violas and lutes, each carefully itemised and detailed for the visitor to enjoy. Italian classical music is continuously being played in the background and the visitor is given the opportunity to purchase some excellent CDs – a place I could spend lots of time in but, alas, I have more calls to make today.

After leaving San Maurizio, I walk across the small campo facing me which looks so austere and under-maintained, and I can't help comparing it with other campos on the island. I have to confess that the immediate area I am now standing in is fairly run down and pretty lifeless, apart from the former church that I have just visited. I am now walking in the direction of Santa Maria dei Giglio, down the Calle Ziguri, and I am about to cross the bridge which spans the Rio S. Maurizio, which I cross and finally reach the next church on my route.

The façade of Santa Maria dei Giglio is absolutely stunning and has to be studied in great detail to fully appreciate its beauty. Even today, when the rain is drizzling down, I can still find time to photograph this edifice and take time to study the detail with a pair of binoculars, as the craftsmanship is phenomenal. A church was first built on this site in the 9th century, the present one being built by Giuseppi Sardi in 1680. Looking at the very Baroque façade, I can see why there was some controversy originally in creating this masterpiece, as the entire face is dedicated to the history of one particular family, named Barbaro. Antonio Barbaro was a wealthy patrician and had a distinguished military and political career in Venice. It was because of his achievements that permission was eventually granted for this monolith, and he was able to commission and design a façade solely to commemorate his close family, a commission that started immediately following his death and at a cost of 30,000 ducats, which was a fortune in the 17th century. Giuseppi Sardi worked entirely from Antonio's instructions and created a façade that can be best described as a collection of statues framed by fluted columns. The statues on the lower level are of Antonio's brothers, each divided by delicate pairs of Corinthian columns. Above, on the middle level, is a statue of Antonio, himself, standing on a sarcophagus, which is framed by marble drapes, and above this are several other statues and statuettes seated over and under an open top pediment. The plinth on the ground and first level depict various battle scenes attributed to Antonio, completing what can only be described as a remarkable work of art.

Internally the finish of Santa Maria dei Giglio is equally as magnificent, as well as having possibly the best natural lighting of any church in Venice. This natural light seems to filter into the building from everywhere, illuminating each piece of precious artwork on display, and even the organ, situated behind the main altar, seems to sparkle with reflected light. Usually, visitors viewing the majority of Venetian churches have to rely on some artificial lighting to view altarpieces and the like, but not this remarkable church. To the right of the nave is what is proudly referred to as the 'treasury', which houses several cabinets of priceless artefacts in gold, together with artwork by Peter Paul Rubens, namely, *'Madonna and Child'* and *'St John the Baptist'*. Tintoretto also has his *'Four Evangelists'* on display in this room together with work by other notable artists. The ceiling of the nave has large canvases by Antonio Zanchi, and the main altar is faced with a decorated scene of *'The Last Supper'* in marble, which is awash with vibrant colours. I simply cannot speak more highly of this outstanding church, as there is so much to digest and enjoy – a must for every traveller to Venice, even on a wet day!

Leaving this priceless building, I now make my way to the Calle Caotorta, which is quite a narrow passageway, and head in the general direction of Campiello Calegheri with the Fondamenta Cristoforo to my left. This short walk will lead me to Calle d. Fenice and, of course, to the exquisite La Fenice opera house.

Before reaching La Fenice, however, the route I am using today actually takes me close to the canal entrance to the opera house, which can be seen to the right when crossing over a small bridge at the west side of the building. Before reaching the grand entrance to La Fenice, having circumnavigated its northern perimeter, I find myself in Campello Mari Della Fenice, having just passed a rather nice restaurant on my left. A few metres further on and I arrive at Campo San Fantin and I am now standing immediately in front of this stunning opera house. The last 10 minutes of my walk were virtually tourist-free and a delight, as there were so many corners and narrow passageways to manoeuvre my way through, and I feel I have seen so much already today and it is still only 2.30pm.

La Fenice really is the climax of my itinerary today, although I still have one other treat in store later, but this masterpiece of architectural achievement can only really be fully appreciated by viewing the interior. Not everyone is fortunate enough to be able to spend an evening here listening to the opera, and for the day visitor, do not despair: fortunately, visitors can explore the building for a few euros and, if you are lucky enough, there are conducted tours at prearranged times. Although I am not going to visit this majestic building today, I have been inside several times in the past, but I will take the reader on a brief tour, starting with the impressive façade. The neo-classical colonnade, which has seven grandiose marble steps leading to the main entrance, has two statues on the façade, which depict *Tragedy* and *Dance* and above these are two masks, namely, *Comedy* and *Tragedy*. The first floor has a fine balcony in the centre of the façade, which is finished in a warm white, and, of course, has *Phoenix* rising from the flames as its centrepiece ('Fenice', meaning 'phoenix', was given this name in the late-16th century following the rebirth of the opera house).

At the end of the 18th century there were seven established theatres in Venice, the grandest being San Benedetto, which stood where the Rossini Cinema stands today, close to Campo Manin. In 1790, the Association (a group of theatregoers) decided to build their own theatre. They then bought some land and selected Giannantonio Selva as the appointed architect to design and build their opera house. Work started in 1791 and the theatre was completed 18 months later! Unfortunately, this building was devastated by fire in 1836, and rebuilding started in 1837; within a year the new building was complete. In 1935 the Association sold their shares in the opera house, and ownership went from private to public, and then later in 1935 major restoration work started to reinstate the building to its former splendour.

La Fenice remained unchanged for over 60 years when, in 1996, it suffered its second fire. There are many stories regarding this fire which range from arson to accident. Whatever, a rebuilding programme was eventually agreed, and in 2003 the building was at last completely rebuilt, other than the façade, which miraculously escaped total damage. Internally, the finish has been reproduced almost exactly to the same specification as the original opera house, although some additions were made and the colour of the walls in the boxes has been changed. The foyer escaped the fire of 1836 and, when eventually restored the following year, became structurally much stronger, thereby protecting the main façade in the 1996 fire. Today it is truly a wonderful sight with its ornate columns and exquisite chandeliers, enhanced by the tastefully decorated walls and ceilings with their deep cornices, which provide the visitor with a taste of the enriched elegance of the past.

The opera house auditorium was completely destroyed and rebuilt to an exact design using similar materials. The vaulted ceiling contains some fine works depicting *The Three Graces*, and *Dance & and Aurora*, and papier-mâché acanthus leaves are everywhere, all of which are finished in 23-carat gold leaf. Throughout the many rows of boxes, there are paintings of cherubs, classical poets and allegories representing history, poetry, philosophy, comedy, tragedy and music, with each individual box being painted in a pastel green. The fairly large orchestra pit can be transformed into an extension of the stage if desired, thereby increasing the capacity of spectators by 104, making a total of 1,126. The former Royal Box was remodelled several times in the 19th century and, following the 1996 fire, was completely rebuilt to the same specification of the one built for the Italian Royal Family of 1866. Next is the Sale Apollinee, being a group of five rooms, which interlink and are used for interval and bar areas. Amazingly, small areas of these rooms survived the 1996 fire and have been carefully included in the reconstruction work, notably the ceiling cornice and some stucco work on the wall panels. The Sala Dante (better known as 'the main bar') once displayed magnificent frescoes on the walls, parts of which were salvaged and reinstated. Obviously, the major part of the frescoes had been completely destroyed, so when restoring these sections the panels have been left incomplete, showing only the surviving pieces. I personally think that this was a marvellous idea, as it now becomes an even greater discussion topic. Next is the Sala Grande, which is the main room of the Sale Apollinee and was formerly used as a ballroom, concert hall and rehearsal room. Incredibly, this room, which again was almost entirely destroyed in the fire, has been reconstructed to its former glory in every manner and form, copying the remarkably high standards of the original craftsmen, even down to the wall coverings. I am so pleased for Venetians that this Mecca of musical delight has been returned to its former glory and I hope that it will provide pleasure for everyone for many years to come.

Whilst whistling Vivaldi's violin concerto from the *Four Seasons*, I move from La Fenice and cross Campo Fantin, where I walk along the Calle delle Veste until I reach the Calle Larga XXII Marzo. What a name for a street! This wide street is again full of designer shops and is generally very busy, especially heading east. As I look to my left, I see the church of San Moise, which stands quite prominently beyond a small bridge.

I am in effect at the end of my journey today, but as I have not entered and explored many buildings en route, and the time is only 2.50pm, I have decided to visit the Correr Museum to view an exhibition of paintings by John Singer Sargent titled 'Sargent and Venice'. Getting to the Correr Museum is so easy, as I simply walk in the direction of San Moise church, walk around the left of the church along the Salizz San Moise and arrive at the Calle larga della Ascensione; the entrance to Correr is then facing me. This exhibition has been running for several weeks now and ends next month, so to avoid completely missing this event I have decided to attend today, as I am so near to the museum. Sargent is an artist whom I greatly admire, as his work has been a tremendous influence on me, especially his landscapes and, more especially, his pieces painted whilst he stayed in Venice. Born in Florence in 1856 to American parents, he studied in Italy and Germany and then went on to Paris. His drawing work is phenomenal; he had the technical ability of a draughtsman and the creative ability of an artist. During the 1880s he produced portraits of many fashionable women of the age, which were exhibited at the Paris Salon, one of which *'Madame X'*, painted in 1884, is probably one of his most famous pieces. Another portrait of his that I really like, and hope to see one day, *'Lady Agnew of Lochnaw'* (1892), which he finished just a couple of years before being elected to the Royal Academy, is a prime example of his natural talent. He moved to London in 1884 and had his first real success with the Royal Academy in 1887, after sending portraits there for some years (having just had my entries for the Summer Collection rejected, I know how he must have felt).

Throughout Sargent's illustrious career, he created around 900 oil paintings and more than 2,000 watercolours of note as well as thousands of sketches and charcoal drawings. Although he is not looked upon as being an 'Impressionist painter', I think that his wonderful watercolours have a feel for this style, especially his landscapes and waterscapes. He often returned to America, where most of his work seems to be exhibited, and where I once had the pleasure of viewing his *'Santa Maria della Salute'* watercolour (1904), in Brooklyn Museum of Art, long before I had ever visited Venice. He worked with and was a friend of Claude Monet at one time, and I would have loved to be a 'fly on the wall' during their time together; can you imagine what creative ideas were discussed over a bottle of wine? Sargent's style is best described as 'Realism', and as I enter the exhibition gallery at the Correr Museum I immediately focus on some marvellous oil paintings one of which is a group of Venetians drinking and enjoying themselves in a bar. In all, there are over 60 works on display, which have been loaned from both private and public collections from all over the world, so I am in for a feast of artistic entertainment at the close of my day- trip to Venice. As I wander through the four main galleries, I become totally engrossed with the works Sargent completed of the Salute between 1902 and 1907, one of which I mentioned earlier, and how I wished I could produce watercolours in this fashion. I try, but I haven't got there yet!

What becomes apparent from Sargent's work in Venice is that he had to paint whilst either sitting or standing on a watercraft of some sort, as there were no digital cameras 'to capture the moment' like there are today, and I can't quite imagine just how he produced so much detail on such an unsteady platform. Looking at the pencil lines, which are clearly visible on some watercolours, I can only assume that some of the detailed drawing work must have been completed in a studio. Clearly, there are many ruled lines that would prove to be impossible to draw, without some stable platform, or perhaps that is why artists of this note are so special. Without labouring on too much about the fine details of art itself, I can say that the scenes from the Rialto Bridge, Palazzo Ducale, Salute, various workshops, cafes and crowded streets kept me spellbound for the best part of an hour and a half, my favourites being, *'Campo San Canciano'* (1882), *'Corner of the Church of San Stae'* (1913), and *'Gondola's off San Giorgio Maggiore'* (1902/03).

Having really enjoyed my brief interlude in the Correr Museum, I now realise that it is 4.35pm and I haven't eaten since breakfast, so I decide to head straight back to Bar S.Lucia and grab a snack and a drink. Once I have finished in the Correr, I simply leave the way I entered, turn left and make my way towards the San Marco pontile. Although I haven't really walked a great distance today, I nevertheless take the vaporetto back to Ferrovia and decide on the No. 82 from San Marco, which after a couple of routine stops gets me to my destination by around 5.00pm. The short walk to the bar takes a few minutes and when I arrive I can sit out front on the Rio terra Lista di Spagna (another wonderful street name) and enjoy my belated lunch and watch the world go by. The earlier rain has now stopped but the humidity is still fairly high and the cool breeze, which is around, is very comforting.

On reflection, my day exploring various locations in San Marco has been very special as this area has lots to offer the tourist, and there are still some very nice little pockets of this sestiere that are peaceful and serene; on the other hand, many tourists do enjoy the hustle and bustle of street markets and shops. Whatever, visitors cannot escape the beauty of San Marco's churches and the wealth of 'hidden history' that presents itself everywhere.

I constantly think to myself when writing this journal, 'what if ?, what if the reader turns right instead of left when following my directions?' Well, the only practical answer I can arrive at is that Venice needs to be explored, and if you get lost, so what? There are always the standard tourist signs to bring the traveller back on track. Providing you are sensible at timekeeping (if it is a day-trip), then I can assure you that your trip to Venice will be more than memorable.

My time at Bar S. Lucia was slightly longer today than on previous occasions, simply because I know there will be a queue at the check-in once I get to the airport, and, quite honestly I would rather watch watercraft sailing down the Grand Canal from the Scalzi Bridge than be part of a 50-metre queue in the airport lounge, even if I do miss my ice cream (the ice cream bar tends to close at 8.00pm sometimes). Eventually, I take the 7.10pm bus back to Marco Polo airport, arrive at 7.35pm and find that I am still in a queue of 10, before my 9.05pm flight home.

At the beginning of this chapter, I mentioned taking some insect repellent wipes with me today. Well, these nasty creatures were still intent on getting me yet again, not, surprisingly, whilst I was enjoying Venice, but in the aircraft coming home; once again, I was able to secure a front seat in the plane and, just before the stewardess closed the cabin door for take off, two mosquito type insects found their way into the cabin. The chap to my left went straight for them with a newspaper, whilst the young lady to my right tried to swot them with her book. Neither were successful, so throughout the 1hr 50min flight home the three of us were on mosquito watch the whole time. Paranoid or what?

Buonasera Venezia

CHAPTER 11
JULY: Castello
'Home to the Pantheon of Venice'

It is hard to believe that it is the middle of summer already, considering the changeable weather we have been experiencing (or is that what we should expect in the future?). Since my last visit to Venice, I have been busy working on some ink and wash sketches, which I hope to include in the journal, and so far I have over 30 to choose from. The problem facing me is that I will probably only be able to publish about 22 in total, so which ones should I choose? During the past year, I have visited so many interesting sestieri, each having its own attractive buildings, streets and squares, that choosing appropriate sketches, which will bring to the reader the full flavour of the 'Serenissima', is proving to be far more difficult than I had ever imagined. Over the past 10 years, I have sketched and painted hundreds of scenes of Venice, but each one was viewed in isolation and usually presented in a colourful format and not as a guide for travellers to enjoy. Each one of the monochrome pieces that I eventually choose will hopefully not just paint a picture of what I have seen but act as an informative guide to this wonderful island.

Making decisions on that level was not a problem for writers

July 2007

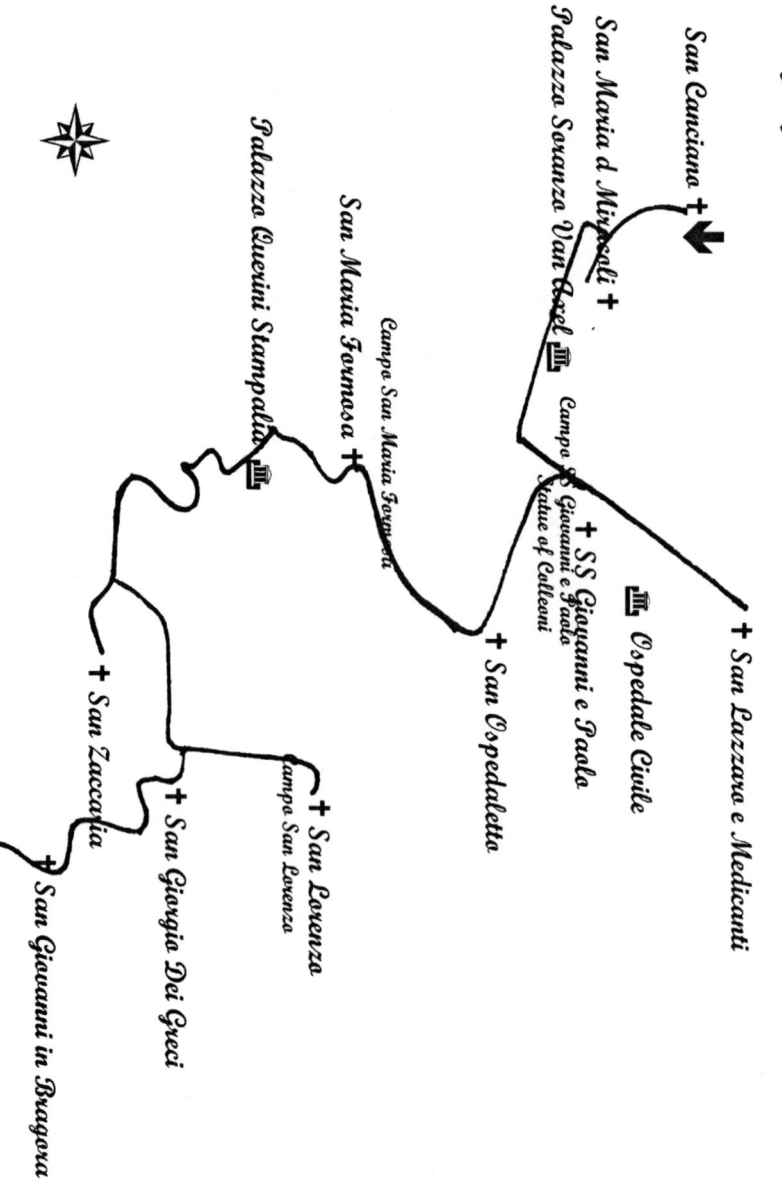

San Canciano †
San Maria d Miracoli †
Palazzo Soranzo Van Axel 🏛
← † San Lazzaro e Medicanti
Campo SS Giovanni e Paolo
🏛 Ospedale Civile
† SS Giovanni e Paola Statue of Colleoni
San Maria Formosa
Campo San Maria Formosa 🏛
Palazzo Querini Stampalla
† San Ospedaletta
† San Zaccaria
† San Lorenzo
Campo San Lorenzo
† San Giorgio Dei Greci
† San Giovanni in Bragora
Riva degli Schiavoni

or artists centuries ago, simply because there were relatively few detailed maps or guides for travellers to use, but can you imagine just how difficult it must have been in planning and choosing a coherent index of place and street names in what was a maze of undeveloped swampland, which would eventually link a mass of small island groups that is now mainland Venice?

Today my journey will take me back to the sestiere of Castello, which was once a group of small islands, one of which was known as Isole Gemini, which grew up around the Arsenale, and today, when linked with the Eastern Region, form the largest of the six Venetian districts. Like all the other five sestieri, Castello has a very vibrant and chequered history, especially when you consider just how important the Arsenale was to the Republic, which incidentally divided the district between the naval yards and the monastic orders occupying the northern area. Today, however, I intend to focus on the western and central areas, which I deliberately avoided visiting in my recent travels. My itinerary will take me to the perimeter of what is known as the Ospedale Civile (hospital sector), where I shall visit several buildings associated with the early Dominican and Franciscan orders, who inaugurated many charitable institutions known as the 'Ospedali'. Whilst on my journey, I shall visit memorials to past Venetian heroes and again enjoy several important and once very active campos, which still accommodate wonderful churches all filled with priceless works of art.

The start of my travels will actually border on the Cannaregio sestiere simply because I have two specific buildings to include which I consider to be of real interest to the reader. Again, in order to complete my full itinerary, it is necessary to backtrack on some short passages en route, which is not a problem, as the scheduled direction I will be taking is certainly an interesting one. Although the journey will end at La Pieta (close to the Piazza San Marco), I hope to avoid the general tourist path, which will almost certainly be crowded at this time of the year.

In order to get the most out of my time in Venice today, I will again take the vaporetto to an area close to the start of my walk, this being the famous Ca D'Oro, where I shall disembark and walk the short distance to San Canciano, which will be my starting point.

Today I am taking my digital camera and recorder, enabling me to use my small shoulder artist's case, which is light and easy to carry. As the journey today is of a reasonable distance, I hope to explore several buildings, and therefore I shall decide to stop for lunch when I find the right restaurant at a convenient time.

* July 11th 2007

This morning I have decided to make my way to Gatwick earlier than usual in view of the recent security restrictions in place, so, having got out of bed at 4.45am, I am on the road to the airport at 5.15am. Upon arrival at Gatwick, I expected to see a heavy police presence and have my car searched or at least checked before parking, but when I arrived it was business as usual. I was, therefore, parked and inside the departure lounge by 6.05am. My flight to Venice was not until 7.45am, so, after getting some breakfast, I sat down to read until it was time to board.

The flight to Marco Polo airport was very comfortable, and it seemed like no time at all before we had arrived and I was being transported to the arrival terminal. Gazing at my watch, I noticed that it was 10.55am, Italian time. Once through airport security, I purchased my ACTV pass and was boarding the No. 5D bus within minutes. The journey to Piazzale Roma, however, seemed to take longer than usual, due to a build-up of traffic on the autoroute at Mestre, which, incidentally, affected my return journey. Having laboured to get to its destination, my bus eventually arrives at Piazzale Roma by 12.05pm, and I make my way quickly to the vaporetto pontile to catch the No. 1 watercraft, which will take me to the Ca'D'Oro on the Grand Canal, where my journey really starts today.

As is quite often the case on my trips to Venice, I seem to end up assisting travellers on the bus with their onward journeys, and today was no exception, resulting in sharing the same vaporetto with a young couple from the UK, as they were heading for the Rialto. Also on the short trip to Ca'D'Oro, I got talking to an American couple who had just arrived and were scheduled to spend a few days in Venice before a week or so trekking around the Dolomites, something I also would dearly like to do one day. By the time I reached my destination, the vaporetto was pretty full, and when I disembarked and said farewell to my fellow travellers, I gazed at the Ca'D'Oro for a few minutes before moving along the Calle Ca'D'Oro, which leads on to the Strada Nova.

The weather here today is fantastic, no sign of the showers that were forecast, just blue skies and a temperature around 20C. As I pass Campo San Sofia, I notice the Traghetto station to my right, which looks as busy as usual, and I continue ahead until I reach Campo dei Apostoli. Surprisingly, there are relatively few tourists around even though it is now 12.30, and I would suggest that this is a great place to stop and eat; there are several really nice trattorias and bars in this area. The campo itself is very attractive as there are several impressive buildings to enjoy and photograph, especially Palazzo Falier, to my right, which lies just beyond a small bridge.

The church of San Apostoli is not one I had planned to visit today, but one that deserves some mention, having an attractive brick façade with three doorways, each with a small pediment above. The main door has a sculptured plaque on display, above which is inscribed some historical detail; I would imagine it records the fact that this church was one of the first churches of the early Venetian settlement in the 9th century.

With the church to my left, I now walk across the campo and make my way down the narrow Calle Langamure until I reach the Calle d. Cason. Ahead of me is a sign which reads 'Hospedale SS. Gio e Paolo, and at this point I turn right and make for the Calle de la Malvasia. This very narrow alley leads me to the Ponte Canciano, and ahead of me is a lovely earth-coloured rendered building, which stands in front of the campanile and directly alongside the church of San Canciano. Although I can't enter the church today, I do know that it is also one of the original churches from the 9th century, which was rebuilt again in the 16th century. Originally the church was dedicated to three Roman brothers killed in a battle in the year AD 304. The façade faces directly onto a building which is in very close proximity, but there is enough space to see that it is a Baroque-style structure with rendered walls and some Istrian stonework on display; it has two large windows either side of and above the ornate portal. I particularly like the main door (which like the belltower is original 10th-century). The weathered door has six heavily moulded fielded panels, which would make a perfect study for a sketch. Above the main doorway pediment there is a beautifully sculptured wall plaque, which, again like San Apostoli, has a text inscription, and is unfortunately so weathered it is difficult to read. However, my research tells me that the church has undergone several restoration projects in the past, the last being in the 18th century. The interior retains a Renaissance appearance and there is a great deal of 16th–18th-century artwork on display by several masters such as Leandro Bassano, Jacopo Tintoretto and Tiberio Tinelli to name but a few. There is an amazing altar created by Longhena for an artisan family called Widman, who, incidentally, built the Palazzo Widman Rezzonico, in the 17th century. Within the immediate vicinity of this parish church several great artists such as Titian, Bassano and Corona all died, and the area I am standing in is wonderfully depicted in a painting by John Singer Sergeant titled 'Ladies Leaving Church in Campo San Canciano' (1882), which I recently viewed at the Correr Exhibition.

Feeling a trifle disappointed about not being able to view the interior of San Canciano today, I move off, reminding myself that it is almost impossible to explore every church I arrive at, as their opening hours vary considerably and, in order to get the most out of my day trips to Venice, I must accept this fact. I can however still take in the surroundings areas and enjoy the wonderful ambience and occasion, knowing that these buildings will still be here when I hopefully revisit on another day. Walking in the direction of Campo San Maria Nova by simply following the blue sign which reads 'Hospedale', I now walk down a narrow alleyway and eventually arrive at Campo San Maria Nova, which is a delightful square with a tree as the centrepiece offering some welcomed shade for all travellers to enjoy. Immediately to my left is a street musician playing a guitar and Jew's harp, and, although his music has a South American flavour, it makes good listening; his audience, who are sitting in the nearby cafes or simply standing in the shade, are certainly appreciative of his talent. As I look directly ahead I can just make out the marble walls of Santa Maria dei Miracoli, which I know is open, as all Chorus churches are throughout the day, so I intend to take full advantage of this opportunity to visit what in my opinion is one of the most beautiful and decoratively finished churches in Venice.

The immediate area surrounding Santa Maria dei Miracoli is extremely attractive; viewed from every angle, the artistry of the marble finish of this church has a unique and overwhelming charm. Although I visited this church last November, whilst travelling through Cannaregio, I simply couldn't resist including it once again today, as it was on my scheduled route. When last here, I didn't get the brilliant summer light reflecting through the windows, illuminating the interior of the church, but today I can see how it really does bring all the marble finished walls to life. I can't think of another church which is completely finished both internally and externally with polished marble and radiates such majestic dignity. As I enter the church, my eye is immediately focused on the abundance of polished marble, which is layered in almost symmetrical accuracy along each side of the single nave. The colours and tones of each piece of marble, separated on three distinct levels, are almost mesmerising and, apart from displaying a certain figurative elegance, it has a unique beauty, which pleases my eye. The ceiling, in contrast, has wonderfully gilded framed paintings which are divided from the walls by an elegant frieze. Even the altar itself stands resplendent, and is accessed by climbing 13 steps. On either side of the chancel stand two small balconies each with their own pulpits. Magnificent is an understatement. Seeing the choir ceiling, which is decorated with carved panels from the Titian school, and enjoying the frescoes of various patron saints in the chancel, becomes a real spectacle which every visitor must surely savour. As I leave the church, I spend some time photographing the exterior of this memorable and glorious building, and I am in awe of the craft and techniques of the marble-work, which probably looks as good today as it did in the late 15th century.

After leaving the church and walking diagonally across the area in front of the façade, I am now in the Calle Castelli, which again is a narrow passageway, and I can see ahead of me a display of beautifully coloured red roses which grace a local garden and serve as a picturesque backdrop in this shaded walk. Arriving at the end of Calle Castelli, I emerge from the shaded alley into sunshine once again and, as I look to my left, I recognise the Palazzo Van Axel, which I am looking forward to visiting. Today I am in luck. Apart from being able to enjoy the interior architecture of this building, I will also get the opportunity to view the work of Rafael Lozano-Hemmer as part of the Mexican Pavilion's exhibition staged for the Biennale di Venice 2007. Although I am quite a traditionalist when it comes to art, I still enjoy all forms of innovation and creativity, and the Biennale International Art Exhibition certainly has a great deal to offer everyone. As the 2007 exhibition is running until the end of November, I intend to visit several galleries sometime in October, but today I can enjoy the contemporary work of this Mexican artist as I explore the Palazzo.

Palazzo Soranzo-Van Axel has an interesting history, as do all of Venice's fabulous buildings, but this one can lay claim to more recent renown than most; erected on the same spot as an earlier Byzantine building, the one we see today was built originally for the Gradingo family and then later bought by Nicolo Soranzo, a former Procurator, in 1473. His family, in turn, owned the palazzo for almost 200 years. From the 16th century onwards both the Venier and Sanudo families owned the building, before it was eventually purchased by the Van Axels in 1665, who were a wealthy family from the Netherlands and lived in Venice from 1628 to 1919. The Van Axel family also owned other properties in Venice and played an important part in the Venetian economy; they lived in this palazzo for 300 years, until it was eventually sold to the Conte Dino Barozzi. Barozzi, who spent a great deal of money restoring the building and bought wonderful 15th-century furnishings and paintings to decorate the interior. The building was last purchased in 1950, by a private owner, which meant that the building has had only six owners since it was first built, a remarkable achievement compared with most other palazzos.

The main façade lies on the Rio della Panada, and therefore having two formal entrances, one from the canal and the other from the street, both of the beautiful façades have 'quadrifora' windows, and there are two external courtyards. The entrance door, which is accessed by walking along a narrow pavement running parallel with the canal, is most interesting, as it dates from the late 14th century, and, apart from having wonderfully engraved panels, it still retains its original metal doorknocker. The immediate area adjacent to the entrance door, and the approach walkway, have featured in many films throughout the years, the most recent being a scene from the 2005 version of *Casanova*. As I enter the palazzo through this remarkable door, I am confronted by an amazing courtyard, which has a fine portico, a wellhead and two very attractive external Gothic staircases. The delightful gardens within the courtyard direct my eye to the portico, which is supported by delicate columns and arches. Under the portico there is a sarcophagus on display and, above it, fixed to the garden wall, is a remarkable wooden carving of the Lion of Venice. Walking up the internal staircase leading to the upper floors, I notice that the walls are simply plastered without any ornate decoration, which works well with the low ceilings with their exposed beams. The internal rooms are obviously not furnished, as the exhibits on display take all of the available space; I am however able to paint a reasonably good picture in my mind of how this interior must have looked in the past. The exhibition itself is most striking. The first room I enter has an exhibit titled *'Wavefunction 2007'*, displaying 50 chairs on pneumatic pedestals which move in wave formation as I walk around them. Apparently, every hour, the chairs move to a performance of Monteverdi's *Lamento d'Arianna*. Quite fantastic. As I move in and out of each room there are other equally interesting pieces on display, my favourites probably being *'Surface Tension'* (1992), depicting a human eye on screen in a darkened room which follows every move I make, and *'Pulse Room'* (2006), in which there are dozens of light bulbs, suspended on cables, that flash when approached and have sensors that record the heartbeat of recent visitors to the room, Creative or what?

Hopefully there will be more of Rafael's work to see when I visit the main Biennale building in October. As I leave the exhibition I return down the external staircase leading to the courtyard and, from the top of the stairs, I can see a very attractive Gothic wooden doorway and windows on the first floor, which are set against the red clay roof tiles of neighbouring buildings, and, just beyond that, the eastern elevation of Santa Maria Miracoli with the tops of its marble walls clearly in view. Magic!

Out through the remarkable doorway which I entered earlier, I now make my way back along the narrow pavement and realise why this location is so special. Apart from being very picturesque, it is very secluded, providing a sense of peace and tranquillity that many have enjoyed for several hundred years. Ahead of me is a small bridge to my left, which I cross and which will eventually bring me to the Calle delle Erbe. Whilst crossing the bridge, I notice the majestic Palazzo Pisani on my right (one of several palazzos with similar names) and as I continue down Calle delle Erbe I come to a group of small shops and find myself in a very narrow lane which leads to yet another small bridge; when I cross over, I see immediately to my left the former Scuola Grande di San Marco. As I walk in the direction of the Scuola, I come to the wonderful bronze monument of Bartolomeo Colleoni, which stands proudly in the Campo SS Giovanni e Paolo. Standing in this campo is an absolute delight for several reasons: firstly, there are very few tourists about; secondly, the entire ambience of this incredible square is so relaxing, yet colourful; and thirdly, there is so much to see and visit in a relatively confined area. Having made my mind up in which order I will visit this group of buildings, I take a short walk along the Fondamenta di Miracoli, which is directly to my left of the Scuola and runs parallel with the canal. The reason for this short diversion is simply that I want to photograph the church of San Lazzaro Mendicanti. This short walk takes a couple of minutes and, on the way, I cross a modern ramp which bridges a spur of the canal for ambulance access. I advise anyone crossing this ramp to be mindful of the surface material; I wasn't, and tripped forward onto my shins, much to the delight of several bargemen standing on the opposite side of the canal. By sheer coincidence, I happened to be walking alongside the main hospital on the island. Fortunately, a quick brush-down was adequate, and once I had got over the embarrassment of my theatricals I walked a further few metres and arrived at the church. The façade of San Lazzaro Mendicanti is entirely finished in Istrian stone and was built to a Renaissance style by Vincenzo Scammozi. Other than that, I have very little information, so, after taking a few photographs, I record yet another church to visit on future trips to Venice.

Walking back to the main campo, I can't help but notice the fleet of ambulances moored to my right, and, as I gaze inside one of these slender motor boat craft, I realise that the interior is not too dissimilar in design to our own ambulances in the UK. I can however imagine just how difficult it must be to get needy passengers on board in an emergency, but then realise that Venetians are boat people and to them it is not a problem. Certainly, getting to the hospital shouldn't be a problem using canals instead of busy roads. Having crossed the ramp on my return without incident, much to the disappointment of the bargemen, I am now back in the main campo, and standing before me is the Scuola Grande di San Marco.

The Scuola is now part of the Ospedali Civile (Civic Hospital) and has been since 1819, so I am very respectful of this fact as I enter the main door. Obviously there are strict security restrictions once inside the building, but tourists are allowed to get a glimpse through the Reception area and can view the immediate surroundings, which clearly identify just what an important Scuola this must have been in its heyday. The Scuola was founded in 1260 and, as its title would suggest, is one of the six grand confraternities of the city, having patrons from several noble families in Venice. It was, however, originally located in the San Croce sestiere, before establishing its current form in this area. It was originally built in 1437 and then damaged by fire in

1485. Pietro Lombardo redesigned its façade, which is in two parts each having its own entry portal. The main doorway is elegantly finished in sculptured stone, as is the elaborate coping above, where there is a blaze of delicate marble on display, the centrepiece being the Lion of Venice. It has many columns, windows, niches and marble statues. The decorative frieze was carved by Tullio Lombardo, the most prominent being the scenes from the life of St Mark portrayed either side of the portal. On the ground floor, either side of the doorways there are what can best be described as isometric designs set into the walls, giving the appearance of a diminishing perspective, which is well worth studying. On the west elevation, whilst I was walking back from San Lazzaro, I noticed the exterior yellow brickwork had virtually no mortar joints; they looked almost dry, but the bonding is remarkably even and each brick has been cast to a remarkable standard. Internally, as one would expect, there have been extensive renovations, the early work completed by Codussi, but, like most of the Scuolas, it was virtually abandoned for many years following the fall of the Republic.

Adjoining the Scuola is the magnificent church (often referred to as a basilica) of SS Giovanni e Paolo. Having visited this huge structure only once in the past, I intend to spend a little time today viewing the treasures on display inside, because of the incredible amount of artistry therein; unfortunately, I can merely summarise, whilst exploring, as there is so much to see and it really has to be viewed first hand because words would not do justice to such beauty. This church is known as 'The Pantheon of Venice', and I can assure you that every visitor who enters its walls will be in for a treat, but I shall start by describing the exterior first. The construction of this massive Gothic brick-built church, sometimes referred to as San Zanipolo, was started in 1343. The building was then enlarged in 1390 and finally consecrated in 1430. However, an earlier church built by the Dominicans was on this site in 1246. One legend has it that the then ruling Doge had a dream of holy doves landing on the then unused land, and decided to build on this spot. The original design was less spectacular than we see today and the size of the structure was originally agreed on more modest lines. Then, in 1458, Gambello built the red brick entrance, having incorporated original columns from a church on Torcello that had previously been demolished. From the main campo you see a mass of red brickwork, which is decorated with finely sculptured Istrian stonework. Across the central part of the façade there is a band of brickwork 2m high, which is corbelled on each course and complements the appearance of the arches below. A large rose window dominates the centre wall, with two smaller windows on either side, which I think emphasises just how huge this building is as well as directing the eye to the stonework which forms the shape of the central nave. Above this stonework are three niches symbolising the Eternal Father, together with the statues of St Peter and St Jerome. On either side of the main entrance there are six recessed niches with arched brickwork, four of which have sarcophagi of former Doges. Incidentally, this church houses the tombs of no less than 25 former Doges. Along the external southern elevation, the red brickwork becomes even more prominent by its voluminous and varied shape, resplendent with statues on display and ornate stonework together with the Apse of the Madonna of Peace, which protrudes at right angles, overlooking part of the campo.

I have to confess that when I first visited this church I wasn't terribly impressed by the exterior finish of the façade. Sure, the sheer size of the structure itself is huge, but compared with the wonderfully decorative Scuola that it sits alongside, it is a little bit of a let down, so I didn't rush to get inside. How wrong I was. As soon as I walked through the main entrance, I was absolutely amazed by what I saw. The inside decoration and artistry are far too splendid for me to describe in any great detail, but I will attempt to describe the layout and highlight a few of the many treasures there are to see. When entering through the main door, you immediately notice the great nave, which has a cross and a vaulted ceiling supported by heavy wooden beams, which in turn are supported by 10 large Istrian stone columns. I suggest the visitor walks a few metres towards the altar and then turns around to view the counter face of the external façade, which itself would compliment any other church in its own right. Along the right aisle is a work by Capuchin, *'Martyrdom the Mecenary'*, and Bellini's *Polytych* of various religious scenes. Next is the Chapel of Salomoni with pieces by Giambattisa Lorenzetti, *'The Infant Christ'* (1587), and *'The Mystic Wedding of St Catherine'* (1699) by Gregorio Lazzarini. Moving on, I reach the Chapel of the Madonna of Peace, with an altarpiece of the *'Virgin and St Hyacinthus'* by Jacopo Palma, and, of course, ceiling decorations by Veronese.

Next in line is the Chapel of St Dominic, resplendent with several 18th-century bas-reliefs on the walls, by Guiseppe Mazza, and a large fresco by Giambattisa Piazetta depicting the *'Apostatises of St Dominic'*. A glorious sight now greets me in the right transept, in the form of a large polychromatic mosaic window (1495) beautifully designed by craftsmen from Murano. Moving on, we come to the Chapel of the Apse, which has a bronze painted altar with two sculptures of the Virgin and John the Evangelist (1585), which can be seen in the background. Alongside this is the Magdalene Chapel, which has an altar displaying statues of St Magdalene flanked by two angels, illuminated by a wonderful mosaic glass window. Moving on again, I arrive at the presbytery itself with its main altar, which is set back above several marble steps and surrounded by funeral monuments attributed to Lombardo and Morosini as well as many other notable artists. To the left of the presbytery is the Trinity Chapel, which has works by Bassano and Salviati. Moving along, to my left is the Chapel of St Pious V, which has a beautiful altar with columns and a small pediment and a battle scene painted by Titian. The left transept has a 24-hour clock (1504) mounted on the wall, which has ornate painting around its face, and its mechanism works in unison with an ancient balance wheel rather than a pendulum, as they were still to be invented.

I now arrive at the largest of the chapels, called the Rosary Chapel, built in honour of the Virgin of the Rosary. This chapel is resplendent with sculptures and magnificent ceiling decorations by Veronese, which were later introduced following devastating fires in the 15th and 16th centuries, which destroyed virtually everything on display. Next we come to the Sacristy, which is a large hall having a stucco-decorated arched ceiling, which in the centre displays a large canvas by Marco Vecellio called *'The Dream of St Dominic'*. Around the ceiling are lunettes depicting various saints, and below are elaborately carved wooden benches. The reason this church is called a basilica is that it is a monolith of a building and has an incredible historical presence, apart from being beautifully decorated, and possesses a great deal of sanctitude within the confines of its walls. As I leave SS Giovanni e Paolo I realise that I shall have to visit this church again and again to fully appreciate its magnitude, as my brief description is very limited and didn't even include the magnificent funeral monuments that are everywhere to be seen.

Coming out of the coolness of the church into the warm bright sunshine I stop to admire the monument to Bartolomeo Colleoni (1400–1476), which stands guard over the square. The bronze statue is said to be one of the finest bronze equestrian pieces in the world, and I can see why it has this claim, as the detail is so realistic. The statue was designed by Andrea Verrochio and completed by Alessandro Leopardi in 1490; incredibly, neither had met with their subject. Colleoni actually requested that his monument should be placed in Piazza San Marco following his death (he bequeathed a fortune to the Republic), but having tentatively agreed to this request when he was alive, the Council decided after his death that they did not want to build monuments on the Piazza. The compromise was a play on words: if not Piazza San Marco then Campo San Marco, and the location of Bartolomeo's monument was finally resolved.

Colleoni was a soldier of fortune, having come from a military family, and had his first engagement at the Battle of Aquila, in 1424, when the kingdom of Naples fought against Alfonso of Aragon. He was born in Bergamo but became a Venetian subject in later life when he served as *Condottiere* for the Venetian government. Throughout the 13th and 14th centuries, cities such as Venice, Florence and Genoa became prosperous through trade but had few armies to defend their wealth from others, including their neighbours. The patriarchs and nobles of these great cities decided to hire companies of soldiers known as 'condotta' to defend their interests, each condotta being championed by a 'condottiere' or captain. Originally these armies were made up of foreigners and were generally disorganised, but they soon developed into efficiently co-ordinated units, which consisted of up to 3,000 mercenary soldiers. Unfortunately, these 'condotollas' worked for the greatest purse and often changed sides, sometimes during a battle! The entire method of warfare between these mercenary groups became somewhat complicated, each contract (condotta) having special periods for renewal, which affected 'the terms of war' as well as the groupings of each unit. Venice did use these mercenaries for land wars but not for naval warfare (*contratto d'assento*), but did retain their contract armies until the end of the 15th century, when national armies from France etc. proved to be too powerful for the division of Italian states with their smaller condottieri armies. Occasionally certain Italian states used their noble princes as condottieri, to gain extra revenue, and warfare became a bargaining exercise rather than a bloodthirsty battle!

Colleoni's army career in Venice started in 1429. After serving with the Napolese, and after returning to Naples once again, he then returned to Venice in 1438 and fought with Erasmo Gattameleta (the then commander in chief of the Venetian army) in the long war against Milan; following that, he went off to Milan where he was imprisoned, and eventually escaped to rejoin the Venetian army in 1455 after which he gained the title of 'Commander in Chief of Venice' although he only actually fought one major campaign in 20 years of service for the 'Serenissima'. He was, however, accredited with some daring escapades, such as bringing the Venetian fleet to the waters of Lake Guarda, using firearms fixed to mobile carts in the battle of Molinella (1466) and escaping from a campanile in Monza using knotted curtains and bedsheets, after having been imprisoned by Filippo Visconti for treason! Venice paid heavily to retain his services, which enabled Colleoni to amass a fortune, and he lived in a lavish castle in Malpaga where he entertained the most noted artists and noblemen of this period. Before he died, he left a fortune of 500,000 ducats to the Venetian state, and later they responded by acknowledging this soldier of Venice by erecting his monument where I now stand.

As I leave the Campo SS Giovanni e Paolo and walk past the wonderful church I have just visited, I take another photograph of the architectural features of the south elevation. Although it is simply a mass of red brickwork, the grouping of the belltower, nave and dome create a spectacular profile with Colleoni's statue in the foreground. The time is now 2.05pm, so I must move on, and as I reach the end of Salizz S. Giovanni e Paolo I now face the church of Santa Maria dei Derelitti, which is generally known as the 'Ospedaletto'. Unfortunately, I have no time to explore this church today. However, I cannot pass without mentioning the façade, which has a bas-relief in the centrepiece depicting a private citizen named B. Cagnoni, who funded its construction. This small church was built by Longhena to a Baroque style and was one of the four hospitals or homes for the elderly and infirm, which was founded in the early part of the 16th century, and also served to educate orphans and abandoned girls. The interior has some works by notable artists, *The Sacrifice of Isaac* (1716) by Tiepolo being just one. In fact, Tiepolo was only 19 years old when he painted his first public work here. Should you get the opportunity to read *The Stones of Venice*, you will see some amusing comments about the sculptured faces on the building façade, which are described by John Ruskin.

From the Ospedaletto I walk towards the Calle Ospedaletto on my right, which leads on to a small bridge, where I cross and eventually arrive at Fondamenta Giovanni Batterano, and to my left is the attractive Palazzo Cavagnis, which is now a hotel.

At the end of this street, I bear right and cross another bridge, which leads me to the Calle Tetta, where once again there is an extremely narrow alleyway leading to the Ponte Tetta. Crossing this small bridge, I turn right following the sign directing me to San Marco, and ahead of me, at the end of the Calle Lunga S. M. Formosa, is the busy Campo San Maria Formosa. This busy square, surrounded by attractive palazzos, houses, and fruit and vegetable stalls is obviously a popular location for tourists, as they are everywhere, most of them resting in the shade offered by the extremely elegant church of Santa Maria Formosa; its elegance is highlighted by the simplicity of the façade, which is finished in Istrian stone and has relatively little decoration. The campo itself sits on what was once an island, one of the original 'Rivo Alto' islands that were colonised by the early Venetians in the 9th century. In fact the church still has canals either side. There is a mix of architectural styles in the campo, which, incidentally, is recorded as being the longest in Venice. Market stalls have been trading here for many centuries, and every morning fresh fruit and vegetables are on sale. The surrounding buildings include several palazzos such as Palazzo Ruzzini-Priuli, Palazzo Dona and the prominent Palazzo Vitturi. The square is very active during the day because of the shops and small market, not forgetting the wonderful restaurant, which extends onto the campo and has an awning to provide lots of shade for its patrons. The Baroque-style campanile has what Ruskin described as 'a grotesque and huge monstrous head' above the door to the tower; it certainly is well positioned for pedestrians to admire. The 18th-century clock on the tower, built by Emmerico Rectinger, was working until the 1970s, but due to poor maintenance schedules the clock stopped after breaking down and has never worked since.

The church has been carefully maintained, and was built by Mauro Codussi in the second half of the 15th century, using the original foundation of an earlier church of the 11th century. The first church on this site was, incidentally, built in the 7th century, being one of the first eight churches founded in Venice. There are two façades to view, one being of Renaissance design, which faces the west canal, the other, a Baroque façade of 1604, which faces the campo. The earlier façade, built in 1542, was funded by a generous donation from the Cappello family in honour of a remarkable victory over the Turks when Vincenzo Cappello was a Venetian admiral. Internally the church has grey and white Istrian stone surfaces and a Latin cross plan that works well with the original Greek cross plan of the earlier design, and there is a cross-vaulted ceiling which centres on the dome. The central nave is flanked by two minor aisles, which have fairly large chapels, which compliment the slender columns and small cupolas that form part of the internal design. As you enter the church, to the right is a 14th-century piece called *'The Virgin and Child'* by Lattanzio Quereni, and on the left side is the *'Virgin of Lepanto'*, which is a very aged Byzantine icon. The far chapel on the right depicts a triptych of the *'Virgin of Mercy'* by Bartolmeo Vivarini completed in the 15th century, which has been recently restored. In the next chapel to the left there is a wonderful 17th-century piece by Jacopo Palma titled *'Piety'* and beyond this chapel, standing over the mullioned window, hangs *'The Last Supper'* by Leandro Bassaro, which he painted at the beginning of the 17th century. On the far right transept, within the chapel of the Scuola dei Bombardieri, is a polyptych (four panels linked together) by Jacopo Palma Vechio, which was completed in the 16th century. Apparently several of the Scuolas had chapels and altars built in various churches in Venice. Traditionally the Doge visited the church every Candlemas following an event in 944 when a number of young girls on their way to church were kidnapped by pirates! The abducted girls were bravely rescued by members of a guild who were based in the church, and as a reward for this heroic act each reigning Doge from that day on was committed annually to visit the church.

As I leave the church of Santa Maria Formosa and walk around the perimeter of the building towards the Calle Querini, the time is 2.25pm and my thoughts go to an article I read recently, stating that the church was hit by an Austrian bomb in 1916, which caused a great deal of damage to the dome. Hard to imagine the carnage of that period, on a day like to today. From Calle Querini I cross a small campo (no name displayed) and I am now facing Palazzo Querini Stampalia. This building is really attractive, the façade finished in a wonderful red colour, having two piano nobiles and ornate gates (water portals) on the ground floor. Although I do not intend to visit this building, it has quite an architectural history and, therefore, deserves some recognition. Palazzo Querini Stampalia is a good example of Renaissance style, originally being built for its owner Nicolo Querini, who incidentally was a great lover of the arts. Several of Nicolo's ancestors took refuge on the Greek island of Stampalia when they were implicated in the Bajamonte Tiepolo plot of 1310; as they eventually owned this island, they later took the title and added it to their name. Today the palazzo is a museum, art gallery and library, which was bequeathed to the city in 1868. The museum displays furniture, porcelain and sculptures of the 15th century, whilst the library contains over 1,000,000 Venetian books and manuscripts. The Pinacoteca Querini Stampalia holds the art gallery on the second floor and contains many masterpieces by notable artists, which are displayed in several rooms. Amongst these artists there are works by Tiepolo *'Presentation at the Temple'*, Longhi's *'Dance of the Furlana'* (1758) and *'Circus'* (1762), Bellini's *'Madonna and Magi'* and some really interesting works displaying the life and times of Venice by Gabriele Bella (1730–-1799) who produced chronicles of Venice in its heyday years of the 18th century. The grounds and gardens of this palazzo were extensively modified by Carlo Scarpa in the 1960s and are fantastic.

Carlo Scarpa (1906–1978) is well worth a mention, as he is very well known for his Venetian architecture of the 20th century. He was a true Venetian architect who was very good at restoration work in relation to aged listed buildings. Scarpa chose architecture as his given profession and completed many notable works as an associate, being extremely sensitive to culture, period and change. Most of his work was within the Veneto region. However, he did produce designs for buildings, gardens and landscaping throughout Italy and in several other countries. Throughout his career he taught drawing and interior decorating at the University of Architecture in Venice. Some of his most notable works include the Accademia Gallery, Palazzo Ca'Foscari, Museum of Castelvecchio (Verona) and, of course, the Fondazione Querini Stampalia.

Moving on from this attractive building, I make my way to the right, which leads me the Ponte e Avogadbo, which is an alternative route to my next chosen building; 'alternative' meaning it has some small shops to view, and on this route my eye is fixed on a series of small iron bridges to my left, each one leading to an entrance door. At the end of this fondamenta, there is a very smart-looking hotel building, which has a wonderful Gothic arch to the left of the main entrance. Continuing along, I walk under some houses which span the street, and above me I can see the extremely old and weathered timber beams which support this structure, and, once through this amazing area, I arrive at Campo San Giovanni Novo. The church of San Giovanni Novo is directly to my left and stands almost forgotten, seeking an identity in its humble surroundings. However, this church, having been built in 1762 by Matteo Lucchesi, is on the site of one of the original 10th-century churches of Venice. Although I cannot get access today, I do know that the church has a single nave with a vaulted ceiling supported by columns. From the outside, the façade is simply red brick facing, keyed to receive a more elaborate finish at a later stage I would imagine. It has a plain portal that has a small pediment above, and there is a single window either side of the main door with a half moon window above the entrance.

As I walk around the north elevation of the church, I arrive at the Calle Fianco Chiesa, and at the end of this street I turn right into the Calle Drio la Chiesa. Continuing along this calle for a short distance, I arrive at a small campo, which is triangular in shape, called San Fillipio Giacomo. This area is really vibrant, with crowds of people enjoying themselves either in the cafes or looking at the wares of the street traders. When I get to the end of Calle dei Chiesa, I turn immediately left, with the campo to my right, and make my way down the Sorportega Provolo, which again is really busy, not surprising as it is only 3.20pm and I am walking parallel with the Lagoon, as I can clearly see 'The Bridge of Sighs' to my right in the distance. Ahead of me is Campo San Provolo, which I quickly pass as I head directly for a narrow calle ahead which has a glorious arch above the opening, displaying a sculptured stone effigy of the Madonna with Saints; once through the archway, I arrive at Campo Zaccaria. This particular campo is in complete contrast to others I have visited today, as it appears to be very peaceful and quiet, which is amazing considering its size and location. Given that the sun is quite warm today, I expected to see lots of tourists sheltering under the large amount of shaded area this campo offers, but not today, so it is all mine, well at least for a few minutes.

The church façade of San Zaccaria is really beautiful. Although predominantly Istrian stone above the ground floor, it stands so graceful with four levels of windows, which are in complete contrast to the ground-floor level, which is finished with wonderful marble panels of pinks and blues, which grace either side of the main door. Seated within these marble panels are two decorative plaques each with two figurines on display. Above the main door is a delicate small arch with a statue above, and there are a further five statues on various levels which form the profile of the roof. The façade is a Renaissance design, which was created by Mauro Codussi in the 15th century; the church itself is actually a blend of Renaissance and Gothic styles. The original church on this site was built in the 9th century, then replaced with a Romanesque-style church and finally rebuilt to the Gothic design we see today.

Antonio Gambello was the architect responsible for the church, but he unfortunately died in 1481 before it was complete, so Codussi was asked to finish it, who changed some of the Gothic design features such as the original pointed arches and spires. This change incorporated what we see today, with the long windows, symmetrical panels and sculptured pilasters. The interior of the church is bright and airy; the apse is encircled by a large cloister with adjoining aisles, which are illuminated from the natural light coming in through the windows. There are three naves each divided by columns, which support a cross-vaulted ceiling, and all the walls are covered with paintings of religious scenes and daily life in Venice centuries ago. One area, in particular, called the Chapel of San Tavasio, which is accessed via the nave, has frescoes by Andrea Castagno, which unfortunately are faded. However, there is also a polyptych by Antonio Vivarini, which is in remarkable condition. Artist Alessandro Vittoria is buried in the church, and his tomb proudly depicts a bust of this fine artist. He is in exalted company, as there are also the tombs of nine former Doges. Giovanni Bellini has a magnificent altarpiece on display, dated 1505, titled *'Madonna and Child with Saints'*, which is said to be one of his finest, and if that is not enough then there are other works on display by Tintoretto, Titian, Van Dyck and Bassano in the 'Sisters' Choir'. The convent attached to the church has quite an eventful past: on one occasion it is said that the 'inmates' of the convent, who were said to be behaving in a lewd manner, pelted officials visiting the building, with bricks! Gaurdi produced a wonderful picture depicting the convent as a 'fashionable salon', which is on display in the Ca' Rezzonico. The nuns themselves were, however, extremely active in creating the ecclesiastical design and artwork for the church and allegedly collected funds and dealt with many projects both to improve the decor of their building and increase their income status. Most of the artwork they received came as gifts from nobility and families whose daughters were 'protected ' by the cloth!

As I leave the campo and head back under the archway of the Madonna, which I previously described, I realise that I have failed to mention that this campo has a gory history, as the Doge Pietro Tradonico was murdered here in 1172, when returning from vespers. Records tell me that Doge Tradonico mismanaged peace negotiations with the Turks and brought the plague back with him on his return from Constantinople. I guess that was motive enough to have displeased his assassins!

Having passed under the arch, I now turn immediately right into Calle Provolo which, after a few metres, leads me onto the Fondamenta dell Osmarin. Walking along this interesting route, I pass Palazzo Priula on my left, which is an attractive Gothic palace having a pale red façade and displaying two piano nobiles one of which has two delicate balconies at either end. Continuing along this passage, I arrive at a junction with two small bridges, which I cross and which take me to my next two buildings and the perfect location for a late lunch. Looking at my watch, I realise that it is 3.35pm and I haven't eaten since breakfast, so I make for a small trattoria, which is located just alongside the Fondamenta San Lorenzo, by the small bridge, which crosses at the intersection between the Rio dei Greci and the Rio San Lorenzo.

As I don't have a great deal of time for lunch today, I settle for a selection of fish for *'primi piatti'* (starters) and pork Milanese for *'secondi piatti'* (main courses) all washed down with a cold beer. Sitting alongside the canal in the shade, watching the world go by, with a glass of beer is wonderful, and when my fish arrives I am not disappointed. The platter consists of many types of wonderful local seafood: king prawns, scallops, calamari, sardines, clams and two other varieties which I couldn't identify, but they were all so delicious, eaten with oil and pepper. The pork in egg and breadcrumbs is one of my favourites and, what's more, I didn't have any fries with it, so the diet that I have carefully adhered to for the past month is still on track. I could quite as easily have sat outside this trattoria all afternoon and evening as it was so comfortable, but I have more interesting places to see, so, after paying my bill, I walk along the Fondamenta Lorenzo to photograph my next location, which is the campo and church of San Lorenzo. After walking about 300m from the trattoria, I reach the small bridge which faces my next campo and, as I look to the church, I immediately see the groups of cats that have commandeered this area. Campo San Lorenzo is rather a nondescript and desolate square; it is quite tidy, but lacking any vibrancy, probably because there is little to see other than the facing church. The church sits at the end of the campo amongst the ageing buildings, its pavement having attractive geometric patterns inlaid in white stone, which I presume indicated the boundaries for markets stalls at one period. The wellhead sits in the centre of the square, almost calling for some live activity, unlike the six steps which lead to the church and which have several small kennels housing the stray cats of the district. Whilst photographing the church, I can see that the brick façade which is waiting to be finished in some form or other looks almost unwanted, and I feel sure that the church itself is in need of some major restoration. There was a church on this site as early as the 7th century, and the one we see today has a single nave, separated by three arches, that was originally designed to separate the nuns' choir from the parishioners, perhaps because the original convent which stands to the left of the church had, like many others in Venice, a reputation for promiscuity in the past. I leave this area feeling slightly sad at the demise of this church, which was deconsecrated and abandoned for many years, and I wonder just how much restoration actually took place following the damage it received when it was bombed in World War II. I do now, however, have a record of the church, which once held the tomb of Marco Polo, which for no apparent reason mysteriously disappeared in 1592 when the church was rebuilt.

Walking back along the fondamenta to the Ponte de Greci, I notice that there is a police station on my right. Not many of them on the island, come to think of it; I haven't seen one policeman out on the streets all day. Once back at the bridge, which I cross over, I turn immediately right, walk a few metres and then enter the gated forecourt of the church of San Giorgio dei Greci. Following the fall of Constantinople in 1453, the Greek population in Venice increased considerably, thereby prompting the need to build a Greek Orthodox Church in the city. Funded by Greek families living in Venice, the church of San Giorgio dei Greci was built between 1539 and 1573 at a cost of 15,000 ducats. Certain conditions were laid down before building work could commence: firstly, the Greek families in Venice were expected to serve in the Venetian army; and, secondly, Greek intellectuals of the community should work in some way for the Republican government. Several architects were involved in the construction of the church, namely Sante Lombardo, Gianantonio Chiona and Bernado Ongarin. As I look at the façade of this engaging and attractive building with its Renaissance design, my eye is instantly attracted to the campanile, which has an incredible lean that, to the untrained eye, looks as though it is about to collapse. It is, in fact, very stable and, judging by its present condition, has been carefully restored, which is good to see, as the rather handsome clock on the belltower itself is a real work of art. The façade faces onto the Rio dei Greci and is finished in Istrian stone. It has two short columns with a pediment above and a large rose window above the main portal, with three circular mosaic effigies inlaid along the narrow frieze above the door. These mosaic decorations continue along the side elevations the full length of the church, but I have to confess they do not have the same resplendent appearance as the façade. Facing the church on the left hand side there is a museum which, unlike the church, is open, but unfortunately I do not have time to explore inside today. To the right of the church is a very attractive courtyard, which it shares with neighbouring buildings. I can imagine this space offering some wonderful shade on hot Venetian days. Internally, craftsmen from the island of Crete undertook most of the decorative work, as Crete was once a Venetian colony for the best part of 400 years. One notable artist who contributed to the decorations was Michael Damaskinos, who was a master iconographer of his time. There is a wonderfully luminous gold-coloured interior with many mosaics and sacred icons on display; one special feature in the Sanctuary is the golden mosaic of Jesus Christ flanked by Mary and John the Baptist. The ceiling has an excellent 16th-century fresco of the *'Last Judgement'* by Giovanni di Cipro, and on one of the side doors there is a glorious mosaic of St George. The whole ambience of this very attractive church can best be described as colourful, peaceful and extremely decorative, and is a credit to Grecian artists. My research tells me that the church was formerly part of a central group of buildings used for training priests, and a nunnery as well as a school for Greek girls.

As I leave the beautiful courtyard of San Giorgio dei Greci, I have one other place to visit today, which is fortuitously on my route home. Having walked back to the Ponte dei Greci, I turn right along the Calle Madonna, turn immediately right into the Salizz d. Greci, then turn almost immediately into Calle Bosello, walk a few metres and arrive in Calle dei Pieta. At the end of Calle dei Pieta I arrive at the Riva degli Schiavoni and immediately to my right is the wonderful building La Pieta, which was once formerly known as Santa Maria della Visitazione. Oddly enough,

I have still to visit this building in its own right, having passed it literally hundreds of times for one reason or another, but its internal architecture is still a mystery. Unfortunately, today is another disappointment, as it is closed again. However, I can provide some information. This splendid Renaissance church, which has a Baroque façade that is not dissimilar to the Gesuati that overlooks the Guidecca, was originally built by the Jesuits between 1494 and 1524. Several architects are credited with both the internal and external design, namely, Francesco Lurano, Mauro Codussi and Tullio Lombardo. Once the Dominicans took over the church in the late 17th century, they built the larger existing church, which abuts La Pieta, thereby demoting Santa Maria della Visitazione to a public library; it did however reopen as a church once again in 1825. Giorgio Massari did eventually rebuild the church, starting in 1745 and the work was almost completed in 1760; unfortunately, the façade was not finished until 1906! Internally there is a single nave, with a flat wooden ceiling, and the church is oval-shaped and devoid of any chapels, which is said to produce amazing acoustic properties, as they apparently act as a buffer against the street noise. Vivaldi himself was said to have had some design input. The high altar is positioned directly below the cupola, and the altarpiece, called *'The Visitation'*, by Piazzetta, provides a wonderful decoration. La Pieta is regarded as both a church and a concert hall. In fact, Vivaldi was said to have written many of his pieces for the orphanage, which was attached to the church. Vivaldi's 'Ospedale at La Pieta' was known as a place to shelter cripples, old people and young women at around the beginning of the 18th century, and the great composer became a resident as well as being choirmaster. After a great deal of restoration work over a period of three years, La Pieta reopened again in 1995, but alas remains an enigma to me, as I have yet to enter and explore this historic building.

Feeling somewhat disappointed about the climax of my journey today, I quickly remind myself that I have visited so many other interesting buildings on my busy itinerary, and for most of the time it had been almost tourist-free, which brings a smile back to my face as I take the short walk to San Zaccaria pontile. During that short walk I was joined by hundreds of tourists making their way back to the watercraft which will take them to their staging posts, so I was quite relieved when I saw the No. 82 vaporetto which was just arriving at San Zaccaria, the time now being 4.55pm. The vaporetto journey back to Ferrovia was an absolute joy, with very few passengers, as it followed the Canale della Guidecca route, which allowed me to cool down and reflect on my wonderful day in the 'Serenissima'. Normally, a trip back up the Grand Canal is so inviting, but today I plumped for some solitude. After just nine stops on my peaceful journey back, I was off the vaporetto and walking towards Bar S. Lucia by 5.35pm and looking forward to sitting outside Enrico's forecourt enjoying a beer before my journey back to the bus terminal. When having a relaxing drink in Enrico's bar, I generally make a few notes of particular events that have occurred during my day's travels which I want reminding of when I eventually write each chapter. Today I couldn't think of any incident that was not captured on my digital recorder, so instead I decided to think of an appropriate quotation for this chapter and again I was stumped for any ideas. Should I direct my thoughts to the boldness of Colleoni, the imperial elegance of SS Giorgio e Paolo or the solitude and humble appearance of San Lorenzo? Having exhausted my quota of descriptive phrases throughout the day, I settled for a quotation I once read which was directed at travel, because that's what I do a great deal of, and settled for one gem by Willa Cather, who once wrote in 1927: *'Men travel faster now, but I do not know if they go to better things.'* I can only respond to Willa by stating that every time I arrive in the 'Serenissima' I find many, many new things to marvel at and enjoy.

After an enjoyable hour talking and soaking up the atmosphere of early evening Cannaregio, I make my way to the bus terminal at Piazzale Roma and when I arrive around 6.45pm the queue waiting for the airport bus is enormous, so large in fact that I felt sure not everyone would get on the first bus that arrived. Evidently there were still traffic problems on the many autoroutes around this part of the Veneto, which converge on Mestre, and as a result slowed traffic down everywhere. When the No. 5 bus did eventually arrive, the three side doors opened and it was almost like 'the opening day of the sales in Oxford Street': everyone was pushing and shoving to get on board, without any respect for their fellow passengers, and I naturally thought that I would have to wait for the next bus. I was wrong. In the melee that took place, several people started arguing with one another, so I simply walked on board the bus stating in a loud voice, *'Non capisco, Inglese'*, just as the bus driver decided to close the doors, I'm not quite sure what one of the people left at the bus stop said to me through the window, probably 'Have a nice journey' but in any event I was on the bus to the airport. I didn't realise just how important getting that particular bus was, as the normal 20-minute journey took an hour, leaving me only 10 minutes to check in at Marco Polo before the desk was closed. Fortunately, the check-in queue was short, and I was in the departure lounge in good time for my 9.05pm flight to Gatwick, which got me home and indoors by 11.00pm UK time.

Before retiring for the evening, for some reason or other I suddenly recalled what a tourist had said to me as I was disembarking from the vaporetto earlier today, and a smile came to my face. He said ' I hope Venice fulfils my expectations; I've been planning this trip for some time.'

Buonasera Venezia

CHAPTER 12
AUGUST: Further East

'Seclusion and Solitude Energized by Art'

August has arrived as speedily as it will depart, and I, like most people, am amazed at the speed in which time arrives and passes. Although my travels to Venice have been fairly extensive during the past 12 months, it seems like only yesterday that I was enjoying my walk in September which crossed three sestieri, took me to the wonderful Frari and, of course, caught a brief glimpse of the treasures that surround Piazza San Marco.

When I look at my map of the 'Serenissima' I realise that although I have provided the reader with many wonderful places to visit, there are still a vast number of other equally interesting places still remaining to be discovered. With that thought in mind, I have decided to escape the main body of tourists and concentrate on three small islands at the far eastern extremes of Venice and at the same time briefly enjoy the Biennale arts at the neighbouring Giardini in the Castello sestiere. At this time of the Venetian season, especially if it is hot, I like nothing better than to visit places of solitude and serenity and simply enjoy the opportunity to wander and explore or just sit down and sketch in the shade. Isola di San Pietro and Isola di San Elena provide the

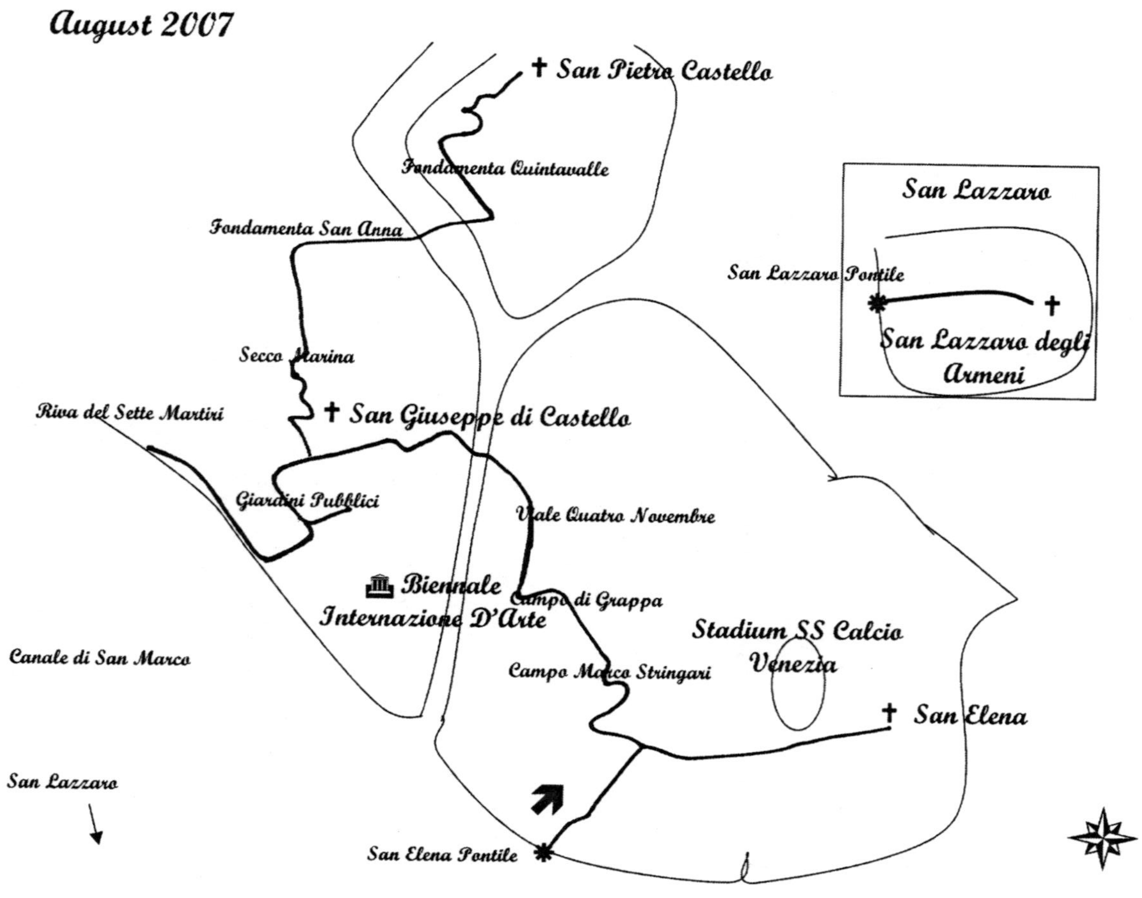
August 2007
San Pietro Castello
Fondamenta Quintavalle
Fondamenta San Anna
Secco Marina
San Giuseppe di Castello
Riva del Sette Martiri
Giardini Pubblici
Viale Quatro Novembre
Biennale
Internazione D'Arte
Campo di Grappa
Stadium SS Calcio
Venezia
Canale di San Marco
Campo Marco Stringari
San Elena
San Lazzaro
San Elena Pontile
San Lazzaro
San Lazzaro Pontile
San Lazzaro degli
Armeni

perfect location for both, even though they cannot compete with the vast number of tourist attractions on offer elsewhere. Having said that, the variety of domestic buildings, greenery and beautiful churches are a sight to be seen, together with the great views of the surrounding Venetian Lagoon.

The third island I intend to visit is the attractive San Lazzaro, which is the monastic headquarters for an order of Armenian Monks who have a creditable history, which I hope to explain in some detail. Finally I shall visit, albeit briefly, the centrepiece of the Venetian Biennale, which is in the Giardini, located on the mainland adjacent to San Elena. If you remember, in February I wrote of the incredible exposition of art that descends upon Venice biennially, bringing exhibitors from all corners of the world. Well, as I mentioned last month, it is in full swing now, so I hope to get a glimpse of what is on offer before my scheduled visit in October. As today's journey requires a fair amount of travel on the vaporetto, I thought it opportune to photograph some really good scenes of the Lagoon, especially those on my return journey from San Lazzaro to Zaccaria, which should bring another dimension to the views of St Giorgio Maggiori and the Piazza San Marco. One other thing I should point out, as I mentioned football long ago in my Introduction, I thought it only fair to mention this subject again, as I shall be passing the Venetian Football Stadium which is on St. Elena. After all, it was football that first brought me to the wonderful 'Serenissima'.

*August 7th 2007

It is with some sadness that I begin to write the final chapter of this journal, as I set off from my home this morning and recall the amazing queues I experienced last September when arriving at

Gatwick and writing the first chapter. A year later, and security issues are still a major concern for all travellers and I still have a healthy respect for the restrictions and protocols that are in place. Today, however, although security is still a major consideration, getting through the strict controls and into the departure lounge proved to be relatively easy. The flight to Marco Polo airport was busy, as one might expect, it being the holiday period, and there were quite a number of children travelling, not surprisingly, as there are wonderful beaches on the Lido. How many other cities are there that can offer superb beaches as well as so much historical interest to discover? Once again my easyJet flight was both comfortable and on time, and by 11.05am Italian time I am first off the plane, through security and within minutes have purchased my ACTV ticket and am sitting on the No. 5 bus to Piazzale Roma.

The weather this morning is around the 29C mark and there is a clear blue sky, which is perfect for my travels today, but I must ensure that I take plenty of liquid on board. Compared to last month, my bus journey from the airport to Venice was amazingly fast, less than 20 minutes, and by 11.45am I am walking to the vaporetto pontile to catch the No. 51, which will take me to Isola di S.Elena. Whilst making my way from the bus terminus, I notice that construction work has restarted at last on the new bridge, which will span the northern extreme of the Grand Canal from the Piazzale Roma side to the land adjacent to the Santa Lucia Railway Station. For some time now I have walked past the two concrete and steel base platforms, which are on either side of the Canal, wondering just when work will eventually resume, and it looks like August 2007 will become a memorable month in the Venetian calendar. Both sides of the new bridge appear to be well under construction since I was last here, as there are large steel sections projecting from the mass of concrete that has waited so long to be rejuvenated. This really is something special, a fourth crossing over the Grand Canal. I look forward to seeing work progress, and would imagine that the pre-assembled steel components could all be in place when I next visit Venice in September.

I must confess that I am looking forward, as always, to my trip on the vaporetto today and not having to make my way through the vast number of tourists in and around Piazza San Marco. This particular ride should take about 30 minutes, and, after a few minutes' wait, the No. 51 arrives, and as I glance at my watch the time is now 11.45am Italian time. Fortunately I am near the front of the queue so I am able to get an open-air seat, which is wonderful on a warm day like today, and also the fact that I will be able to get a good view of my journey along the Canale del Giudecca, which will bring me to the open waters of the Lagoon. There are relatively few stops en route, the vaporetto calling at Santa Marta, Zattere and Giardini Esposizione, before arriving at San Elena at 12.20, and, interestingly enough, my fellow passengers appear to be a mixture of either locals and professional people and, strangely enough, no tourists.

Once off the vaporetto, I walk through a rather nice park towards the Viale Quattro Novembre, which I cross over and continue walking along the Calle Rovereto. After walking a short distance, I turn right into Calle del Carnaro and very soon again I see before me the impressive façade of the Hotel St. Elena. At this point, the calle then dog-legs to the left. As I continue walking I can now see the church of San Elena in the distance, but before reaching it I have to cross a wide wooden bridge which spans the Rio dell S. Elena. Once over the bridge I am now standing adjacent to the perimeter walls of the Stadium SS Calcio Venezia. Like La Fenice, the football team that play in this stadium hope to rise from the ashes after a history of calamitous disasters culminating in relegation from the Seria B League after going bust, and at present sit in the Fourth Division. I sympathise with this club and their supporters as I am well aware just how difficult it must be to become a great team once again, having followed my beloved Chelsea for over 50 years through the good and bad times. I feel quite depressed when I look at the outside appearance of the stadium walls, as it reminds me of a deserted prison, having tangled barbed wire fixed to the top of the perimeter walls, and an amazing amount of graffiti on display. A. C. Venice may not have the most impressive team or stadium in Italy, but I can't think of any other football club that has such an impressive view that spectators can enjoy from the high terracing. Not having experienced a football match in Venice (as they normally play on Sundays), I suspect that the journey on the vaporetto transporting both home and away supporters to the San Elena pontile could be a pretty eventful occasion. It is difficult to imagine hundreds or even thousands of black, orange and green scarves being waived when the supporters both arrive and leave by boat, not to mention the surprise it must be for tourists enjoying the seclusion of this charming island, as I am today. As I pass the stadium on my left and walk down the long avenue towards San Elena church, I can't imagine anything destroying the tranquillity of this area. Can you visualise sitting on the banks of the River Thames at Runnymede and suddenly hearing the applause of thousands of supporters when a goal is scored? Obviously, the indigenous population of this island and the church community are far more understanding of this sport than most, and a happy compromise exists between everyone.

Unfortunately, when I reach San Elena church, at the end of this short avenue, it is closed to visitors at this time of the day. Not a complete disaster, as I have some history of this isolated building, which was built in the early 13th century when the bodily remains of St Elena were transported from the East to Venice. In later years Olivetan Monks, who resided nearby, rebuilt the original church, and it was eventually consecrated in the early 16th century. The Olivetan Monks were a branch of the 'white monks' of the Benedictine order and were founded in1319 by St Bernard Ptolemy, who was formerly a philosopher from Sienna. This particular order were noted for their solitude and austerity and lived on a staple diet of bread, water and wine, sleeping on straw mattresses and wearing rough fabric gowns. St Bernard Ptolemy died in 1348 whilst devoting his time exclusively to the needs of the victims of the plague, which he in turn succumbed to. At one time, San Elena held many rich treasures and was considered to be an extremely important religious site. Unfortunately, it was deconsecrated and stripped of its treasures in 1807, for reasons I have yet to discover, but was eventually reopened in the late 1920s. Even though the church is not open at this time of day, it is possible to take a look through the iron grills which form part of the external garden wall, and I can clearly see the attractive layout of a private campo, which I suspect belongs to the adjoining convent. The colonnade around this campo has some wonderful arches supported by short columns set on a small raised wall.

Having taken some photographs of the church, I notice from the door signage that it is open between 5 and 7pm Monday to Saturday. Therefore I have decided to revisit in November when

I will be staying overnight on one of my future visits to Venice. Making my way back along the avenue with the football stadium to my right, I cross over the wooden bridge and continue walking until I reach Calle Passarella. After walking down this calle, I reach the delightful Campo Marco Stringari, which has grass areas divided into four sections, with a shaded seated arrangement as the centrepiece, and I notice lots of cats lazing around in the shade, again producing a scene of absolute serenity and peace. Continuing along the Calle del Sabotino, which is a reasonably long street, it is worth mentioning how attractive certain houses are along this route, a mixture of brightly coloured exteriors most of which I guess were built between the 19th and 20th centuries, which remind me of a similar small Italian town, whose name escapes me, in northern Tuscany. I am continually amazed just how deserted the main streets are, and as I cross Campo d Grappa and reach the Viale Quarto Novembre once again, I realise that I have arrived at the far end of this long street which I crossed over earlier.

Having mentioned the word 'grappa', I cannot resist the opportunity to mention the values of this splendid Italian national drink, which I hasten to add is one of my favourites. For those of you who are not familiar with grappa, let me explain. Grappa is a unique Italian drink that has been around since the Middle Ages, which is traditionally made from 'pomace' (discarded grape seeds, stalks and stems). Known as 'firewater' by many Italians, it is either drunk neat or added to espresso coffee and, although an acquired taste, is today becoming more popular around the world. It was originally distilled in a small town in the Veneto called Bassano del Grappa, when it was then made from a grouping of the byproducts from several varieties of local grapes. Today it is generally made from a single grape variety and distilled in a similar manner to sherries or brandies: distillation takes place after gentle heating, which allows the mixture to evaporate, leaving a very potent end product, and occasionally a little syrup is added for sweetening. In more recent times radical changes have been introduced in the making of grappa whereby 'selected' single grape varieties have been introduced called 'monovitigno', following which various other base ingredients such as apricot, peach and pear, to name a few, are also added for flavour. Served chilled in a small 'shot' glass after a meal (good for the digestion), grappa can be either sipped slowly or swallowed in one shot, remembering always to toast the occasion by saying 'Salute'.

I continue my journey after my short aperitif commercial and take the left turning, which runs alongside a well-watered triangular grassed area, which will eventually lead me to a bridge which spans the Rio del Giardini. Whilst walking over this wooden bridge with its iron balustrade, I can clearly see the church of San Pietro di Castello to my right, although somewhat in the distance. I must acknowledge that the view from this bridge is extremely picturesque. There are small two-storey buildings fronting the canal, which serve as a perfect mooring station for the many small craft on display. Just above the roof level of these attractive houses, I can clearly see the white campanile and domed roof of San Pietro di Castello as the sun cascades on this historical site. I now turn left into the Palado S. Antonio, walk a few metres and then turn right into Rio terra San Giuseppe. I pass the Institute Nautical Technico, which is currently undergoing some restoration work, and find that I am now entering Campo S. Giuseppe. This area is very familiar to me, as I remember passing through here last February and remarked on that occasion that there is a wonderfully descriptive Canaletto painting of the church of Giuseppe Di Castello and the campo, which I am now facing. Unfortunately, today, as in February, I am unable to enter the church as it is closed, but not abandoned as I previously thought.

I move on across the small canal and make my way along the adjacent Corte Solda until I reach the Secco Marina. Once again I cross over this wide street and continue down the Calle Correda until I reach the Fondamenta S. Anna. This particular concourse is in fact the street which eventually becomes Via Giuseppe Garibaldi, which I also featured in February's chapter. The local surroundings are what you would expect from a discreet island in the 'Serenissima', quiet, inviting and very parochial, and arguably the perfect scene for rambling and exploring both the architecture and culture of its inhabitants. When I arrive at Fondamenta S. Anna, I take a right and walk along this narrow street. Ahead of me is the bridge which crosses the Canale San Pietro. Having crossed the bridge, I turn left into Fondamenta Quintavalle and follow this snaking path until I finally arrive at Campo San Pietro. The campo is set in a wonderfully lush grassed square, which is the home of the almost isolated campanile that has a slight lean, but then what tower in Venice doesn't have a lean? This campanile is, however, different from most others, as it has been clad entirely with Istrian stone and stands mighty and majestic in this serene location. This one-off campanile is the work of Mauro Codussi, which replaced the original in the 15th century and has a solid fluted shaft with the normal three opening windows surrounding the bell housing. As I face the church itself, I am amazed to find such a magnificent edifice in such a remote part of the 'Serenissima', but there is a good reason for this, as I will endeavour to explain.

I refer to San Pietro di Castello as a church when in fact it is a basilica in its own right, and was the most important religious building until Basilica San Marco was constructed, as the sestiere of Castello was one of the original islands which made up the Rivoalto, and once formed part of the major populated area long before Venice became a city. In the 7th century a temple was built on this spot funded by a wealthy merchant named Samacali, which was dedicated to St Sergio and St Bacco, and a century later the first church of St Pietro was built in place of the temple. Over the centuries that followed, St Pietro became the most important church of Venice, at the same time becoming the first seat of the Bishopric, following which, in 1451, the Pope appointed the Bishop of Castello, Lorenzo Giustiniani to be Patriarch of Venice. The original church had been extensively extended and modified over the centuries, but succumbed to fire and was eventually demolished. The façade of the existing basilica is the work of Andrea Palladio, who unfortunately died before it was completed. However, one of his followers, Francesco Smeraldi, completed the task in line with Palladio's designs. The façade is dominated by four large columns and has cross keys in the centre of the gable with double festoons moulded above each of the three doors. In between the columns on either side of the main door are two niches simply waiting to accommodate some statuettes to complete the façade. The interior is absolutely amazing as it has so much light entering through the windows that every piece of artwork on display can be enjoyed, as the detail on each piece can be clearly seen. The layout forms a Latin cross, with three naves and a cross-vaulted ceiling. The dome itself is supported by four arches each resting on Corinthian capitals, with the centre nave ending with a long presbytery.

As I start to explore the interior, I have decided to work my way around the basilica from right to left, and the first treasure I come to is the Altar of the Cross, followed by the Altar of the Madonna of Health. The latter altar represents the *'Heavenly Father in Glory with Angels'* by Tizianello (1570–1650), who was a nephew of Titian, and just below this is the icon of the *'Madonna of Graces called of Health'*, which is dated around the 13th century. Moving to the altar of St Peter, which has magnificent red and grey marble columns with decorative yellow sculptured tops supporting several cherubs, there are also two statues, on either side, of Isaiah and Jeremiah. The altarpiece of *'St Peter on the Throne with Saints Nicolas, Andrew, Jacopo and Anthony'* is by Marco Basaiti and was completed in the 15th century. Next is the altar of St Ellen, which was built for Francesco Morosini, a Procurator, which has an altarpiece called *'Virgin in Glory and Saints Ellen and Francis, and Thomas the Apostle'*, completed by Francesco Ruschi in the 17th century. At the far end of the nave sits the Chapel of the Most Holy Sacrament with a masterful fresco in the vaulted area depicting Jesus appearing to the Apostles, again 17th century. There are also two canvases, one *'The Adoration of the Magi'* by Ricchi, and the other a far more dramatic piece called *'The Chastisement of the Snakes'* by Pietro Liberi. The chapel itself has four graceful marble columns with a crown of ornately crafted stonework. Arguably one of the most magnificent altars in Venice is the Main Altar of this basilica, with its distinguished presbytery area reserved for priests, which to my mind significantly contributes to the overall design. The 16th-century walnut choir seats, by Sansovino, and the Patriarchal Throne, also 16th century, provide a fitting accompaniment to the overall appearance of the main altar, which was designed by Baldassare Longhena in 1649 and built by Clementi Moli. There are several cherubs and angels, which support the urn, designed in precious sculptured marbles of white, yellow and red, and above the Main Altar itself, are gilded copper panels, which represent the three theological virtues. The urn contains the relics of St Lorenzo Giustiniani (1380–1455) and behind the altar itself are laid the tombs of three patriarchs, namely, Giovanni Tiepolo, Alvise Foscari and Alvise Sagredo. Looking up to the magnificent frescoes by Gerolamo Pellengrini (1624–1760), I can see *'The Apotheosis of the Saint'* and *'The Most Holy Trinity in Glory'*. The walls contain canvases by Bellucci and Lazzarini amongst others, and I should mention again just how good the natural lighting is in this edifice, as it allows me to see each of these masterpieces in detail.

Moving on from the Main Altar, I am now standing in front of the Chapel of The Cross. Again, the sheer beauty and craftsmanship of this altar would compliment any other church it was positioned in, as it displays peach-coloured marble columns which are enhanced by a Byzantine Cross, in copper and wood, which sits above the altar itself. There are two remarkable canvases on the altar walls by Giovanni Solimena and a beautiful fresco on the ceiling. In the 17th century Cardinal Francesco Vendarim commissioned Longhena to build the adjoining chapel, which is again of Baroque design, having black and grey sculptured marble enhanced with some stonework, together with another classical feature namely, the seating incorporated on either side. Michele Ungaro is attributed as being the sculptor of this fine chapel, which displays eight statues representing the ecclesiastical virtues conferred upon its benefactor, namely; cleverness, astronomy, poetry, generosity, strength, virtue, theology and agriculture. This apparent self-appraisal tells me that this particular cardinal was a very busy person! Sitting adjacent to the Vendarim Chapel is the small but equally beautiful Chapel Lando, which was erected by the Bishop Marco Lando in 1425. This particular chapel is Gothic in design and has wonderful mosaic work, especially the altar step, which is accredited to the Romanesque period.

Heading back along the left nave, I reach the Altar of the Immaculate, which was originally sited in the Church of Corpus Domini and which, unfortunately, was demolished by the French during their occupation; this particular chapel is in Baroque style with four distinct columns in Greek marble. The next altar is that of St John the Evangelist, displaying a glorious altarpiece by Padoranimo (1588–1648). Finally I arrive at the last altar in this amazing basilica, which is that of St Anthony, again Baroque in style, with a fairly modern statue of the saint set against a background of gold mosaic. Lastly, as I leave this basilica, which really is one of the finest buildings I have visited in Venice, I notice the two large canvases which are positioned each side of the main door depicting *'The Supper of Jesus and His Disciples'*, by Jacopo Beltrame, and *'The Supper of the Hebrew Passover with Jesus in the House of Simone il Furiseo'*, by Piero Malombra. What a finale! Having thoroughly enjoyed my visit to this amazing building, I would totally recommend visitors to Venice to explore St Pietro di Castello, as I have.

I now make my way back along the route I came earlier, but, before leaving the square, I notice a small archway, which leads to a rather forlorn but nevertheless attractive small campo, which has a wonderful portico encompassing this quiet oasis. Each sculptured arch is attractive in its design and is supported by delicate columns; this really is a charming area, but in need of some careful restoration.

Retracing my steps back to the vaporetto pontile, I remember that I have to get to Giardini Exposizione in order to catch my next waterbus which will take me to San Zaccaria, but, before doing so, I have decided to get some information regarding the Biennale. Therefore, once I reach the church of San Giuseppe di Castello, I make my way through the campo into the park, where I arrive at the Biennale Internazionale D' Arte, . Fortunately, the time is still only 1.35pm, but I only have enough time on this occasion to get details of this event, which I intend to visit before November. But for readers of this journal I can give a brief resume of the Biennale 2007 to give a flavour of what's in store.

When Biennale is in town, there are scores of events throughout the city of Venice, which form part of this amazing spectacle of contemporary art. There are three prime centres which focus on this event, the Giardini, the Arsenale/Corderie and, finally, Tronchetto. To enjoy and see all that is on display this year would take several days, but I would suggest starting at the Giardini International Pavilion where it is possible to view contemporary art from at least 30 countries throughout the world; each one of these artistic creations is magical and, as the programme suggests, 'Keep your ears and eyes open for surprises'. I would imagine that three hours in the Giardini is enough, and would suggest, therefore, moving on to the Corderie (Ropery), which can be located by heading in the general direction of the Arsenale and simply aiming for the Via Giuseppe Garibaldi; and then coming off at the Calle D. Forno. Inside the Corderie there is a large African section among many other exhibitors, and one might expect to be in there for at least a day to capture most of the pavilions. I hope to make several more trips to Venice before the Biennale finishes at the end of November and I hope eventually get to the Cornice Art Fair at Tronchetto (conveniently located near Piazzale Roma). Finally, the choice of remaining venues is quite endless, as there will be exhibitions at the Correr Museum, Guggenheim Museum, Palazzo Grassi and Ca'Pesaro, which are just a few of those on offer throughout Venice. Even though I haven't really entered the full spirit of Biennale, my appetite has been whetted for future visits, and as I make my way to the vaporetto pontile, having collected my programme of events, I notice that the No. 5 waterbus is about to arrive and my thoughts now focus on my next 'port of call', which will be the island of San Lazzaro.

Before I can make my way to San Lazzaro I have to get to San Zaccaria, and as the time is now 2.20pm I feel comfortable knowing that the short vaporetto journey will get me to the No. 20 watercraft pontile in good time for my onward journey. Trips from San Zaccaria to San Lazzaro are tightly scheduled so I have to be there in good time, knowing that there will probably be a queue forming already for the 2.45pm trip. Timing is important when visiting San Lazzaro, as there are limited tours available and visitors are encouraged to arrive for the 3.20pm tour, which is hosted by one of the Armenian monks who reside on the island.

Upon arriving at San Lazzaro after a 15-minute journey on the vaporetto, I was surprised to see just how new the surrounding landing-stage area and walled terraces were. I guess I was expecting to see century-old brickwork and stonework. I wasn't disappointed, however, when I discovered the main buildings and church which were considerably older.

Historically, the Armenians have been resident in Venice for many centuries; in the early years, they were mainly moneylenders and artisans, having their own church close to Piazza San Marco. San Lazzaro was originally a leper colony between the 12th and 17th centuries, before developing into a monastery. Manug di Pietro, known as 'Mekhitar', arrived on the island in the early 18th century after being driven out of Morea by the Turks, and became the Armenian leader, forming the current Armenian monastery. The 'Mekhitarian' Monastery was then founded, and today the island has a wonderful church, gallery, museum, library, and accommodation for its followers, in addition to a fairly comprehensive printing shop. As I walk towards the main building, I can't help but notice the pleasant gardens, which are beautifully maintained and encompass the entire area, in addition to the wide variety of trees and shrubs that have been carefully positioned to create a picture of complete tranquillity. Positioned majestically in the gardens along the short walk to the main building is a wonderful statue of Mekhitar that welcomes the visitor to the island. The entrance to the monastery is accessed through a small doorway where visitors are greeted by monks who act as hosts for the tour, which, incidentally, will cost 6 euros, but is worth every penny. Once the assembled visitors are grouped, a multilingual monk then leads the tour party to the cloister, which encompasses yet another attractive garden that has manicured lawns, small trees and colourful flowers. The portico around the garden is made up of many shapely arches supported by slender stone columns that in turn support the ornate building structure above. Moving along the portico, I arrive at the steps of the church, which lead into a small room containing several artefacts of historical value together with three frescoes depicting Mekhitar by the artist Noe' Bordigon.

The church itself was built around 1400 and has been restored several times since, having a main altar together with several other equally magnificent side altars, which have been dedicated to *'The Holy Cross'* (1738), *'St Gregory'* (1737), *'The Virgin Mary'* (1735) and *'St Anthony'* (1737). Whilst the lighting levels of the church are good, considering the age and design of the building, it is not until the lighting is switched on that the visitor can fully appreciate the wonderful marble, stone and glass that decorate the interior. The High Altar has two frescoes by Paolo Paoletti depicting *'St Peter and St Paul'*, and within the Sanctuary of the church stand two marble altars; one dedicated to the *'Virgin Mary'* the other to *'St Anthony'*, which are both Baroque in design. Above the arches of the sanctuary are colourful mosaic portraits of Armenian saints, each meticulously caricatured and crafted by masters of this technique. I particularly like the stained glass rose window, which displays a dove in the centre; even on a dull day, the light entering the church is wonderful.

From the Sanctuary the tour now moves on to the Refectory, which was built in 1739. The decor is relatively sparse, and our guide is quick to point out that absolute silence is observed in this room whenever the monks or students dine. The dining tables are laid out in a modest and prescribed fashion. However, the artwork that is displayed on the walls is masterful, particularly a painting of *'The Last Supper'*, which was painted by Pietro Novelli in 1780. From the refectory my tour party are taken upstairs to a long and wide corridor, which provides an excellent location for the art gallery that is on view. The collection in this Armenian gallery is fantastic. As an artist, I could spend hours enjoying what is on display, as there are so many variations of styles and schools to enjoy. Those I particularly like are a collection of sketches of

Armenian folk, which are finished in a variety of mediums. The floor that we are currently standing in also contains several other rooms which have many other art treasures, far too numerous to describe, but all of outstanding quality. I should also point out the wonderful libraries situated in this area which contain thousands of books, periodicals and newspapers, all of which form the largest collection of this type of work in the world.

Next, I find myself in the Archaeological Museum, which houses treasures from both Armenian and Indian art displaying handcrafted work, which has been exquisitely tooled and fashioned. The ceiling in this section is certainly worth mentioning, as it has a fantastic painting by Tiepollo called *'Justice and Peace'* as well as other portraits on the walls of Doge Alvise Mocenigo and Napoleon III. After climbing some steps and having passed the main library, I arrive at a large hall in which several unusual artefacts can be seen, such as an Egyptian mummy and a funeral mask, but the most striking feature of this room must be the plaster statuette of Napoleon's son, by Antonio Canova. Moving on yet again, I enter a library and study room which was used extensively by Lord Byron when he studied here between 1816 and 1817, and a portrait of this remarkable man sits above the doorway to the room. The tour of this interesting building ends with my group being taken to the recently constructed *'Manuscripts Hall'* (1970), which has been impressively designed to exhibit a vast collection of manuscripts, silverwork, ornate bindings and coins. I should add that the hall itself is circular in shape and designed with split-levels that have finished surfaces which compliment both what is on display and the historical heritage of this group of buildings.

With the tour now over, I make my way back, following the prescribed route, and eventually arrive at the cloister, where I quickly purchase a cold drink from an available machine, which incidentally was a bargain at 0.50 euros, as my thirst buds reminded me that they needed quenching. I must confess that I thoroughly enjoyed my first ever tour of San Lazzaro and would highly recommend this trip when visiting Venice. But be mindful of the visiting times for both the vaporetto and the monastery.

Having returned on the No.20 vaporetto to San Zaccaria, I now make my way to the pontile where I can catch the No. 42 back to Ferrovia, which will get me there by about 5.40pm, and will allow me adequate time to have a beer and snack at Bar S. Lucia. Also, if time permits, I shall book a room today at Santa Chiara Hotel for an extended visit I shall be making in November, and perhaps get the opportunity to have a chat with the manager about progress with the journal. As always, having a refreshing drink at Bar S. Lucia is the perfect finale to my day in Venice. I also learned that Enrico will be refurbishing his bar later this year, which I look forward to seeing, and while sitting outside the bar under the canopy I gaze across Campo San Geremia and notice an artist at work. Last month, when I was sitting in this same spot, I noticed the same artist working on a graphite/charcoal scene of Venice and thought just how good her work was, and today I am equally impressed by the piece she is currently working on. The range of work on display seems to vary from intricate sketches of tracery from parts of historic buildings to the landscape scenes of canals and waterways throughout this wonderful city, and I do hope that she gets lots of admirers and customers, as I know just how difficult it must be to make a living as an artist. Having spent a really pleasant hour enjoying my drink and cooling down in the early evening twilight, I realise that it is 6.55pm and my bus leaves Piazzale Roma at 7.10pm.

The journey back to Marco Polo airport was equally as quick as the earlier morning journey, and I arrived at the easyJet departure desk by 7.40pm and was through security in a matter of minutes. Having some time to spare before my 9.05pm flight home, I decide to sit for a while in the upper waiting lounge and enjoy the view across the airport into the Lagoon. This area is great for viewing, as passengers are able to see quite clearly the panoramic profiles of both Burano and Torcello in the distance. Whilst gazing on this scene, I cannot help thinking to myself just how much global change has evolved since the early settlers from the mainland decided to inhabit the swamp-infested landmass of the Lagoon. Having said that, although most civilised countries throughout the world now embrace all that the 21st century has to offer, mankind is not so different to those refugees who populated the Lagoon settlements in the 7th century. Like those early settlers, there are still many people today throughout the world who seek refuge on a permanent basis rather than as temporary exiles, but unlike the Venetian settlers evading the onslaught from Lombardy, there are very few uncharted areas today that can sustain such a mass exodus.

After a comfortable flight back to Gatwick, I arrive home at 11.00pm and unload my backpack, having decided to sit down and quietly reminisce on my day, as I usually do. Today however was slightly different, in as much as I remind myself that this really is the last chapter of this journal. Yes, I know I have to write about today's events and there are still several sketches to produce before I choose which ones will be featured, not forgetting the index which needs compiling. However, I still feel a sense of emptiness rather than jubilation. I guess the prime expectation for most writers is to finish their book as soon as possible, especially those who have publishers' deadlines to meet. My goals are slightly different, I guess, as I feel that this journal, which will have taken me over a year to complete, is simply a passage in time and there is still so much more to discover, to paint, to write and, of course, to enjoy in the 'Serenissima'.

My son Anthony once asked me what I will do next once the journal is finished, and without any hesitation I replied 'Easy, I will do it all again.' 'Do it all again?' he asked in a questionable manner. 'Yes', I said. 'Venice has become part of me and there is so much more to discover.'

Fino ad allora. Buonasera Venezia

INDEX

A

Accademia 10, 17, 18, 24, 29, 36, 52, 53, 55, 57, 58, 59, 60, 63, 64, 77, 84, 102, 123, 323, 348, 351, 408
Acqua Alta 80, 122, 156, 164, 266, 269
ACTV 4, 16, 33, 34, 80, 113, 158, 195, 196, 238, 242, 265, 272, 283, 324, 360, 388, 424
Adriatic 33, 179, 180, 242, 265, 266, 268, 272, 274, 276, 277, 278, 284
Ala Napoleonica 20, 156, 165, 166
Alexandria 155, 173
Armenian Monks 423, 436
Arsenale 52, 163, 164, 167, 169, 195, 199, 200, 201, 202, 204, 205, 212, 369, 387, 435
Arsenalotti 200

B

Bacino Orseolo 7, 20, 22, 145, 279
Bambini, Nicolo 333
Bar S. Lucia x, 26, 71, 81, 106, 137, 138, 143, 189, 190, 223, 240, 241, 258, 282, 302, 355, 382, 417, 440
Basaiti, Marco 432, 451
Basilica San Marco 22, 102, 156, 172, 180, 212, 253, 279, 316, 431
Bassano, Jacopo 300, 451
Bellini, Giovanni 60, 233, 411, 451
Bellini, Jacopo 123
Benedictine 274, 299, 427
Biblioteca Nazionale Marciana 159
Biennale Internazionale D'Arte 211, 435
Bonaparte, Napoleon 5, 58, 111, 167
Bratto 15
Briganto 205
Burano xvii, 34, 168, 221, 225, 227, 241, 242, 243, 244, 245, 246, 248, 249, 250, 251, 256, 257, 258, 259, 261, 360, 441
Byron, Lord 17, 275, 439
Byzantine xix, 31, 37, 38, 43, 44, 52, 64, 155, 174, 180, 200, 231, 233, 250, 253, 273, 326, 366, 393, 406, 433

C

Ca' da Mosto 319
Ca' Rezzonico 37, 337, 338, 339, 344, 411
Café Florian 165
Café Quadri 171
Campanile 11, 15, 91, 126, 133, 175, 233, 235, 246, 249, 250, 255, 256, 258, 283, 301, 302, 325, 326, 328, 331, 390, 403, 405, 414, 429, 430
Campo del Mori 90
Campo San Toma 15
Canal, Giovanni Antonio (Canaletto) 168
Canale di Cannaregio 11

Canal della Giudecca 271
Cannaregio 6, 11, 38, 69, 72, 75, 78, 82, 83, 84, 87, 90, 98, 100, 101, 105, 106, 107, 227, 229, 240, 279, 282, 335, 347, 368, 387, 392, 418
Canova, Antonio 168, 372, 439, 452
Carmelite 107, 331, 332
Carnevale 107, 331, 332
Carpaccio, Vittore 62, 170, 451
Carriera, Rosalba 62, 340, 451
Casanova, Giacomo 216
Casino Municipale 276
Castellani 335, 336, 345
Castello 6, 105, 180, 193, 197, 207, 208, 211, 309, 335, 336, 369, 385, 387, 421, 429, 430, 431, 434, 435
Ca D'Oro 388
Chorus Ticket 131
Codussi, Mauro 40, 97, 105, 123, 133, 171, 406, 410, 416, 430
Colleoni, Bartolomeo 396, 402
Condottiere 402
Constantinople 161, 174, 180, 231, 249, 412, 414
Convents 58, 294, 295, 296
Corderie 435
Cornaro, Caterina 67, 97, 362
Corradini, Antonio 342, 452
Correr Museum 129, 338, 359, 379, 380, 381, 436
Council of Ten 118, 178, 186

D

Da' Mosto, Francesco 44, 282
Damaskinos, Michael 415
De Medici, Cosimo 301
Doge Agnolo Partecipazio 299
Doge Alvise Mocenigo 439
Doge Andrea Dandolo 177
Doge Andrea Gritti 53, 181
Doge Francesco Erizzo 199

Doge Francesco Foscari 15, 70, 181, 182, 183
Doge Leonardo Dona 163
Doge Leonardo Loredan 162
Doge Lodovico Manin 181
Doge Marino Falier 181, 188
Doge Marino Grimani 208, 244
Doge Otto Orseolo 180
Doge Pietro Candiano 180
Doge Pietro Gradenigo 181
Doge Pietro Grimani 181
Doge Pietro Orseolo 179
Doge Pietro Tradonico 125, 411
Doge Sebastiano Ziani 180, 301
Doge Vitale Michiel 180
Dolomites 6, 32, 237, 302, 389
Dorsoduro 6, 214, 321, 323, 324, 326, 335

E

Eastern District 193
Erberia 48, 49
Evelyn, John 202

F

Festa della Madonna della Salute 354
Festa del Redentore 292
Fondaco dei Turchi 128, 129
Foscarini, Antonio 131
Franco, Veronica 217
Frari (Santa Maria Gloriosa) 7, 12, 13, 14, 15, 60, 112, 116, 121, 123, 124, 125, 140, 148, 168, 241, 315, 421
Friscata 205
Fusta 205

G

Galuppi, Baldassare 246
Garibaldi, Giussepe 195, 209, 211, 430, 435
Gesuati 346, 347, 416

Gesuiti 78, 98, 99, 100, 227, 237, 239, 240, 347, 348
Ghetto 72, 78, 85, 86, 87, 88, 89, 189, 284
Giadini Pubblici 206, 211
Giardinetti Reali 19, 54, 158
Giardini Esposizione 207, 425
Giardino Papadopoli 111, 114, 241
Giudecca xvii, 34, 62, 214, 244, 263, 264, 271, 275, 279, 282, 283, 284, 285, 287, 289, 292, 294, 299, 303, 360, 425
Gothic xix, 15, 31, 42, 53, 54, 91, 95, 98, 102, 115, 122, 123, 132, 170, 182, 198, 234, 252, 277, 288, 293, 296, 328, 331, 345, 367, 371, 372, 394, 395, 398, 408, 410, 412, 434
Granai di Terranova 159
Grand Hotel Excelsior 277
Grappa 257, 428, 429
Guardi, Franchese 62, 216, 344
Guardi, Francheso 451
Guggenheim, Peggy 191, 301, 348, 349, 350, 351

H

Hansen, Harald 279
Hellenic Institute 38
Henry III, of France 202, 218
H M S Victory 204

I

International Legion 210
Isola di San Elena 421
Isola di San Pietro 421

J

Jewish Cemetery 273, 274

L

Lace 219, 222, 244, 245

Lagoon xix, 3, 6, 22, 23, 33, 34, 39, 78, 80, 82, 90, 91, 98, 100, 107, 129, 156, 158, 159, 161, 162, 168, 177, 182, 193, 196, 197, 200, 202, 206, 207, 211, 213, 214, 225, 230, 237, 238, 241, 242, 243, 245, 250, 255, 258, 261, 263, 265, 266, 267, 268, 269, 270, 271, 273, 275, 277, 278, 283, 284, 288, 293, 294, 302, 326, 336, 369, 409, 423, 425, 441
Lazzaretto 275
Lazzarini, Gregorio 334, 400
La Fenice 357, 359, 375, 376, 377, 379, 426
La Grazia 275
La Pieta 275
La Volta 51
Liberia Sansoviniana 160, 165
Lido xvii, 34, 98, 153, 156, 167, 180, 206, 214, 263, 264, 265, 266, 270, 271, 272, 273, 274, 275, 277, 278, 280, 282, 283, 292, 424
Logetta 163
Lombardo, Pietro 57, 83, 102, 122, 372, 398, 452
Lombardo, Tullio 40, 97, 199, 361, 398, 416, 452
Longhena, Baldassare 68, 353, 433, 452
Longhi, Alesandro 451
Longhi, Alessandro 451
Longhi, Pietro 43, 451
Lotto, Lorenzo 128, 331, 451

M

Madonna dell Orto 78, 91, 92, 93
Malamocco 153, 172, 272, 277
Malombra, Piero 434
Manin, Daniele 195, 209, 367
Marghera 6, 27, 268, 296, 368

Masks 214, 215, 219, 220, 298, 376
Massari, Giorgio 52, 171, 338, 347, 416, 452
Mazzini, Giuseppe 209
Mekhitar 437
Merceria 172, 189, 357, 360, 361, 362, 363, 364, 365
Moli, Clementi 433
Molo 160, 161, 196, 197, 206, 212, 271, 279
Morosini, Morosina 244
Mose (Barrier) 270
Mulino Stucky 271, 285, 293, 296
Murano xvii, 11, 34, 56, 57, 83, 168, 213, 225, 227, 229, 230, 231, 232, 233, 234, 236, 237, 242, 243, 250, 255, 312, 343, 400
Museo Marciano 174, 175
Museo Storico Navale 202

N

Nicolotti 327
Northern Islands 225, 237, 238, 239, 243, 244, 258, 261

O

Olivetan Monks 427
Oratorio dei Crociferi 98, 240
Orseolo, Orso 252
Ospedali Civile 397

P

Palanca 284, 293, 297
Palazzo Agnusdio 132
Palazzo Arnaldi 115
Palazzo Balbi 52, 65
Palazzo Barbarbo 53
Palazzo Barbarigo 56
Palazzo Belloni Battagia 69
Palazzo Ca'Corner della Regina 42, 67
Palazzo Calbo Crotta 37
Palazzo Camerlenghi 48, 280, 281
Palazzo Ca da Mosto 44
Palazzo Contarini dei Bovolo 366

Palazzo Contarini Fasan 54
Palazzo Corner Mocenigo 125
Palazzo Corner Spinelli 40
Palazzo Dario 56, 57
Palazzo Da Mula 234
Palazzo Ducale 20, 22, 23, 39, 52, 155, 156, 157, 160, 163, 172, 177, 181, 182, 183, 188, 189, 197, 200, 206, 279, 316, 372, 381
Palazzo Falier 52, 390
Palazzo Flangini 38
Palazzo Fontana Rezzonico 41
Palazzo Foscani Contarini 70
Palazzo Gargonzi 125
Palazzo Giustinian 236
Palazzo Grassi 52, 436
Palazzo Grimani 51
Palazzo Gritti 69, 70, 197
Palazzo Gritti Pisani 53
Palazzo Labia 11, 78, 81, 229
Palazzo Lezze 94
Palazzo Loredan 64, 370, 371
Palazzo Mafetti 125
Palazzo Manin Dolfin 50
Palazzo Marcello 115
Palazzo Mastrelli 90
Palazzo Mocenigo 17, 275
Palazzo Papodopoli 51, 66
Palazzo Querini 38, 39, 407
Palazzo Querini Stampalia 407
Palazzo Sagredo 43, 433
Palazzo Salviati 55, 56, 146
Palazzo Savorgnan 69, 85, 107
Palazzo Seriman 98
Palazzo Soranzo 125, 393
Palazzo Surian 83
Palazzo Van Axel 393
Palazzo Vendramin Calergi 40
Palladio, Andrea 186, 286, 289, 431, 452
Palma the Younger 11, 249, 364
Paoletti, Paolo 438
Patriarchs 64, 187, 216, 219, 284, 363, 367, 402, 433
Pavement 37, 97, 130, 155, 164, 176,

208, 213, 246, 250, 251, 288, 370, 394, 395, 413
Pellegrini, Gerolamo 451
Pescheria 33, 49
Piatti, Sante 333
Piazza, Paolo 290
Piazzale Roma xiii, xviii, 4, 5, 6, 7, 16, 23, 24, 26, 33, 35, 39, 69, 73, 80, 104, 107, 111, 114, 139, 156, 158, 166, 167, 189, 190, 195, 196, 207, 222, 227, 229, 240, 242, 258, 265, 271, 273, 279, 283, 302, 324, 355, 360, 389, 418, 424, 436, 441
Piazza San Marco 7, 15, 18, 19, 20, 21, 22, 54, 55, 70, 142, 153, 155, 157, 158, 167, 193, 212, 215, 221, 275, 279, 287, 302, 361, 362, 365, 388, 402, 421, 423, 425, 437
Piazzetta 61, 131, 156, 162, 164, 182, 197, 334, 347, 416
Piazzetta, Giambattisa 131, 347
Pietra del Bando 174
Plague 24, 117, 118, 205, 218, 220, 248, 289, 290, 323, 332, 352, 353, 354, 412, 427
Ponte dei Pugni 305, 335, 337, 345
Ponte della Liberta 5, 6, 80, 196, 223, 273
Ponte della Paglia 22, 23
Porta della Carta 182
Procuratie Nuove 156, 159, 165, 168, 169
Procuratie Vecchi 20, 55, 156, 165, 168, 170, 171
Ptolemy, Bernard 427

R

Redentore 263, 284, 286, 289, 292, 298, 347, 353
Regatta 51
Renaissance xix, 31, 39, 40, 48, 52, 56, 65, 66, 69, 83, 97, 102, 119, 120, 122, 123, 125, 133, 160, 165, 167, 171, 197, 199, 200, 233, 298, 299, 328, 329, 331, 361, 366, 371, 372, 391, 397, 406, 407, 410, 414, 416
Rialto 17, 24, 29, 36, 37, 45, 46, 47, 48, 49, 50, 61, 65, 66, 78, 85, 96, 105, 106, 111, 112, 133, 134, 135, 136, 152, 155, 159, 161, 172, 189, 196, 280, 281, 285, 323, 343, 357, 360, 361, 362, 365, 381, 389
Ridotto 216, 219, 344
Rio e Bacino Orseolo 7, 20, 22
Ristorante All Vecio Pipa 256
Rood Screen 8
Ruskin, John xvi, 10, 31, 51, 54, 57, 129, 184, 404

S

S. Maria Elisabetta 271
Saint Fosca 253
Saint Roch 117, 120
Salviati, Antonio 232
Sansovino, Jacopo 50, 159, 163, 164, 173, 177, 185, 328, 361, 364, 452
Santa Chiara Hotel 9, 26, 80, 139, 143, 229, 241, 265, 324, 440
Santa Lucia Station 64, 81
Santa Maria Assunta 78, 98, 147, 252
Santa Maria Degli Angeli 235
Santa Maria dei Giglio 374, 375
Santa Maria dei Miracoli 102, 392
Santa Maria della Salute 18, 149, 351, 380
Santa Maria e Donato 146, 235
Santa Maria Formosa 144, 405, 407
Santa Maria Mater Domini 132
Santo Stefano 370, 371
San Angelo Raffaele 327
San Apostoli 97, 390
San Canciano 101, 381, 388, 390, 391
San Cassiano 112, 132, 133
San Cosima 263, 294
San Croce 294, 397

San Elena 421, 423, 425, 426, 427
San Eufemia 284
San Francesco de Paola 211
San Geminiano 165, 166
San Geremia 11, 38, 69, 71, 440
San Giacomo Di Rialto 47
San Giobbe 83, 84, 92
San Giorgio dei Greci 414, 415
San Giorgio Maggiore xvii, 34, 206, 214, 231, 263, 279, 282, 283, 293, 297, 298, 299, 301, 302, 317, 330, 381
San Giovanni Crisostomo 78, 104, 105, 189
San Giovanni Elemosinario 112, 134
San Giovanni Evangelista 122
San Giovanni in Bragora 197, 198
San Giovanni Novo 409
San Giuseppe Di Castello 435
San Lazzaro xvii, 275, 293, 396, 397, 398, 423, 436, 437, 440
San Lazzaro Mendecanti xvii, 275, 293, 396, 397, 398, 423, 436, 437, 440
San Lorenzo 412, 413, 417
San Marco (Sestieri) 3, 6, 18, 19, 22, 35, 36, 42, 45, 46, 49, 50, 51, 53, 54, 55, 68, 111, 142, 156, 158, 167, 189, 335, 357, 365, 370, 382, 396, 397
San Maria dei Carmini 330, 331
San Maria dei Derelitti (Ospedaletto) 404
San Martino 199, 243, 246, 247, 249
San Marziale 93, 94
San Michele 100, 167, 213, 237
San Nicolo 273, 274, 324, 325, 326, 336
San Nicolo Mendicoli 325
San Pietro di Castello 336, 429, 431
San Pietro Martire 233, 234
San Polo 3, 6, 13, 46, 109, 111, 112, 114, 123, 124, 125, 127, 133, 335, 368
San Polo (Sestieri) 3, 6, 13, 46, 109, 111, 112, 114, 123, 124, 125, 127, 133, 335, 368
San Rocco 15, 112, 116, 117, 118, 120, 121, 122, 123
San Sebastiano 328, 330
San Servolo 275, 302
San Simeon Piccolo 9, 10
San Stae 69, 112, 130, 131, 132, 135, 381
San Teodoro (Column) 20, 156, 161
San Trovaso 345, 346
San Zaccaria 278, 344, 410, 417, 435, 436, 440
San Zulian 364
Sardi, Giuseppe 361, 452
Sargent, John Singer 359, 379
Scala dei Censori 183, 184
Scalzi 9, 10, 12, 37, 70, 71, 72, 73, 80, 139, 223, 239, 241, 279, 281, 302, 382
Scalzi (Church) 9, 10, 12, 37, 70, 71, 72, 73, 80, 139, 223, 239, 241, 279, 281, 302, 382
Scamozzi, Vincenzo 40, 164, 208, 299, 361, 452
Scarpa, Carlo 59, 60, 61, 62, 408, 452
Scarpagnino, Antonio 118, 371, 452
Scuola dei Merletti 244
Scuola dell Angelo Custode 98
Scuola Grande dei Carmini 332
Scuola Grande dei San Marco 112, 116, 117, 118, 120, 122, 307, 330, 332, 396, 397
Scuola Grande San Rocco 116, 120
Sessola, Sacca 275
Smeraldi, Francesco 431
Sotoportego Del Banco Giro 47
Southern Islands 261, 282, 283, 302
Spavento, Giorgio 361, 366, 452
SS Giovanni e Paolo 396, 398, 401, 404
Stadium SS Calcio Venezia 426

T

Tafur, Pero 201
Tetrachs 174
The Stones of Venice 31, 404
The Treasury 177
Three Masts (Piazza San Marco) 161
Tiepolo 39, 51, 56, 61, 81, 97, 119, 126, 131, 178, 248, 333, 334, 338, 340, 341, 342, 343, 347, 348, 404, 407, 408, 433, 451
Tintoretto, Jacopo 60, 90, 331, 348, 391, 451
Titian 14, 15, 60, 99, 119, 160, 174, 176, 185, 280, 328, 329, 330, 354, 361, 391, 392, 401, 411, 432
Tizianello 432
Torcello 34, 168, 225, 227, 230, 241, 242, 243, 244, 246, 247, 248, 249, 250, 251, 254, 255, 256, 257, 258, 294, 301, 399, 441
Torre dell Orologia 156
Toso, Pietro 232
Tourist Office 158
Turner, JMW x

V

Vendarim, Francesco 433
Venetian Constitution 155, 178, 181, 182
Venice Film Festival 276
Veronese, Paolo 60, 328, 329, 364, 451
Villino Canonica 206
Visconti, Pietro 339
Vittoria, Alessandro 65, 185, 208, 364, 411
Vivaldi, Antonio 104
Vivarini, Antonio 411, 451

W

Wagner 40
Wetlands 267

Z

Zattere 271, 292, 346, 369, 425

Zecca 19, 156, 159, 161
Zitelle 263, 284, 285, 286, 287, 294

EPILOGUE

I simply cannot end this journal of Venice without remembering and thanking the scores of painters, sculptors and architects of the past who have made my journal possible; without their supreme skills this beautiful Venice, as we know it today, would simply not exist. Although I have continuously praised each of these masters throughout my travels this past year, I feel that I have only provided a brief resume of some of their achievements, and not given a more biographical account of their wonderfully productive lives. Looking at the list of names below, I feel extremely humble and hope that I have not understated the accomplished work they have all achieved.

Painters: Marco Basaiti (1449–1512), Jacopo Bassano (1515–1592), Gentile Bellini (1429–1507), Giovanni Bellini (1430–1516), Vittore Carpaccio (1460–1526), Rosalba Carriera (1675–1757), Francheso Guardi (1712–1793), Gregono Lazzarini (1655–1730), Alesandro Longhi (1733–1813), Pietro Longhi (1701–1785), Lorenzo Lotto (1480–1556), Paolo Paoletti (1671–17350, Gerolamo Pellegrini (1624–1670), Giovanni Tiepolo (1696–1770), Jacopo Tintoretto (1518–1594), Tiziano Vecelli (1485–15760, Paolo Veronese (1528–1588), Antonio Vivarini (1440–1480).

Architects: Pietro Lombardo (1435–1515), Baldassare Longhena (1598–1682), Giorgio Massari (1687–1766), Andrea Palladio (1508–1580), Jacopo Sansovino (1480–1570), Giuseppe Sardi (1680–1753), Vincenzo Scamozzi (1548–1616), Carlo Scarpa (1906–1978), Antonio Scarpagnino (1505–1549), Giorgio Spavento (? –1509).

Sculptors/Artists: Antonio Canova (1757–1822), Antonio Corradini (1668–1752), Tullio Lombardo (1455–1532).

Knowing that there are so many other master artists who have contributed to the evolution of Venice who are not even mentioned in this book, I am also eternally grateful for their contribution. Given the opportunity to explore and write a second journal, I will make every effort to include those who have not featured above, who have also provided so much for every visitor to the 'Serenissima' to see and enjoy today, as well as in the past.

Printed in the United Kingdom
by Lightning Source UK Ltd.
129687UK00002BF/9/P